Fundamentals of Child Counseling

Donald B. Keat

Houghton Mifflin · Boston

Atlanta
Dallas
Geneva, Illinois
Hopewell, New Jersey
Palo Alto
London

Printed in the U.S.A.

Library of Congress Catalog Card Number: 73-11774

ISBIN: 0-395-17827-4

Fundamentals of Child Counseling

To Marilyn, Preston,
Megan, Brandon, and Justin

Contents

This book is for persons concerned with children. It is intended to acquaint the reader with the fundamental techniques as well as the more advanced procedures for counseling children. The writing represents a wide variety of approaches to working not only with the child, but also with the persons and environments that influence the child. Throughout the book, the primary focus remains on "the world's most valuable resource and its best hope for the future" (John F. Kennedy, address on July 25, 1963), the child as a prized and valuable human being.

The text is primarily for elementary counselors-in-training or for those already practicing in the schools, but it can also be used as a supplementary text in the fields of secondary school guidance counseling, school psychology, child psychology, teaching, and school administration. It can be used as a basic text for courses in elementary school guidance and counseling or for the seminar-practicum which most universities offer for students during their internships; for the practitioners, this book should serve to update perspectives and provide many useful and innovative procedures.

As a supplementary text in the field of guidance, the text can be used for courses in the organization and administration of secondary school guidance programs, with a focus on the chapters on administration and coordination of counseling programs; or it can be used in independent study courses where students concentrate on one area (for example, appraisal as outlined in Chapter Two, or individual counseling approaches as described in Chapter Three). School psychologists will find Chapter Two and the chapters on treatment (Three, Four, Five, and Six) especially relevant to their work. Child psychology majors, if their interests are in the applied clinical areas, will find the chapters on individual and group procedures for children and adults beneficial. Those who are oriented toward theoretical research will find the material on counseling theory in Chapter Three and on current research in Chapter Eleven to be helpful.

Teachers and teachers-in-training will find supplementary material on classroom group meetings, classroom management, confluent education, career orientation, and home and school intervention strategies in Chapters Five through Nine. Chapters Five through Eight and Chapter Ten also relate to the work of elementary school principals and other administrators.

The order of presentation is based on practicality; the techniques are offered for students and practitioners who are interested in becoming effective counselors. The sequence of chapters reflects my own bias. I feel that effective appraisal should be completed before proceeding with intervention strategies with individual children or with most types of group counseling (i.e., with children, parents, and teachers).

In the later chapters the role of the counselor as an agent of change is stressed. Moving out of the office into other sectors of the school, the home, and the community, the counselor deals with environmental modification. Later in the book aspects of administration and coordination of counseling programs are dealt with. The final chapter covers the present state of research in the field of counseling.

I would like to acknowledge the help and influence of some special people who have shared their life space, time, and ideas with me during my professional development and/or the writing of this book.

First of all, there is Ed Herr. Without Ed the book might never have materialized. His encouragement was ever present and his communicative skill provided a high-level model. The excellence of his ideas and writing can be perused in Chapter Eight of this book, which he contributed. Bob Shute helped by surveying and cataloguing the contents of the *Elementary School Guidance and Counseling Journal*. Many useful ideas were provided by Jack Frost for Chapters One, Four, and Five. With regard to Chapter Two, the chapter on appraisal, Stan Baker's testing knowledge provided helpful input, the learning disability references supplied by Al Mastantuono were useful, Walter MacGinitie's early encouragement and test knowledge skills are reflected, and Roy Hackman's expertise in the area of test development was especially influential. Although Chapter Three mainly represents approaches I've found useful in my years of counseling, it was influenced by my first professional model, Charlie Morris, such broadminded analytic therapists as Irv Schulman and Al Gerstein, the radical approaches of Ed Silverman, the existential philosophy and counseling of Sandy Macdonald, and the broad spectrum of behavioristic techniques developed by my more recent model, Arnold Lazarus. One of the senior members of the faculty at Penn State, George Hudson, is the staff expert-in-residence on groups, and as such provided me with references and constructive comments on the group scene. Mary Linda Merriam provided inspiration as well as material from her work for inclusion in Chapter Five. John Bellanti's brainstorming on adult groups and Bill Logan's parent group examples were helpful. Over the past couple of years it has been stimulating to work with an elementary school counselor-collaborator *par excellence* (for Chapter Six), Fred Leubuscher.

Chapter Seven owes much to the 1972 graduating class of elementary counseling students at Penn State. Although Iva McDuffy and I got the project started, Dale Malecki and Linda Leaman Selkowitz really pushed the affective curriculum book (Keat, et al 1972) to fruition. I am grateful to John Swisher whose grantsmanship enabled me to work in an ongoing affective education project (see Chapter Seven) for the past two years. Jim Kelz, our department community expert, offered numerous sources which were useful in preparing Chapter Nine, and Dave Faber also provided some ideas for Chapter Nine. The wealth of experience and wisdom of George Hudson was again helpful in organizing my thoughts for Chapter Ten. And finally, the research chapter (Chapter Eleven) was enhanced by some materials provided by Stan Baker (coordinator of the local self-study project) and the guidance staff of the State College Area Schools. In particular, the support, positive reinforcement and constructive review of the entire manuscript by Jim Muro is appreciated.

The manuscript went through numerous typings, and I'd like to acknowledge the efforts of those who worked diligently on it during the past year: Betty Blazer (The Boss), Andi Glassman, Ginny Henning, Lynda King, Dottie Oliver, Kathy Spicer, Bob Strong, and Janis Weinberg.

Finally, I would like to acknowledge the help received from my family. First of all, my father's career contribution to public education as teacher, principal, and superintendent influenced me to combine training in psychology with education in order to work in this joint capacity in the schools. My mother taught me the intrinsic value of caring for and helping others. And my mother-in-law, Mary Sterner, I wish to thank for engaging me in many stimulating discussions providing the elementary school principal's perspective. Saving the best for last, I'd like to acknowledge the efforts of my wonderful wife Marilyn. For well over ten years now she has attempted to make my English understandable. Her editing work as well as many worthwhile ideas are incorporated into this book. It is to her and our children that this book is dedicated.

Donald B. Keat II
University Park, Pa.

Fundamentals of Child Counseling

1

The child counselor works in a helping relationship with children during their elementary school years, caring for them in a special way. As a result of his specialized training, to be described in this book, the counselor can be an effective helper.

One definition of the guidance function (Peters, Shertzer and Van Hoose, 1965) states that guidance sustains and develops the pupil's self intellectually and affectively. That is, the purpose of guidance is to assist all children to grow and develop within a wide framework of normality. Dinkmeyer and Caldwell (1970) are perhaps the staunchest advocates of personalizing and humanizing the guidance process for all students (i.e., "developmental guidance").

The main thrust of such a process should be the "personalized" development of the child and primary prevention of problems. This assertion is based on the assumption that prevention is easier and better than subsequent cure. Thus it is important to be prepared to complement the efforts of classroom teachers. Since the child's growth and development are largely shaped by environmental influences, it is essential to recognize the effects of significant persons (e.g., parents, teachers, peers) and various systematic characteristics of the school on the child, and to acknowledge their relationship to guidance strategies.

The concept of elementary school guidance as a preventive force (Muro, 1970) is especially important in the prevention of delinquency and student dropout, and in the curtailment of aberrant mental health. Elementary school guidance can help both to identify those pupils whose lifestyles render them potential candidates for counseling and to muster the resources of the individual

An Overview of Elementary School Counseling and the Counselor

and his environment to overcome such obstacles. More importantly, perhaps, elementary school guidance programs can create within the school and among the relevant adults, both teachers and parents, a sensitivity to the emerging individuality of each pupil. This sensitivity can be reflected in positive and constructive environments for growth and learning that meet the individual needs of children.

With the emergence of larger school districts and the resulting need for comprehensive guidance services, it is necessary that elementary school guidance programs be attuned not only to the individual histories of students but also to their futures. Elementary school children need to increase their self awareness in relation to the educational and vocational options that will be available to them in the future. Joint counselor/teacher efforts in curriculum development and small-group activities designed to enhance student self knowledge, as well as heighten sensitivity to the social-educational-occupational systems, will help in this process.

There are also times when the counselor must undertake educative, remedial, and/or therapeutic procedures: appraisal, individual and group counseling strategies, teacher and parent group meetings, and other environmental change plans should be part of the counselor's repertoire. All children are distressed occasionally by comparatively minor and common problems resolvable by wise and understanding parents and teachers. But other children are sometimes overwhelmed by real or imagined problems that need the immediate attention of a skilled professional who can deal effectively with the individual, his behavior, and his environment. To determine the seriousness of his problems, the child should not be treated "strand by strand" (Smith, 1967) but as a whole child, with individual complexities. The elementary school counselor in his various roles can assist in making differential treatment plans only if he is professionally equipped to identify negative characteristics and foster positive development. This book attempts to develop the "technical eclecticism" (Lazarus, 1967)· that equips counselors to make use of any methods they think will be useful in practice and with which they are competent. In addition, the counselor must understand the interaction between pupil and environment sufficiently well to assist, through a collaborative relationship, those who are models of behavior and provide appropriate reinforcements. Further, the counselor needs to be able to coordinate available resources in such a way as to facilitate total pupil development.

Finally, the enhancement approach must be considered. This approach emphasizes the counselor's role as a consultant or collaborator. In this role, the counselor must develop awareness and skill in dealing with the major life environments of the child. In particular, such procedures as curriculum changes, behavioral change strategies for families, and contingency management (i.e., controlling the relationship between a response and its environmental consequences) in the classroom are used to enhance the potential of all children.

Role and Function of the Elementary School Counselor

While there will obviously be variation in the expectations of elementary school counselors from district to district, the counselor may be said to fill seven major roles: counseling, consultation or collaboration, coordination, communication, curriculum development, fostering child growth and development, and teaching coping behavior. Three of these roles (counseling, consultation, and coordination) were originally delineated in the joint statement of the Association for Counselor Education and Supervision and the American School Counselor Association (APGA, 1969). Two more (curriculum and communication) were suggested by Stamm and Nissman (1971). It now seems appropriate to expand the counselor's roles and functions to embrace the seven C's of elementary counseling, by proposing that he also be a child development expert and teacher of coping behavior.

Counseling

It is assumed that the elementary school counselor will counsel individual children, groups of children, and significant adults. The focus of these counseling relationships will be determined largely by individual and group needs, the availability and system of referral, and the degree to which consultation with teachers and parents is effective. It is imperative that the counseling relationship, whether it be with the children or important adults, retain its place at the core of the counselor's role. Thus, the stance taken in this book agrees with that of other writers (Muro, 1970; Boy, 1972) who feel that counseling should be the counselor's primary function. Thus, Chapter Three is devoted to the topic of individual counseling with children. Other chapters deal with group counseling of children (Chapter Four) and of parents and teachers (Chapter Five).

Collaboration or Consultation

In the collaborating or consulting role it is assumed that the counselor's knowledge of individual behavior will be used primarily to complement teacher efforts to identify student needs through the use of available objective and subjective information, implement positive classroom climates, individualize experiences for particular students to meet their particular needs (e.g., coping with problems), to create constructive behavioral models and reinforcement schedules, and to develop experiences that emphasize self understanding and are in keeping with the nature of educational and vocational development. Consultative relationships will also concentrate on helping teachers, parents, and possibly administrators to come to grips with the influences that they, collectively and individually, exert on students. How these influences are transmitted and how they can be positively manifested will be discussed. Chapter Five focuses on types of collaboration that result in development of working relationships among the significant adults in a child's life.

Coordination

The role of coordinator assumes that there are available within the school system and the community psychological, social work, and health services that can be activated for specific purposes. Through his consultative and counseling roles, the elementary counselor should be sensitive to needs for these supportive services and should be the focal point for their appropriate application. Chapter Ten deals with the coordination of the services of various members of the guidance team.

Communication

Communication, as it is defined in this book, has a broad conceptual base. The primary focus is on the counselor's ability to communicate with the child by using the child's own language and media (i.e., play materials). Secondly, communication skills that facilitate exchanges between adults (e.g., teacher-counselor, counselor-parent) are important. Both Chapters Three (communication with children) and Five (communication skills between adults) are concerned with the development of this skill.

Curriculum

If the counselor's work is to have an effect on the daily lives of the children in his elementary school, he must influence the curriculum. The counselor's primary area of concern is the emotional life of the child. By integrating an affective curriculum (e.g., Dinkmeyer, 1970) with the overemphasized cognitive one, the counselor can have a positive day-to-day impact on the lives of children. If he attempts to generate "confluent education" (the term used for the integration of the affective and cognitive elements in learning [Brown, 1971]) the counselor must introduce teaching procedures using relevant materials and also develop inservice procedures to help teachers develop their own skills and materials. Chapter Seven is devoted to this important topic in developmental guidance.

Fostering Child Growth and Development

The counselor should fulfill the role of expert in child growth and development. Such expertise is crucial for work with children and for much conference activity with parents and teachers. Chapter Six focuses on the knowledge a counselor should possess in order to function as a child expert in consultation with both teachers and parents.

Teaching Coping Behaviors

Coping behavior can be taught in several ways. At times the counselor can serve as a role model for children—for example, demonstrating how one copes with a situation effectively. In other instances coping behavior can be learned in a counseling session. Coping skills can be gained through individual and/or group counseling (Chapters Three and Four) in which the child is helped to undo rigid defense patterns and to learn more efficient and effective ways of protecting himself. In addition, some of the topics covered in an affective curriculum (Chapter Seven) can help the child to develop effective means of coping.

Education of Elementary School Counselors

The process of educating a person to become an elementary school counselor encompasses a spectrum of considerations. The topic has been dealt with specifically (University of Maine) by Muro

(1970) as well as more generally by Dimick and Huff (1970). Some of the topics which should be considered are selection of candidates, the importance of elementary school teaching experience (e.g., see Hudson, 1961; Dilley, 1972; Boller, 1972), selective progressive retention of students, a program of courses which will prepare students for his or her profession, and finally some way of evaluating the program so that each subsequent program is an improvement over that which preceded it. A model of such a program is the current program at The Pennsylvania State University. The details of the program can be examined in Appendix A of this volume. In addition, the School Counselor Attitude Inventory (Baker, 1971; Baker & Hansen, 1972) which is used in The Penn State screening process is reprinted in Appendix B. This scale is also administered at the end of the program in order to investigate changes in the counselor's attitudes after exposure to the program. Finally, with regard to program evaluation, the questionnaire which we use for feedback at the end of the year is included in Appendix C. Responses to this questionnaire are used to implement changes for the next year's class.

Guidance Learnings

The following nine guidance learnings can be viewed as potentially desirable in the development of the child. They are listed here for the consideration of the guidance counselor and teacher, as well as other adults who may be working with the child. That is, whenever such areas are touched upon in an existing situation —whether it be curriculum, a counseling session, or some other situation—they are to be positively reinforced and enhanced in some way. The following guidance learnings are gleaned from numerous sources (Hill and Luckey, 1969; Dinkmeyer, 1970; Besell, 1970; and Brown, 1971):

1. Understanding and accepting oneself. This category comprises what is generally accepted as the most important task for a person in life: the development of a positive self concept and realistic expectations for oneself. Indeed, when we meet children with various difficulties, this is the one area in which there is usually a deficiency. Therefore, the development of self understanding, self concept, and self image are all important areas that need to be enhanced by the counselor and by the teacher in curriculum development.

2. Becoming aware of and understanding feelings and emotions. Perls (1969) has said that awareness by and of itself can be curative and can have a therapeutic effect. Awareness can and should

lead to understanding of the child's feelings and emotions. Then the child should learn to appropriately label his feelings. The final step is the appropriate expression of these feelings through such means as sublimation, catharsis, or pure verbalization. This includes the expression of both positive and negative feelings.

3. Understanding human behavior: emotional maturity. Perls (1969) formulated the concept that maturation is the transition from environmental support to self support. Hill and Luckey (1969) preface each of their guidance learnings with the statement "the child must mature." Effective understanding of human behavior implies the gaining not only of insight but also of the ability to make behavioral changes. It includes such capacities as handling stressful situations and utilizing appropriate outlets for tensions.

4. Developing responsibility for oneself. This is the ability to accept responsibility for the consequences of one's own behavior and for the best possible use of one's abilities. Much of what Glasser (1965, 1969) describes as the core of education for responsibility belongs in this category. That is, responsibility is the ability to fulfill one's needs and to do so in a way that does not deprive others of the ability to fulfill their needs. Individual and group counseling are the most effective forms of treatment for deficiency in this area. In addition, Glasser (1969) advocates *teacher-run meetings* with the entire classroom of children in order to implement this guidance learning for the child.

5. Establishing interpersonal relationships: understanding others and participating in social groups. This guidance goal means learning how to get along with and live with others. Human relationships are the core of a person's life and need to be fostered. The popularity of the "group" as a forum for working out problems reflects the fact that people have not learned how to relate to others and are reaching out to meet people in the controlled atmosphere of a group. Among the skills that can be learned are cooperation, conflict resolution, acceptance of deviance, and working within a group.

6. Understanding choices, making decisions, and solving problems. These skills have to do with the child's planfulness (Super & Overstreet, 1960). Independence of action is an attribute that contributes to effective decision making. In order to gain the necessary decision-making skills, the child should be guided through innumerable situations in which he must choose between alternatives. This method can be implemented from the time the child

is in kindergarten, introducing increasingly complex decision-making skills. In addition, the child should develop the ability to solve his own problems, such as how to get along with others. For example, experiencing "social-problem-solving" meetings (Glasser, 1969). The crucial consideration is how to achieve a sound balance between support and the development of the child's sense of responsibility.

7. Demonstrating adjustment capacities. Included in this category are coping skills, independence, and self reliance. This might be considered "life adjustment education" or learning how to balance one's defense mechanisms. Balance is always the crucial consideration in the personality makeup of individuals. That is, we all have coping strategies, but we only become concerned when they are out of balance. For example, we are concerned when a child continually escapes into fantasy and does not meet the demands of reality. At times the therapeutic strategy will be to uncover defensive maneuvers, while in other situations it may be necessary to support existing defenses and help the person develop more effective coping skills.

8. Developing appreciation of the world of education and some understanding of the world of work. This process initially involves the development of basically positive attitudes toward the educational system in which the child finds himself. Then there is the process of "vocationalization" (Herr & Cramer, 1972) which goes on throughout the elementary school years as the child develops values, knowledge and skills that feed into effective vocational behavior.

9. Developing a sense of values and ideals. The process involves the individual's views of what is most important in life, the goals he strives for, and the values and ideas he develops in the course of living. "Character education" is the overall term for this area of development. The author is in accord with Miel & Brogan (1957), who have said:

> We need a world with fewer hostile people and more warm and friendly ones, fewer lonely people and more who can communicate with others, fewer incapable people and more who know how to act responsibly, fewer people who don't care and more who have concern for the common welfare.

These, then, are the main guidance learnings for the elementary school child. The list could undoubtedly be extended. But for our purposes, these learnings will serve as the working model for meeting the needs of children.

**A Model for the
Elementary School Counselor** ————————————————————

In these days of accountability, the construction of behavioral objectives for the counselor should be considered. Behavioral objectives are goals or behaviors that approximate what the counselor will or ought to do on his job. Mager (1962) has identified three basic steps in the writing of instructional objectives. They are: (a) identifying by name the terminal behavior i.e., "the behavior you would like your learner to be able to demonstrate at the time your influence over him ends," [Mager, 1962, p. 2.] (b) describing the important conditions under which the behavior is expected to occur; (c) specifying the criteria of acceptable performance by describing how the learner must perform to be considered adequate. Gronlund's (1970) approach more closely fits the paradigm used in this chapter: to state the general goal and then to consider some specific behaviors that contribute toward this goal. Finally, the various means of evaluating particular objectives are considered. Silvern's (1965) approach is similar to that utilized here, i.e., (1) objectives are stated; (2) procedures, activities, and experiences are explored; and (3) some evaluative possibilities are considered. Similar types of goals have recently been delineated by Herr and Cramer (1972) and Horan (1972) in specifying behavioral goals for counseling.

The following model developed by Frost (1972) illustrates how the elementary counselor can develop measurable behavioral objectives to evaluate the effectiveness of his guidance program. This outline was developed to help plan and evaluate developmental counseling services at a university laboratory school (adapted from Frost [1972]. Reprinted with permission of the author).

Need (purpose, related to student needs): All children encounter normal developmental problems in the process of growing up. Every child occasionally needs help from an understanding, non-authoritative adult to assist him in self understanding; decision making; and school, home and social-personal adjustments. Therefore, counseling services should be available to all students who request this assistance.

Goal (What hope to accomplish): To provide effective counseling services to all children who request counseling during the school year.

Performance Objectives (behavioral objectives, including a statement of time and proficiency level): All students in the school who request counseling from the counselor will be provided individual counseling and group counseling by the counselor during the regular school term. The effectiveness will be measured by a survey of all students in this school to be conducted at the end of the regular school term. As a result of these counseling sessions, 80% of the students who participated in the sessions will indicate that counseling assisted them with some developmental problem they were experiencing, as measured by a survey of all students in this school who participated in one or more counseling sessions with the counselor.

Management Objective (to indicate what will be done, when it will be done, and the desired outcome): The counselor will conduct one or more individual or group counseling sessions during the regular school term with all students requesting counseling in order to assist them in coping with the normal developmental problems they are experiencing.

Activities (experiences designed to meet or contribute toward meeting a stated objective):

1. Make classroom visits to encourage self referral
2. Develop self referral request forms
3. Consult with teachers concerning self referral problems
4. Make a PTA presentation to describe developmental counseling to parents.
5. Develop surveys to evaluate stated objectives
6. Conduct counseling sessions
7. Evaluate the counseling services

Resources (Materials, equipment, supplies, and resource persons to be used):

1. Role statement: "The Elementary School Counselor"
2. Guidance in the Elementary School; a State Department or APGA publication
3. Self referral request form and posters in classroom
4. Survey form: "Availability of Counselor for Self-Referral Counseling Services"
5. Survey form: "Survey of Pupils' Attitudes Toward Counseling"

Evaluation (methods used to determine if the stated objectives have been met): The counselor will survey all students in the Laboratory School to determine if every student who requested counseling has had at least one counseling session with the counselor. The counselor will survey all students who have participated in counseling to determine whether they feel these sessions have been helpful to them.

With the objective of accountability in mind, refer to the behavioral objectives for each chapter listed in Table 1-1. These objectives are intended as a summary of what is to follow in the rest of the book. Also described in Table 1-1 are experiences/activ-

Table 1-1 *Plan of the Book: Behavioral Objectives, Experiences, Evaluation*

CHAPTER NUMBER	BEHAVIORAL OBJECTIVES	EXPERIENCES	EVALUATION
1	To gain an understanding of the roles of the elementary counselor, to foster guidance learnings for children, to be adequately prepared to render and to be accountable for the services offered in an environment conducive to confluent education.	School observation, including daily reports and logs; readings, lectures, role-playing in class.	Quality of reading, quality of writing, contribution to discussions, feedback from school intern supervisor and teachers.
2	To acquire the ability to use subjective and objective child study procedures to appraise individual children, to become proficient in objective methods of child evaluation for individual and group use, and to give feedback to significant persons.	Development of an appraisal procedure; administration of tests to children; interpretation of tests to child, parents, teachers, administrators.	Instructor evaluation of competence in appraisal, field-testing evaluations by supervisor, participation in a role-playing test session, observation of student in school, individual supervision.
3	To develop an appropriate level of ability to perform effective individual counseling with children: to gain an understanding of theories of counseling; then to shape one's own personal approach to techniques for counseling children.	Readings in counseling theory, film observation, listening to tapes of counseling, performance of individual counseling with children.	University supervisor appraisal and field feedback from school counselor, behavioral changes in children.
4	To develop the competency to make child counseling groups effective: to know how to initiate a group as well as to plan the actual practice of child group counseling.	Readings, observation of video tapes of groups, initiation of a small group in the school, conducting of a meeting(s) in the classroom with the teacher.	Field feedback and personal observation, feedback from school teacher and counselor supervisor.

	Objective	Experience	Evaluation
5	To gain knowledge and skill in running parent conferences (groups), teacher groups and classroom guidance groups; and to conduct such groups.	Readings, behavior rehearsal, running of a conference with a parent (perhaps including the child), planning of a structured parent education group, listening to tapes of teacher groups, and conducting of a teacher group with the university supervisor.	School supervisor consultation, quality of rehearsal, assessment of plans, tape critique(s) of groups.
6	To develop skills in collaboration-consultation: this includes implementation of classroom evaluation procedures, interpretation of child growth and development, consultation with teachers regarding classroom contingency management procedures, inservice collaboration, and staff case conferences.	Lectures, readings, discussions, demonstrations, observations, role-playing implementation, and group meetings in school.	Feedback from teachers, evaluation by supervisors of effectiveness, extent of readings, school supervisor's feedback on effectiveness of intern's program, supervision of proposed program(s).
7	To develop the ability to contribute to the maximum growth and development of all elementary school children through confluent education. To plan and implement an affective curriculum in the classroom.	Planning and coordination with an interested teacher(s), training of the teacher(s) to use the materials, utilization of affective materials in the classroom.	Quality of planned program, competence with materials in the classroom, teacher and supervisor feedback.
8	To be able to collect, analyze, disseminate and interpret appropriate information for use with individuals and groups of clients in facilitating decision making about future educational and occupational goals.	Lectures, readings, job analysis exercises.	Examinations on content, utilization of the actual materials, development and presentation of a project.

Table 1-1 (Continued)

CHAPTER NUMBER	BEHAVIORAL OBJECTIVES	EXPERIENCES	EVALUATION
9	To develop the ability to use pupil personnel services and community resources that contribute to the maximum growth and development of all elementary school children; to be aware of and to develop such community resources; to develop action interventions for school, home, and community.	Involvement in action programs during field experience; focus on school, home and community interventions.	Adequacy of programs implemented and quality of report to group on referral sources in community and action programs initiated.
10	To develop the ability to coordinate and work cooperatively with the staff in the schools; to establish objectives and strategies for guidance services in order to organize and implement new programs, manage and coordinate existing ones.	Lectures, readings, group meetings with school staff, personal contacts.	Extent of classroom participation in discussions, quality of presentation of a model for the organization and administration of an elementary guidance program, school supervisor feedback.
11	To develop the ability to conduct continuous evaluation of all phases of elementary school programs: to be able to formulate evaluative criteria appropriate to the counselor's setting; to collect, analyze and interpret appropriate data; and to report the results of such research studies.	Readings, lectures, development of a research project.	Accuracy of computations regarding reliability, validity, norms, group project presentation, quality of Master's papers. These Master's papers are usually action-research oriented and involve before-after measures of the effects of such programs as child groups, parent groups, confluent education procedures in the classroom.

ities and means of evaluating the educational components of the projected behavioral competencies of the counselor-in-training. The experiences and evaluative methods listed suggest ways to use the following chapters in an elementary counselor training program.

——————————————————————— **Summary**

This chapter has introduced several concepts basic to elementary guidance and counseling. First, a general rationale was presented, with guidance seen as preventative, educative, and enhancive.

Second, the seven major roles of the counselor were delineated as the seven C's of counseling, consultation or collaboration, coordination, communication, curricular development, child growth and development, and teacher of coping behavior.

Third, the education of the elementary school counselor was considered. This section involved a brief summary of topics with more details of an operating program being provided in three appendices.

Fourth, nine important guidance learnings for the child were discussed. They were: understanding and acceptance of self, awareness of feelings, emotional maturity, development of responsibility, understanding of others, development of problem-solving skills, increasing adjustment capacities, appreciation of the world of education and work, and development of a sense of values.

Fifth, a model for the preparation of behavioral objectives for the elementary guidance program was presented. This model was based upon the appraisal of the needs of the school and included goals, performance and management objectives, activities, resources, and evaluation.

Finally, the overall plan of the book was outlined in a table listing each chapter number and delineating the corresponding behavioral objectives, experiences, and the means of evaluating these objectives as they are reflected in the preparation of elementary school counselors.

——————————————————————— **References**

American Personnel and Guidance Association. *The elementary school counselor in today's schools.* Washington, D.C.: APGA, 1969.

Baker, S. B. The development of an instrument to measure school counselor attitudes toward client problems on a status quo-change agent scale. Unpublished doctoral dissertation, State University of New York at Buffalo, 1971.

Baker, S. B., & Hansen, J. C. School counselor attitudes on a status quo-change agent measurement scale. *The School Counselor*, 1972, **19**, 243–248.

Bessell, H. *Methods in human development: theory manual*. San Diego: Human Development Training Institute, 1970.

Boller, J. D. Counselor certification: Who still needs teaching experience? *Personnel and Guidance Journal*, 1972, **50**, 388–391.

Boy, A. V. The elementary school counselor's role dilemma. *The School Counselor*, 1972, **19**, 167–172.

Brown, G. *Human teaching for human learning: an introduction to confluent education*. New York: Viking Press, 1971.

Dilley, J. Counselors without teaching experience can be successful. *The School Counselor*, 1972, **20**, 132–133.

Dimick, K. M., & Huff, V. E. *Child counseling*. Dubuque, Iowa: William C. Brown, 1970.

Dinkmeyer, D. *Developing understanding of self and others*. Circle Pines, Minn.: American Guidance Service, 1970.

Dinkmeyer, D., and Caldwell, E. *Developmental counseling and guidance: a comprehensive school approach*. New York: McGraw-Hill, 1970.

Frost, J. M. Plan and evaluation for developmental counseling services at the Jones-Jaggers laboratory school. Unpublished manuscript, Western Kentucky University, 1972.

Glasser, W. *Reality therapy*. New York: Harper & Row, 1965.

Glasser, W. *Schools without failure*. New York: Harper & Row, 1969.

Gronlund, N. E. *Stating behavioral objectives for classroom instruction*. New York: Macmillan, 1970.

Herr, E. L., and Cramer, S. H. *Vocational guidance and career development in the schools: toward a systems approach*. Boston: Houghton Mifflin, 1972.

Hill, G. E., & Luckey, E. B. *Guidance for children in elementary schools*. New York: Appleton-Century-Crofts, 1969.

Horan, J. Behavioral goals in systematic counselor education. *Counselor Education and Supervision*, 1972, **11**, 162–170.

Hudson, G. R. Counselors need teaching experience. *Counselor Education and Supervision*, 1961, **0**, 24–27.

Lazarus, A. A. In support of technical eclecticism. *Psychological Reports*, 1967, **21**, 415–416.

Mager, R. F. *Preparing instructional objectives*. Palo Alto, Cal.: Fearson, 1962.

Miel, A., and Brogan, P. *More than social studies: a view of social learning in the elementary school*. Englewood Cliffs, N.J.: Prentice-Hall, 1957.

Muro, J. *The counselor's work in the elementary school*. Scranton, Penn.: International Textbook Company, 1970.

Perls, F. *Gestalt therapy verbatim*. Lafayette, Cal.: Real People Press, 1969.

Peters, H. J., Shertzer, B., & Van Hoose, W. *Guidance in elementary schools*. Chicago: Rand McNally, 1965.

Silvern, L. C. Systems analysis and synthesis in training and education. *Automated Education Newsletter*, 1965, 1C1–1C25.

Smith, H. M. Preventing difficulties through elementary school guidance. *Elementary School Guidance and Counseling*, 1967, 1, 8–14.

Stamm, M. L., and Nissman, D. *New dimensions in elementary guidance*. New York: Richards Rosen Press, 1971.

Super, D. E., and Overstreet, P. L. *The vocational maturity of ninth-grade boys*. New York: Teachers College, Columbia University, 1960.

2

This chapter will focus on a variety of procedures that counselors, teachers, and administrators can use in evaluating children. With appropriate training, counselors, teachers, and other individuals in the schools can learn to use these procedures. With the current stress on the need for accountability, the counselor should be able to utilize quantifiable procedures to help in the understanding of children. This is especially true at a time when cutbacks are taking place throughout the school systems. Indeed, if the counselor is to survive professionally, he must be able to demonstrate his special competencies in a quantifiable way so that administrators will consider them worthwhile and relevant to the school.

The counselor's goal is not to become primarily a tester or psychometrician but to develop the necessary skills to meet the immediate needs of the school's personnel. In this the author agrees with Muro (1970). Muro and Oelke's study (1967) indicated that teachers often need help with the appraisal of the individual child. The existing situation in most schools is that when some form of individual appraisal is needed, the referral is made to a school psychologist. In many instances, the actual testing takes up to six months. This lapse wastes valuable time. Therefore, appropriate placements may not take place until a much later and inappropriate time. In the meantime the child may have experienced failure that has lessened the possibility of future success in working with him.

There are a few classic surveys of tests in the area of counseling. Goldman (1971) covers, as do most of the major sources, important basic concepts such as the foundations of test interpretation and the various kinds of "bridges" from tests to the individual

Individual and Group
Appraisal Procedures for Children

(also see Keat & Hackman, 1972). He also presents two brief elementary school cases. Cronbach (1970) does a monumental job of covering numerous forms of tests, including some of the relevant individual scales such as the Wechsler and Binet. Anastasi (1968) surveys numerous kinds of tests. Super and Crites' classic for counselors (1962) focusses on the use of tests to appraise the vocational fitness of persons older than the elementary school-age child.

This chapter is designed to meet the needs of practitioners functioning in the elementary school. It provides various procedures that can be utilized by the counselor or another trained person. The author advocates precision testing to answer relevant questions about the individual child. Precision testing can be focused on personal needs or problems in order to formulate remedial approaches. In the latter case, essential diagnosis is often important for educational placement of the child in particular classroom settings or even intra-classroom groupings.

Of course, after differential evaluation is charted, the primary concern of the counselor is to choose a course of action. He may choose counseling, covered in Chapters Three, Four, and Five, or actual classroom implementations, discussed in Chapters Six, Seven, and Eight. In reality, there is little need for diagnostic evaluation if no remedial, educative, and/or therapeutic procedures are to follow. The viewpoint of the author is that action should be preceded by stocktaking. That is, one does not blindly plunge ahead to change things, with a paucity of information. Instead, one proceeds from a background of knowledge about the child. Bateman's (1967) paradigm is useful here. That is, some of this background information, such as a case history, can be etiological. Or it can be gathered by means of a task-analysis approach such as that organized under the rubric of behavioral modification. Or it can be diagnostic-remedial, utilizing test procedures to determine the best next course of action. Of course, treatment plans should follow assessment procedures. One without the other is incomplete.

This chapter will describe procedures that can be utilized by a counselor. It will proceed from the more general approach such as the case history, behavioral analysis, and the child interview to specific individual appraisal techniques. Individual appraisal (idiographic) procedures will be described in the areas of intellect, coordination (both fine and gross motor coordination), speech and hearing, reading, achievement, learning disabilities, personality, and social maturity. Group (nomothetic) approaches to intellectual assessment, achievement evaluation, reading tests, learning disabilities, motivation and interest assessment, interpersonal and/or social relations situations, and personality will be described. In all of these areas an attempt will be made either to delineate specific procedures one can adopt or to indicate sources of detailed descriptions of the implementation of particular procedures. The emphasis will be on techniques and procedures that have been used by the author and thus are believed to be practical for other counselors to use in school.

Individual Appraisal

The practitioner should have a general outline or case history within which to organize his data about the child's lifestyle. Various ways to organize this outline are available. Some can be found in such sources as Muro (1970, pp. 199–200), and Hill and Luckey (1969, pp. 183–185). The following case outline can serve as a general format for organizing data about a child.

Case History

1. Name
2. Age
3. Grade
4. School
5. Appraisal of the Situation, or Why Child was Referred
This category delineates why the child is being singled out for counseling, that is, the types of problems he presents that indicate the necessity for individual consideration.
6. Physical Status

a. Early development: this category includes such things as adverse history (for example, birth trauma), feeding schedules, toilet training, and sexual identification.

b. Health record: this category includes illnesses other than the "normal" childhood ones.

c. Present physical conditions: this category includes the child's assets and limitations, mannerisms, and other relevant data.

7. Educational Situation

a. Progress history: this category can include such things as anecdotal records and cumulative file information.

b. Child's present school situation.

c. Relationships with teachers.

d. Relationships with peers.

8. Home and Family Constellation

a. Family characteristics and chronology.

   1. Members' ages and education.

   2. Interactions and climate of the family. This can be investigated by means of *The Life Style Inventory* (Mosak & Shulman, 1971), in which the child's relationships to his siblings and parents are delineated on the basis of an interview with the child and/or the parents.

b. Environment: this rubric encompasses the community and the neighborhood in which the child lives in addition to the school environment.

9. Social and Peer Relationships

a. Relationships with adults.

b. Relationships with peers.

c. Social skills.

10. Objective Test Data Available

These data include measurements of such things as intellectual level, gross and fine motor coordination, speech, reading, achievement, learning disabilities, personality and motivational analysis.

11. Interviews and Subjective Data

This category includes records of such things as attitudes toward school, home, self, and others. Dengrove (1972) suggests that the child also write a self evaluation ("What kind of person are you?" is a possible title), identify what he would like to change about himself, list fears and angers, and write an autobiography.

Behavioral Diagnosis Format

An extremely useful format for observing behavior is the paradigm developed by Kanfer and Saslow (1969). A somewhat abbreviated outline of this format follows.

1. Initial Analysis of the Problem Situation
a. Behavior excesses: subcategories include (1) frequency; (2) intensity; (3) duration, and (4) occurrence (i.e, under conditions when its socially sanctioned frequency approaches zero).
b. Behavioral deficit: a given desirable behavior fails to occur (1) with sufficient frequency; (2) with adequate intensity; (3) in appropriate form, or (4) under socially expected conditions.
c. Behavioral assets: this category includes nonproblematic behavior and that which the person does well.

2. Clarification of the Problem Situation (the Environment)
a. Are the problematic responses categorized as behavioral excess or deficit?
b. Which persons or groups object to (or support) the behavior?
c. What consequences does the problem have for the client and others?
d. Under what conditions do the behaviors occur?
e. What satisfactions continue if problematic behaviors are sustained (gains maintained)?

3. Motivational Analysis
a. How does the child rank incentives? Incentives are the reinforcing events in the child's life and are measured by such scales as A *Reinforcement Survey Schedule For Children* (Keat, 1972) (see Appendix D).
b. What are reinforcers and under what conditions are they effective?
c. What reinforcing events are realistically useful for teaching new interpersonal skills?
d. List major aversive stimuli for the child, both immediately and in the future.

4. Developmental Analysis
This category involves analysis of notable biological (for example, vision and hearing), sociological (the child's present milieu and the congruency of his roles at home and school), and behavioral changes.

5. Analysis of Self Control
This category involves an analysis of situations, consequences, persons, or reinforcers that influence the child's self controlling behaviors.

6. Analysis of Social Relationships
In this category are listed significant persons who are responsive and provoking. An especially important consideration regarding

the social environment is finding means by which people who influence the patient can participate in treatment.

7. Analysis of the Social-Cultural-Physical Environment
This category has to do with the norms and behavioral environment of the person and the supports the milieu offers for changes in attitudes and values.

Kanfer and Saslow (1969) provide a more complete analysis of the details of each of these seven categories. Nevertheless, this outline can serve as a broad conceptual scheme by means of which one can delineate the various relevant behaviors.

Anna Freud's Diagnostic Profile

Another valuable diagnostic profile was developed by Anna Freud (1965). The reader is again referred to the original source for a more complete analysis. The useful and unique components of this approach are the assessment of the ego functions of memory, reality-testing, synthesis, controlled motility, speech, perceptual-motor functions, tension, concentration abilities, and the like. These characteristics are generally measured by the results of intelligence tests and observation. Another major consideration is the organization of the child's defenses. Are his coping skills age-adequate, too primitive, or too precocious? A final area of concern embraces the child's frustration tolerance level, sublimation potential, overall attitudes toward anxiety, and an evaluation of his developmental forces—are they primarily progressive or regressive in nature? The counselor needs to determine whether the child is different enough to merit special attention.

Child Observations

Another necessary factor in the appraisal of children is a means of organizing one's observations. That is, what are some meaningful categories for grouping their behaviors? The following list of characteristics is one type of categorization (adapted from Goodman and Sours, 1967) for organizing one's observations of the child.

1. Size and Appearance. This is the place for general observation of the child's appearance and physical characteristics.

2. Motility. Motility is the child's level of motor behavior. One can learn by observing the child's walk and his other behaviors whether he is hyper- or hypoactive.

3. Coordination. This category includes both fine and gross motor coordination, which can be evaluated by means to be

delineated later in this chapter. Certain gross observations can be made by a person who observes the child in his life settings (i.e., classroom teachers work daily with fine perceptual-motor coordination and physical education teachers deal with gross motor coordination).

4. Speech.   This category involves the child's receptive capabilities and expressive output skills.

5. Intellectual Level.   The child's intellectual capacity can be determined by talking with him to determine his information level, attention span, and vocabulary, and can also be evaluated psychometrically.

6. Thought Life of the Child.   This category has to do with his thoughts about good and bad, right and wrong, and his perceptions of various phenomena.

7. Emotional Reactions.   This category involves the range of the child's affect, or feelings and moods, and the range of their expression.

8. Manner of Relating.   This phenomenon can be observed during the interview with the counselor or gleaned from reports of relationships in school or with peers.

9. Coping Mechanisms.   These are the child's usual methods of defending himself against his life encounters, including such mechanisms as projection, avoidance, denial, escape into fantasy, and the like.

10. Fantasies and Dreams.   Depending on the skill of the counselor, he may want to engage in analysis of the content of the child's dreams.

11. Play.   The importance of play is perhaps the major factor that distinguishes working with children from working with adults. One should be able to judge the child's ability to initiate play activities, the movement of play activities (for example, fragmentary or goal directed), the appropriateness of his play, the level of maturity indicated by his choice of toys, the duration and creativity of his play with toys, and the mode and intensity of his expression of aggression.

Diagnostic Evaluation of the Child: General Procedures

The process of diagnosis should be viewed as an initial evaluative stage that precedes plans for helping the child. It is actually the process of coming to know and understand the child. In a more comprehensive vein, the approach advocated in this text is based on two of Woody's (1969, p. 77) points: "The present functioning or characteristics should be evaluated and described" (Chapter Two of this text) and "a treatment approach recommended" (Chapters Three, Four, Five, Six, Seven, Eight, Nine, and Ten).

The following outline is provided to guide the counselor in the office evaluation of a child. A format for observation and actual questions is provided for the counselor to use.

Office Evaluation of Child

1. The Child-Counselor Introduction. The counselor should greet the child by name and introduce himself to the child, using whatever title he feels is appropriate in the situation. He should explain what is to follow: that there are toys in the playroom-office and that he and the child are going there to play.

2. Reaction to Separation from the Mother or Teacher. This tells one much about the child's interactions with adults. This is a more prevalent difficulty in working with pre-school and kindergarten-age children than it is with older children.

3. The Office Evaluation. Here the child should become aware of the relationship between why he is coming in and what he is doing. One should ask the child why he visits the counselor: "Do you know why you are here today?" There are two schools of thought about the next step. Some counselors (e.g., Sullivan, 1954) say that the child should be simply told in behavioral terms why he is there: e.g., because he is not doing well in school, is wetting the bed, or whatever the reason. The other approach holds that the child knows why he is there and that it need not be clearly delineated at this time. The reasons will come up during the course of the interview or during the second session. The author normally does not introduce the subject at this time but allows the child freedom to do what he chooses. The reasons for the child's visits are usually dealt with during the first few sessions. During the office contact the following phenomena should be evaluated.

a. Child's play. The counselor should look for common aspects of content, how the child adheres to reality, and the nature of his thinking on a fantasy level. (During the evaluative session note-taking is usually permissible, but no notes should be taken during counseling hours). The nature of the child's affect (e.g., happy, sad, mad, etc.) during play and the patterns of this play should also be noted. Of course, the counselor should have a comprehensive knowledge of child development. A broad conceptual outline for this kind of understanding and for teacher consultation is detailed in Chapter Six.

b. Child's maturation. Maturation encompasses physical characteristics, motor development, speech, visual-motor integration, ideational-conceptual abilities, and the like. Depending upon one's orientation, this analysis can focus on the level of psychosexual development, ego or superego development, or a more behavioral orientation. During the office evaluation the counselor can normally collect data on the above-mentioned topics.

4. Child interview. Some evaluation is carried out by means of direct questions about the child's situation. These kinds of questions are typified by the "lifestyle interview" generally conducted by Adlerians (Herman, 1971). Lifestyle questions focus on determining the child's psychological position in the family. Among such questions are: "You are one of how many children?" "What kind of kid was Denise when she was growing up?" "Compared to the other children in the family, who is the most intelligent?" "Who is the least intelligent?" "Who got the best grades in school?" "What is your favorite subject in grade school?" "Who is the most industrious?" "Who had a temper?" "Who is the most sensitive?" "Who had the most friends?" These are fairly directive questions that focus on how the child's lifestyle has developed during the growing-up period. Subsequent questions concentrate on the family situation and the child's memories of his parents. For example, "What kind of person is Mother (Father)?" "Early recollections" are also probed in the lifestyle interview; the child is asked to think back as far as he can remember and to tell what he remembers. These and other direct questions are outlined in *The Life Style Inventory* (Mosak & Shulman, 1971).

During the child's individual interview, one can also ask various types of projective interview questions. Examples of such questions follow; of course, the counselor can invent his own questions to probe into the concerns of the particular interview. In the area of interests one can ask such things as "What would you rather have than anything else in all the world? Your second choice? Your third choice?" "What would you like most to do? Why?" "What would you like most to be? Why?" The author likes to ask, "If you could change something about yourself, what would it be?" Projective questions that focus on the school are "What subjects do you like best, worst (least)?" "What teachers do you like best and least?" In the area of fears, some questions are: "All people are afraid of something. What are you afraid of most?" "What were you most afraid of when you were a little child?" Earliest memories can be tapped by "What is the first thing in your life you can remember?" "How old were you then?" "What is the most pleasant memory you have?" "What is the most unpleasant memory you have?" To get at the child's fantasies or wishes, you can ask, "If you could be anything you wished, no matter what it was, what would you like most to be?" Then there is the traditional three-wish question, based on the story of Aladdin's lamp in which the child is asked to name his three wishes. If he does not know the story, the counselor can tell it to him. Aggression is another area we quite often want some information about. Questions that tap this area are: "What annoys you or irritates you most easily? Tell me about it." "Does it take much to get you angry enough to fight?" "What makes you angry the quickest?" "How does this make you want to behave?" To inquire into dreams one can ask: "Describe a pleasant dream you have had." "Tell me about any nightmare you have had." A further favorite question of many practitioners is "If you were going to be changed into an animal, what kind would you choose to be? Tell me about it." Another question, to determine what the child generally does during the course of a day, is "Tell me what your usual day is like." One need only draw on one's own ingenuity and creativity to develop more questions. Goodman and Sours (1967, Appendix A) list a series of questions that can provide some further leads for the counselor.

Child Observation   The counselor may want also to observe the child in a group. In a small group, many of the characteristics identified in the individual analysis are visible in relief, among them reaction to separation from mother or the classroom, initial reaction to the playroom, speech patterns, motor development, gross and fine coordination, activity level, attention span, frustration tolerance, fantasy development, play patterns, and relationships with play materials, other children, the counselor, and the playroom.

The child is often observed in the classroom. Certain behavioral observation procedures can be utilized in this situation. One of the useful methods of observing and recording child behavior in the classroom has been described by Werry and Quay (1969). In this format the observer records behaviors for 20 seconds and then rests 10 seconds. This process is kept up for 15 minutes. Behavior is recorded by occurrence rather than duration, and is thus a frequency count. The ideal is to take as many samples of behavior as possible. Werry and Quay identify three kinds of behavior:

1. Deviant Behaviors
a. Being out of one's seat (without permission or when the activity, though permitted, is prolonged).
b. Making physical contact with or disturbing others directly.
c. Making audible noise.
d. Turning in one's seat (90 degrees or more).
e. Vocalization (answering without permission, swearing, and the like).
f. Isolation (timeout).
g. Other deviant behaviors.

2. Attending Behaviors or on task–off task activity
a. Attending.   The child must have eye contact with the task or the teacher for not less than 15 out of the 20 seconds.
b. Irrelevant activity, not on the assigned task.
c. Daydreaming (more than 5 seconds out of 20).

3. Contact with the Teacher
a. Teacher-initiated positive contact.
b. Teacher-initiated negative contact.
c. Pupil-initiated positive contact with teacher.
d. Pupil-initiated negative contact.

Individual or Idiographic Appraisal Techniques

Measuring Intellectual Level

The intellectual level of the child is perhaps the most pervasive and generalized characteristic to influence his daily functioning, whether it be in interpersonal relationships, school, home, or in whatever capacity he must function. The two major individual intelligence tests are the Wechsler Intelligence Scale for Children (WISC) (Wechsler, 1949) and the Stanford-Binet Intelligence Scale (Terman and Merrill, 1960). Recently the WISC was extrapolated to a test with similar subtests entitled the Wechsler Pre-school and Primary Scale of Intelligence (WPPSI) (Wechsler, 1967), making the Wechsler useful for testing children from ages four to six and one-half. The WISC itself is generally regarded appropriate for ages five to sixteen, although statistical questions sometimes reflect adversely upon its use prior to age eight. Therefore, the Stanford-Binet is quite often used with preschoolers (ages two through six or seven). For eight-year-olds and older, the Wechsler is definitely the instrument preferred by most trained clinicians. In the area of interpretation, some more recently published books have updated Wechsler's standardizations. One book is the *Clinical Interpretation of the WISC* by Glasser and Zimmerman (1967). Another, by Ferindon and Jacobson (1969), concerns the educational interpretation of the WISC. Although these instruments are generally considered to be in the realm of the school psychologist, counselors with appropriate training can make use of them. Indeed, certain graduate programs (e.g., Muro, 1970) do include individual intelligence testing in the curriculum. The primary purpose of this section is to describe alternative procedures that can be used in lieu of intelligence tests, which require approximately one hour to administer.

One very quick method is to use the vocabulary list from the Stanford-Binet (Terman and Merrill, 1960). The child's level of verbal functioning, which has been determined to be the best indicator of intelligence, can be estimated by the examiner by asking the child to define the first 15 words from the Stanford-Binet vocabulary list. If the child appropriately (scoring based on examples given in the manual) answers the first six items (orange, envelope, straw, puddle, tap, gown), he has attained the six-year-old level of vocabulary. If he answers two more (roar, eyelash), he has attained the eight-year-old level. If he answers three more (Mars, juggler, scorch) he has attained the ten-year-old level. If he can correctly define four more words (lecture, skill, brunette, muzzle), he has attained the twelve-year-old level of functioning according to the vocabulary test of the Stanford-Binet.

The *Slosson Intelligence Test* (SIT) (Slosson, 1963), a scale that has adapted a great many items from the Stanford-Binet, may be administered within a brief period of time (10 to 20 minutes to give and score). By also using Gesell items (Gesell, Amatruda, 1947), it has extended coverage of items from infancy to adulthood. The test items for the elementary school years (ages 5–12) draw on vocabulary, information, comprehension, recognition of similarities and differences between objects, memory for sentences and numbers (both forward and backward), verbal analogies, arithmetic concepts, and perceptual-motor functioning. After reading the introductory remarks, the examiner simply administers items (mostly verbal questions) in order to determine the mental age (MA) of the child. The Intelligence Quotient (I.Q.) is then determined either by dividing the MA by the chronological age (CA) or by using the "I.Q. Finder."

Another quick inventory is the *Peabody Picture Vocabulary Test* (PPVT) (Dunn, 1965). This test takes only 10 to 15 minutes to administer and is particularly appropriate for use with children who cannot respond to the Stanford-Binet vocabulary words. This test provides norms for children from age 2 years 3 months to 18 years 5 months. The child is simply asked to indicate which of four pictures illustrates the word the examiner has spoken. The *PPVT* gives a quick estimate of a child's level of intellectual functioning in the area of picture identification. The scores derived are intelligence quotient, percentile score, and mental age.

A similar pictorial test that provides the examiner with an intelligence quotient is the *Quick Test* (Ammons and Ammons, 1962). It is somewhat quicker than the *PPVT*, taking from three to ten minutes to administer. The Quick Test is normed from two years up to nineteen years of age. It is designed for quick screening of verbal-perceptual intelligence in practical situations. The subject is required to choose the illustration of the indicated word from a series of pictures. This type of test (i.e., PPVT, SIT or Quick Test) can be used as a quick screening inventory for many of the cases referred for testing. Thus, the number of individual children referred for the Wechsler and Stanford-Binet can be reduced. If a more reliable and valid measure is needed, the child can be referred for individual testing with the Wechsler or Stanford-Binet if the counselor is not trained in these procedures.

Coordination Tests

Coordination tests might be considered neurological exams for children and are generally an extension of the mental status examination for children described by Goodman and Sours (1967). This area is a key one because it provides information that can be programmed into the child's educational environment. That is, it can help determine the kinds of remediation procedures that will help the child gain greater proficiencies in his deficient areas. Coordination evaluation also aids in the diagnosis of minimal brain dysfunction. That is, it is part of the comprehensive approach that evaluates intelligence, learning deficits, and perceptual-motor deficiencies. For more information about the minimal brain-disordered child and his diagnosis, the interested reader is initially referred to a book by Deutsch and Schumer (1970). The following is an outline of informal procedures the author uses to evaluate the child's functioning in fine and gross motor coordination areas.

1. General Observations
One should note here such things as the child's attention span, distractability, walk, and speech.

2. Motility

An important consideration is the child's level of activity on the hyper-hypo activity continuum. Ask the child to sit as still and as quietly as he can for two minutes. The minimal brain dysfunction child has no tolerance for this kind of game. The neurotic hyperactive child is likely to ask how long the interview will last and to be concerned about how he is supposed to be doing. The organically based hyperactive child is generally unconcerned about the length of the interview (Goodman and Sours, 1967).

3. Fine Perceptual Motor Evaluation

Activities in this category to be considered under another heading, include the Bender (1946) or the Benton (1963) and handwriting. Among the play activities that draw on fine perceptual-motor functioning are pick-up sticks, jacks, unwrapping candy and gum, and various kinds of drawing, to be discussed at length later. One can also ask the child to fold a paper, place it in an envelope, seal it, and then describe how he would mail it. This is similar to part of a comprehension task in an intelligence evaluation.

4. Reading

Informal assessment can be accomplished by using the word list from Lerner (1971). In addition, one can draw up a page of letters and numbers for him to recognize and talk about. For formal assessment, the author uses Gray's (1963) oral reading paragraphs.

5. Gross Motor Coordination (Informal Techniques)

A series of exercises the author generally asks the child to do to determine gross motor skills is as follows:

a. Extension of the arms with the eyes closed. Wide divergence of the arms, wide difference in the arm levels, or finger span fanning indicates some disturbance (Clements & Peters, 1962).

b. Passive rotation of the head with the eyes closed. Abnormal indicators are wide divergence or convergence of the arms, a dropping of the chin toward the arms, or rotation of the body at the shoulders or hips. If the entire body whirls to the turning of the head, or if there is extreme rigidity or resistance, difficulty with this task is indicated (Clements & Peters, 1962).

c. Walking. The child is instructed to walk on his heels while you observe the hands or face. Other tasks are the toe walk and the heel-to-toe walk (sometimes along a line).

d. Hopping on the right foot and then on the left foot. Skipping is also included here.

e. Standing on the right foot and then on the left foot (for observation of balance).

f. Playing catch with various sizes of balls. Kicking a ball should also be included here.

g. Games of various types that use motor functions, such as ring-around-the-rosie and hopscotch. The child's ability to ride a bicycle or swim can be reported or observed. The child can be asked to do various calisthenics such as push-ups, jumping-jacks, deep knee bends, following-the-leader, or "Simon says." Some of these games can be observed in the classroom as well as on the playground or in the office.

h. Tests of hearing or the cranial nerve. One can use a wrist or stopwatch and ask the child when he can hear it approaching him. Visual acuteness can also be assessed by asking the child how many fingers one is holding up at various distances. This procedure is for a gross indicator, and a nurse should be called upon for finer visual discrimination measures. To test eye dominance the child can be handed a roll of paper; the hand he uses to grab it and which eye is used to sight it should be noted. Another exercise is to ask the child to slowly chew gum on one side of the mouth and then the other. Further neurological examination procedures are described by Ilg and Ames (1964) under the headings of single and double commands. Interested readers are referred to this text for delineations of these tasks. They include right-and-left discrimination tasks as well as simple single commands. Norms are presented for the five- to ten-year-old range. Double commands (Ilg & Ames, 1964, pp. 175–181) are more complicated and require the child to do such things as putting his right middle finger against his left cheek. These are some of the major procedures a counselor can use to determine the child's gross motor coordination capacities. Assessment of these skills is often necessary to complete the picture of the child's strengths and weaknesses.

6. Gross Motor Coordination (Formal Techniques)
One formal type of evaluation includes both fine and gross motor coordination tests. This is the *Purdue Perceptual Motor Survey* by Roach and Kephart (1966). This survey is designed for the practitioner or teacher "to identify those children who do not possess perceptual-motor abilities necessary for acquiring academic skills by the usual instructional methods" (Roach & Kephart, 1966, pp. iii). The norms provided for this test are for grades 1 to 4. The five major groupings for the eleven subtests in the survey are balance and posture, body image and differentiation, perceptual-motor matching, ocular control, and form perception. The eleven subtests in the survey are the walking board, jumping,

identification of body parts, imitation of movements, obstacle course, Kraus-Weber (Kraus & Hirschland, 1954) test of physical fitness, angels in the snow, a chalkboard procedure, rhythmic writing, ocular pursuit, and reproduction of the Gesell copy forms (Ilg & Ames, 1964, p. 378).

7. Fine Perceptual Motor Evaluation (Formal Procedures)
Bender Motor Gestalt Test still utilizes designs developed by Loretta Bender (1938) over 30 years ago. The plates are available from the American Ortho-Psychiatric Association (Bender, 1946). The adaptation that has made this test most relevant and applicable for work with young children is the work of Koppitz (1964). Administration takes approximately five to fifteen minutes, depending upon the child. Koppitz's main contribution has been to norm this test for children from ages five to ten and to develop an objective scoring system based on more than 1,200 public-school children. The developmental drawing age is determined on the basis of scores on 25 criteria for the nine designs presented. The directions and procedures are relatively simple.

The child is simply told, "I have nine cards here with designs on them for you to copy. Here is the first one. Now go ahead and make one just like it." The child copies on an $8\frac{1}{2} \times 11''$ piece of plain white paper the nine designs presented to him. The second phase of the examination that the author uses focuses on recall. The child is simply asked to draw again all the forms he can remember. It has been generally assumed by those using this instrument that four or five designs is the average number of recall. This estimate, however, is based upon adult performance. Recent recall norms developed by Felty (1972) have indicated that the average number varies with the grade of the child as follows: For fifteen third-graders the mean number of designs recalled was 3.6 (ranging from 1 to 7). The sixth-grade mean recall score was 4.5 (ranging from 2.5 to 7). Scoring was based on a simple count of accurate designs, giving half-credit for partial recall of designs. It should also be noted, however, that the rural population tested also ranged six months to one year below the Koppitz (1964) norm group in their drawing ages. A third phase of the examination is to attempt to determine whether the child has a receptive or expressive disturbance, or a combination of both. The child is presented with designs he has seriously distorted in the copy phase. If he makes the same error(s) again, he is asked if he can perceive the difference between his drawings and the stimulus designs. If the child cannot see his errors when they are pointed out to him, it indicates that the disturbance is primarily one of visual perception of the receptive sort. If the child can perceive that the designs are different but has difficulty reproducing what he perceives, this tends to indicate an expressive disturbance. The primary use of the Bender is to determine a drawing age and to investigate specific perceptual-motor deficiencies in the child. Koppitz (1964) uses the test in such other areas as mental retardation and achievement. She has also developed indicators for scoring emotional disturbance in a young child (Koppitz, 1964).

Gesell Copy Forms (Ilg & Ames, 1964)   These stimuli have been available in various forms for quite a while. They are based on Gesell's (1941, 1947) original work and also appear on the Stanford-Binet test as indicators of intellectual functioning at various age levels. These designs are used primarily as informal indicators of the perceptual-motor achievement of the child. The norms generally accepted for these copy forms are that the child copy a circle by age three, reproduce a cross (a plus sign) at age four, make a square at five, replicate a triangle at six, and copy a diamond at seven. The child is given a copy form on a card and is asked to copy it on the plain paper. The instructions are simply to "make one like this on the paper."

Benton Visual Retention Test (1963)   This test taps visual memory or the recall of designs. There are three forms of the test. The one the author primarily uses is Form A. The child is instructed to look at the design for ten seconds; then the design is removed and he is asked to draw what he remembers. Administration time for the test is about ten minutes. The directions for administration of Form A are "You will be shown a card on which there are one or more figures. Study the card for ten seconds and then I will remove the card and you draw what you have seen." Norms are provided for the ten designs for ages eight to fourteen, and interpretative ranges (e.g., low average) are included for these scores. The two scores obtained are the number correctly reproduced and the total number of errors. Types of errors scored are omission, distortion, perseveration, rotation, misplacement, and incorrect size.

Frostig Developmental Test of Visual Perception (Frostig, Lefever, & Whittlesey, 1966)   This is a formal test for the child aged four to eight, intended as a screening procedure for preschoolers and kindergarten and first-grade children. It can also be useful as a clinical evaluation procedure for older children who suffer from learning difficulties. Administration time is between 30 and 45 minutes. It can be administered to the individual child or to a group of children. The five phenomena examined by this test are eye-motor coordination, figure-ground relationships, constancy of shape, position in space, and spatial relationships. The test is directly tied into a remedial procedure. That is, after the perceptual functions are measured, the remedial procedures used in Frostig's own developmental perceptual program can be implemented. These materials are available from the Follett Corporation (Chicago).

Figure Drawings Figure drawings have been used a great deal over the past 50 years. The classic work in this area was done by Florence Goodenough (1926). For many practicing clinicians, this test is still the basic method of acquiring a rough estimate of a child's drawing age (scores yield drawing ages from 3 years 6 months to 13 years 6 months). There appeared more recently a revision and extension of the Goodenough draw-a-man test (Harris, 1963). This approach offers considerable refinement in scoring. Norms are provided for ages three to fifteen and yield standard scores (mean = 100; standard deviation = 15). The basic premise of the draw-a-man approach is that drawing reflects the child's intellectual maturity. Directions for Harris' version ask the child to make a picture of a man, a woman, and finally himself. As can be surmised, the administration time is fairly brief. It has been the author's experience that this drawing procedure provides a fairly reliable estimate of the intellectual level of the child when administered the same day as the individual intelligence procedure.

Machover (1948) has done much to develop the personality-projective aspects of figure drawings. Despite Harris' findings that this is not a productive avenue for personality appraisal, it seems that some relevant information can be gleaned by utilizing the child inquiry questions from Machover's (1948) outline. Questions that the author asks are, "What is the child or person in the picture doing?" "What is the best (worst) part of the body?" "What does the person worry about?" "Does he have many friends?" "How much does he enjoy his family?" and "How does he like school?" This line of questioning can lead one to consider various other components of the child's personality relevant to his adjustment. In practice, one quite often finds that a child will verbally identify the person pictured as himself. Other children do not do so. In the latter case, the child is directly interviewed during the course of the examination to investigate his conscious awareness of where he personally stands with regard to the questions just cited involving peer friendship, family relationships, and school functionings.

The House-Tree-Person (H-T-P) Test (Buck, 1950) is used by numerous practitioners. In addition to the drawing of a person discussed above, the child is asked to draw a house and a tree as well as he can. Numerous inferences about the child's personality can then be drawn by a trained examiner on the basis of the child's drawings and the post-drawing interrogation procedure (Buck, 1950).

Other procedures, such as instructing the child to draw a family, have been developed. One recent approach developed by Burns and Kaufman (1970) asks the child to draw "a picture of everyone in your family, including you, doing something. Try to draw whole people, not cartoons or stick people. Remember, make everyone doing something—some kind of action." The kinetic family-drawing procedure avoids the sometimes inert figures encountered in the draw-a-person, house-tree-person, and draw-a-family procedures.

Another drawing procedure that focuses on family relationships has been developed by Leubuscher (1972). This is the so-called "supper-time drawing," in which the counselor fills in the seating arrangement around the family table. (If the family snacks all over the livingroom, consider the table edges as the four walls.)

Figure 2-1 *Supper-time drawing. Counselor fills in seating arrangement according to child's description. Lines of communication can then be drawn around the table.*

After the seating arrangement is determined, the child is to indicate whom he talks to most, in descending order. Lines of communication can be drawn around the table. Inquiry is then made about the kinds of things each person talks about. This procedure investigates the kinds of things the family does during one of the major occasions on which they are together in the home. Further lines of questioning can focus on the kinds of things the family members do together.

Speech and Hearing Tests

Many speech disorders can be evaluated by the teacher through informal talk and classroom observation (Smith, 1969). More formally, the *Illinois Test of Psycholinguistic Abilities* (Kirk et al., 1968) tests expressive and receptive functioning. Another test that can be administered by a counselor in order to rapidly identify those children most in need of speech therapy is the *Riley Articulation and Language Test* (Riley, 1966). Administration time is from one to two minutes and norms are provided for kindergarten, first grade and second grade. Subtest A measures articulation and is composed of eight words that have been used in previous articulation tests and contain the desired phonemes in the initial or final position. Subtest B (sentence repetition) consists of six sentences that have an increasing number of syllables. That is, the first sentences are the easiest and the last sentences the hardest. The examiner can note various substitutions, distortions, and omissions produced by the child when he attempts to reproduce either sounds and words or a complete sentence. Separate scores for articulation and sentence repetition are yielded. It should only be used for preliminary probing; further diagnostic testing, if needed, should be done by a speech and hearing specialist. If such a person is not available, one can utilize a more time-consuming procedure such as *The Templin-Darley Tests of Articulation* (Templin & Darley, 1960).

A screening procedure for hearing that can be used at the kindergarten and first-grade level is the *Kindergarten Auditory Screening Test* (Katz, 1971), which takes approximately one-half hour to administer. The three subtests focus on auditory skills that are important for scholastic success. They are:

1. A speech in environmental noise subtest in which words are spoken against variable decibels of background noise.

2. A phonemic synthesis subtest that utilizes a multiple-choice picture format.

3. A same/different subtest in which the child must decide

whether two spoken words are the same: the norms are presented on a pass-borderline-fail basis.

If the child fails one of the three subtests, he is considered to have failed and to be able to benefit from an auditory training program.

Reading Tests

Formal reading inventories are usually an excellent way to begin the diagnostic enterprise. A useful little paperback in this idiom is *Informal Reading Inventories*, by Johnson and Kress (1965), which provides an outline of procedures. Criteria are established for the various reading levels, such as the independent level, instructional level, frustration level, and the hearing comprehension level.

Lerner (1971, pp. 52–53) has provided an extremely useful listing of words selected from several basal readers, which can serve as an informal graded word reading list for the elementary school years. The procedure is as follows:

1. Type a list of words for each grade on a separate card.

2. Duplicate the entire list on a single sheet of paper.

3. Have the child read the words from the card while the examiner marks errors on the sheet. The examiner should note the child's method of analyzing and pronouncing difficult words.

4. Have the child read from increasingly difficult lists until he misses three words. This is the frustration level (too difficult). Two words missed is the instructional level, at which the child should be able to read with help. One word missed indicates the independent reading level, at which the child can read alone.

Pre-Primer

see	dog	down	boy
run	at	you	
me	come	said	

Primer

day	under	little	blue
from	house	came	
all	ready	you	

Grade 1

about	catch	boats	hold
sang	across	hard	
guess	live	longer	

Grade 2

hungry	trick	himself	leading
loud	chair	color	
stones	hopped	straight	

Grade 3

arrow	castle	safety	happiness
wrist	learned	yesterday	
bottom	washed	delight	

Grade 4

brilliant	grammar	terrify	agent
credit	jingle	wrench	
examine	ruby	mayor	

Grade 5

career	grieve	procession	volcano
cultivate	jostle	sociable	
essential	obscure	triangular	

Grade 6

buoyant	incubator	prophesy	vague
determination	ludicrous	sanctuary	
gauntlet	offensive	tapestry	

An individual inventory is the *Gray Oral Reading Test* (1963). This test can generally be completed in a matter of five to ten minutes. Passages are provided for the pre-primer level to the adult level, and total scores are converted to grade equivalents (grades 1.1 to 12.0). An important aspect of this type of test is that it enables the examiner to determine the types of errors made by the child. Kinds of errors identified for scoring are those of aid with a word, gross and partial mispronunciation, omission, insertion, substitution, repetition, and changes in word order. Each passage is timed and there are four comprehension questions at the end of each paragraph. Some guides to interpretation are provided in the manual which allow the examiner to specify the child's particular type of difficulty.

Another type of reading inventory attempts to determine reading readiness. There has been a need for an inventory that draws on the skills, but not the symbols, used in reading. Children are often found to be failing a task that is not diagnosed until after they have experienced considerable failure. The reversal of failure feelings is more difficult than prevention. Kinsbourne has standardized a test that can be utilized with pre-schoolers. It is called *MARK II* (Kinsbourne, 1972). The first two subtests of the three in this test are accompanied by norms for 20 children in kindergarten (Conklin, 1972), 192 first-grade males, and 175 first-grade females (Kinsbourne, 1972). The test sections that utilize nonsense forms and shapes, called visual discrimination tests, are composed of the following sections: discrimination and retention of form, discrimination and retention of orientation, discrimination and retention of sequence. The auditory, or phoneme discrimination, test is composed of work-pair repetition, same-different discrimination, phoneme-word repetition, sound discrimination in the word, and three-phoneme sequence repetition. The administration time is from thirty minutes to one hour. The third section of the test, called paired association, utilizes the nonsense shapes as well as nonsense syllables. This aspect of the test is in the early developmental stage. Although MARK II appears promising, there needs to be further collection of norms and data to determine its applicability.

Achievement Tests

Teacher-made tests, are, of course, the primary informal means of evaluating achievement. The counselor should nevertheless have some informal and formal methods for evaluating achievement. Parts of the Gesell procedures (Ilg & Ames, 1964) indicate norms for children from five to ten in the following areas. On paper-and-pencil tests, the child is asked to print letters, his name and address, and the numbers he knows. Time orientation is evaluated by asking the child the month and year. A further indication of achievement is to ask each child to name all the animals he can think of until he is stopped (Ilg & Ames, 1964). This was an item on the old form of the Stanford-Binet intelligence test (Terman & Merrill, 1937). By using these procedures and asking questions the counselor can determine informally the child's achievement level.

A more formalized and quick procedure (15 to 20 minutes) is the *Wide Range Achievement Test* (Jastak & Jastak, 1965). Level 1 of this test covers children from 5 years through 11 years 11 months. It is composed of tasks in three areas: reading, writing, and arithmetic. The reading section simply requires recognition and naming of letters and pronounciation of words. Therefore, the author generally omits the reading part and administers the other two. In the spelling section, words are dictated and the child writes them. The arithmetic tasks are presented both orally and in written form. Scores yielded on the *Wide Range Achievement Test* are grade equivalents, standard scores (mean of 100 and standard deviation of 15), and percentiles.

Learning Disabilities

In spite of the fact that there is no general agreement about the nature of learning disabilities, Kirk and Bateman's (1962) definition is generally agreed to be the best. It states that "a learning disability refers to a retardation, disorder, or delayed development in one or more of the processes of speech, language, reading, writing, arithmetic, or other school subjects resulting from a psychological handicap caused by possible cerebral dysfunction and/or emotional or behavioral disturbances." Thus, this is a broad type of disorder. Many of the tests previously mentioned and those to be discussed on the following pages can be conceived of as instruments for the diagnosis of learning disabilities.

The screening of learning disabilities can be one of the primary functions of the counselor. The pupil rating scale to be described was developed by Myklebust (1971) and is a relatively quick screening procedure that can be used by the teacher to rate her pupils in the classroom. Norms are presented for third- and fourth-grade children (ages seven to ten). Five tests comprise this scale. Auditory comprehension involves comprehension of word meanings, adherence to instructions, comprehension of class discussions, and retention of information. The area of spoken language tests vocabulary, grammar, word recall, storytelling, and the formulation of ideas. The orientation test evaluates judgments of time, skills, space orientation, judgments of relationships, and knowledge of directions. Motor coordination has to do with general coordination, balance, and manual dexterity. Personal-social behavior includes cooperation, attention, organization, adjustment to new situations, social acceptance, responsibility, completion of assignments, and tactfulness. Once the general screening procedure is completed and a child seems to need further evaluation, a more comprehensive procedure can be used.

One relatively informal procedure, suggested by Valett (1967), tests 53 basic learning abilities grouped under the major rubrics of gross motor development, sensory-motor integration, perceptual-motor skills, language development, conceptual skills, and social skills. Thus the overall testing time can be extensive unless precision testing is used and the examiner focuses on the problem areas. The actual tasks are grouped according to level of difficulty for ages 5–8, 8–10, and 10–12. More important than the "psychoeducational evaluation of basic learning abilities" (Valett, 1968), however, is the content of Valett's handbook, which describes activities for the remediation of learning disabilities (Valett, 1967).

The *Illinois Test of Psycholinguistic Abilities* (ITPA) (Kirk, McCarthy and Kirk, 1968) can be used to appraise learning disabilities in a more formal fashion. The ITPA is a relatively involved test composed of twelve subtests. Norms based on the scores of 1,000 average school children are presented for ages 2 years 4 months to 10 years three months. Initially, the ITPA can take an hour and a half to administer. With practice, however, this time can be lowered to about 45 minutes. It is similar to the Stanford-Binet in that the counselor needs to establish a basal (i.e., level at which a certain number of items are passed) and a ceiling (i.e., level at which a certain number of items are failed) and can therefore administer less than the entire test. Subjects are listed below so that the reader can determine their relevance to any particular child under consideration for evaluation.

1. Auditory Reception. Such questions as "Do dogs eat?" and "Do bicycles eat?" are responded to by "yes-no" answers.

2. Visual Reception. The examiner shows the child a picture and then turns the page and the child must point to the one of the four items pictured that matches the first picture. This is similar to the picture memory subtest of the Stanford-Binet (Terman & Merrill, 1960) at the three-year level.

3. Visual Sequential Memories. The child observes a sequence card (5 seconds), the card is removed, and the child is asked to replicate it by placing corresponding chips (with designs) on the tray in the same order.

4. Auditory Association. This is a verbal analogy test. For example, "A dog has hair, a fish has _____."

5. Auditory Sequential Memory. This is a digit-span test in which the person repeats a sequence of digits (from two to eight numbers long). It is similar to the digit-span of the Wechsler Intelligence Scale for Children (Wechsler, 1949).

6. Visual Association. The child points to one of four peripheral pictures most closely associated with a central picture.

7. Visual Closure. This is a picture identification task in which the child is to point to all the specified objects (e.g., dogs) he can find in 30 seconds.

8. Verbal Expression. The child describes five objects (nail, ball, block, envelope, and button) by saying something about each one after instructions from the examiner to "tell me all about this."

9. Grammatic Closure. The examiner reads incomplete state-

ments to the child, points to pictures, and stops when the child is to supply the missing word.

10. Manual Expression.   The child is to demonstrate the use of the pictured objects by showing (pretending) the examiner what to do with the object (e.g., coffee pot and cup).

11. Auditory Closure.   The child is recited words with significant sounds omitted, for example, -isher-an. He is supposed to supply the completed word.

12. Sound Blending.   The examiner recites successive sounds and the subject is asked to verbalize the whole word or nonsense word.

The major useful scores gleaned from this test are the psycholinguistic age for each subtest and a scale score for each subtest (mean of 36 and standard deviation of 6). Of course, this test leads to a detailed profile analysis of the types of skills described above. These skills are related to a wide range of functions including intelligence, perceptual-motor functions, and the like. It should be noted that numerous remedial activities have been developed for use after weaknesses are discerned on the diagnostic ITPA. For procedures to overcome particular learning disabilities one should refer to such sources as Karnes, *et al.* (1966), Valett (1967, 1968), & Lerner (1971).

Personality Tests

Procedures that enable the counselor to assess the child's personality can be crucial in determining his adjustment and coping capacities. Therefore, it is important to look at various procedures that can be used to appraise the personal aspect of the child's functioning. In many cases the counselor's primary concern will be to determine the emotional status of the child. The following procedures make possible this type of appraisal.

1. Thematic Methods.   The Children's Apperception Test—Form H (Bellack, Bellack & Hurvich, 1965) uses pictures of children in ambiguous situations, which the child is asked to describe. These tests are for children aged 5 to 10; administration time depends both on the number of pictures selected (from a total of 20) and on the length of the child's story. The child is instructed that this is a story-telling game in which the child is to make up a story for each picture the examiner shows him. "Tell what has happened before and what is happening now. Say what the people are feeling and thinking and how it will come out. You make up any kind of story you please." Pictures in this series

draw on the child's relationships around the dinnertable, in games, with siblings and mother, at a picnic, seeing parents in bed, in the bathroom, and so on. Much can be learned from the child's descriptions of the characters' thoughts, feelings and actions. It has been found productive to use any kind of picture suitable to tap the particular area the examiner wants information about. Such a book as *Family* by Mead and Heyman (1965) offers a wealth of pictures for which the child can make up stories. There are pictures in this book of mothers and children, fathers and children, brothers and sisters, grandparents, children alone, friends, and so on. The counselor can thus choose numerous kinds of pictures to stimulate the fantasies of the child. This can, of course, be an aspect of either diagnosis or counseling work (e.g., the self-disclosure procedure).

2. Sentence Completion.   Sentence completion is the process of providing the stem of a sentence and asking the child to complete it. His answers indicate his feelings about the subjects of the statements. For example, one can simply say a single word, e.g., "mother" or "father." To this stem the child adds the rest of the sentence. There are numerous informal forms of sentence completion (see Chapter Four in this text). In any particular situation, the author utilizes such sentence stems (relevant to the particular case) as the following: "I feel . . . a mother is more likely than a father to" "A sister . . ." "My father . . ." "If only fathers would . . ." "My friends . . ." "I am afraid . . ." "I worry about . . ." and the like. Thus the counselor can choose the stems to suit the situation and elicit reactions about matters that are important to the child. In addition, formal sentence completion tests are available. One of these is the Forer Structured Sentence Completion Test (Forer, 1957). This test is composed of a series of 100 stems, which the child is directed to finish. Among them are "School is . . ." "I wish that school . . ." "I feel guilty about . . ." "I am afraid of . . ." "I feel like running away when . . ." and others.

3. Drawings.   The "squiggle" game has been described in a recent book by Winnicott (1971). The counselor explains, "I shut my eyes and go like this on the paper and you turn it into something, and then it is your turn and you do the same thing and I turn it into something." The counselor first draws something on the paper with his eyes closed. Then the child is to complete the drawing, say what it is, and talk a bit about it. Next the child makes a "squiggle" on the paper, which the therapist is to complete. This exchange of drawings goes on, allowing the

counselor to gain some insight into what is going on in the child's mind. Winnicott gives various illustrations of types of children aged from 21 months of age up to 16 years. The cases in the textbooks are illustrated with detailed squiggles and descriptions of the interchanges between counselor and child. This procedure enables one to gain information about the child before consulting with the parents about him. Another interesting procedure has been developed by Leaman (1972). It requires a piece of paper with a stick man drawn in the center and a series of men drawn around the periphery. The child is asked to label the center one as himself, and then to recall a recent event (for example, a fight) and label the smaller stick figures with the names of other children involved in the fight. Then the child is to explain, step by step, what happened before and during the fight. As he describes it, he draws arrows from figure to figure, numbering in sequence the interchanges between himself and the other children. The counselor records the numbers on a separate sheet of paper. In the example given in Figure 2-2, the following numbers explain the interchanges.

1. Jim told Steve that he should not let Don play with the car.
2. Don asked Steve if he could play with the car.
3. Steve said no.
4. Don kicked Steve.
5. Jim said he was going to tell the teacher.
6. Don told Jim that he had better not tell the teacher.

Once the interaction and the details of the actual fight have been described, the counselor can go on to explore alternative responses the child could have made. These are listed on the paper. For example, in this case some alternative responses of the child were:

1. Could hit Steve gently.
2. Tell the teacher that Steve would not let him play with his car.
3. Ask Steve nicely—please.
4. Ask Steve why he can't play with his car.
5. Find another toy to play with.

In other words, this technique combines a diagnostic procedure that attempts to concretize an action-interaction between the child and his environment with a treatment situation in which the child is to consider alternative responses that are more appropriate than the ones he made. If the child does not come up

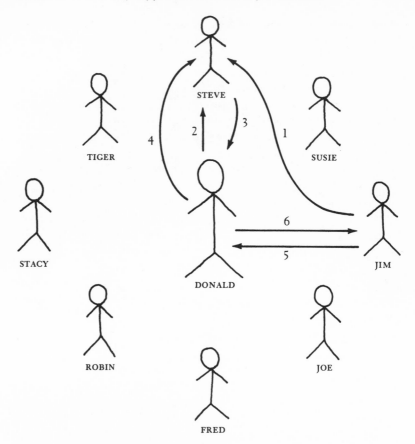

Figure 2-2 *The "stick man procedure" attempts to determine the interaction between the child and his environment in a given situation.*

with appropriate alternatives, then the counselor can suggest some additional ones. Finally, a procedure such as role-playing can be used to rehearse more adaptive responses.

The Make-a-Family Test (Malecki, 1972) utilizes materials similar to "the family materials" published by Milton Bradley (1967). It consists of a large felt board and felt characters representing adults in the child's life, children, and various figures such as houses, cars, trees, and balls. The examiner asks the child to "make a family." The examiner is to remain relatively noncommittal during this test, reflecting the child's feelings and encouraging him to make his family. The examiner can record the child's reactions, choices of characters and objects, and the placement of each. When he has finished, the child can be asked such questions as, "Would you like to tell me all about this?" His answers reflect the interrelationships and dynamics of his family.

4. Self Concept. One's self concept is his image of himself. It is considered by many to be the single most important variable in an individual's life. "We can conclude that the parents of children with high self-esteem are concerned and attentive ('accepting') toward their children, that they structure the worlds ('limits') of their children along lines they believe to be proper and appropriate, and that they permit relatively great freedom within the structures ('respect') they have established" (Coopersmith, 1967, p. 236). Means of measuring self concept vary from asking pupils to describe the kind of persons they are (would like to be) in compositions to more formal assessment procedures.

An 80-item self concept scale has been published by Piers and Harris (1969). This test can be individually administered (in 15 to 20 minutes) below the third grade and individually or group administered from third grade on; for group testing in grades 3 to 6, one should read the instructions aloud and repeat each of the items once. Although norms with percentiles and stanines are available for grades 4 to 12, one is encouraged to develop local norms.

Another useful scale for children has been developed by Coopersmith (1959, 1967). This 58-item inventory (see Coopersmith, 1967, Appendix A, pp. 265–266) examines four areas: peers, parents, school, and personal interests. Although the items were reworded for use with 8–10-year-olds, the norms (means and standard deviations) are from a fifth- and sixth-grade population.

Another self concept scale uses 30 adjectives which the child uses to rate himself as he is and as he would like to be (by Bledsoe & Garrison, reported by Fox, Luszki, & Schmuck, 1966, pp. 99–101). This tool gives the examiner a picture of how positively the child sees himself and also of the discrepancy between his self image and what he would like to be.

In order to investigate the self orientation of younger children, Ziller, Long and Henderson (reported by Johnson & Bommarito, 1971) developed a pre-school scale (ages 3 to 8) that takes about 10 minutes to administer individually. The child uses gummed labels on chosen points or points his finger to indicate his answers. Among the areas this test measures are esteem, dependency, identification, skin color, and size realism.

Measuring Social Development

The classic and most important work in the area of social maturity was done by Edgar Doll (1953), whose social maturity scale is a means for someone familiar with the child to evaluate his development in this area. The ages covered are from birth up to and over the age of 25. More recently, Doll has developed the *Preschool Attainment Record* (PAR) (Doll, 1966), which allows evaluation of the child's development from birth up to 7 years of age. The PAR thus covers the crucial years for evaluation of the child's intellectual and social readiness for entrance into school—that is, the years from 4 through 7. This test allows for a rather broad evaluation of numerous kinds of skills, such as the gross motor skills of ambulation, the fine visual motor skills of manipulation, the verbal or communicative skills, ability to get along with others ("rapport"), and self help skills necessary for such tasks as cleaning up ("responsibility"). Further, the PAR attempts to appraise the child's intellectual level in the areas of information, ideation, and creativity. Thus, by interviewing a parent or teacher who knows the child very well, the counselor can compile a summary profile of these kinds of achievement and compute a social quotient indicating the child's developmental expectations and accomplishments in particular skills.

Barclay (1966) sees the uses of sociometry as threefold: (1) sociometric scores can be used in conjunction with teachers' ratings to provide a basis for screening and assessing social desirability factors; (2) the procedure generates teacher interest and involvement; (3) it can be utilized as a criterion for behavior change before and after active interventions. The topic of sociometry is too broad to be covered here; for detailed expositions see Gronlund (1959) and chapters in Dinkmeyer and Caldwell (1970) and Fox *et al.* (1966). Certain basic considerations, however, should be mentioned. It is important to examine the major life areas of school (e.g., "If you could sit next to three children in your class, whom would you choose?"), playground (e.g., "If you could play with three children in your class, who would you choose?"), and home (e.g., "What persons would you like to invite to a party at your home?"). Sociometry usually uses some form of matrix and sociogram to organize the data. This map can help the teacher to visualize the child's relationships more clearly and to organize group activities in a more meaningful personal-social way.

Group or Nomothetic Appraisal

The first part of this chapter introduces individual or idiographic approaches to working with children. The subject of the second part, group approaches to assessment, is generally adequately covered in most other elementary guidance books. Furthermore, it is relatively comprehensively covered in test courses in graduate programs in counselor training. That is, by their very nature these courses generally concentrate on group tests that can be utilized in the schools. Therefore, this section will be comparatively brief by contrast to the first section. Various relevant tests will be listed under selected areas of evaluation. Only if the approaches are unique or deserving of special attention will detailed descriptions comparable to those in the first part of this chapter be included.

A notable contribution in this area of test evaluation has been edited by Ralph Hoepfner (1970). This publication, produced by the UCLA Graduate School of Education, provides a comprehensive listing of test evaluations for the elementary school. The tests are grouped according to the goals of elementary school education and measure such areas as affective learning, cognitive learning, and skills in language, foreign languages, mathematics, music, physical education, reading, religion, science, social studies, and so forth. For each test there is an evaluation of measurement validity, examinee appropriateness, administrative usability, and the norms' technical excellence. If the examiner wants an evaluation of a test he is considering for a particular grade level (they are grouped for grades 1, 3, 5, and 6), he can use this book to ascertain its important measurement criteria.

Another useful source, edited by Johnson and Bommarito (1971), is a compilation of more than 300 measures that are not available from test publishers. The scales are classified in ten categories: cognition, personality and emotional characteristics, children's perceptions of environment, self concept, characteristics of the environment, motor skills and sensory perception, physical attributes, other attitudes and interests, social behavior, and other measures (a potpourri of tests that do not fit into the other categories).

The following sections contain brief listings of particular tests that are often used in the schools and are relevant to educational programming. The tests represent a selective listing, in order of use by elementary school districts in Pennsylvania, previously published in the Guidance Keynotes (Pennsylvania Department of Public Instruction, 1967). After listing the title, its grade appropriateness and publisher will be cited.

Intelligence Tests

Intelligence is generally considered to bear on the child's capacity to learn and to deal with new situations. Therefore, the results of intelligence tests are often used for placement and grouping of students. In addition, knowledge of these results also affects the expectations of teachers and counselors for particular children.

1. California Short Form Test of Mental Maturity. Grades K–1, 1–3, 4–8. California Test Bureau.

2. Otis-Lennon Mental Ability Test. K.5–6.9. Harcourt Brace Jovanovich.

3. Lorge-Thorndike Intelligence Tests. Grades K–1, 2–3, 4–6. Houghton Mifflin.

4. Primary Mental Abilities Test. K–1, 2–6. Science Research Associates.

5. Kuhlmann-Anderson Intelligence Tests. K, 1, 2, 3, 4, 5, 6. Personnel Press.

Achievement Tests

Achievement tests attempt to measure the child's attainments in certain subject-matter areas. They can therefore be used to supplement teacher-made tests.

1. Stanford Achievement Test. Primary (grades 1–3) yields 5 scores; Elementary (grades 3–4) yields 6 scores; Intermediate (grades 5–6) yields 9 scores. Harcourt, Brace & World.

2. Iowa Tests of Basic Skills. Grades 3–9. This test yields 15 scores. Houghton Mifflin.

3. Metropolitan Achievement Tests. Grades 1.5–6. This test yields scores in four major areas. Harcourt, Brace & World.

4. California Achievement Test. Grades 1–2, 3–4, 4–6. This test yields 11 scores. California Test Bureau.

Reading Tests

Reading is perhaps the most basic academic skill in the elementary school. Therefore, all the achievement tests cited above measure reading. There are, however, several other commonly used scales, among them:

1. Gates-MacGinitie Reading Tests. Grades 1, 2, 3, 2.5–3, 4.5–6. Teachers College Press.

2. SRA Achievement Series. Grades 1–2, 2–4, 4–9. Science Research Associates.

Motivation and Interests

There are two main scales that measure motivation and interests. The initial one is a reinforcement survey schedule for children

(Keat, 1972). Norms are available for grades 4, 5, and 6. In addition, there are individual case studies for children in grades K–3. Used in any fashion, this inventory provides the parent, counselor, or teacher with a system of rewards ("reinforcement menu") of value to the particular child, allowing him to develop a reinforcement program for the child that will maintain his interests and thus possibly motivate him to achieve in other areas.

An interest inventory entitled "What I Like To Do," published by Science Research Associates, measures (for grades 4–7) preferences in art, music, social studies, active play, quiet play, manual arts, home arts, and science.

Personality Inventories

The nature of the child makes this type of group measurement extremely difficult during the elementary school years. Therefore, there are only a few tests that seem useful.

1. Early School Personality Questionnaire (ESPQ). Ages 6–8. Institute for Personality and Ability Testing (1966). The ESPQ and the next test are based on the work of Cattell and the 16-factor personality inventory.

2. Children's Personality Questionnaire. Ages 8–12. Institute for Personality and Ability Testing (1968).

3. California Test of Personality. Grades K–3, 4–8. This test yields 15 scores. California Test Bureau (1953).

These are some of the inventories that can be used in group appraisal work with children. For a more detailed development of these areas, the interested reader is referred to one of the classic texts in testing, such as Cronbach's (1970), and sections in the elementary guidance texts of Shane, Shane, Gibson, & Munger (1971) and Muro (1970).

Another comprehensive source on testing is the Guidance Monograph Series published by Houghton Mifflin. In particular, the monograph on school testing programs (Bauernfeind, 1968) discusses sources of information about standardized tests and various considerations involved in the development of testing programs in the schools. Other areas covered in the Guidance Monograph Series are interest tests; personality inventories; intelligence, aptitude, and achievement tests; and various other statistical concepts in testing. It is assumed, of course, that the counselor-in-training will have attained sophisticated understanding of reliability, validity, and practicality so that he can determine from perusal of a manual the feasibility of particular evaluation instruments for the school in which he is working. In addition, it is expected that the counselor will have the skills to develop local norms if they are relevant and applicable.

Summary

This chapter has attempted to provide a basis on which to develop an individualized assessment schedule for elementary school children. Therefore, the focus has been on the development of individual techniques. The emphasis was on individual, not group, procedures—though group tests were listed. It is felt that the counselor should have sufficient background in tests and measurements and statistics to evaluate group tests by examining the manual. Therefore, this chapter has introduced types of procedures of which counselors are generally unaware. After using such procedures, the counselor can make assessments and educational recommendations to be implemented in the regular classroom. The implementation procedures for particular areas of the educational program will be considered in Chapters Seven and Eight. After particular educational difficulties or personality disorders are identified on the basis of the counselor's appraisal, various kinds of subsequent action are covered in Chapters Three (individual counseling), Four (child group counseling), Five (parent and teacher groups), Six (classroom collaboration), and Nine (environmental considerations). Effective counseling and school or environmental modification strategies must be based on an evaluation of the child's current functioning, both intrapsychically and in his environments.

References

Ammons, R. B., & Ammons, C. H. *Quick test.* Missoula, Mont.: Psychological Test Specialists, 1962.

Anastasi, A. *Psychological testing.* New York: Macmillan, 1968.

Barclay, J. R. Sociometry: Rationale and technique for effecting behavior change in the elementary school. *Personnel and Guidance Journal,* 1966, **44,** 1067–1076.

Bateman, B. Three approaches to diagnosis and educational planning for children with learning disabilities. *Academic Therapy,* 1966–67, **11,** 215–222.

Bauernfeind, R. H. *Building a school testing program.* Boston: Houghton Mifflin, 1968.

Bellak, L., Bellak, S. S., & Hurvich, M. S. *Children's Apperception Test—Human Figures.* Larchmont, N.Y.: C.P.S. Company, 1965.

Bender, L. *A visual motor gestalt test and its clinical use.* New York: American Orthopsychiatric Association, 1938.

Bender, L. *Bender Motor Gestalt Test*. Cards and manual of instructions. New York: American Orthopsychiatric Association, 1946.

Benton, A. *The Revised Visual Retention Test*. New York: The Psychological Corporation, 1963.

Bradley, M. *The family*. Springfield, Mass.: Milton Bradley Company, 1967.

Buck, J. N. *House-Tree-Person Test*. Beverly Hills, Cal.: Western Psychological Services, 1950.

Burns, R. C., & Kaufman, S. H. *Kinetic family drawings*. New York: Brunner/Mazel, 1970.

Clements, S. D., & Peters, J. E. Minimal brain dysfunction in the school-age child. *Archives of General Psychiatry*, 1962, 6, 185–197.

Conklin, N. A. A study of the potential use of the Mark II as a predictor of reading readiness in a sample of kindergarten children. Unpublished masters thesis, Pennsylvania State University, 1972.

Coopersmith, S. A method of determining types of self-esteem. *Journal of Abnormal and Social Psychology*, 1959, **59**, 87–94.

Coopersmith, S. *The antecedents of self-esteem*. San Francisco: W. H. Freeman, 1967.

Cronbach, L. J. *Essentials of psychological testing*. New York: Harper & Row, 1970.

Dengrove, E. Practical behavioral diagnosis. In A. A. Lazarus (Ed.), *Clinical Behavior Therapy*. New York: Brunner/Mazel, 1972, pp. 73–86.

Deutsch, C. P., & Schumer, F. *Brain-damaged children*. New York: Brunner/Mazel, 1970.

Dinkmeyer, D., & Caldwell, E. *Developmental counseling and guidance: A comprehensive school approach*. New York: McGraw-Hill, 1970.

Doll, E. A. *The measurement of social competence*. Minneapolis, Minn.: Educational Test Bureau, 1953.

Doll, E. A. *Preschool Attainment Record*. Circle Pines, Minn.: American Guidance Service, 1966.

Dunn, L. M. *Peabody Picture Vocabulary Test*. Circle Pines, Minn.: American Guidance Service, 1965.

Felty, S. Bender-Gestalt Recall. Unpublished masters thesis, Pennsylvania State University, 1972.

Ferinden, W. E., & Jacobson, S. *Educational interpretation of the Wechsler Intelligence Scale for Children*. Linden, N.J.: Remediation Associates, 1969.

Forer, B. R. *The Forer Structured Sentence Completion Test*. Santa Monica, Cal.: Western Psychological Services, 1957.

Fox, R., Luszki, M., & Schmuck, R. *Diagnosing classroom learning environments*. Chicago: Science Research Associates, 1966.

Freud, A. *Normality and pathology in childhood*. New York: International Universities Press, 1965.

Frostig, M., Lefever, W., & Wittlesey, J. *Developmental Test of*

Visual Perception. Palo Alto, Cal.: Consulting Psychologists Press, 1966.

Gesell, A., Halverson, H. M., Thompson, H., Ilg, F. L., Castner, B. M., Ames, L. B., & Amatruda, C. S. *The first five years of life.* New York: Harper & Row, 1940.

Gesell, A., & Amatruda, C. S. *Developmental diagnosis: normal and abnormal child development.* New York: Hoeber, 1947.

Glasser, A. J., & Zimmerman, I. L. *Clinical interpretation of the Wechsler Intelligence Scale for Children.* New York: Grune and Stratton, 1967.

Goldman, L. *Using tests in counseling.* New York: Appleton-Century-Crofts, 1971.

Goodenough, F. *Measurement of intelligence by drawings.* New York: Harcourt, Brace & World, 1926.

Goodman, J. D., & Sours, J. A. *The Child Mental Status Examination.* New York: Basic Books, 1967.

Gray, W. S. *Gray Oral Reading Tests.* Indianapolis, Ind.: Bobbs-Merrill, 1963.

Gronlund, N. E. *Sociometry in the classroom.* New York: Harper & Brothers, 1959.

Harris, D. B. *Children's drawings as measures of intellectual maturity.* New York: Harcourt, Brace & World, 1963.

Herman, I. *Adlerian psychology.* Chicago: Alfred Adler Institute, 1971.

Hill, G. E., & Luckey, E. B. *Guidance for children in elementary schools.* New York: Appleton-Century-Crofts, 1969.

Hoepfner, R. *C.S.E. Elementary school test evaluations.* Los Angeles: Center for the Study of Evaluation, 1970.

Ilg, F. L., & Ames, L. B. *School readiness.* New York: Harper & Row, 1964.

Jastak, J. F., & Jastak, S. R. *The Wide Range Achievement Test.* Wilmington, Del.: Guidance Associates, 1965.

Johnson, M. S., & Kress, R. A. *Informal reading inventories.* Newark, Del.: International Reading Association, 1965.

Johnson, O. G., & Bommarito, J. W. *Tests and measurements in child development: a handbook.* San Francisco: Jossey-Bass, 1971.

Kanfer, F. H., & Saslow, G. Behavioral diagnosis. In C. Franks (Ed.), *Behavior Therapy: Appraisal and Status.* New York: McGraw-Hill, 1969, pp. 417–444.

Karnes, M., Hodgins, A., Hertig, L., Solberg, C., Morris, J., Heggemeier, M., & Lorenz, C. *Activities for developing psycholinguistic skills with preschool culturally disadvantaged children.* Urbana, Ill.: Institute for Research on Exceptional Children, 1966. (Available from Educational Resources Information Center.)

Katz, J. *Kindergarten Auditory Screening Test.* Chicago: Follett, 1971.

Keat, D. B. *A reinforcement survey schedule for children.* University Park, Penn.: Author, 1972.

Keat, D. B., & Hackman, R. B. A method of clustering persons' profiles for counseling. *Measurement and Evaluation in Guidance*, 1972, **5**, 373–378.

Kinsbourne, M. *Mark II*. Unpublished test, Duke University, 1972.

Kirk, S. A., McCarthy, J. J., & Kirk, W. D. *Illinois Test of Psycholinguistic Abilities*. Urbana, Ill.: University of Illinois Press, 1968.

Kirk, S. A., & Bateman, B. Diagnosis and remediation of learning disabilities. *Exceptional Children*, 1962, **29**, 73.

Koppitz, E. M. *The Bender Gestalt Test for Young Children*. New York: Grune, & Stratton, 1964.

Kraus, H. O., Hirschland, R. P. Minimum muscular fitness tests in school children. *Research Quarterly*, 1954, **25**, 178–188.

Leman, L. *The Stick-man Procedure*. Unpublished test, Pennsylvania State University, 1972.

Lerner, J. W. *Children with learning disabilities: diagnosis and teaching strategies*. Boston: Houghton Mifflin, 1971.

Leubuscher, F. Family supper-time drawing procedure. Unpublished manuscript, Pennsylvania State University, 1972.

Machover, K. *Personality projection in the drawing of the human figure*. Springfield, Ill.: Charles C Thomas, 1948.

Malecki, D. *Make-A-Family Test*. Unpublished test, Pennsylvania State University, 1972.

Mead, M., & Heyman, K. *Family*. New York: Macmillan, 1965.

Mosak, H. H., & Shulman, B. H. *The Life Style Inventory*. Chicago: Alfred Adler Institute, 1971.

Muro, J. J. *The counselor's work in the elementary school*. Scranton, Penn.: International Textbook Company, 1970.

Muro, J. J., & Oelke, M. C. Guidance needs in elementary schools— cue to the preparation of counselors. *Counselor Education and Supervision*, 1967, 7, 7–12.

Myklebust, H. R. *The Pupil Rating Scale: Screening for Learning Disabilities*. New York: Grune & Stratton, 1971.

Pennsylvania Department of Public Instruction. *Keynotes*. Harrisburg, Penn.: 1967, **1**, 1–5.

Piers, E. V., & Harris, D. B. *The Piers-Harris Children's Self Concept Scale (The Way I Feel About Myself)*. Nashville, Tenn.: Counselor Recordings and Tests, 1969.

Riley, G. D. *The Riley Articulation and Language Test*. Beverly Hills, Cal.: Western Psychological Services, 1966.

Roach, E. G., & Kephart, N. C. *The Purdue Perceptual-Motor Survey*. Columbus, Ohio: Charles E. Merrill, 1966.

Shane, J., Shane, H., Gibson, R., & Munger, P. *Guiding human development: the counselor and the teacher in the elementary school*. Worthington, Ohio: Charles A. Jones Publishing Co., 1971.

Slosson, R. L. *Slosson Intelligence Test*. East Aurora, N.Y.: Slosson Educational Publications, 1963.

Smith, R. M. (Ed.) *Teacher diagnosis of educational difficulties*. Columbus, Ohio: Charles E. Merrill, 1969.

Sullivan, H. S. *The psychiatric interview.* New York: Norton, 1954.

Super, D. E., & Crites, J. O. *Appraising vocational fitness.* New York: Harper & Row, 1962.

Templin, M. C., & Darley, F. L. *The Templin-Darley Tests of Articulation.* Iowa City: State University of Iowa, 1960.

Terman, L. M., & Merrill, M. A. *Measuring intelligence.* Boston: Houghton Mifflin, 1937.

Terman, L. M., & Merrill, M. A. *Stanford-Binet Intelligence Scale: manual for the third revision, Form L-M.* Boston: Houghton Mifflin, 1960.

Valett, R. E. *The remediation of learning disabilities: a handbook of psychoeducational resource programs.* Belmont, Cal.: Fearon, 1967.

Valett, R. E. *A psychoeducational inventory of basic learning abilities.* Belmont, Cal.: Fearon, 1968.

Wechsler, D. *Wechsler Intelligence Scale for Children.* New York: Psychological Corporation, 1949.

Wechsler, D. *Wechsler Preschool and Primary Scale of Intelligence.* New York: Psychological Corporation, 1967.

Werry, J. S., & Quay, H. C. Observing the classroom behavior of elementary school children. *Exceptional Children,* 1969, **35**, 461–470.

Winnicott, D. W. *Therapeutic consultations in child psychiatry.* New York: Basic Books, 1971.

Woody, R. H. *Behavioral problem children in the schools.* New York: Appleton-Century-Crofts, 1969.

3

Brammer and Shostrom (1968) discuss a viewpoint of "emerging eclecticism" in which the counselor develops a unique flexible but workable and consistent pattern. Each counselor must, therefore, assume responsibility for developing his own approach to counseling. Dimick and Huff (1970) talk about the evolution of an individual's own theory as an essential aspect of becoming a counselor and state that the counselor must grow and expand his personal theories so that his efforts make a significant difference to the client. Lazarus (1971a) advocates a flexible and "personalistic" system of counseling. In this approach one must search continuously for new, empirically useful techniques capable of achieving constructive therapeutic ends. Woody (1971) advocates "psychobehavioral" counseling as technical eclecticism with a special emphasis on the use of both conditioning and insight techniques. The role of the counselor is to be significantly responsible for counseling or therapeutic action and for the changes that take place.

Theory

The personalistic approach advocated in this book can be termed an A-to-I approach to theory. That is, the author utilizes techniques gleaned from a variety of theories. These theories will be delineated alphabetically from A to I, each letter representing the initial letter of a theoretical approach. Table 3-1 presents the building blocks of counseling from his perspective. That is, the main (but not only) function is listed on the left. The levels represent different types of theoretical approaches which are related

A Broad Spectrum of Counseling
Techniques for Use With
Individual Children

to the functions. Explanations for each of the theoretical approaches follows.

Analytic

Analytic theory is the basic foundation for much of counseling. Psychoanalytic thought is so pervasive in psychological thinking today that one cannot ignore it. Especially in the area of child work, the major contributors have been members of the various analytic camps. As a matter of fact, even such widely used child-rearing books as Spock's (1968) are couched in analytic terminology. A quick review of a few of the basic concepts derived from psychoanalytic theory must include: the personality systems of id, ego, and superego; the defense or coping mechanisms of the ego, such as sublimation, repression, regression, rationalization, displacement, projection, fixation; and the stages of development, i.e., oral, anal, phallic, oedipal, latency, and puberty. These stages form the basis for Erikson's (1963) psychosocial theory to be discussed in Chapter Six. Among the counseling procedures that can be utilized with children are free association, listening to dream content, awareness and interpretation of the transference relationship, and control of countertransference (e.g., the counselor feeling sleepy when working with a child). The most important contributor from an analytic viewpoint is Anna Freud, Sigmund Freud's daughter. In her classic work on the psychoanalytic treatment of children (1946), Freud states that the counselor should primarily be useful, interesting, and a powerful person who is indispensable to the child. In her discussion of methods, she touches upon the use of daydreams in child work, the importance of drawing for communication, the role of transference in child analysis, and the educational functions of the child's counselor. This earlier treatment was updated (Freud, 1965) in her delineation of the goals of child counseling as the reduction of anxiety and the dissolution of crippling defenses. In addition, counseling is to provide outlets for drives that need relief. Smirnoff (1971) has compared the views of the two most important child analysts, Anna Freud and Melanie Klein (1960). In the author's view, the analytic approach has the most to offer in regard to appraisal and/or understanding of the child. Where more efficient treatment procedures are desired (or needed, as in the schools), however, one must turn to other approaches.

Behavioristic

Woody (1971) makes a strong case for "psychobehavioral" counseling, or the integration of behavioral and insight-oriented therapies (analytic approaches). Behavioral procedures have direct relevance to work with children because they focus on the client's behaviors, which are sometimes easier to deal with than verbalizations. This is especially true of work with the younger child; verbal approaches are not very effective, because he is still functioning on a predominately behavioral basis. Using approaches based upon learning theory, one must distinguish between the role of behavior modifier, as outlined in Chapter Six, and that of the behavioral counselor described in this chapter. The behavioral counselor is a person who deals directly, on an operant or respondent level, with a client in a one-to-one relationship. In this sense, behavioral counseling can be seen as interventionistic in that some direct intrusion is made into the life of the child. Once the evaluation of a child is complete, the behaviorist can chose among a variety of procedures that can be effective with

Table 3-1 *Main Functions of Various Theoretical Approaches*

APPROACH	MAIN FUNCTION
Behavioristic Individualistic Factor–Reality	Action Orientations
Client-Centered	Basis for Counseling
Analytic Developmental	Understanding
Existential Gestalt Humanistic	Theory

children. Some of the behavioral methods that will be discussed in detail in the course of this chapter are systematic desensitization, assertive training, behavior rehearsal, reward systems, modeling, behavioral contracting and cognitive restructuring.

Client-centered

This approach has its basis in the work of Carl Rogers. It should be noted that Rogers' early experience was with children and that he wrote a book (1939) on the treatment of the child. In this book Rogers contrasts his approach with the analytic process. He states that relationship therapy "places its major emphasis on the curative power of the emotional relationship itself rather than on any insight gained by the individual through the interpretation of his past experiences" (1939, p. 340). Rogers' more recent book (1951) contains a chapter on the client-centered approach to play therapy (Dorfman, 1951). In this approach, it should be emphasized, the relationship is the key to therapeutic change. Axline's (1947, 1964) approach will be examined later in this chapter when relationship counseling is discussed. In the author's view, the relationship is a necessary condition to therapeutic change and therefore precedes much of the behavioristic work.

Developmental

In work with children, especially, developmental considerations must be kept in mind. If one can recognize a child's developmental conceptual stage, it can help to understand his level of functioning. Erikson (1963), one of the great child analysts of our time, has delineated the eight ages of man. His theory will be discussed in Chapter Six. The term "developmental" also has a broader conceptual meaning than Erikson gives it, encompassing such developmental tasks as those of Havighurst (1953). Dinkmeyer and Caldwell view developmental guidance as "the organized effort of the school to personalize and humanize the educational process for all students" (1970, p. 3). This aspect of counseling will be covered in later chapters on the development of curricula and other broad avenues of work with children.

Existential

This approach is primarily of philosophical interest. Its major theorist has been Rollo May (May, Angel & Ellenberger, 1958; May, 1969). In the latter book, May delineates his stages of treatment as: (1) development of the wish, or eliciting awareness of the needs and desires of the person; (2) movement from wish to will, in which awareness becomes self consciousness and the wish is incorporated on a higher level of consciousness; and (3) decision. May views the decision as a pattern of acting and living that is empowered by wishes, asserted by will, and responsive to and responsible for the other persons who are important to one's self and realization of long-term goals. Another contributor, Moustakas (1966), has collected an interesting series of readings in existential child therapy.

Factor, or Trait-factor

This approach holds that man is a compendium of his patterns of abilities, and that assessment is therefore crucial. In Chapter Two, the importance of child evaluation was espoused. The case study is important to this approach. In particular, the reality-therapy approach of Glasser (1965, 1969, 1972) can be conceived of as belonging under this rubric. One of Glasser's important messages is that one person who cares could be sufficient for the child's growth and continued investment in life. The counselor can be this person who meets the basic needs (factors) of the child to be loved, to love, and to feel positive self worth. The goal at the start of treatment (viewed by Glasser as a special kind of teaching or training) is to achieve involvement or establish a relationship with the child. The second stage is that the counselor rejects behavior that is unrealistic but still accepts the child and maintains involvement with him. The third step, somewhat behavioristic in nature, is teaching the child better ways to fulfill his needs within the confines of reality. Gronert (1970) has advocated coordination of the behavioral approach with reality therapy (Glasser, 1965). Hawes (1969) develops this approach in another article. The procedure advocated by Glasser that has particular relevance to the schools is the classroom meeting (Glasser, 1969). There are three types of meetings, which will be discussed in Chapter Five.

Gestalt

Gestalt theory focuses on the here-now, the function of awareness in counseling, and expanding human awareness. Fritz Perls (1969) is the major advocate of this approach. Some of Perls' approaches have been adapted to child work by Lederman (1969). The foundation of Gestalt counseling is to focus on the now and the how, or the ongoing process. Shostrom (1967) has attempted to popularize some of the Gestalt principles. His book includes a chapter on children and parents and the types of manipulative children. There is Freddy-the-Fox, who begins life as a crier and becomes a Junior Calculator who gets other people to do things for him; Tom-the-Tough, who uses hate and fear to control people and becomes a Junior Bully. Finally, Carl-the-Competitor is a combination of Tom and Freddy who views winning (being one-up) as the most important thing in life.

Humanistic

This approach is characterized by concern for the human experience. The existential (May *et al.* 1958) and client-centered approaches (Rogers, 1961) could easily be grouped under this heading. Even Skinner (1971) considers himself a humanist. The person is the focus of attention, and emphasis is on the qualities that are distinctively human. The worth of man and an interest in the development of authenticity in the child are central (Button, 1969). Most counselors undeniably have this orientation.

Individualistic

The Individual Psychology approach was initiated by Alfred Adler and is today called Dreikurian. Rudolph Dreikurs (1968) has attempted to deal with the classroom setting, and delineated the basic principles of child encouragement (Dinkmeyer & Dreikurs, 1963). Of particular interest here are the child's four goals or mistaken motivations (Dreikurs & Soltz, 1964; Soltz, 1967), which serve as the basis for treatment. These are: (1) *attention*, which can be active constructive, represented by cute remarks; passive constructive, as in such behaviors as excessive neatness, conscientiousness, and attempts to be a model child. Active destructive tendencies are showing off, clowning, and obtrusiveness. Passive destructive behaviors are instability, tearfulness, lack of stamina, bashfulness, eating difficulties, and performance difficulties. (2) *The power struggle* is more intense than attention-getting behavior. Active destructive examples are temper tantrums, contradicting, masturbation, untruthfulness, and dawdling. Passive destructive behavioral phenomena are laziness, stubbornness, disobedience, and forgiving. (3) *Revenge.* Active destructive revenge behaviors, which hurt others, are stealing and bedwetting. Passive destructive acts are reluctance and passivity. (4) *Displaying inadequacy or giving up.* The only form of such behavior is passive destructive; examples are stupidity and indolence. The Dreikurian approach advocates numerous procedures for counseling. Two techniques the author has found particularly helpful are the "bathroom technique" and the family council meeting (Dreikurs & Soltz, 1964). It should be noted that Dinkmeyer's (e.g., Dinkmeyer & Caldwell, 1970) approach is mainly based upon individual psychology.

The foregoing illustrates a broad spectrum of theoretical influences. The emphasis thus far has been on theory, although sources of related techniques have been mentioned (e.g., Brown, 1972). The task of the counselor is to personally incorporate appropriate aspects of the various approaches into one's repertoire and to develop one's own personalistic approach in order to carry out effective counseling with children.

The Counseling Environment

The Playroom

The playroom is any place where the child participates in play in one-to-one interaction with the counselor. There is, of course, usually a discrepancy between the ideal and the feasible. This is especially so in schools, where the counselor may be called upon to work in the boiler room, the nurse's office, a storage closet, the library, or any other space available at the particular time one is meeting with a child. Erikson writes that play is "the royal road to the understanding of the infantile ego's efforts at synthesis" (1963, p. 209). Faust declares that the play process "is the relationship between the child and counselor, with play as a major vehicle for the relationship, which makes it possible for the child to effect changes within himself" (1968, p. 154). Ginott states that "the child's play is his talk and the toys are his words" (1961, p. 51). Thus play is the child's natural medium of expression and it is crucial for the counselor to be trained in play techniques (Nelson, 1966, 1967; Waterland, 1970; Myrick & Haldin, 1971).

Some general characteristics of an adequate playroom follow. It should be approximately 10 feet by 15 feet or larger. This provides enough space for the counselor to engage in such activities as jumping rope or playing catch. Table and chairs should be available for the primary-aged child (ages 5 to 8). Younger children need smaller chairs and tables so that they can work at their own level and have their feet on the floor, which enhances their feelings of security. Intermediate-aged children can usually function with a standard-size desk (with a pull-out leaf) and chair. The room should also possess a tape recorder, for the recording of sessions whenever appropriate and for such procedures as mutual story-telling (Gardner, 1971), to be discussed later in this chapter. Other desirable materials are a painting easel, piano, foam pillows, punching bag, Bobo (or Superman), a variety of sizes of balls, relevant books for bibliotherapy (to be discussed later in this chapter) and a chalkboard. In addition, it is advantageous to have water, a sandbox, and climbing equipment available or readily accessible during the hour. The rest of the basic equipment of the playroom will be various kinds of toys, to be covered in the following paragraphs.

The Playbag

The playbag is an essential concept for most elementary school counselors, who may have to change rooms or move from one building to another either within one day or on different days of the week. By making play materials portable, the itinerant counselor can have a stable repertoire of stimuli to which to expose children. The playbag concept involves the counselor in carrying a bagful of toys. The bag can be anything the counselor has access to. Counselors have used shopping bags, duffel bags or briefcases.

There are a variety of toys that facilitate the establishment of contact with the child, among them puppets, dolls and doll families, phones, a typewriter, and numerous types of pencil drawings, crayon work or paintings. Toys that help the child to replicate real-life (reality-testing) experiences are a variety of animals, traffic setups, cars and trucks, play money, a variety of school-room toys, and housekeeping equipment. Toys that evoke or encourage catharsis include pegboards, block houses, tool kits, a medicine ball, nails (for driving), wood (for sawing), and craft supplies for such activities as knitting and weaving. Play media that develop or enhance self-concept are those that allow the child to master such tasks as building models, constructing with Lincoln logs, setting up erector sets, doing puzzles, and pasting and cutting paper. Materials that allow for the sublimation of aggressive drives are sand, water, paints, clay, cooking utensils, equipment for writing poems and stories, Playdough, toss games, Sure Shot Hockey, dart boards, and checkers. Games that aid in the development of gross motor coordination and thus enhance the self-concept include Follow the Leader, Hokey Pokey, Simon Says, hopping, jumping, and a variety of ball games. In all of these activities it is important to use the natural resources of the school. Physical education facilities, outdoor play equipment, the art room, and music facilities can be used. The library should have a variety of books appropriate for bibliotherapy. The counselor should have some voice in the choice and purchase of library materials. Films on such topics as educational objectives, the development of values, and orientation to vocations should also be available. Many of these materials can be organized and carried in the playbag. For more comprehensive discussion of play materials, the interested reader can refer to chapters in Axline's (1947) and Ginott's (1961) books. The approach advocated in this book is essentially technique-oriented, stressing the importance of tailoring specific techniques to specific problems (Krumboltz & Hosford, 1967; Lazarus, 1971a). Using this approach, one fits the procedure to the particular client and/or problem presented. That is, one does not operate within the confines of any particular viewpoint but does what is best for the client. The counselor, therefore, may employ any effective technique—Lazarus' (1967) "technical eclecticism."

Establishing the Relationship

Relationship approaches are based on the work of Rogers (1939), Allen (1942), Axline (1947), and Dorfman (1951). Axline (1947), in particular, has delineated the basic principles of the client-centered approach.

1. The deliberate establishment of a positive relationship (induced by providing the child with social approval, smiling behaviors, and other rewarding contingencies)

2. Acceptance of the child as he is

3. Permissiveness, allowing the child freedom to express his feelings completely

4. Recognition and reflection of the child's feelings by the therapist so that he gains insight into his behavior

5. The child's responsibility for his own choices in problem-solving behavior

6. Sanction for the child to lead the way and the therapist to follow

7. Gradual process, which the counselor does not attempt to hurry things along

8. Certain limits, necessary to anchor counseling to the world of reality and to make the child aware of his responsibility in the relationship

In support of this position, Moustakas (1959) argues that the relationship is both the means and the end of therapeutic change. He states that the relationship between the therapist and the child is the essential dimension, and perhaps the only significant one, in the therapeutic process and in all interhuman growth. Thus this dimension is of vital importance. The crucial question, of course, is how to establish a relationship with the child. This question cannot be answered easily, and the answer varies with each particular child. The counselor must care for the child and attempt to find out what is reinforcing to the child. Once this is determined, the counselor can proceed to establish some kind of positive relationship with the child based on his own and the child's personalities. The relationship could range from saying hello to the child periodically, to building a model or an engine over months of time, or to becoming more deeply involved emotionally during contacts extending over a year. There are no quick, easy routes to such a relationship. The counselor must confirm his standing with the child and relate to him in some positive fashion that is uniquely and personally meaningful. The author feels that relationship approaches have been effective in about one-quarter of his cases. That is, in about a quarter of one's cases a counselor can expect that the relationship itself will be a necessary and sufficient condition for therapeutic change. It is especially important in the case of emotionally deprived children, who can grow as a result of a relationship with a significant other person. In the other three-quarters of the author's hundreds of cases, however, the relationship was necessary but proved insufficient for improvement (Lazarus, 1969) or for the promotion of desired behavioral change (Hosford, 1969). In cases such as these, Lazarus believes that additional techniques are necessary. Therefore, he favors the broad spectrum approach. What follows is an application of such an approach, delineating various kinds of procedures necessary for implementing change with children.

Relaxation Exercises

Although relaxation is most often used with adults as part of the systematic desensitization procedure, learning to relax often serves young children as a means of overcoming anxiety (Woody, 1969; Bergland & Chal, 1972; Keat, 1972c). One can use three kinds of approaches to relaxation with children. First, the breathing component can be introduced not only as essential for relaxation but also as being very useful for such games as running and riding a bicycle. Children can be won over to breathing techniques if they can see their practical application to activities of daily importance to them. By becoming proficient in breathing, they can compete more successfully with peers in the gross motor activities that are generally highly valued in the peer culture. It can be pointed out that this is the procedure many basketball players use just before taking a foul shot (i.e., expel a deep breath, then shoot). After the child learns deep diaphragm breathing, he can be gradually led to relax. One useful technique is to have the child say some kind of syllable as he is expelling air. The counselor should tell the child to inhale as deeply as possible and then to pronounce some kind of syllable, such as an "s" (hissing sound) or an "aw" or "um," as he slowly expels the air from his lungs. In this way the counselor can check the quantity of air expelled. The counselor can also use such motivational devices as a contest to see who can expel air for the longest period of time.

Secondly, certain isometric exercises (Wittenberg, 1964) can be used to express aggressive urges and also to learn about the tension-relaxation paradigm. While this process is related to assertive training in that it deals with the expression of aggression, it is also useful for dispelling tension by such means as "directed muscular activity" (Lazarus, 1971a). It is a good type of exercise to use in conjunction with other tension-relaxation procedures to be described and with those delineated by Wolpe and Lazarus (1966, Appendix 4). The basic principle of isometric exercises is to direct physical energy against an immovable force. This can include activities such as lifting up on the seat on which one is sitting, pushing against the wall, pushing one's hands against each other, and clenching a fist. These exercises have great attraction for children when they are told that the Green Bay Packers and other professional athletes use them to increase their physical fitness for participation in athletics.

Finally, relaxation training can focus directly on the particular presenting problems of the child. For example, a child may have difficulty going to sleep or confronting an examination. In either instance, the use of direct relaxation can help the child to cope better with the tension-producing situation. In the first case, the child can do a series of relaxation exercises just before going to bed. Relaxation exercises can also inhibit the anxiety produced by an examination situation by having the child practice them prior to or periodically during the test.

Systematic Desensitization

As the reader is probably aware, controlled tension and deep muscle relaxation are the first steps in the process of systematic desensitization (Wolpe & Lazarus, 1966; Wolpe, 1969; Lazarus, 1971a). In addition to the relaxation exercises to be discussed here, Wolpe and Lazarus' book includes four pages of explicit exercises (1966, Appendix 4). Lazarus (1971b) also has recorded a series of cassettes on relaxation exercises.

Relaxation exercises can be focused on the primary area of tension in the child. For example, when a child is having psychosomatic complaints centering in his stomach, this can be the focal point for efforts at relaxation. The second step in the traditional systematic desensitization paradigm is the construction of hierarchies of anxiety. This involves making up a list of graded steps for approaching the phenomenon that evokes anxiety. Although this process can be accomplished with adults through imagery, it is generally preferable with children to practice desensitization "in vivo." This real-life approach to a nine-year-old child's school phobia is described by Lazarus, Davison, and Polefka (1965). The author used similar procedures with a child who had not attended school for over one year (Keat, 1974). In setting up a systematic approach, the hierarchy of experiences that gradually led up to approaching the school was as follows:

1. The child was visited at home in order to establish an anxiety-inhibiting relationship.

2. The child was taken out to eat so that he would associate leaving his house with a pleasant experience.

3. He came alone to the counselor's office and the counselor took him home after the appointment.

4. He was taken to school and introduced to the school counselor so that he would know a supportive person there to whom he could turn if he became too upset.

5. The child was to attend school on a half-day basis.

6. He was reinforced for coming to the office for his appointment.

7. He was introduced into a small activity counseling group of children.

8. A behavioral contract was established with him that divided the behavioral goals into very small units (the contracting procedure will be discussed later in this chapter).

9. He was taken to school on the first day of his contract.

10. His behaviors—from getting out of bed to eating breakfast to leaving the house and finally to attending school—were systematically rewarded.

11. His school attendance was maintained by constant support and reinforcements from the counselor (green stamps) and his mother (money).

Each child has his own reinforcement menu. Various lists of reinforcers are available in other sources (e.g., Blackham & Silberman, 1971; Madsen & Madsen, 1972).

The final phase of systematic desensitization is to counteract anxiety with relaxation exercises while the child works his way through the series of steps described above. Relaxation procedures and rewards were used to help the child complete the component parts of his contract. Both respondent (classical) and operant conditioning procedures were necessary in this particular case, because the school phobia was composed of two factors: that is, avoidance behavior was motivated by fear of school and maintained by various secondary reinforcers emanating from the mother. Bugg (1972) reports on several cases in which systematic desensitization was effective with school-aged children suffering from test anxiety and fears of public speaking.

Assertive Training

With an inhibited person who responds to interpersonal situations by withdrawing, it is theorized that each time assertive responses are enacted, they will reciprocally inhibit the anxiety associated with a given action, and thereby the habit of anxiety responses (Wolpe, 1958; Wolpe & Lazarus, 1966; Wolpe, 1969). Therefore, when the counselor has a child whose primary mode of behavior is withdrawn or passive, the child should be continually encouraged to perform stronger actions on his own behalf. That is, standing up for one's rights is important in gaining "emotional freedom" (Lazarus, 1971a).

The goal with such a withdrawn child, therefore, could be to encourage the expression of suppressed angry feelings (Keat, 1972c). It is often necessary to lead children gently and systematically toward more assertive responses. This can be done in two ways. First, assertiveness can be practiced during the counseling session. For example, the child may want to do something in particular. The counselor will have given him a reinforcement survey schedule (Keat, 1972a) or discerned the child's reward system from the interviews. The child may, for example, want to build a model during the counseling hour but be reticent about articulating his desires; he needs to be encouraged to voice his sentiments and stand up for his own rights. Specifically, he can be encouraged to express his wishes more quickly during the session. The author (Keat, 1972c) counseled one child who would consume an entire session without stating his desires. He was constantly encouraged to speak up sooner and, as a result, his ability to voice his preferences increased.

In order for such improvements to carry over into the natural environment, the child can be assigned various tasks to carry out in his daily living. These include such "psychological homework" tasks as insisting upon his rights in interactions with other people. This could mean such things as enlisting the aid of his father in constructing a model. The child should be prepared to behaviorally rehearse (to be discussed later in this chapter) various reactions to various hypothetical responses from his father. Whatever the father's reaction, it is very unlikely to be as bad as the child imagines. The parents, of course, must also be prepared for behavioral changes so that they will not sabotage the efforts of the counselor. The child's real-life behavior, of course, is much more difficult to assess than his assertiveness during the counseling hour. Both behavior rehearsal and psychological homework are necessary aspects of assertive training because progress must be generalized to the child's daily life.

Behavior Rehearsal

Behavior rehearsal is used to teach the child new behaviors and to counteract the anxiety-producing aspects of the situations he encounters. Generally, the nature of the referral suggests particular problems that might be discussed and rehearsed during the hour. Such situations as getting along with peers or approaching someone for help with a task are examples. The counselor and child can examine the problem, identify appropriate response patterns to help solve it, and then rehearse the situation so that the child can practice effective behavior. This procedure is generally known in the literature as role-playing, but has the added dimension of role-reversal.

Initially, the stage is set by a clear exposition of the problem that is bothering the child.

COUNSELOR: We've been talking about some of the difficulties which you have in standing up for your rights.

CHARLIE: Yeah, I guess so.

COUNSELOR: What is one situation which is bothering you most now?

CHARLIE: I guess it's that my father never does anything with me.

COUNSELOR: What is it you would like him to do with you?

CHARLIE: I don't know. I guess that maybe he could help me with my model sometimes when I get stuck.

COUNSELOR: Have you ever asked him to help you with the model?

CHARLIE: No.

COUNSELOR: Why?

CHARLIE: Because he's always so busy.

This child is failing to stand up for his rights. He anticipates that his father will reject him because he is too busy, but he is too inhibited to ask. The first step, after delineating the problem situation, is to find out how he would approach the situation.

COUNSELOR: Charlie, let's try to see what you might do in this situation. Let's make believe that I'm your father and you be yourself. The scene is that you have finally gotten up enough nerve to approach your father about working with you on your model.

CHARLIE: You're going to act like my father?

COUNSELOR: That's right. And you be yourself.

CHARLIE: Umm. Aaaa. Hi, Dad. How're you doing?

COUNSELOR: (Father) Fine. And you?

CHARLIE: O.K., I guess. Aaa. See you later, Dad.

It may be difficult to induce an inhibited child to act out a role. If the child does not have an appropriate repertoire of responses to cope with such a situation, he must be taught the kinds of things he might say. One usually elicits more response on the first several attempts with a more verbal child. When confronted with a withdrawn child, one may either encourage the child to work on the problem or move directly into some type of teaching situation (role-reversal, modeling) in which the counselor attempts to enlarge the child's repertoire of responses. In this situation, the counselor chose the latter course.

COUNSELOR: O.K., Charlie. It seems that you have some difficulty in approaching your father. Let's try something else awhile. Let me be you and you act as you think your father would. O.K.?

CHARLIE: Maybe (long pause). I guess I can do it.

COUNSELOR: All right, let's try it: Hi, Dad. How're you doing?

CHARLIE: (Father) Rotten. Can't you see that I'm busy?

COUNSELOR: Yes. You really seem to have a lot of work to do.

CHARLIE: Yeah. Go away and leave me alone.

COUNSELOR: All right. But can I check with you again in a little while to see if you can help me with my model? I'm stuck now and sure could use your help.

CHARLIE: O.K. In a little while.

This is what the child expects to happen. Charlie thinks that his father will reject his advances outright. But, since he expects the worst, almost any outcome is better than anticipating failure and not trying. In this situation, the counselor as Charlie has at least managed a hopeful call-back closure that leaves the door open for future approaches. It would now be appropriate to reverse roles, so that Charlie can play himself using the counselor's model responses.

The counselor's next task is to attempt to anticipate most of the possible responses the child might have to use. The father's responses could range from the anticipated rejection to saying "Not now, but later," to answering positively.

COUNSELOR: O.K. Now you be yourself again and I'll be your father.

CHARLIE: (After several sessions of rehearsal) Hi, Dad. How's it going?

COUNSELOR: Pretty bad. How are things with you?

CHARLIE: All right. But right now I'm stuck on my model. Could you help me with it sometime?

COUNSELOR: Sure. Why not now? I'm at a good stopping-point.

"Nothing ventured, nothing gained." The child who does not ask for what he wants is unfortunate. By using assertive training combined with behavior rehearsal, the counselor can help the withdrawn child to emerge from his shell. In this procedure an attempt is made to anticipate the major possible reactions to the child's request, have him practice what the counselor models, and reverse roles, thereby developing a repertoire of responses that can enable him to cope better with any eventuality. As he achieves success, more positive approaches should generalize to other situations.

It has been noted that in many cases behavior rehearsal is "significantly more effective in resolving specific social and interpersonal problems than direct advice or nondirective therapy" (Lazarus, 1966). Developmental considerations should be kept in mind when working with behavior rehearsal. It has been the author's experience that this technique is more effective with the intermediate elementary school child (e.g., Gittleman, 1965) than with primary grade children. It does, nevertheless, add a useful reality dimension to the treatment of all children's problems. That is, instead of dealing with the troublesome situations in his imagination, the child can act out and attempt to work through his behavioral approaches to particular kinds of problems.

Modeling

Modeling is the tendency of the child to imitate or copy the behavior of a model. Modeling plays an exceedingly important role in the learning of behaviors. Such learning can take place in a situation like that described above in which the child observed the counselor's behavior. The child's current functioning is, of course, in large part the result of modeling on peers and adults.

He usually copies behavior he agrees with or likes. For a more comprehensive treatment of modeling, the reader is referred to Bandura (1969), who has done considerable research on this phenomenon.

With respect to counseling procedures, modeling has more relevance to group counseling (to be discussed in Chapter Four). Modeling can, of course, occur in response to films or video tapes. Therefore, the importance of TV-viewing in the life of the child should be recognized. Eron, Huesmann, Lefkowitz, and Walder (1972) "demonstrated that there is a probable causative influence of watching television programs in the early formative years on later aggression" (p. 263). Who is a more potent model for children than an admired athlete? They want to copy the very dress and movements of such a hero. Modeling can also take place as a result of reading about the specific behaviors of someone else. The counselor can give the child stories appropriate to his level that bear on the behaviors the counselor is attempting to modify.

Treatment procedures in the area of copying behavior can induce the child to identify and talk about particular social situations that create difficulty for him. After these situations have been defined, they can be worked through during the course of counseling. The counselor can modify and model particular behaviors and responses until those that are most appropriate for the child become apparent. The child can practice these behaviors. Thus, modeling is an integral aspect of behavior rehearsal as well as being important for learning to cope with life.

Motor Coordination Training

Motor coordination training can focus on both the fine and gross motor areas. If the child is deemed to be functioning below age expectancy on various types of tasks, training in these tasks and consequent increases in skill in the fine perceptual motor area can enhance his self image. An example of an approach that can be used in counseling is model-building. As the child works on a model, he engages in verbal interaction and is reinforced with encouragement and praise. For many elementary school-age children, the work task also affords some distance from the counselor, alleviating some of the pressure for continued verbal interaction. Without such pressure, conversation typically flows more freely. Therefore, model-building may not only enhance self esteem but also enable the flow of conversation to move more freely.

Many children have gross motor coordination difficulties. Counseling can involve training in these skills. (Another approach, however, is to deprecate physical skills and focus on other areas in which the child has greater potential; e.g., play down psychomotor skills and encourage cognitive capacities.) One can engage in numerous exercises with the child, such as playing catch with a medicine ball. An additional benefit of such exercise is the incidental "directed muscular activity" (Lazarus, 1971a), which inhibits the child's anxiety. Skill with balls will enhance the counselor's value as a role model for children of elementary school age. This is especially important if the male parental figure is relatively absent from the home situation. The counselor can partially fill the void of the absent parent by behaving in ways the child can model. With a model, the child may become more proficient in these skills and thus become acceptable to other children who look upon a child who lacks these skills as deserving of exclusion from the peer group.

Cognitive Restructuring

Lazarus (1971), discussing approaches typically outside the confines of behavior therapy, focuses on various kinds of endeavors whose goal is cognitive restructuring. These procedures are intended to alter how the child thinks and to correct his misconceptions. There are four basic approaches to cognitive restructuring with children.

The first approach is to encourage the child to label his feelings and express them verbally. Incapacity in this area is, of course, a general deficiency of our civilization (and educational system) and one of the goals of the developmental counselor is to teach children what feelings are and to sanction their expression in appropriate ways. It is often necessary to provide a kind of multiple-choice format for the child. For example, one can suggest possible reactions to particular emotional stimuli. For example, "Do you feel glad, sad, mad or scared about that?" The next step is to learn to associate particular physiological and emotional states with these verbal labels. Many children are inhibited in the expression of these feelings; it needs to be emphasized that it is acceptable to express them in particular places. Indeed, counseling sometimes concentrates on learning the appropriate places to say and do particular things so that the child can increase his judgment and become more effective at handling emotions.

A second approach is the rational method of helping children to understand the nature of their own thoughts about their problems. This process is labelled by Ellis (1962) "the ABC Theory of personality and of emotional disturbance." This theory stresses that it is the thoughts that occur at point B in time, rather than the event at point A, that cause a reaction at point C. By knowing the kinds of responses (A) that other persons might make, the child can become aware of, and alter, his self defeating assumptions (B) by changing his "internalized sentences" (Ellis & Harper, 1961; Ellis, 1962; Glicken, 1968). In one particular case (Keat, 1972c), the child was telling himself irrational things about the magnitude of his physical disability, a repaired and practically unnoticeable cleft palate.

COUNSELOR: Let's see what the other children are saying to you. What do they call you?

CHARLIE: Usually two names. Either Bugs Bunny or Lippy.

COUNSELOR: How do you feel when they say this?

CHARLIE: Bad.

COUNSELOR: Let me guess what you're telling yourself. Other kids call me Bugs Bunny or Lippy, so I must be pretty funny-looking.

CHARLIE: Yeah.

COUNSELOR: What's so great about what they think? How do they rate to say how you look?

CHARLIE: Don't know.

COUNSELOR: Well, they're not really so hot. Let's see about the Bugs Bunny bit. Look at my teeth (counselor shows his crooked teeth). Whose do you think are worse? Mine or yours? (Some counselors use a mirror at this stage to show the client how he looks.)

CHARLIE: Yours.

COUNSELOR: O.K. That's the reality of it. My teeth are worse off than yours. Now what's so bad about yours?

CHARLIE: Not much.

COUNSELOR: Right. You know the saying "sticks and stones?"

CHARLIE: Yeah.

COUNSELOR: What's the rest?

CHARLIE: You know it.

COUNSELOR: Yeah. But I want to hear you say it.

CHARLIE: What's that again?

COUNSELOR: Sticks and stones will break your bones but . . .

CHARLIE: Yeah.

COUNSELOR: What's the rest?

CHARLIE: Names will never hurt me.

COUNSELOR: That's it. But that's not what you're telling yourself. Names do hurt you now. But they shouldn't. So now, what should you say?

CHARLIE: Names won't hurt me.

COUNSELOR: That's right. And also, I feel sorry for others who have to pick on you to feel good. It's really their problem if they need to make fun of you.

In this case, four attitudes were restructured cognitively. The child was: (1) told not to value others' opinions so much; (2) confronted with reality; (3) told alternative sentences to say to himself; (4) taught to project the pathology onto the other children rather than absorbing it as his problem. By using one's self as a guide to one's own feelings of self esteem, the child has a more stable means for evaluating himself. In reality, some of the most physically beautiful people consider themselves ugly. Marilyn Monroe is a classic example of a person who did not incorporate other's aesthetic evaluations into her own feelings of self worth. She died a lonely and unhappy woman. Physical attributes are basically what a person tells himself they are. His perceptions are, of course, influenced by environmental feedback, but the crucial dimension is what the person tells himself about himself.

Thirdly, "emotive imagery" techniques can be used. The three classic cases using this approach, described by Lazarus and Abramovitz (1962), were with children aged 8, 10, and 14. The general procedures are as follows:

1. The circumstances of the child's fears are ascertained and a graded hierarchy is drawn up (from most- to least-feared situation).

2. The counselor identifies the child's hero images (models).

3. The child is to close his eyes and imagine a sequence of events similar to those of his everyday life but to introduce his hero into the anxiety situation.

4. The child is to approach the situation slowly and systematically (imaginatively). If anxiety is indicated, the stimulus is withdrawn. The procedure is repeated, as in the process of systematic desensitization, until the most threatening phenomenon in the hierarchy can be tolerated.

These procedures can be used to counteract a variety of fears, including fears of dogs (Lazarus & Abramovitz, 1962), darkness (Lazarus *et al.*, 1962), school (Lazarus *et al.*, 1962) and the dentist (Lazarus, 1971). In the case of Charlie (Keat, 1972c), the child's hero-image (an astronaut) was established. Then he imagined a sequence of events close to his everyday life, but introduced the astronaut, as a person who could do whatever he desired in an anxiety-free fashion, into the imaginative situation. Making believe that he was the astronaut, Charlie could behave in ways he could not manage on his own. Once his anxiety was dissipated, the child could see that he could handle the situation himself.

The fourth procedure is bibliotherapy, which can be mainly an educative service about certain subjects the parents have difficulty confronting. Sex education is a common example. Passages in a variety of books can be discussed with the child. The books, of course, need to be geared to the reading level of the child. With younger children (4–8), the counselor can read the passages aloud. Older children (9–12) can read materials themselves, either with the counselor or with their parents. The author has used books on sex (Pomeroy, 1968), divorce (Gardner, 1971), and brain dysfunction (Gardner, 1972). Other topics, in the realm of affective education, will be listed in Chapter Seven. These topics involve such matters as child conflicts, peer difficulties, fear of failure, and the like. Bibliotherapeutic procedures assume that once the cognitions of the child are restructured, behavioral change will follow.

Behavioral Contracting

Behavioral contracting is a procedure in which the counselor draws up a written agreement with the client specifying the behavior of each for a stated period of time. The contents of the contract generally involve goals and rewards for the child. Several types of contracts have been reported in the literature. For example, Tharp and Wetzel (1969) utilized a contract in which an adolescent repaid his stepfather for an automobile with improved home behaviors; Dinoff and Rickard (1969) used mutually agreed-upon goals in formulating a contract with campers; Kiersay (1969) drew up a detailed educational contract in which limits were agreed upon and the role of each participant was clearly delineated; Homme, Csanyi, Gonzales and Rechs (1970) reported the use of daily contracts in the classroom. Finally, another form of behavior contract reported by Hill and Luckey (1969) had as its purpose helping the child regain self esteem and identity through self control and improvements in his own behavior.

Behavioral contracts should focus upon events that can be broken down into observable behaviors. After a goal or observable behavior is agreed upon, the various reinforcement contingencies for the child should be delineated. In practice, the author outlines a contract in the following way. The date is recorded on the left-hand side. In the center part of the page, goals for each day are listed. Finally, the child's reward is indicated on the right-hand side. Thus the contract's elements are the time factor, behavioral goals, and rewards. Rewards can be marks or tokens that the child can save for a particular book or toy he wants. The major persons in the child's life, including his mother and father, teacher, and counselor, should be reinforcing agents. In addition, it is a good idea to draw up the contract for a stated period of time, such as one week, after which time it will be evaluated and possibly revised. At the next appointment, the child can bring in the contract and his reward accomplishments can be tallied. Although the counselor can arrange for separate rewards from the parents and teacher, the other major rewarders in the child's environment should be gradually incorporated into the contract. This can be done through individual and parent group discussions in which the parents are made aware of the contract's contingencies.

The author has used behavioral contracts with numerous types of children. One was the case of Harry, discussed earlier (Keat, 1974), the child who had not attended school for over a year. In Harry's case, the child's main goal was to buy a guitar with trading stamps. Subgoals, which could be attained prior to the guitar, were a Beatles songbook or records. The child was rewarded with a page of stamps for getting out of bed, eating breakfast, going outside, seeing someone outside of his home, and eventually entering the school. This type of reward (like money) has the additional benefit of being divisible into discrete units. That is, stamps can be awarded in any amount. Of course, social reinforcement and rewards are given concurrently with the tangible rewards provided for in the contract.

In the case mentioned above (Keat, 1974), a combination of operant and classical conditioning approaches was used. The incorporation of trading stamps into the behavioral contract seems to have been the single most effective procedure in the achievement of the end goal of school attendance for the child. Daily goals were established, and the child was rewarded with stamps when he met these goals. After several months the child was maintaining daily school attendance.

In another case of the author's, a fifth-grade child was rewarded with Green Stamps for a less encompassing type of behavior. This child did a comic-like trip down the aisle every time he entered the classroom. It was felt that this was done to gain the attention of his classmates. This particular case involved two kinds of procedures. The first was modification of both the attention-getting

```
Persons:  Harry, Dr. K., Mrs. Z.


Goals:  To obtain with Green Stamps
        A) a guitar; or
        B) a Beatles songbook; or
        C) Beatles records


        Date                      Goal                      Reward


        11/12          Visit Guidance Office,           Green Stamps
                       establish contact

        11/13          Up by 7:30 a.m.                  Green Stamps

        11/14          Up by 9 a.m., eat                Failed -- no reward
                       breakfast

        11/15          Up by 9 a.m., eat                Green Stamps
                       breakfast, go outside,
                       play or see someone

        11/16          Up by 7:15 a.m., eat             Green Stamps
                       breakfast; Dr. K. to pick
                       up at 8:10 a.m. to take
                       to school

        11/17          Up and to school                 Green Stamps

        11/18          Up and to school                 Green Stamps

        11/19          Up, to school, in to             Green Stamps
                       see Dr. K.
```

Figure 3-1 *Harry's Contract*

behavior and lack of concentration in the classroom. The second component was "card-carrying" (Sanborn & Schuster, 1969), a process in which a child who behaves as his contract stipulates is rewarded with a mark on his card. In addition, he receives social reinforcement from the teacher. This card is to be carried home for an appropriate reward from his mother or father. In schools whose students go home for lunch, it can be done on a half-day basis. If the child eats his lunch at school and the parents are the persons who bestow rewards, the child can take the card home after school. This is a kind of behavioral "report card" that has the advantage of being used every day. Of course, this procedure requires the cooperation and involvement of both parents and teachers. In this particular case, the child made significant behavioral gains as a result of behavior modification and card-carrying procedures. Such gains often generalize to related subject matter areas.

A similar use of the contract helped a child who was overly aggressive. The third-grade child had been referred for counseling because of excessively aggressive behavior, including hitting and shoving other children on the playground and while waiting for the bus. The child was also periodically aggressive toward a younger sister. After the counselor carried out baseline (i.e., the usual level of behavioral occurrence) observations in the home and in the school, he was ready to attempt to modify the behavior by establishing a contract with the child. The child's reinforcement contingencies were determined through interviews with him and by the use of the reinforcement survey schedule (Keat, 1972a). With all the contingencies in mind, the counselor drew up an agreement with the child. This was a collaborative and co-operative venture in which the child was asked to reflect upon the terms of the contract and to identify the things that were rewarding for him. Thus, the child could correct the observations of the teacher and his parents, who may have misconceived what was rewarding to him. The contract was to operate in the home and in school. In the home, it was addressed to aggressive behavior toward the younger sister; in the school, the problem was aggressive behavior toward other children. The child was to be rewarded in the home with released time to play cards with his mother upon receiving a certain number of points for appropriate behaviors. In school the teacher was to keep track of the child's behavior and give both social (e.g., attention, praise) and tangible (tally marks or stars) rewards when he behaved appropriately during the selected time periods (e.g., completing assigned work in class). The child was given the rewarding contingencies of his choice of cleaning the blackboard, being responsible for the classroom television, playing a ball-roll game or a ring-toss game. These and other rewarding activities had been identified in interviews with the child in which he spoke of them as reinforcing for him. The contract can be checked weekly with the counselor and modifications appropriate to the results can be negotiated. In this way the behavioral contract is generalizable to the home and to peer activities in the school. After the aggressive behaviors in this case were appropriately modified, the focus shifted to the child's study habits. The counselor can serve as a reinforcing agent for one of the child's payoffs. In this situation, when the child had achieved enough points for nonaggressive behavior or attention to his study tasks, points were redeemable for time playing basketball with the counselor.

It is important in this procedure that the child be rewarded for minimal gains at the outset. The behavioral contract allows everyone involved to know what is expected of the child and what behavior is being rewarded. As a result, behavioral gains can be more clearly identified and quantified. Behavioral change can be noted and the child rewarded correspondingly.

Reinforcement

Reinforcement is considered to have occurred when contingent use of a stimulus results in the increase or maintenance of a dependent behavior. In operational terms, a positive reinforcer is any stimulus that acts to strengthen (or maintain) the behavior (response) it follows. Positive reinforcement is generally the preferred mode of operation for working with children in the schools.

Negative reinforcement means "the removal of a negative reinforcer or aversive stimulus as a consequence of the response" (Sulzer & Mayer, 1972, p. 292). Aversive stimuli should be used sparingly if at all, in the schools.

One of the most valuable techniques is the withdrawal of reinforcement. According to this procedure, a person who is potentially reinforcing for another person refuses to give recognition or acceptance to a specific behavior. For example, if the child is not behaving appropriately during counseling or in a classroom, he can be ignored. The theory is that the frequency of this maladaptive behavior will decrease. Also, previously given rewards, such as special recognition, can be withdrawn. These procedures can be used in both individual group counseling and in the classroom. The application to a group of the withdrawal of positive reinforcement will be discussed in Chapter Six. Krumboltz and Krumboltz (1972) provide an interesting example: a child ignored being called "Shorty," and this epithet quickly disappeared from his peers' vocabulary.

Another procedure, basically a withdrawal of reward, is "timeout." The timeout procedure involves withdrawing the child from a situation in which undesirable reinforcement may be occurring. When the child behaves in an inappropriate fashion, he is removed from the potential reinforcing situation and isolated. This timeout should be for a specified period of time (for example, five minutes) and should be directly related to the inappropriate behavior. The child should be placed in an isolated situation in which no other external stimulation is available. Thus, sending the child out into the hall is an inappropriate timeout device. More appropriate are special isolated places that can be constructed in the classroom or the home in which the child has nothing to do. In a sense, timeout is the opposite of the "bathroom technique" (Dreikurs & Soltz, 1964); in the former the child is removed from the rewarding situation, while in the latter the rewarder is removed from the scene because the parent withdraws from the conflict and goes to the bathroom which is stocked with literature and a radio to aid in the isolation process.

Over the past thirty years, numerous aversive conditioning devices or apparatuses have been used in the treatment of enuresis. The classic article is by Mowrer and Mowrer (1938). Yates (1970) presents an excellent summary of procedures for use in enuresis and encopresis. Recent evidence (Turner, Young, & Rachman, 1970) tends to support the use of a simple conditioning apparatus, such as the Wee-Alert sheets available from Sears (Tough, Hawkins, McArthur, & Ravenswaay, 1971). On the whole, however, the author tends to steer clear of the use of mechanical apparatus (Keat, 1972b).

Another approach that seems useful in the treatment of encopresis is "restitution" (Foxx & Azrin, 1972), which educates the child to assume responsibility for his behavior. Thus, if a child soils his pants, he can be trained to clean up the mess. This is generally quite aversive to the child. If the child learns to accept responsibility for his act, the frequency of inappropriate elimination should decrease.

In all such approaches, it is important to keep in mind the desirability of a balanced approach. Therefore, combined positive and negative reinforcement is generally advisable. The world is not characterized by an endless stream of positive reinforcement; it is important that children at times be exposed to reality in the form of negative reinforcements. Often the most effective procedure is a combination of positive and negative reinforcement procedures. For example, a child might be conditioned to give up thumbsucking by being rewarded when the behavior does not occur, and denied a reward when he sucks his thumb. In addition, the child could be isolated in timeout when he sucks his thumb. Other procedures are to offer verbal reinforcement, to grant points (tokens) for appropriate behavior, and to offer some kind of reward for achieving the final behavioral goal.

These procedures are generalizable and applicable to a broad range of problems. Another approach is to deal with specific problems. The problem-centered approach is described by the Blackham and Silberman book (1971), Ullman and Krasner (1965), Graziano (1971), Madsen and Madsen (1972), and Krumboltz and Krumboltz (1972). The last book is technique-oriented, and the index referencing makes it possible to identify useful approaches to many types of problems.

Mutual Storytelling

Mutual storytelling is based on a book by Gardner (1971). The child first tells a story, which is recorded on the tape machine. Then the counselor surmises the meaning of the story and tells one of his own. The counselor's story describes the same characters in a similar setting, but introduces healthier adaptations, coping methods, and resolutions of the conflicts exhibited by the child's story. This is an excellent way to use the tape recorder, which is quite often present in the counselor's office, in a therapeutic fashion. Gardner documents his description of mutual storytelling with numerous transcripts of sessions with children. In this way, he illustrates the use of the technique in various phases of treatment. One section describes the use of mutual storytelling to treat such common problems as anger inhibition, low self esteem, minimal brain dysfunction, and reactions to such events as divorce.

Directions and procedures are clearly described in Gardner's book. Nevertheless, some basic technique modifications can be utilized. One modification the author has used is illustrated by the following tape transcript. The technique was introduced in the usual way (e.g., "Tell a story with a beginning, a middle and an end. Then mention the lesson of the story"). After the child told her story, the counselor began his. The child was allowed to prompt and correct the counselor and to engage in a more active dialogue than is encouraged in Gardner's procedure. This procedure keeps the child active and helps her to formulate more healthy adaptations of things to do and think about. This procedure seems more appropriate for younger children, keeping them involved in the stories rather than requiring them to sit back and listen while the counselor talks. It should be noted that this child's primary reason for referral by both the school and the family was stealing. This is the first story she told in treatment and was recorded only a minute or two after her initial entrance into the counseling room.

CHILD: Hello. Welcome to my story. This is Jane, and this is a police story, and I'm goinna tell it right and wrong. How to cross the street. Look both ways and listen for any cars, and see if you don't hear any cars, then you can cross the street. Now that's one thing you should do. And here's another thing. Don't accept gifts from strangers. Don't take candy from them, don't accept rides from them. And what else? Don't stay after school. Go home first and then if you want to play at school you can, but go home first and ask your mother first; and don't go through dark alleys. Go straight home. The end.

In response, the author told this story.

COUNSELOR: This is Dr. Keat. I'm going to tell a story something like Jane told today. This is a police story. The police story says: Be careful when you cross streets, look both ways, always be careful so you don't get hurt or nobody else gets hurt. And you should . . .

CHILD: (Prompting)   And go home after school.

COUNSELOR: If you want to go out to play after school you should go home and ask your mother first if it's O. K. if you go out so that she gives you her permission and knows where you are. Because your mother's concerned about what you're doing, where you are, and what you're up to. So if you don't ask her, then she doesn't know where you are—if you don't go home and ask her right after school—so you should always go home after school and ask her if you want to go see a friend.

CHILD: (Providing a cue)   Dark alleys.

COUNSELOR: Oh, yeah, that's a good one. Don't go through dark alleys. What can happen in dark alleys?

CHILD: Well, if you go through dark alleys, maybe you could get lost, and not find your way home. So you should always not go through dark alleys. O. K. O. K. And what else. Don't accept any rides or gifts from strangers. So, and remember always that the policeman is your friend. Don't be afraid to talk to him or tell him that you're lost. Don't be afraid to talk to him. O. K. The end.

COUNSELOR: So the policeman can help look after things for you, and take care of you too. Some people think that the policeman is just a man who gives them a hard time or something, if they do something wrong. But they can also help you.

Then Jane told a reality-based story about an experience with a policeman in California. The story just cited represents her attempt to work through a variety of conflicts: initially, her relationship with her mother and the external controls her mother exerts over her, generalized to another external control agent, policemen. She was attempting to resolve her feelings about threatening external forces. These vary from unsureness of her position (being lost) to concern about doing things wrong. The counselor initially attempted to clarify her concerns and then to present some of her conceptions in a more positive light (i.e., policemen can also be helpful) in order to help her restructure her thoughts.

Another way to vary the usual mutual storytelling procedure (i.e., the child tells his story first and then the counselor relates his adaptation) is to have the child and counselor move into an action-oriented approach to the lesson (moral) of the story. The shift can be suggested either by the counselor or initiated by the child. An example of this transition follows (Keat and Maki, 1974):

COUNSELOR: Alright. Nan's decided that we're going to make up a play about Jack the turtle and Bill the man who had the flat tire. Nan, what are we going to do?

CHILD: Well, I'm going to make Jack the turtle and Miss Maki's going to make Bill in the play and then she's going to make him get mad in the play and I'm going to go over and say "I'll help you" and I'll jack the car up and he can change the tire.

The theoretical rationale for such an approach is based in role-playing procedures such as behavioral rehearsal. A label for this particular procedure could be "mirrored fantasy" because the counselor often reflects the content of the fantasy during role-playing. By such techniques the child can integrate behaviors with thoughts and thus obtain greater therapeutic benefits. A detailed example of such a procedure with an eight-and-a-half-year-old fearful girl is provided in an article by Keat and Maki (1974).

Blackboard Drawing

Procedures that use blackboards have special relevance for the school. A child must learn to function at a blackboard, and there is usually one available in the school. The disadvantage of such procedures is that blackboard drawings cannot usually be kept from one interview to another. Quite often the less inhibited child is attracted to the blackboard. Maclay (1970) has written about the use of blackboard drawing in work with children. Interpretation should follow lines similar to that of other forms of drawing and painting.

One elementary school-aged child referred for stealing (Maclay, 1970) drew a fat boy with a large head, hair on end and arms outstretched in despair, facing a cannon manned by two soldiers. The cannon had been fired and the shot was striking the fat boy. After the interview, the boy requested that his mother see the drawing and showed it to her gleefully. This drawing provided the stimulus for future discussion about how badly he was being treated and pushed around, his feelings that others hated him, and the aggression he felt toward others. The mother became more aware of his underlying emotions and began to deal with him more understandingly.

Activity Counseling

Bettie McComb (1972) has described an individual counseling procedure for the elementary school child which she terms "activity counseling." It is very similar to what the author does in play counseling with children. After the child is referred to the counselor, he is observed in the classroom. During one-to-one contact, he and the counselor talk about special projects the children can undertake, such as painting, sewing, letter-cutting, and so on. As they work together in the ensuing sessions, the child and the counselor find out much more about each other. The activity gradually progresses toward completion. It is important for the child to acquire skills that he had not previously possessed. The difference between McComb's procedure and the author's is that once the project is completed, McComb suggests that the child and the counselor arrange with the teacher to present it to the class. The child receives additional benefits and reinforcements from this procedure. As he talks about the project he may receive attention and admiration from his classmates. This additional bonus enhances the child's feelings of self worth.

Use of the Child as Consultant

Strean (1970) has discussed the use of the patient as a consultant in therapy. He asks the child what he considers worthwhile to do in the course of treatment. The author has found it useful to discuss the child's views of the solution to his problem. An example follows:

COUNSELOR: What would you change in order to help with your problems?

CHILD: I don't know, that's a hard decision. I might change myself so I could get rid of three or four of my problems. I might change myself so I was perfect. Then my mother wouldn't have any reason to yell at me.

COUNSELOR: Three or four of your problems. Would you tell some more about the things you would change?

CHILD: Well, well, I would never say anything at all bad or do anything at all bad. Then my mother wouldn't have anybody to . . . anything to yell at me about. I'd be better at sports. Do things like that—be, have more friends. Things like that.

In two brief statements, this ten-year-old boy delineated his problems and some possible solutions. The core of his difficulty was a destructive mother-son relationship. His solution was to be good, perhaps too good, in order to meet expectations. This situation required concurrent counseling of mother and son. His second main reason for referral was difficulty getting along with peers. His solution was to be better at sports and to have more friends. This outlook, of course, required some cognitive restructuring regarding the importance of sports and some actual education about the kinds of behavior that lead to friendships.

Parent Involvement

There are various approaches to parental involvement, which is often necessary to implement behavioral change with children. Indeed, the man who started it all was Sigmund Freud (1959), in his 1909 consultation through the mail with Little Hans' father. Since that time there have been numerous reports by other analysts of the use of parents in the treatment of children (e.g., Borstein, 1935; Schwarz, 1950; Kolansky, 1960). From a client-centered viewpoint, the filial therapy approach (Guerney, 1964) seems especially useful with pre-school and primary-grade children. This approach involves training (individually or in a group) parents to conduct relationship play experiences with their young children. Guerney (1969) has collected numerous articles on the use of parents as behavioral counselors.

One of the initial reports with a primarily behavioristic orientation was by Williams (1959), who used parents to eradicate temper tantrums. Russo (1964) has published a more explicit report on the use of parents to carry out operant conditioning. Other approaches (e.g., Wahler, Winkel, Peterson & Morrison, 1965) focus on behavior modification principles and on the training of mothers as social reinforcers to eliminate deviant behavior in young children (ages 4–6). A program described by Patterson, McNeal, Hawkins and Phelps (1967) utilizes such media as programmed textbooks for parents (Patterson & Gullion, 1968). Some of these procedures (i.e., parent groups) will be addressed further in Chapter Five. Through the use of social learning books in parent education (Barten & Barten, 1973), parents are generally better able to comprehend their role and to provide appropriate reinforcers to sustain desired behaviors in their children. As such behaviors are pinpointed, counselor and parents can chart behaviors for the parents to implement in their interactions with the child.

The author attempts to design unique programs for each situation. That is, if the primary difficulty appears to be parent-child relationships, discussions are combined with reading of books such as Axline's (1947, 1964). If the trouble seems to involve communication between parent and child, books like Gordon's (1970) or Ginott's (1965) can be used. With situations in which the parent can benefit from understanding the child's motivations and possible ways to deal with them, Dreikurs and Soltz (1964) provide stimulating reading. For more specific problems (e.g., eating, sleeping, negativism, and the like), the author uses such books as the following with parents: Smith and Smith (1964); Patterson and Gullion (1968); Wittes and Radin (1969); Madsen and Madsen (1972). These bibliotherapeutic readings are combined with discussions to enable parents to cope more effectively with their children.

Summary

This chapter has had three main objectives: to delineate a personalistic theoretical orientation to counseling; to describe the setting for counseling and to recommend a collection of materials for use in child work; and, finally, to present a broad spectrum of techniques useful for child counselors.

From the theoretical perspective, useful ideas from nine major theories were presented. These were: analytic, behavioristic, client-centered, developmental, existential, factor (trait-factor), gestalt, humanistic, and individualistic. The counselor's development of a flexible and personalistic system was advocated.

Secondly, the playroom setting and playbag materials were described. These play materials should facilitate the development of a relationship, enhance reality-testing skills, encourage catharsis, sublimate aggressive drives, and enhance the child's self concept. Individual play-activity counseling can be integrated into the child's classroom functioning.

Finally, a broad spectrum of counseling procedures was described. The approach advocated was to expand one's knowledge of techniques in order to increase one's repertoire. Then one can utilize whatever procedure seems suitable for the presenting problem. Techniques described included the establishment of the relationship, relaxation exercises, systematic desensitization, assertive training, behavior rehearsal, modeling, motor coordination training, cognitive restructuring, behavioral contracting, reinforcement, mutual storytelling, blackboard drawing, activity counseling, the use of the child as a consultant about his case, and parental involvement.

References

Allen, F. H. *Psychotherapy with children.* New York: Norton, 1942.

Axline, V. *Play therapy.* Cambridge, Mass.: Houghton Mifflin, 1947.

Axline, V. *Dibs: in search of self.* Boston: Houghton Mifflin, 1964.

Bandura, A. *Principles of behavior modification.* New York: Holt, Rinehart & Winston, 1969.

Barten, H. H., & Barten, S. S. (Eds.) *Children and their parents in brief therapy.* New York: Behavioral Publications, 1973.

Bergland, B. W., & Chal, A. H. Relaxation training and a junior high behavior problem. *The School Counselor,* 1972, **19,** 288–293.

Blackham, G. J., & Silberman, A. *Modification of child behavior.* Belmont, Cal.: Wadsworth, 1971.

Bornstein, B. Phobia in a two-and-a-half-year-old child. *Psychoanalytic Quarterly,* 1935, 4, 93–119.

Brammer, L. M., and Shostrom, E. L. *Therapeutic psychology: fundamentals of actualization counseling and psychotherapy.* Englewood Cliffs, N.J.: Prentice-Hall, 1968.

Brown, B. M. The multiple techniques of broad spectrum psychotherapy. In A. A. Lazarus (Ed.), *Clinical behavior therapy.* New York: Brunner Mazel, 1972, pp. 174–226.

Browning, R. M., & Stover, D. O. *Behavior modification in child treatment.* Chicago: Aldine-Atherton, 1971.

Bugg, C. A. Systematic desensitization: a technique worth trying. *Personnel and Guidance Journal,* 1972, **50,** 823–828.

Button, A. D. *The authentic child.* New York: Random House, 1969.

Dimick, K. M., & Huff, V. E. *Child Counseling.* Dubuque, Iowa: William C. Brown, 1970.

Dinkmeyer, D., & Caldwell, E. *Developmental counseling and guidance.* New York: McGraw-Hill, 1970.

Dinkmeyer, D., & Dreikurs, R. *Encouraging children to learn.* Englewood Cliffs, N.J.: Prentice-Hall, 1963.

Dinoff, M., & Rickard, H. C. Learning that privileges entail responsibilities. In J. D. Krumboltz, & C. E. Thoresen (Eds.), *Behavioral counseling: cases and techniques.* New York: Holt, Rinehart & Winston, 1969, pp. 124–129.

Dorfman, E. Play Therapy. In C. R. Rogers, *Client-centered therapy.* Boston: Houghton Mifflin, 1951, 235–277.

Dreikurs, R. Psychology in the classroom. New York: Harper & Row, 1968.

Dreikurs, R., & Soltz, V. *Children: the challenge.* New York: Hawthorn, 1964.

Ellis, A. *Reason and emotion in psychotherapy.* New York: Lyle Stuart, 1962.

Ellis, A., & Harper, R. A. *A guide to rational living.* Englewood Cliffs, N.J.: Prentice-Hall, 1961.

Erikson, E. H. *Childhood and Society.* New York: W. W. Norton, 1963.

Eron, L. D., Huesmann, L. R., Lefkowitz, M. M., & Walder, L. O. Does television violence cause aggression? *American Psychologist*, 1972, **27**, 253–263.

Faust, V. *The counselor-consultant in the elementary school.* Boston: Houghton Mifflin, 1968.

Foxx, R. M., & Azrin, N. H. Restitution: A method of eliminating aggressive-disruptive behavior of retarded and brain damaged patients. *Behavior Research & Therapy*, 1972, **10**, 15–27.

Freud, A. *The psychoanalytic treatment of children.* New York: International Universities Press, 1946.

Freud, A. *Normality and pathology in childhood.* New York: International Universities Press, 1965.

Freud, S. Analysis of a phobia in a five-year-old boy. *Collected Papers*, vol. 3. New York: Basic Books, 1959.

Gardner, R. A. *The boys' and girls' book about brain dysfunction.* New York: Science House, 1972.

Gardner, R. A. *The boys' and girls' book about divorce.* New York: Science House, 1970.

Gardner, R. A. *Therapeutic communication with children.* New York: Science House, 1971.

Ginott, H. G. *Group psychotherapy with children.* New York: McGraw-Hill, 1961.

Ginott, H. G. *Between parent and child.* New York: Macmillan, 1965.

Gittelman, M. Behavior rehearsal as a technique in child treatment. *Journal of Child Psychology and Psychiatry*, 1965, **6**, 251–255.

Glasser, W. *Reality therapy.* New York: Harper & Row, 1965.

Glasser, W. *Schools without failure.* New York: Harper & Row, 1969.

Glasser, W. *The identity society.* New York: Harper & Row, 1972.

Glicken, M. D. Rational counseling: a dynamic approach to children. *Elementary School Guidance and Counseling*, 1968, **2**, 261–67.

Gordon, T. *Parent effectiveness training.* New York: Wyden, 1970.

Graziano, A. M. *Behavior therapy with children.* Chicago: Aldine-Atherton, 1971.

Gronert, R. R. Combining a behavioral approach with reality therapy. *Elementary School Guidance and Counseling*, 1970, **5**, 104–112.

Guerney, B. Filial therapy: description and rationale. *Journal of Consulting Psychology*, 1964, **28**, 304–310.

Guerney, B. (Ed.) *Psychotherapeutic agents: New roles for nonprofessionals, parents and teachers.* New York: Holt, Rinehart & Winston, 1969.

Havighurst, R. J. *Human development and education.* New York: Longmans, 1953.

Hawes, R. M. Reality therapy: an approach to encourage individual and social responsibility in the elementary school. *Elementary School Guidance and Counseling*, 1969, **4**, 120–127.

Hill, G. E., and Luckey, E. B. *Guidance for children in elementary schools.* New York: Appleton-Century-Crofts, 1969.

Homme, L., Csanyi, A. P., Gonzales, M. A., & Rechs, J. R. *How to* use contingency contracting in the classroom. Champaign, Ill.: Research Press, 1970.

Hosford, R. E. Behavioral counseling: a contemporary overview. *The Counseling Psychologist*, 1969, **1**, 1–33.

Keat, D. B. A reinforcement survey schedule for children. University Park, Penn.: Author, 1972a.

Keat, D. B. Review of "Advances in behavior therapy", by Rubin, R. D., Fensterheim, H., Lazarus, A. A., & Franks, C. M. (Eds.). *Behavior Therapy*, 1972b, **3**, 135–137.

Keat, D. B. Broad-spectrum behavior therapy with children: a case presentation. *Behavior Therapy*, 1972c, **3**, pp. 454–459.

Keat, D. B. Behavioral counseling with an adolescent: The green-stamp case. *Pennsylvania Personnel and Guidance Association Journal*, 1974, **2**, in press.

Keat, D. B., and Maki, K. D. Variations on the mutual storytelling theme. *International Journal of Child Psychotherapy*, 1974, **3**, in press.

Kiersay, D. W. Systematic exclusion: eliminating chronic classroom disruptions. In J. D. Krumboltz, & C. E. Thoresen, (Eds.), *Behavioral counseling: cases and techniques*. New York: Holt, Rinehart & Winston, 1969, pp. 89–114.

Klein, M. *The psychoanalysis of children*. New York: Grove Press, 1960.

Kolansky, H. Treatment of a three-year-old girl's severe neurosis—stammering and insect phobia. In *The Psychoanalytic Study of the Child*, vol. XV. New York: International Universities Press, 1960.

Krumboltz, J. D., & Hosford, R. E. Behavioral counseling in the elementary school. *Elementary School Guidance and Counseling*, 1967, **1**, 27–40.

Krumboltz, J. D., & Krumboltz, H. B. *Changing children's behavior*. Englewood Cliffs, N.J.: Prentice-Hall, 1972.

Krumboltz, J. D., & Thoresen, G. E. *Behavioral counseling: cases and techniques*. New York: Holt, Rinehart & Winston, 1969.

Lazarus, A. A. Broad spectrum behavior therapy and the treatment of agoraphobia. *Behavior Research and Therapy*, 1966a, **4**, 95–97.

Lazarus, A. A. Behavior rehearsal vs. non-directive therapy vs. advice in effecting behavior change. *Behavior Research and Therapy*, 1966b, **4**, 209–212.

Lazarus, A. A. In support of technical eclecticism. *Psychological Reports*, 1967, **21**, 415–416.

Lazarus, A. A. Relationship therapy: often necessary but usually insufficient. *The Counseling Psychologist*, 1969, **1**, 25–27.

Lazarus, A. A. *Behavior therapy and beyond*. New York: McGraw-Hill, 1971a.

Lazarus, A. A. *Relaxation exercises*. Chicago: Instructional Dynamics Incorporated, 1971b.

Lazarus, A. A., & Abramovitz, A. The use of "emotive imagery" in the treatment of children's phobias. *Journal of Mental Science,* 1962, **108**, 191–195.

Lazarus, A., Davison, G., & Polefka. Classical and operant factors in the treatment of a school phobia. *Journal of Abnormal Psychology,* 1965, **70**, 225–229.

Lederman, J. *Anger and the rocking chair.* New York: McGraw-Hill, 1969.

Maclay, D. *Treatment for children.* New York: Science House, 1970.

Madsen, C. K., & Madsen, C. H. *Parents/Children/Discipline.* Boston: Allyn & Bacon, 1972.

May, R. *Love and will.* New York: Norton, 1968.

May, R., Angel, E., & Ellenberger, H. F. (Eds.) *Existence: A new dimension in psychiatry and psychology.* New York: Basic Books, 1958.

McComb, B. Activity counseling: an individual counseling procedure for the elementary school child. Unpublished manuscript, Nova Elementary School, Fort Lauderdale, Fla., 1972.

Moustakas, C. *Psychotherapy with children: the living relationship.* New York: Harper & Row, 1959.

Moustakas, C. (Ed.) *Existential child therapy.* New York: Basic Books, 1966.

Mowrer, O. H., & Mowrer, W. A. Enuresis: a method for its study and treatment. *American Journal of Orthopsychiatry,* 1938, **8**, 436–447.

Myrick, R. D., & Haldin, W. A study of play process in counseling. *Elementary School Guidance and Counseling,* 1971, **5**, 256–65.

Nelson, R. C. Elementary school counseling with unstructured play media. *Personnel and Guidance Journal,* 1966, **1**, 24–27.

Nelson, R. C. Pros and cons of using play media in counseling. *Elementary School Guidance and Counseling,* 1967, **2**, 143–147.

Patterson, G. R., and Gullion, E. *Living with Children.* Champaign, Ill.: Research Press, 1968.

Patterson, G. R., McNeal, S., Hawkins, N. & Phelps, R. Reprogramming the social environment. *Journal of Child Psychology and Psychiatry,* 1967, **8**, 181–195.

Perls, F. S. *Gestalt therapy verbatim.* Lafayette, Cal.: Real People Press, 1969.

Pomeroy, W. B. *Boys and sex.* New York: Delacorte Press, 1968.

Rogers, C. R. *The clinical treatment of the problem child.* Boston: Houghton Mifflin, 1939.

Rogers, C. R. *Client-centered therapy.* Boston: Houghton Mifflin, 1951.

Rogers, C. R. *On becoming a person.* Boston: Houghton Mifflin, 1961.

Russo, S. Adaptations in behavioral therapy with children. *Behavior Research and Therapy,* 1964, **2**, 43–47.

Sanborn, B., & Schuster, W. Establishing reinforcement techniques in the classroom. In J. D. Krumboltz, and C. E. Thoresen (Eds.),

Behavioral counseling: cases and techniques. New York: Holt, Rinehart & Winston, 1969, pp. 131–152.

Schwarz, H. The mother in the consulting room: notes on the psychoanalytic treatment of two young children. In *The psychoanalytic study of the child,* vol. 5. New York: International Universities Press, 1950, pp. 343–357.

Shostrom, E. L. *Man, the manipulator.* New York: Bantam Books, 1967.

Skinner, B. F. Humanistic behaviorism. *The Humanist,* 1971, **31,** 35.

Smirnoff, V. *The scope of child analysis.* New York: International Universities Press, 1971.

Smith, J. M., & Smith, D. *Child management: a program for parents and teachers.* Ann Arbor, Mich.: Ann Arbor Publishers, 1964.

Soltz, V. *Study group leader's manual:* for use with *Children: The challenge.* Chicago: Alfred Adler Institute, 1967.

Spock, B. *Baby and child care.* New York: Pocket Books, 1968.

Strean, H. S. The use of the patient as consultant. In H. S. Strean (Ed.), *New approaches in child guidance.* Metuchen, N.J.: Scarecrow Press, 1970, 53–63.

Sulzer, B., & Mayer, G. R. *Behavior modification procedures for school personnel.* Hinsdale, Ill.: Dryden Press, 1972.

Tharp, R. G., & Wetzel, R. J. *Behavior modification in the natural environment.* New York: Academic Press, 1969.

Tough, J. H., Hawkins, R. P., McArthur, M. M., & Ravenswaay, S. V. Modification of enuretic behavior by punishment: a new use for an old device. *Behavior Therapy,* 1971, **2,** 567–574.

Turner, R. K., Young, G. C., & Rachman, S. Treatment of nocturnal enuresis by conditioning techniques. *Behaviour research and therapy,* 1970, 8, 367–381.

Ullmann, L. P., & Krasner, L. *Case studies in behavior modification.* New York: Holt, Rinehart & Winston, 1965.

Wahler, R. G., Winkel, G. H., Peterson, R. F., & Morrison, D. C. Mothers as behavior therapists for their own children. *Behavior Research and Therapy,* 1965, **3,** 113–134.

Waterland, J. C. Actions instead of words: play therapy for the young child. *Elementary School Guidance and Counseling,* 1970, **4,** 180–187.

Williams, C. D. The elimination of tantrum behavior by extinction procedures. *Journal of Abnormal and Social Psychology,* 1959, **59,** 269.

Wittenberg, H. *Isometrics.* New York: Award Books, 1964.

Wittes, G., & Radin, N. *The reinforcement approach.* San Rafael, Cal.: Dimensions Publishing Company, 1969.

Wolpe, J. *Psychotherapy by Reciprocal Inhibition.* Stanford, Cal.: Stanford University Press, 1958.

Wolpe, J. *The practice of behavior therapy.* New York: Pergamon Press, 1959.

Wolpe, J., & Lazarus, A. *Behavior therapy techniques.* New York: Pergamon Press, 1966.

Woody, R. *Behavioral problem children in the schools.* New York: Appleton-Century-Crofts, 1969.

Woody, R. *Psychobehavioral counseling and therapy.* New York: Appleton-Century-Crofts, 1971.

Yates, A. J. *Behavior therapy.* New York: Wiley, 1970.

4

There are times when it is more appropriate to work with children in groups than individually. The counselor is often confronted with deciding what to do with a group of children. In addition, he must consider the children's ages, the sex composition of the group, the length and frequency of meetings, the group's size, and its goals.

The focus of this chapter is group *counseling*. Group *guidance* will be covered in Chapter Five (teacher-conducted classroom meetings or group guidance sessions), Chapter Seven (classroom implementation of affective curriculum materials), and Chapter Eight (vocational orientation programs that can be implemented in the elementary schools).

It is important initially to define group counseling. Group counseling has been described as

> a dynamic, interpersonal process through which individuals within the normal range of adjustment work within a peer group and with a professionally trained counselor, exploring problems and feelings in an attempt to modify attitudes so that they are better able to deal with developmental problems (Cohn, Combs, Gibian & Sniffen, 1963, p. 355–356).

A further elaboration of the key phrases in this definition was made in a more recent article which focuses on the key phrases of the dynamic interpersonal process: dealing with individuals within the normal range of adjustment, working with a peer group, working with a professionally trained counselor, exploring problems and feelings in an attempt to modify their attitudes, and the final aspect of dealing with the developmental problems (Cox & Herr, 1968). Among other definitions of group counseling is the following:

Group Counseling With Children

Group counseling is a dynamic interpersonal process focusing on conscious thought and behavior and involving the therapy functions of permissiveness, orientation to reality, catharsis, and mutual trust, caring, understanding, acceptance and support. The therapy functions are created and nurtured in a small group through the sharing of personal concerns with one's peers and the counselor(s). The group counselees are basically normal individuals with various concerns which are not debilitating to the extent of requiring extensive personality change. The group counselees may utilize the group interaction to increase understanding and acceptance of values and goals and to learn and/or unlearn certain attitudes or behaviors (Gazda, Duncan, & Meadows, 1967, p. 305).

Mahler has defined group counseling as the process of using group interaction to facilitate deeper self understanding and self acceptance. There is a need for a climate of mutual respect and acceptance, so that individuals can loosen their defenses sufficiently to explore both the meaning of behavior and new ways of behaving. The concerns and problems encountered are centered in the developmental tasks of each member rather than on pathological blocks and distortions of reality (Mahler, 1969, p. 11).

Developmental considerations are especially important because different approaches are necessary with different age groups. In particular, certain authors advocate play procedures for children in the lower grade levels. "It is thus advocated that such techniques as play therapy fit the lower grade level much better than do the more verbal group counseling approaches" (Cox & Herr, 1968, p. 63). In addition, different developmental tasks are being worked through at different ages (Gazda, 1971). This chapter will deal primarily with children aged 5–12.

While the major emphasis of this chapter is on group counseling, one should be aware of the difference between group counseling and group guidance. Muro and Freeman (1968) describe group guidance as having to do with "all aspects of the guidance program that are content centered and involve such counselor activities as dispensing occupational and educational information, planning and conducting orientation programs, group follow-up meetings, and group testing" (Muro & Freeman, 1968, p. 44).

Another important distinction should be made between play therapy and play media. Play therapy is the utilization of play, in the presence of the counselor, to help a child get rid of tensions, cope with problems more appropriately, and so on. Play media are the materials used in the playroom. In application, of course, they are interrelated in that play media facilitate the play process.

Group counseling is increasingly being preferred to individual counseling. Faust (1968) advances two arguments in support of group counseling. The first is economic. The second, however, is based on the belief that what children learn is learned in groups and that new learning (or unlearning) might therefore best be effected in groups. Sonstegard's (1968) view is that the use of groups enhances the learning process of the child by helping him to redirect his mistaken goals; this is the Dreikurian outlook. Carkhuff (1969) has developed group training as a preferred mode of treatment for problems in living that are interpersonal in nature. Although his approach focuses primarily on the training of parents (already discussed in Chapter Three and also to be covered in Chapter Five), its theoretical underpinning has important ramifications for group counseling. In summary, Carkhuff proposes that the core of functioning (or dysfunctioning) and the core of the helping process (learning or relearning) are interpersonal. Therefore, he supports group processes as the best mode of treating difficulties in interpersonal functioning. From this viewpoint, the group situation can be viewed as a learning laboratory in which the child gets a chance to try out *in vivo* some of the skills he is using inappropriately in his real-life environment. It should be mentioned, however, that a child may be in individual counseling and group counseling concurrently. Quite often a natural outgrowth of individual counseling is a transfer into group counseling. The placement of the child is based upon the counselor's intensive knowledge of him as a result of individual contacts. The counselor must decide whether to continue both modes of counseling or only one. For some children, whose lives are already too organized or who need personal attention, individual counseling may be indicated. Most children, however, can gain something positive from a constructive group counseling experience.

––– **Theory**

The sections that follow have to do with theories of child group counseling. Among the topics discussed are the conduct of the group (the role of leadership), group goals (purposes and objectives), and phases of the group process. This theoretical section is intended to provide the backdrop against which one can consider the actual implementation of a child counseling group.

Conducting the Group

Deciding on the nature of the group and facilitating its functioning has been described as the conductor's role (Walton, 1971). The term "conductor" seems to suggest the way in which the counselor selects group members, manages the group by means of appropriate interventions, and in a variety of ways orchestrates the unfolding of events. There are numerous viewpoints on the role of the counselor in groups. Dinkmeyer (1968) considers it important that leaders be experienced in individual counseling because understanding of personality dynamics and characteristics central to individual helping relationships is also fundamental in group work. Gibb (1947) describes leadership as a function of social interaction, relative to the situation, flourishing in a problem situation, and determined by and directed toward an objective goal of the group. Warters (1960) identifies the basic functions of the leader as helping the group set and define goals and progress toward achievement of these goals, and maintaining the group itself. Kemp (1964) discusses the historical bases of group leadership from the authoritarian, democratic, and group-centered viewpoints, with examples given of each type of approach. Dinkmeyer and Muro (1971) state that among the primary functions of the group leader are to promote interactions, resolve conflicts, and guide the group through a number of techniques that encourage movement toward accepted goals. Rose (1972) says that the leader initially functions as a guide who structures and leads but gradually recedes and lets the group take over.

In the final analysis, of course, the role of the conductor is very much a function of the counselor's personality and philosophy of counseling. The view favored by the author, whose practical manifestations will be elaborated in this chapter, is client-centered within a behavioral paradigm. This means that the group has a framework but that within it there is room to use client-centered approaches with the individual child and with groups of interacting children.

Group Goals, Purposes and Objectives

Dinkmeyer and Caldwell (1970, p. 138) identify the goals of developmental group counseling as being to help each member of the group to:

1. Know and understand himself.
2. Develop self acceptance and a feeling of being worthwhile in his own right.
3. Develop methods of coping with the developmental tasks of life.
4. Develop increased self direction and better problem-solving and decision-making abilities.
5. Develop sensitivity to the needs of others, thus becoming more aware of his role in relationship to others, and a better ability to identify with the feelings of those around him. As he becomes more aware of self, he can be more responsible for his impact upon other human beings.

Hansen and Stevic (1969) discuss four purposes of group work: to help with transitions in school; to undertake extra-class activity to enhance self understanding; to discuss general concerns as a prelude to individual counseling; and to help pupils learn that other children have similar concerns. These goals can be approached from a behavioral viewpoint. In Rose's (1972) chapter on plans for treatment, he discusses such behavioral goals as modifying the frequency of overt manifestation of affect among members; increasing or decreasing general or specific intragroup interaction; planning group activities and the modification of group goals; reducing intragroup competition; increasing the attractiveness of the group; increasing various members' participation in the group and decreasing others'; lessening physical abuse such as hitting and stealing and fighting within the group; and other, more easily quantifiable, goals and behaviors. The advantage of this type of goal is that it can be stated behaviorally; thus it is possible to measure the effects of changes resulting from the group process.

The Process and Phases of the Group

Goldman (1962) describes the roles of content and process in group work. Group content topics ranged from the traditional school subject matter, to school-related topics, to nonschool topics. He sees the process as three-leveled: the leader plans topics and lectures, the leader and group members collaborate in planning topics, topics originate with group members. Given this paradigm, the level of group interaction in this chapter would generally be considered to be levels five through eight. That is, the content topics can involve school-related or nonschool subjects. The process results both from collaboration and from the suggestions of group members. The procedures used are discussions, role-playing, and talk about attitudes, opinions, feelings, and needs.

As was stressed in Chapter Three, the counselor's relationships with the various children in the group are at the core of the process. Ohlsen (1970) supports this viewpoint strongly and devotes much of his work to the development of a relationship with the child. This is the foundation upon which the rest of group work can be built. Hansen (1971) discusses the stages in the life of the group. These are:

1. Stage one is the initiation of the group, in which the group members get acquainted. Goals are established, but there is generally little organization or group structure at this stage.

2. Stage two is conflict and confrontation, and deals with issues related to the satisfaction of the group members with the group and its operation.

3. Stage three is the development of cohesiveness, which causes the members to drop certain preconceptions and attempt to find more adaptive kinds of behavior.

4. Stage four is production, in which the established view directs itself toward the goals that have been agreed upon.

5. Stage five is termination. When children in groups have established personal bonds and reached some of the goals of the group, they have mixed feelings about separation. This ambivalence needs to be worked through in the termination of a group.

Warner (1971) identifies the stages in the counseling process as (1) engagement, (2) commitment, and (3) behavior-modifying experiences.

From the Adlerian viewpoint (Dinkmeyer, 1968) and that of Dreikurs and Sonstegard (1968), there are four phases:

Table 4–1 *Interaction of Content and Process in Group Guidance, Group Counseling and Group Therapy*

Content	PROCESS		
	LEVEL I	LEVEL II	LEVEL III
	Leader plans topics	Leaders and group members collaborate in planning topics	Topics originate with group members
	Lecture and recitation	Discussions, projects, panels, visits	Free discussion, role-playing
	Facts and skills emphasized	Attitudes and opinions emphasized	Feelings and needs emphasized
	Units in regular classes	Separate guidance groups meet on schedule	Groups organized as needed, meet as needed
Type A Usual school subject matter: mathematics, English, etc.	1	4	7
Type B School-related topics: the world of work, choosing a college, how to study, etc.	2	5	8
Type C Non-school topics: dating behavior, parent-child relations, handling frustrations, etc.	3	6	9

Reprinted from Leo Goldman, "Group Guidance: Content and Process," *Personnel and Guidance Journal,* February 1962, p. 519, figure 1. Copyright 1962 American Personnel and Guidance Association. Reprinted with permission.

1. The establishment and maintenance of appropriate relationships.

2. An examination of the purpose of each group member's actions or behaviors.

3. The revelation to each child of the goals he is pursuing (psychological disclosure).

4. A reorientation and redirection for the child.

Gazda (1971) has also enumerated stages in group development. Stage 1 is an exploratory period in which the group members introduce themselves and describe what they hope to achieve during the course of the group. Stage 2 is transitional and begins when one or more counselees begin to self disclose at a deeper level. Stage 3 is an active period in which worker production comes out of the group's functioning. Gazda (1971) makes an extremely important point here; he states that, in the final analysis, counselee action is goal-related and dependent upon behavioral modifications to be employed outside of the group setting. This process is encouraged by assigning homework to be done and reported on to the group at the next session (Gazda, 1971). The final stage is terminal, and involves the tapering off of counselee self disclosures and reinforcement of the growth of the group members during the course of the group meetings.

For counselors who are sports-minded, Cox and Herr (1968) make an analogy from baseball to the life of a group. On the way to first base, the members are busy becoming a group. This involves getting acquainted, figuring out what the counselor is going to do, and deciding whether to become a member of the group. In the trip to second base, the members test the group they have tentatively joined, indulging in a kind of trial-and-error exposure during which they open up and then withdraw. On the way to third base, the now-functioning group begins to gain social insights from the interchange and interaction. This ventilation has the effect of relieving tensions and anxieties. In addition, other group members acquire new ideas that broaden their perspectives. During the final dash for home the insight-equipped members attempt to put these understandings into action, both within the group and outside it. Once the goal has been accomplished, the group begins to dissolve. The counselor may recap the game by outlining the benefits derived from it.

Forming the Group

The counselor who is called upon or desires to institute a group must address a variety of considerations. These include group composition, group size, the counseling setting, the length and frequency of contacts, referral, and behavioral assessment. The following pages examine these subjects.

Group Composition

In thinking about the composition of groups, both fantasy and reality need to be considered. That is, what is the ideal situation and what is the reality that dictates the identities of the children and the kind of facilities available for the group meeting? The ideal group would seem to be composed of heterogenous individuals, with respect to behavior. However, one usually notes regression toward the mean of average behavior in group members. This means that the group should be balanced with regard to such characteristics as active behavior and withdrawal. In addition, of course, some type(s) of model children should be included. These models illustrate appropriate behaviors for the other children to observe.

Various authors, notably Ginott (1961), have described several kinds of persons who should be included and some who should be excluded. Dinkmeyer and Muro (1971) have summarized these observations. Among the children who should ideally be included in the group are compulsive children, effeminate boys, restricted children, do-gooders, children with specific fears, and those with conduct problems. Children who should be excluded are those who have experienced a trauma such as death or divorce, severe sibling rivalry, those who steal, and those who give evidence of a lack of conscience or other kinds of sociopathic tendencies. The author has included in groups some children who have experienced divorce, others who are going through severe sibling rivalry, and others who steal. Such children were included because their problems can be dealt with in group counseling. Thus, such lists are not meant to be prescriptive but to be used as tentative guides.

With respect to age, the group's composition should be more or less homogeneous. This is more difficult to accomplish than it would appear. For example, one should consider the phases Redl (1966) discusses with regard to stages. What is the maturational congruency of the child with regard to the various facets of his development? This includes consideration of the child's chronological age, mental age, and social development. The author has led a group with a chronological age range of three years. For example, one group included a child who was nearly ten and others whose ages ranged from seven to nine. This older child was included because her social development and intellectual maturity were similar to those of a younger child. Therefore, although chronological age can be used as a rough guide for grouping, the counselor should not make the mistake that many educators have tended to make of grouping the children on the basis of chronological age alone. Overall developmental considerations must be taken into account. As a general rule of thumb, a span of two years is an appropriate range for grouping children of elementary school age.

Sex composition is another area of concern in arranging a group. Because most children during the elementary school years are in the latency period, authors have generally agreed that it is best to treat them in separate groups. For example, Ohlsen has "conceded that it may be wise to treat girls and boys of the latency period in separate groups" (1968, p. 291). Dinkmeyer and Caldwell (1970) consider single-sex groups preferable in grades 1 to 6. Yunker writes, "When counseling primary school children, unisexual groupings would possess distinct advantages" (1970, p. 176). Most authors support single-sex grouping during the elementary school years, and all groups in this age range that the author has run have been composed of children of the same sex.

Group Size

The number of children in a group depends on several variables. One is the nature of their disorders. For example, with children who are withdrawn, the number could be larger than average. With behaviorally disordered children who are aggressive and acting out, it is necessary to have fewer members in the group. There the literature offers numerous suggestions about group size. Cox and Herr (1968) suggest five to ten in a group; Combs, Cohn, Gibian and Sniffen (1963), four to six; Dinkmeyer and Muro (1971), five to six; Mayer and Baker (1967), five to six; Hansen and Stevic (1969), four to six; Peters, Shertzer and Van Hoose (1965), four to eight; Faust (1968), three to four for primary-age children and up to six in the intermediate grades. The author's experience has led him to develop the following guidelines: If the counselor is handling the group by himself, the advisable number is from three to five or six children. If, however, there is to be a co-counselor, six to ten children could be handled in the group. It is generally advisable for the co-counselor to be of the opposite sex, if possible, to simulate the family situation in which children interact with two people of different sexes.

The Counseling Setting

As was observed in Chapter Three, the counseling setting will be dictated by the resources of the school. Sometimes reality requires that the group meet in a storage room, cafeteria, auditorium, or whatever other space is available. Of course, it is ideal to have a facility that is consistently available and that the counselor can equip with his normal working tools. The room should be long enough so that approximately eight to ten children can gather there, and large enough so that the children can play catch with various kinds of balls (e.g., a minimum of 12 by 24 feet). The room can be dual-purpose, providing space for play and for materials such as fingerpaints, clay, easels, a blackboard, and a variety of games. The chairs (of appropriate size so that the children's feet touch the floor) should be set up in an approximate circle. An alternative is to place a mattress or blanket on the floor. The latter arrangement is sometimes more relaxing for the children.

Length and Frequency of Sessions

The length of group sessions necessarily varies with the age of the children. For the 5–8 age range, the author has generally found 40 to 60 minutes to be a satisfactory length of time. For ages 9–12, the length can be increased from 1 to 1½ hours. The frequency of sessions is often dictated by reality. Although some authors (e.g., Gazda, 1971) recommend two group sessions equally spaced through the week, reality (e.g., counselor and child time) often requires that these meetings take place once a week.

Referral and Behavioral Assessment

How a child joins a group varies with the situation. The child is often referred by the teacher because of some behavioral disorder. Or the counselor can establish credibility with several classes of children and be deluged with requests to join the group. Whatever the reason for considering a child for the group, the counselor's task remains one of reaching children in need (e.g., the withdrawn child who might remain uncontacted by these two referral strategies) and composing a viable group.

Rose has stated that "the purpose of assessment is the collection of data and the statement of the problem in such a way that its formulation points to appropriate corrective procedures" (Rose, 1972, p. 30). Once the appropriate assessment is made, the goal of the group can be delineated. Does the child need help with social skills and getting along with others? Is the problem a behavioral one? Are tutoring skills needed? Just what is the presenting rationale for the group? Behavioral assessment can be accomplished by various means. One is the individual interview, in which the child talks to the counselor and focuses on his problem or concerns. The data from the interview help formulate the reason(s) for assigning the child to a particular group. Another aspect of assessment is determining what is reinforcing for the child. A reinforcement survey schedule (Keat, 1972) or menu (Daley, 1969) can be used with children prior to the outset of the group and/or during the initial group session.

Another aspect of assessment is monitoring or charting behavior. Monitoring is counting manifestations of behavior to determine just how much a child engages in a particular behavior. Although the count can be made by the counselor during the session, the author considers it preferable to have other persons do the tabulation, if practical. If the group meets behind a one-way mirror, the observers can be given sheets to time the child's behaviors (Cline, 1972, p. 42). For example, an active child count might monitor such actions as turning around in the seat, rocking, getting up, and leaving the room. Once such baseline data are acquired, changes in behavior can also be charted. The counselor will also have some subjective impressions of the nature of these kinds of behaviors. Reality is quite often difficult to chart. However, one may often analyze tapes after the sessions are over. If this is not possible, the counselor may have to rely upon his own subjective impressions.

Another procedure for evaluating group members is to interview them and discuss such topics as their concerns, willingness to discuss their concerns with a group, interest in helping others with their problems, and willingness to change their own behaviors.

The foregoing are some considerations that are normally dealt with before the group meets. Now let us move on to the initiation of the group and look at some of the techniques and methods that can be used with a group of children.

―――――――――――――――――――――――――――― **Implementation**

This section deals with some of the important techniques and media of group counseling. Initially, the counselor must get things rolling. In the talk or interview section, numerous kinds of tasks can be carried out. In the activities section, toys and other media are available. The counselor may wish to make a formal statement or set of agreements (i.e., contracts) about what the child is expected to do over a given period of time in return for a given reward. The contract can be a simple statement about participating in the group and abiding by certain limits during the group session, or it can involve carrying out assignments, such as homework, outside the group. Contracts were discussed in Chapter

Three; in the group they can take the form of group agreements, in conjunction with individual agreements. These contracts can bear on such matters as general rules of operation, and specific tasks the child might perform outside of the group during the upcoming week. Rose (1972) has discussed both contracts and behavioral assignments. Dinkmeyer and Muro (1971) give a brief illustration of a contract between the group and a particular member of the group. This type of procedure allows for focusing of goals during the course of the group's meetings. In addition, it can provide some material for discussion during the group talk section. That is, children can discuss what they are doing in and out of the group and whether or not they meet the terms of the contract that the group initially agreed upon.

Getting Started

The counselor is now concerned about the implementation of a group. It is important for everyone involved to have some idea about the group's purposes and reasons for participating in it. The purposes involve why the children are there and what they plan to do while they are in the group. Dinkmeyer and Caldwell (1970) discuss the initiation of counseling and list considerations for getting started. After get-acquainted introductions, the group moves on to talk about concerns, problems, and reasons for being there. In addition, Dinkmeyer and Caldwell stress stating of the rules of the game, or limits within which the group should function. Frost (1972) lists the following guidelines for group members to adhere to:

1. Everything we talk about is to be considered confidential. You are not to tell anyone what we talk about in this group.

2. We are here to help each other. This is a place where we can talk about anything. However, we must listen carefully to others and try to help them. This means you should not try to dominate the group by doing all the talking.

3. Only one person will talk at a time. You don't have to raise your hand but should wait until others have finished talking before you begin.

4. The counselor is the leader of the group, but is also a member. He performs his functions from within the group. The counselor will attempt to keep the discussion moving, clarify or answer questions, and at other times he will be a deep listener.

5. Once a topic is being discussed we stick to the topic until we feel it is time to discuss a new topic.

6. The group exists to help us gain a better understanding of ourselves and how we affect others.

Examples of some interactions from an initial session follow. During the get-acquainted section, the counselor asks the children to tell their names.

COUNSELOR: O.K. Let's get started by each of us telling our names so that we can get to know each other. Some of you know each other already and you all know who I am. (The first two children proceed to give their real first names.)

CHILD C: I don't want to be called C, I want to be called Rider.

COUNSELOR: Oh, why's that?

CHILD C: Because I'm a tomboy. (This was followed by some vague explanations. The real reason for changing her name was not clear until the third session when C's sister revealed that C was leaving her two sisters and mother to live with her father in another state. She was therefore starting to separate out from the family by changing her identity.)

COUNSELOR: Anyone else ever feel like changing their name sometimes?

CHILD D: Yeah, but Rider is a weird name.

COUNSELOR: What would you change your name to?

CHILD D: I like it the way it is.

COUNSELOR: Sometimes we like to change it to be like a different person, like make-believe.

CHILD B: What about you?

COUNSELOR: Sometimes I would like to change my name. You put me on the spot. I guess, somebody that I like, look up to, admire. Arnold. (Laughs from the children). Guess you don't know who Arnold is. The name itself is not so important but that it should be the name of someone we like or would like to be like.

CHILD E: Jeanie.

COUNSELOR: Magical one?

CHILD E: Jeanie, I dream of Jeanie.

CHILD B: Samantha. Some children call me Sam.

COUNSELOR: Do you know why? (A dangerous question at this stage. The child is not yet ready for self disclosures to the group.)

CHILD B: Don't know.

COUNSELOR: Would you like to be called B or Samantha?

CHILD B: Sam. And how about you? (indicating the co-counselor)

CO-COUNSELOR: I like my own name.

In this initial get-acquainted section, the group members not only got to know each other's preferred names, but were also exposed to some identification and/or modeling theory. Child B, a quiet and withdrawn child, got caught up in talking about names and started to conduct the group by asking both the counselor and co-counselor what they preferred to be called!

The second aspect of the initial group session is discussion of what the group will be doing during the meeting hours.

COUNSELOR: What is your idea of what we are to be doing during our time together?

CHILD A: Play games.

CHILD C: Fill in those papers (referring to the reinforcement survey schedules on a table in the corner of the room).

CHILD E: Eat ice cream and candy.

COUNSELOR: Probably not ice cream, but we do have candy and some things like that. The papers are there because we want to figure out what you like best.

CHILD E: Candy!

COUNSELOR: Anybody else have any ideas?

CHILD B: Play with puppets.

CHILD D: Play games. Careers.

COUNSELOR: Careers. I'm not familiar with that one. But you can bring it in and teach us how to play. We'll teach you some, and you can teach us some. We'll help each other learn new things. Anybody else have any ideas? (No response for about 15 seconds.) I'll give you some idea what's going to happen because you're probably curious about this. Well, first we're going to sit down and talk awhile about some things that are on our minds. This can be something like getting along with others, what's going on in school, what we like to do best. After we talk awhile, then we will probably have a story. Miss Conklin has a story to share with us today. Then after we discuss this we will play some games. Sometimes these will be all together or you can choose to play whatever you like.

The final issue which should be covered in the initial session is why the children are in the group. Here the conductor may choose either to "lay the cards on the table" (Sullivan, 1954), let the group suggest reasons, or let them come up during the group process.

COUNSELOR: Does anyone have any idea why we are here?

CHILD F: To play.

CHILD A: To talk about our troubles and problems. (This is a child who was also in individual counseling with the counselor.)

COUNSELOR: Yes, our worries and concerns. Anything on our minds which we are concerned about, talk about.

CHILD C: Find out what to do about things.

COUNSELOR: Yes, to find out solutions to our troubles, like if you have trouble with your mother, what can you do about it (a leading question, to guide the children into talking about a particular topic).

Talk First, Play Later

Activity group counseling is basically identical with what Gazda labels "activity-interview group counseling" (1971, p. 116). It is a composite of activity group therapy (*à la* Slavson) and talk or an interview within the group. The author prefers to call it an activity group counseling session. The actual sequence of events is different from that suggested by Gazda (1971) and Blakeman and Day (1969), all of whom suggest beginning with a game or activity and then initiating the interview group counseling. The author's approach focuses on the first interactions that occur during the talk phase of the verbal session. Experience indicates that it is more beneficial to begin with the talk or interview and then to move into games and activities. In this fashion, children can be more easily focused at the beginning of the session. That is, they are usually willing to sit down for a while to discuss things and then to move to some activity. If the children immediately begin an activity, it is sometimes difficult to lure them to sit down and talk about things (especially with behaviorally disordered boys). Also, by following talk with activities the counselor can make some desirable activities contingent upon the child's performance during the talk session. In one instance, a boy who started a fight during the talk section of the group session was asked to leave the group. He was forbidden from participating in the more pleasurable portion of the session. This brings up the issue of limits. The counselor can either state these limits initially or deal with them as they come up. The following exchange illustrates the latter approach:

Child A is out of her seat and has one of the games in her hands.

COUNSELOR: You know one of the things that we have in here, A, is when we're sitting here and talking we need to sit down and talk or we don't get the lollypops.

CHILD A: Oh!

COUNSELOR: That's one of the rules.

CHILD D: You should of told us.

COUNSELOR: Oh, we didn't tell you that because it didn't happen till now (4th session). She's the first to do it.

Child A quickly moves back into her seat.

Bibliocounseling

The use of literature during the talk section of the meeting has been called by various names. Anderson and Schmidt (1967) called this "story-book" counseling. The author prefers to call it bibliocounseling, and has developed a guide to affective materials that can be used in such counseling groups (Keat *et al.*, 1972). Actually, any children's stories suitable for the purpose can be used in the group. Some of these stories can come from structured materials such as are available in Developing Understanding of Self and Others (Dinkmeyer, 1970) or from the Human Development Training Institute (Bessel & Palomares, 1970). These stories are generally selected to focus on concerns of the group and can deal with such topics as friends, sharing, sibling rivalry, problem solving, decision making, and the like. Thus the only limitation is the counselor's awareness of, and the availability of, various sources of literature for children. Literature can be used to initiate and structure the talk section of the meeting around particular topics the counselor deems appropriate for the group.

The following example is from the third session of a group. It draws on a previous story, a commonly known tale, and finally a new story.

COUNSELOR: Remember some of the group talk rules from the last story last week?

CHILD D: Don't clam up.

COUNSELOR: Clarissa said don't clam up. Any other ones?

CHILD D: Stick to the point.

COUNSELOR: Who said that?

CHILD C: The swordfish.

COUNSELOR: Spike, the swordfish. Any other characters?

CHILD A: Raise your hand.

COUNSELOR: Yes, but we don't want to use that one because it makes it too much like school. Remember, one of you has a pet like the other one.

CHILD A: Turtle.

COUNSELOR: Said listen carefully. Soupy said this. Any of you ever read a story about a turtle?

CHILD A: Of the hare and the tortoise.

CHILD C: We have a record on it.

COUNSELOR: You know what the lesson of that story is?

CHILD C: Mm hm. I forgot.

CHILD D: Keep steady.

COUNSELOR: Right. The rabbit was faster but stopped to eat and sleep, but the turtle kept steady and plodded along and finally won. Now we have another story for today.

CO-COUNSELOR: (Starts reading "Gordo and Molly" from Dinkmeyer, 1970). "Both boys pulled and fell on the floor still holding on to the block." What do you think's going to happen next?

CHILD D: Somebody's gonna get hurt.

CO-COUNSELOR: Somebody might get hurt!

COUNSELOR: What happened that one day, remember, when both wanted the same lollypop?

CHILD D: And it dropped.

CHILD C: That was A's.

COUNSELOR: When two people want the same thing and fight over it, well, one's gonna get hurt, or something like a broken lollypop, so it's better to share it.

CHILD D: Neither of them have it.

COUNSELOR: Fighting over it neither can use it. What could they do?

CHILD D: Break it.

CHILD A: Share it. Put all together and build something together.

The story goes on. The story serves as a springboard for discussion. In this example, the first page of the story provided the stimulus. The counselor related the story to an incident from the previous week that had to do with sharing lollypops. Then the group was asked for solutions to the real-life situation as well as the storybook one. It is important that whenever problems come up solutions should be solicited from the children.

Problem-solving Exercises

Another procedure the counselor can use with the group is to set up a problem situation and encourage the children to work out solutions to it. These situations can be conjured up by the counselor prior to or during the session, or can be taken from published sources (e.g., Dinkmeyer, 1970). The following problem-solving situation is primarily from the latter source, although it was personalized by the co-counselor.

COUNSELOR: Remember, we have talked a lot about problems and how you solve them, and she has something to talk to us about.

CO-COUNSELOR: I have a problem story. A story I heard about a problem, and I'm going to tell it to you. You can help me solve it. There were some girls who were going to play jump-rope. They didn't know how. Sue (last in line) said to Mary, "Oh you can't jump because you're too fat," and the next girl came up and she said, "Karen you can't jump, you're too stupid," and another girl came up and she said another nasty thing. The other girls said they didn't like this and they wanted her to stop, and then it was Sue's turn and one of the girls said, "Oh you can't jump either, you're too dumb." Sue got upset. She ran away and started to cry. What do you think of that?

CHILD A: Well, maybe because she said all of those nasty things to the other girls.

CHILD D: Yeah, she shouldn't do that if she didn't want them to do it to her.

CHILD A: But just because she did it, it didn't mean they have to do it to her!

CO-COUNSELOR: Do you think the other girls liked playing with Sue?

CHILD F: No.

CHILD D: Because she told them mean things.

CO-COUNSELOR: Any other reasons? (No response.) How do you think they felt?

CHILD A: Sad.

CHILD D: They didn't like that—so they had a right to call her those things because . . .

CHILD A: And they were brave. They didn't run away, and I wouldn't pay attention.

CO-COUNSELOR: So you'd just ignore it.

CHILD D: And that can't hurt you really, couldn't really hurt you.

COUNSELOR: It's like that old saying "Sticks and stones . . ."

CHILD D: Yeah. "Sticks and stones may break your bones but names will never hurt you."

A discussion followed about how people feel when they are called names. One of the children called the counselor fat (a safe epithet because of his thinness) and there was some personalizing of feelings. A particularly interesting incident occurred in the hall after the session. One of the girls told the co-counselor that she had bad breath. The counselor related this to the group by asking the girl how she thought the co-counselor felt.

Modeling and Behavior Rehearsal

There are certain similarities between the use of modeling and behavior rehearsal in individual counseling (discussed in Chapter Three) and in a group. But the presence of other group members makes the group setting for behavioral practice more like reality. A variety of models are available in the group. The therapist is always present. In addition, a guest can be brought in to serve as a model for the group. He or she might be a person who is idealized and looked up to for skill in sports. The conductor should as a rule include in the group a model(s) child for the other children to emulate. A further way of introducing a model to the group is through the use of audio- or videotape films. Hansen, Niland and Zani (1969) found that the use of models in group counseling served to strengthen learning about social behavior, and that models who are socially successful appear to be more effective reinforcers than does a counselor.

Behavior rehearsal—Lazarus' (1966) term for role-playing—implies that the client should imitate the behavior that he has observed in the model. Its purpose is to allow the client to practice in a protected situation so that he will be less anxious and therefore more likely to succeed in reality. A further distinction can be made. Corsini (1966) defines psychodrama and sociodrama somewhat differently. Role-playing is, of course, an aspect of both psychodrama and sociodrama. Psychodrama is the role-playing by a person of his own past, present, or future situation. Sociodrama is a role-playing situation that focuses on the shared problem of the group. In behavior rehearsal, appropriate behavior is usually exhibited to the child by a model or by the counselor acting as a model. Next, the child is to rehearse or practice the model's behavior. Then the child can be assigned the homework of carrying out the desired behavior in his life. Another way of structuring rehearsal is to use literary sourcebooks. The children can act out behaviors described in a story. Example behaviors should be selected that illustrate more adaptive coping behaviors than the child's.

Another approach, described by Boyd and Youssi (1958), uses open-ended problem stories that deal with home situations. Fulmer (1971) discusses such further interventions as spontaneous improvisation, play and feedback, directions from the director of the group, and other nonverbal exercises. Rehearsal can focus on particular behaviors, like helping and sharing behavior (Staub, 1971). Other appropriate areas are interpersonal relationships and decision making (Gamsky & Gamsky, 1971).

The following transcript illustrates the effect of the group's model (Child D), the counselors as aides to problem solving, role-playing, and the use of role reversal in helping children appreciate how others feel. The goals are to help the children to express feelings and cope with an anxiety-provoking situation.

CO-COUNSELOR: Role-playing is part talking and part acting.

CHILD A: Drama.

CO-COUNSELOR: What else do you think it might be?

CHILD F: Nothing.

CHILD A: I done it in my school.

CO-COUNSELOR: Good, you'll be able to help us. Everybody gets to help in this. Everybody's afraid sometimes.

CHILD A: Yeah, or another.

CO-COUNSELOR: Who can tell me a time they're afraid?

CHILD F: Never.

CHILD D: Oh, you're afraid sometimes.

COUNSELOR: I'm afraid everyday. There's at least one time I'm afraid of something.

CHILD C: She's afraid of lightning.

CHILD F: I'm not.

CHILD A: Was too. She was bawlin one day because it was lightning.

CHILD D: Guess what? You're afraid when you go to the park and lose your mommy.

CO-COUNSELOR: That's what we'll talk about when we're role playing. What's something that you're afraid of?

CHILD A: Oh, oh, Oh! I'm afraid of my turtle dying.

CO-COUNSELOR: What do you do when you're afraid?

COUNSELOR: A lot of times I get scared—like when I'm under water too long and can't get a breath.

CHILD A: Oh, I could stay under the water for 10 minutes.

CHILD D: Without lifting your head out?

CHILD A: Yes.

COUNSELOR: That would be a world record, wouldn't it?

CHILD A: I can swim from one end of the pool to the other.

CHILD D: Yes, I'd like to see it without lifting your head out.

CHILD A: I can.

CO-COUNSELOR: So what some people are afraid of others aren't.

CHILD A: I'm afraid of the high dive.

CHILD D: So am I.

CHILD A: When you go down the water spanks you (a continuation of discussion of diving and heights of boards).

CO-COUNSELOR: (Breaking into the discussion after about one minute.) Well, this time I'd like you to imagine a situation that's scary. I'd like you to imagine that you went to a department store with your mother and went to the toy department.

CHILD A: And you were so interested in the toys that you lost your momma!

CO-COUNSELOR: All right. You've lost your mother, and you've looked around and she was gone. What would you think happened?

CHILD G: His mother was gone to another store.

CHILD D: Probably not to another store but to someplace in the same store. Don't think she would leave him there.

CO-COUNSELOR: You don't think she would have left him there on purpose but was someplace else in the store.

CHILD D: At the arts festival, told to meet us at the big tree if we got lost because there were so many people there.

CHILD A: And once at the carnival I got lost with my mom.

CO-COUNSELOR: What did you do?

CHILD A: I looked for her and found her.

CO-COUNSELOR: Well I'd like you to pretend that we're going into the store and I'm the mother and you're the children. And we're going to the toy department and I'm going to lose you in the toy department. And I want you to show me how you'll act. O.K. I'm mother and here are my six children. Here's the toy department. What do you see?

CHILD D: Cars.

CO-COUNSELOR: Mother goes away. You can't see her. Are you worried? What do you do now?

CHILD A: Look.

CO-COUNSELOR: What else?

CHILD D: Help, Mommy! (hollering)

CO-COUNSELOR: You might call for her.

CHILD C: You could get to the office and call her.

CO-COUNSELOR: Let's think of some other things.

COUNSELOR: You came up with some pretty good things: looking farther and going to the office.

CHILD D: You could go up to the desk and ask. Or you could stay at the toy desk because she would probably come back there to look for you after she found what she wanted.

COUNSELOR: Stay right where you were.

CO-COUNSELOR: How would mother feel?

CHILD D: Annoyed at herself, because left alone.

CO-COUNSELOR: Now let's switch roles and you be the mothers. You're going to the store to buy dresses, go by toy department to look at dresses. Now you've discovered that your child isn't with you. What would you do?

CHILD G: Go to the candy store to look farther.

CHILD A: I would go to the toy department.

CO-COUNSELOR: How'd mother feel when she found child?

CHILD D: Happy and angry that he didn't come with her.

CO-COUNSELOR: Might also be relieved. Do any of you know what role-playing is?

CHILD D: Acting out.

CHILD G: Doing different kinds of things that happen to people.

CHILD D: And figuring out how people feel and learning better ways to act and solve the problems.

Child D (the child model) provided a lot of input about coping with stress. Most of her responses, with one exception (yelling in the store), were quite adaptive. The counselor and co-counselor also aided in the problem-solving process by summarizing the children's suggestions and introducing new ones. The role-playing of the children in the illustration helps to get them in touch with their feelings in such a situation. Role reversal helps them to appreciate the feelings of others. The final step is to have the children rehearse more appropriate coping behaviors.

"Transactional analysis (TA) is offered as a method of group therapy because it is a rational, indigenous approach derived from the group situation itself" (Berne, 1961). Berne (1966) later published a systematic treatise on the use of TA in groups. More recently, Harris (1969) has given this approach even wider exposure. Another possible way to utilize TA theory is with gestalt-oriented experiments (James & Jongeward, 1971).

Transactional analysis, as applied to children, can be illustrated by the following example from Dennis Marks discussed by Harris (1969). Marks works with children in a circle. They make a contract to learn about the three active elements (P-A-C) in each person's makeup, i.e., the Parent (life as observed and taught during one's first five years); the Adult (the reality-computer that makes decisions after processing information), and the Child (spontaneous emotions and feelings). The conductor then helps the children identify which part is talking when a group member makes a statement. The youngsters can learn to identify words and actions in this way:

To the crash of rock music:
PARENT: That horrible stuff kids listen to today.
ADULT: It's hard for me to think or talk when the music is so loud.
CHILD: That makes me want to dance (James & Jongeward, 1971, p. 22).

The children repeat "I'm O.K.—You're O.K." at the beginning and end of each session. This phrase is to become their key to turn off emotions and turn on their mature adult responses.

Marks reports (in Harris, 1969, p. 173) on a "youngster" who was trembling with rage and attempting to hit everyone around him. Marks went over to him and restrained him by holding him tightly. The child was screaming, "Leave me alone." After 20 seconds, Dr. Marks (M) said to Tom (T):

M: Now, Tom, how am I restraining you? Is this Parent, Adult or Child?
T (shouting):   Parent!
M: Not really, Tom. I'm not spanking you. That would be Parent. And I'm not fighting with you. What would that be?
T: That would be Child.
M: So how am I restraining you, with my Parent, Adult or Child?
T: With your Adult.
M: O.K. That's good, Tom. Now we'll show these people how

we can do it. Now you take my hand and we'll say what we always say.

T(taking hand and mumbling):   "I'm O.K.—You're O.K."

The reported result was a transformation from a furious child to a relatively calm one in three minutes. Marks' objective was "to modify his behavior and get past the episode" (Harris, 1969, p. 174). This was achieved by turning off the Child and turning on the Adult.

Use of Pictures

Another device one can use to stimulate talk during the group session is pictures. This use of this procedure in connection with diagnosis was discussed in Chapter Two, but it can be used equally satisfactorily in the therapeutic dimension of self disclosure. The pictures can be from a book (Mead & Hayman, 1965), magazine, or newspaper. Keat and Keat (1973) have photographed and made use of pictures that illustrate the central concerns of a child's life. These include children on playgrounds, alone, in stressful situations with a mother, feeling guilty, playing with a group of peers, with grandparents, with fathers, and so on. These pictures serve as a stimulus for the child's fantasies. This procedure is thus best understood as one that encourages children to talk about problems that might be threatening on a personal level. An impersonal picture can impel the child to free-associate. This is a projective technique used as a therapeutic procedure.

The counselor can use a direct or indirect approach to introduce the pictures to the group. The direct approach is to show the pictures to the group at the appropriate time. The indirect approach is simply to leave the pictures conspicuously in the room. When the children see them, they are quite often fascinated by them. This is the counselor's lead; the approach is illustrated below.

COUNSELOR: I see G would like to do something else. (Child G has picked up the pictures from under the counselor's chair and is inspecting them.) (Keat & Keat, 1973; Bellack & Bellack, 1965.) What would you like to do, G?

CHILD G: Oh.

COUNSELOR: Would you like to show the people some pictures? Why don't you show them the pictures and see if they can make up a story about them. Now for this story I would like You to think about what people you see, how they got to be there, what they are thinking and feeling and doing there, and how the story will end.

CHILD A: There's a mommy and a daddy there.

COUNSELOR: There's a mom and a dad on there. What else?

CHILD D: Mommy and a boy?

COUNSELOR: Someone else tell us something about how they got there, what they are thinking and doing.

CHILD A: They're going shopping, the mommy and the daddy and the baby.

CHILD C: They're coming back from shopping; got their milk, and are going home.

COUNSELOR: O.K., so they went shopping, got their milk, and are going to take it home now. How do they feel about this?

CHILD C: They like to do it, because it's food.

COUNSELOR: It's food and that's good. Anything else?

CHILD A: They're glad to be together, going shopping and that stuff.

COUNSELOR: They seem to be happy doing things together. And how does it all end up?

CHILD A: They go home and live happily ever after.

COUNSELOR: After they have a good time shopping they go home and enjoy their life.

This transcript from a session with young girls (ages 7–9) reveals their responses to a thematic card (Bellack & Bellack, 1965). The card (number 4) shows a woman carrying a basket containing some milk bottles, with a baby over her shoulder and another child riding a tricycle behind her. The two girls who perceived the child in the picture as a father lived alone with their divorced mother. Their wish-fulfillment story probably represents their desire to have their daddy back to do things with them. When this happens in their story, the family can live happily ever after (as fairy tales often end).

The Use of Mirrors

The use of mirrors possesses both verbal and physical aspects. The verbal part is a technique for reflecting a person's feelings. The physical component is the use of an actual mirror to induce children to look at themselves. Counseling for self concept improvement is an extremely important activity. Self concept assessment was discussed in Chapter Two; in Chapter Three a mirror could have been used to get Charlie to look at his mouth more realistically as an aspect of cognitive restructuring; and the core of Chapter Seven is enhancement of the self concept of children.

The use of mirroring procedures has been discussed by Myrick and Moni (1972). They ask children to look in the mirror and describe what they see. Other leads include "As you look at yourself in the mirror, tell me what you like best" and "What doesn't the mirror know about you?"

Another interesting technique devised by the same authors (Myrick & Moni, 1972) is the Magic Box (a small box filled with a mirror to reflect the face of anyone looking into the box). The procedure centers around the question, "Who is the most special person in the world?" First, the teacher reads a story about the importance of individuality (e.g., Vreeken, 1959; or Exupéry, 1943). Then the children trace their hands and draw pictures of themselves. Next, they take turns looking inside the Magic Box to discover the special person ("It's me!"). Finally, a group discussion about the "most special person" takes place. At this time it is announced that the drawings of themselves will be placed in a special place (the library) with signs reading, "We are special persons! You are too!"

The Use of Incomplete Sentences

The use of incomplete sentences can serve as a stimulus for both intraindividual introspection and interindividual group discussion. The procedure the author uses is to pass out a page listing a series of sentence stems. One can use standardized sentence completion items or make up one's own series of stimulus stems. These should be chosen to deal with important areas in the life of the child. For elementary school-aged children, the author generally uses the following list (see Figure 4-1).

The transcript on p. 123 illustrates the use of incomplete sentences with a group. The counselor can choose either to focus on the immediate responses the stems stimulate or to elicit as many responses as possible and discuss them later. In this example, the counselor attempts to move the group through the sentences at a steady pace, sharing responses as they proceed.

CHILD D: What's that? Oh, I know what it is. We did that at camp.

COUNSELOR: We're just going to try a couple of these.

CHILD F: Can we have these to take home?

COUNSELOR: Yes, you can keep the pencils and pads (rewards for working on the task).

CHILDREN: Yay! Yay!

COUNSELOR: What I'd like you to do is read this and write out how you feel. "I like . . ." and then just finish that sentence. Whatever you like.

Instructions: Complete each sentence in your own words. Write down the first thing you think of or feel.

I like _____.

I am very _____.

My mother _____.

My father _____.

At bedtime _____.

Boys _____.

Girls _____.

My greatest fear _____.

In school _____.

My teachers _____.

I hate _____.

I wish _____.

I am very _____.

Most dreams _____.

Children are the most trouble when _____.

The kind of animal I would like to be is _____.

A person usually fails when _____.

My family _____.

I get annoyed when _____.

When someone tells me what to do I _____.

If I can't get what I want I _____.

I'd like most to be _____.

I daydream about _____.

When I came into the group I _____.

Right now I feel _____.

Figure 4–1 *Sentence Completion*

CHILD D: I like candy.

CHILD A: Turtles.

CHILD D: Kitty cats. Arlo, I married Arlo, my cat.

COUNSELOR: Next one to do (skipping over some, to use the available time on items particularly relevant to the situation) . . . Skip to "In school," what do you say about "In school," say whatever you like.

CHILD A: I didn't like anything. (The rest write down their responses.)

COUNSELOR (moving on):   Next, "I hate . . ."

CHILD F: Homework.

COUNSELOR: "I hate homework," and how about you, A.

CHILD A: I hate homework.

COUNSELOR: Another one hates homework.

CHILD C: I hate school.

COUNSELOR: O.K. Let's do the next one. "I wish . . ." Make-believe you had Aladdin's lamp and could wish anything you wanted to. You would say "I wish that I . . ."

CHILD D: I like you (referring to counselor). Well, I do.

CHILD C: I wish I was a boy.

COUNSELOR: "When someone tells me what to do I . . ." What do you do, A?

CHILD A: Don't do it (laughs).

CHILD D: I do do it. I don't know, it depends on what they tell me. Sometimes I don't do it and sometimes I do do it.

COUNSELOR: Sometimes I don't do it and sometimes I do do it.

COUNSELOR: "When I came into this group I . . ."

CHILD A: Excited.

CHILD C: Nothing.

CHILD F: Happy.

CHILD D: Nervous.

COUNSELOR: Well, everyone seemed to feel different about starting the group. And "Right now I feel . . ."

CHILD F: Happy.

CHILD C: Like playing any kind of sport.

CHILD D: Mixed-up.

CHILD A: Happy.

CHILD E: Happy.

The main themes that emerged involved interests, feelings toward school, desires, responses to outside direction, and past and current feelings about the group. Any of these topics can provide the stimulus for fruitful discussion.

The Use of Music

The use of music for therapeutic purposes has been said to have three principal goals:

1 The establishment or reestablishment of interpersonal relationships
2 The bringing about of self-esteem through self-actualization
3 The utilization of the unique potential of rhythm to energize
and bring order (Gaston, 1968, p. v).

Although music therapy has been used primarily with deviant
populations of children (e.g., Nordoff & Robbins, 1965; Gaston,
1968; Assagioli, 1971). However, it has additional therapeutic
uses that the elementary counselor can either carry out himself
in groups (to supplement the regular work of the music teacher)
or in conjunction with the music teacher in the classroom. The
approaches to be discussed vary from receptive listening to active
participation.

Three receptive-listening approaches will be discussed first.
First, children can close their eyes as a mood-invoking musical
selection is played (for some ideas on musical selections, see
Capurso, Fisichelli, Gilman, Gutheit, Wright, & Paperte, 1952;
and Heussenstamm, 1971). Each child can then describe what he
felt or imagined while listening to the music. One can also have
the children paint or draw what they feel as the music is playing.

Secondly, one can play records that deal with feelings or philosophies of life and then discuss these with the group. Some
examples of such records (for the intermediate or middle-school
level) are:

On the idea of self concept: "You are the only one like you"
("You Are Special," from *Misterogers knows that you are special*,
Small World Records, 4RS-1252).

On showing emotions: "*A man ain't supposed to cry*" (title
song by Joe Williams, Roulette-R-52005). "But I Was Cool"
(Oscar Brown, Jr. *Sin and Soul*, Columbia, CL1577).

Third, if the counselor can play the piano or guitar, he might
use an approach similar to Marian McPartland's (Balliett, 1973),
using music that reflects different emotions and having children
learn to label the emotions. McPartland gets the children to stand
around the piano and sing. For example, "Raindrops Keep Fallin'
on My Head" is appropriate for six-year-olds; and "Hey Jude"
(see Okun, 1970, for arrangements) for ten-year-olds. On the
second chorus, the children begin clapping and finally hop around
and laugh (catharsis!).

This brings us to the realm of active participation, the basic
form of which is sing-along. Sing-alongs can use records (e.g.,
Over 40 of the World's Greatest Children's Songs, RCA Camden,
CAL1017), or songbooks (e.g., Nelson, 1967; Winn, Miller, &
Alcorn, 1966, Rogers, 1970). This type of singing fosters involve-

ment melodically and encourages the children to keep time rhythmically (with feet and/or hands) as they sing.

Rhythmics is even more effectively introduced by the use of such primitive instruments as drums, bells, claves, maracas, and the like. The author has led groups of pre-school and primary-aged children around singing, shouting, and banging drums and sticks. Besides having fun, the children were being taught co-ordination (hitting drums) and cooperation (marching around in line), and they were directing their muscular activity in a positive fashion.

Use of Materials, Facilities and Games

Lifton (1966) has stated that interest is maximized at the elementary level by the use of games, activities, and puns. The author would agree especially about the first two procedures. Many of the kinds of toys discussed in Chapter Three are also relevant here. The toy room may be stocked with schoolroom toys and a blackboard, real-life toys such as dolls and animals, and toys that help children release aggression and enhance their self concepts. Other materials and facilities found in most schools are record players, workbenches and tables, the industrial arts shop, home economics facilities (for those interested in cooking), a craft room, the gymnasium, the swimming pool, and various athletic fields. The availability of such resources, of course, varies with the school. The primary difficulty is likely to be scheduling. The use of these natural settings with a counselee stresses that the counselor can leave the confines of the counseling room. While a somewhat private room is required for the talk section of the meeting, the activity part can take place in almost any area.

There are two basic ways of organizing the activity part of the session. The author prefers to move from the structured group talk section of the meeting to a structured activity section, which requires that all members participate together. Structured group activity necessitates cooperation with others in order to play a game. This kind of game can take up about one-third to one-half of the section. There is a great variety of games that can be played by children in groups. For a list of 65 such games and the purpose, equipment, number of children, the appropriate grade level, and rules for each, the interested reader is referred to Keat *et al* (1972, pp. 41–62). After the structured section, the natural movement is to a free choice of activities. Free play can give the group members decision-making practice, and allows one to observe how the children interact. Equipment should be available for group games that four people can play, card games, drawing activities, puppets and dolls, and a variety of other endeavors. Unstructured play is generally the most pleasing part of the group session, and thus allows the meeting to end on a pleasurable note. The children are more likely to look forward to coming back the next week.

Sometimes games can be viewed as a remediation for fine or gross motor coordination problems. One such group sensory motor activity program has been described by Painter (1968). Games were played that focused on perceptual-motor capacities the child needed to improve. For example, "Simon Says" was played to develop visual and auditory dynamics. These added benefits of physical activities are sometimes overlooked, unless the group focuses on this kind of remediation.

Thus, some kinds of motor activity can have specialized remediative effects. In addition, they can direct physical and mental energies in a cathartic fashion; the releasing effects of directed muscular activity have been discussed. Further, greater muscular coordination skills, and probable consequent peer acceptance, can influence the self image of the child.

An example of how one can combine involvement activities outside the counseling room with group counseling in the school is provided by Frost (1973), who describes the use of an elementary-guidance club to develop "Team Action for Leadership and Learning" (Frost, 1973, p. 189). Fifth- and sixth-grade teachers were asked to identify pupils of average or above average ability, who had leadership potential but were disinterested in school. The selected pupils (and their parents) then organized activities consistent with their strengths and interests. Among these activities were acting as greeters at a parent test-interpretation meeting, going through the junior-high registration process, staging a potluck dinner, and visiting various outside sites (e.g., the telephone company, the university museum, a school for the blind). For small-group activities, the club was divided into groups of four or five. Sessions were held weekly and lasted 30 to 40 minutes. It was felt that the small group provided a safe environment in which the members could risk trying out new or modified behaviors. In addition, the small group was also used as a setting to deal with the purposes of the club, to plan learning experiences for the small group, and to choose activities to suggest to the large group for decision making.

Summary

This chapter has discussed the facilitation of small groups of elementary school children, focusing on theory, formation of the group, and implementation. Group counseling was defined, the counselor's role as group conductor discussed, a variety of group goals presented, and the stages of groups investigated. In connection with forming the group, the following factors were discussed: group composition, group size, the length and frequency of sessions, the counseling setting, referral and behavioral assessment. The bulk of the chapter stressed the practice of child group counseling and covered getting started, talking first and playing later, bibliocounseling, the use of problem-solving exercises, modeling and behavioral rehearsal, transactional analysis, pictures to stimulate self disclosure, mirrors to enhance self image, incomplete sentences to encourage talk about important life areas, music to elicit directed muscular activity (coordination and catharsis) and facilitate cooperation, and child group counseling activities both in the school building (play media) and outside (club functions) the school.

References

Anderson, J., & Schmidt, W. I. A time for feelings. *Elementary School Guidance and Counseling,* 1967, 1, 47–56.

Assagioli, R. *Psychosynthesis.* New York: Viking, 1971.

Balliett, W. The key of D is daffodil yellow. *The New Yorker,* 1973, 48, 43–57.

Bellack, L., & Bellack, S. *Children's Apperception Test—Human Figures.* Larchmont, N.Y.: C.P.S. Inc., 1965.

Berne, E. *Transactional analysis in psychotherapy.* New York: Grove Press, 1961.

Berne, E. *Principles of group treatment.* New York: Oxford University Press, 1966.

Bessell, H., & Palomares, V. *Methods in human development.* San Diego, Cal.: Human Development Training Institute, 1970.

Blakeman, J. D., & Day, S. R. Activity group counseling. In G. M. Gazda (Ed.), *Theories and methods of group counseling in the schools.* Springfield, Ill.: Charles C. Thomas, 1969, pp. 56–85.

Boyd, A., & Youssi, M. Peer group regulates role playing. *School Counselor,* 1958, 6, 11–18.

Capurso, A., Fisichelli, V., Gilman, L., Gutheil, E., Wright, J., & Paperte, F. *Music and your emotions.* New York: Liveright, 1952.

Carkhuff, R. R. *Helping and human relations—Volume II: Practice and research.* New York: Holt, Rinehart & Winston, 1969.

Cline, D. W. Video tape documentation of behavioral change in children. *American Journal of Orthopsychiatry,* 1972, 42, 40–47.

Cohn, B., Combs, C., Gibian, E. J., & Sniffen, A. M. Group counseling, an orientation. *Personnel and Guidance Journal,* 1963, 17, 355–358.

Combs, C., Cohn, B., Gibian, E., & Sniffen, A. Group counseling: applying the technique. *The School Counselor*, 1963, **11**, 12–18.

Corsini, R. J. *Roleplaying in psychotherapy*. Chicago: Aldine, 1966.

Cox, R. F., & Herr, E. L. *Group techniques in guidance*. Harrisburg, Penn.: Department of Public Instruction, 1968.

Daley, M. F. The reinforcement menu: Finding effective reinforcers. In J. D. Krumboltz, & C. E. Thoresen (Eds.), *Behavioral counseling: cases and techniques*. New York: Holt, Rinehart & Winston, 1969, pp. 42–45.

Dinkmeyer, D. C. (Ed.) *Guidance and counseling in the elementary school*. New York: Holt, Rinehart & Winston, 1968.

Dinkmeyer, D. C. *Developing Understanding of Self and Others*. Circle Pines, Minn.: American Guidance Services, 1970.

Dinkmeyer, D. C., & Caldwell, E. *Developmental counseling and guidance: a comprehensive school approach*. New York: McGraw-Hill, 1970.

Dinkmeyer, D. C., & Muro, J. J. *Group counseling: theory and practice*. Itasca, Ill.: Peacock, 1971.

Dreikurs, R., & Sonstegard, M. Rationale of group counseling. In D. Dinkmeyer (Ed.), *Guidance and counseling in the elementary school*. New York: Holt, Rinehart & Winston, 1968, pp. 278–287.

Exupéry, A. S. *The little prince*. New York: Harcourt, Brace Janovich, 1943.

Faust, V. *The counselor-consultant in the elementary school*. Boston: Houghton Mifflin, 1968.

Frost, J. M. Counseling outcomes with fourth, fifth and sixth grade pupils. Unpublished doctoral dissertation, Wayne State University, 1972.

Frost, J. M. The elementary-school counselor and his work with groups. In W. Van Hoose, J. Pietrofesa, & J. Carlson. *Elementary-school guidance and counseling: a composite view*. Boston: Houghton Mifflin, 1973, pp. 187–201.

Fulmer, D. W. *Counseling: Group theory and system*. Scranton, Penn.: International Textbook Company, 1971.

Gamsky, I., & Gamsky, N. Role playing in the elementary school classroom. *Elementary School Guidance and Counseling*, 1971, **6**, 62–63.

Gaston, E. T. (Ed.) *Music in therapy*. New York: Macmillan, 1968.

Gazda, G. M. *Group counseling: a developmental approach*. Boston: Allyn & Bacon, 1971.

Gazda, G. M., Duncan, J., & Meadows, M. E. Group counseling and group procedures, Report of a survey. *Counselor Education and Supervision*, 1967, **6**, 305–310.

Gibb, C. A. The principles and traits of leadership. *Journal of Abnormal and Social Psychology*, 1947, **42**, 267–284.

Ginott, H. G. *Group psychotherapy with children*. New York: McGraw-Hill, 1961.

Goldman, L. Group guidance: content and process. *Personnel and Guidance Journal*, 1962, **15**, 518–522.

Hansen, J. C. Life stages of a group. In J. C. Hansen, & S. H. Cramer (Eds.), *Group guidance and counseling in the schools.* New York: Appleton-Century-Crofts, 1971, pp. 261–267.

Hansen, J. C., Niland, T. M., & Zani, L. P. Model reinforcement in group counseling with elementary school children. *Personnel and Guidance Journal,* 1969, **47,** 741–744.

Hansen, J. C., & Stevic, R. R. *Elementary school guidance.* New York: Macmillan, 1969.

Harris, T. A. *I'm O.K.—You're O.K.* New York: Harper & Row, 1969.

Heussenstamm, F. K. I dig rock n' roll music: A counselor's listening guide. *The School Counselor,* 1971, **18,** 198–204.

James, M., & Jongeward, D. *Born to win: transactional analysis with gestalt experiments.* Reading, Mass.: Addison-Wesley, 1971.

Keat, D. B. A reinforcement survey schedule for children. University Park, Penn.: Author, 1972.

Keat, D. B., Anderson, S., Conklin, N., Elias, R., Faber, D., Felty, S., Gerba, J., Kochenash, J., Logan, W., Malecki, D., Martino, P., McDuffy, I., Schmerling, G., Schuh, C., & Selkowitz, L. *Helping children to feel. a guide to affective curriculum materials for the elementary school.* State College, Penn.: Counselor Education Press, 1972.

Keat, D., & Keat, M. A procedure for child appraisal and self-disclosure. Unpublished manuscript, Pennsylvania State University Counselor Education Library, 1973.

Kemp, C. G. Bases of group leadership. *Personnel and Guidance Journal,* 1964, **42,** 760–766.

Lazarus, A. A. Behavior rehearsal vs. non-directive therapy vs. advice in effecting behavior change. *Behavior Research and Therapy,* 1966, **4,** 209–212.

Lifton, W. *Working with groups,* 2nd ed. New York: Wiley, 1966.

Mahler, C. *Group counseling in the schools,* Boston: Houghton Mifflin, 1969.

Mayer, G. R., & Baker, P. Group counseling with elementary school children: a look at size. *Elementary School Guidance and Counseling,* 1967, **1,** 140–145.

Mead, M., & Heyman, K. *Family.* New York: Macmillan, 1965.

Muro, J. *The counselor's work in the elementary school.* Scranton, Penn.: International Textbook Company, 1970.

Muro, J. & Freeman, S. (Eds.) *Readings in group counseling.* Scranton, Penn.: International Textbook Company, 1968.

Myrick, R., & Moni, L. The counselor's workshop: helping children look at themselves. *Elementary School Guidance and Counseling,* 1972, **6,** 287–290.

Nelson, D. *190 children's songs.* New York: Robbins Music Corporation, 1967.

Nordoff, P., & Robbins, C. *Music therapy for handicapped children.* New York: Music Publishers Holding Corporation (for Rudolf Steiner Publications), 1965.

Ohlsen, M. Counseling children in groups. In D. Dinkmeyer (Ed.), *Guidance and counseling in the elementary school.* New York: Holt, Rinehart, & Winston, 1968, pp. 288–294.

Ohlsen, M. *Group counseling.* New York: Holt, Rinehart, & Winston, 1970.

Okun, M. (Ed.) *The New York Times great songs of the sixties.* Chicago: Quadrangle Books, 1971.

Painter, G. Remediation of maladaptive behavior and psycholinguistic deficits in a group sensory-motor activity program. *Academic Therapy Quarterly,* 1968, **3**, 233–24.

Peters, H. J., Shertzer, B., & Van Hoose, W. *Guidance in elementary schools.* Chicago: Rand McNally, 1965.

Redl, F. *When we deal with children.* New York: The Free Press, 1966.

Rogers, F. *Misterrogers' songbook.* New York: Random House, 1970.

Rose, S. D. *Treating children in groups.* San Francisco: Jossey-Bass, 1972.

Sonstegard, M. Mechanisms and practical techniques in group counseling in the elementary school. In J. Muro & S. Freeman (Eds.), *Readings in group counseling.* Scranton, Penn.: International Textbook Company, 1968, pp. 127–136.

Staub, E. The use of role playing and induction in children's learning of helping and sharing behavior. *Child Development,* 1971, **42**, 805–816.

Sullivan, H. S. *The psychiatric interview.* New York: Norton, 1954.

Vreeken, E. *The boy who would not say his name.* Chicago: Follett, 1959.

Walton, H. (Ed.) *Small group psychotherapy.* Middlesex, England: Penguin, 1971.

Warner, R. W. The role of the group in the process of counseling. In J. C. Hanson & S. H. Cramer (Eds.), *Group guidance and counseling in the schools.* New York: Appleton-Century-Crofts, 1971, pp. 289–296.

Warters, J. *Group guidance: principles and practices.* New York: McGraw-Hill, 1960.

Winn, M., Miller, A., & Alcorn, J. *The fireside book of children's songs.* New York: Simon & Schuster, 1966.

Yunker, J. A. Essential organization components of group counseling in the primary grades. *Elementary School Guidance and Counseling,* 1970, **4**, 172–179.

5

A variety of types of groups will be discussed in this chapter. Because it is necessary to deal with the characteristics of the child's major life environment, the home, the counselor must occasionally meet with groups of parents and siblings, who are important influences upon the child. There are a variety of ways for the counselor to deal with such groups (see Frost, 1973). This chapter will discuss ways for the counselor to handle open parent group meetings, parent group meetings that focus on parent effectiveness needs, and more structured parent education groups that use a specific book or a teaching approach. Suggestions will also be made for family counseling with the parents and siblings of the identified client (the child).

Teacher groups have been conducted by counselors relatively less often than have parent groups. One rationale for more teacher groups is that they provide an opportunity to affect a large number of children significantly—the teacher molds one of the major life environments of children. A teacher group can focus either on self-enhancement or on the skills necessary for classroom management and group meetings.

Group meetings of administrators are extremely rare (Watson, 1969). Dreikurs and Chernuff (1970) propose that teachers and parents participate in study groups together, and Guerney and Merriam (1972) push this approach even further. The democratic type of group includes parents, teachers, administrators, and counselors. The purpose of such a group is to train adults to work more effectively with children in their particular capacities.

The final topic of the chapter will be child guidance groups in classroom. This approach has been discussed by various writers, including Faust (1968) and Glasser (1969). A somewhat more

Parent, Teacher, Administrator
and Child Guidance Groups

democratic approach is elaborated in the work of Guerney and Merriam (1972). Their procedure, to be discussed in this chapter, to training group leaders is to involve all the significant persons in the planning and conduct of group meetings.

Parent Groups

Grams (1966) advocates the involvement of the schools in parent groups. "Parent education in the schools can be sharply focused upon those aspects of parent role behavior which we agree relate directly to the learning process" (Grams, 1966, p. 77). This approach is carried out by organizing the parents into "classes." It is generally advisable to label these groups "classes" or "meetings" in order to encourage the involvement of as many parents as possible. In such groups one does not necessarily focus on problems, although the parent with a problem is more likely to be motivated to join.

The Open Group

In an open group, the counselor starts the session with a projective question. For example, the counselor might say, "Are there any questions or concerns which you have today?" The parents respond to this question, and the ensuing discussion moves in whatever direction the parents lead it. That is, the group takes over after the initial question and whatever the members are motivated to discuss becomes the topic of the session.

The Semi-structured Group

Another kind of parent group counseling is somewhat more highly structured. This is the type of parent group with which counselors tend to feel most at ease. The structure can take numerous forms. For example, the counselor can write down some ideas on a large pad, visible to all present, and discuss these ideas with the parents. These ideas may be a series of concepts likely to stimulate talk, or to goad the parents to think and discuss. Another procedure is to have the parents read a small brochure (e.g., Dreikurs & Goldman, 1964) before the group meets. There are, of course, many other ways to provide some structure for the group. Some excerpts from a series of five sessions follow, illustrating some of the ways the counselor can structure the group situation to provide meaningful direction. Such a structure has the added advantage of putting the counselor at ease; he can prepare prior to and even during the group meeting to implement particular ideas and concepts.

Ways of Structuring the Parent Group

COUNSELOR: As I explained in the letter, this is an opportunity for us to get you together to talk about some of your concerns as parents, and perhaps to share some of your ideas and help each other. You have a big responsibility to your child, and we hope to figure out some ways to help you with the job of being parents. The letter was sent to all parents, so you weren't singled out. The group was open to everyone. So, I'm glad you decided to participate. These groups will be informal. We'll be meeting for five weeks and hope we will get to know each other. Do you have any questions? (silence) Things we are going to talk about will be whatever is on your mind. Probably the best way to get started is to introduce ourselves, tell a bit about yourself, and tell us about your children. (After giving their names, the parents describe the individual problems of their children, and discuss such general issues as school starting age, working mothers, the heredity-environment issue, the importance of peers, boy-girl developmental differences, classroom grouping, siblings learning from each other, and the like.)

Listing Concerns to Focus the Discussion

COUNSELOR: It might be helpful for us to make a list of general concerns, as parents, that you might like to get into. [This is the second session.] This will help us to get some general ideas, of things to go into more deeply and should help us in dealing with these kinds of concerns.

PARENT A: Well I think we've talked about everything there is to talk about. So, you might as well break out the other tapes (from past sessions) and play them again. Dig into it a little deeper.

COUNSELOR: Get back into some of the topics. Maybe we can help ourselves out.

PARENT F: Rewarding the children for what they do.

COUNSELOR: Rewards, yeah, that was one of the things we talked about.

PARENT A: Kindergarten. Whether kindergarten helps or not.

COUNSELOR: The influence of kindergarten.

PARENT B: The differences between boys and girls.

COUNSELOR: I'll stick a fifty-cent word up here on the tablet. Developmental differences: how children develop through the years, and boy-girl differences.

PARENT A: And between the first and second, this could enter into the same category.

PARENT B: Like divided classes for the different abilities.

COUNSELOR: That's a good point, B. Here's a good area. That's the order in the family. Whether first, middle, or last can be an important influence on their development. What are some of the other things?

PARENT D: Teasing.

PARENT B: Punishment. If you have rewards you have to have punishment.

COUNSELOR: That's a good one, B. They certainly fit together.

PARENT B: They almost have to.

COUNSELOR: A, you were talking about a situation with your child.

PARENT A: That's my problem, not his.

The ensuing discussion focuses on what to tell a child about ganging-up on the situation to which A was referring.

Discussing a Problem Situation

COUNSELOR: Now, I'm going to give you a situation (Gordon, 1970). I'm going to read what a child says. Then I'd like you to write down how you might respond to that if it was your child saying it. O.K.?

Let's suppose you have a ten-year-old daughter and this is what she says to you: "I don't know what's wrong with me. Ginny used to like me but now she doesn't. She never comes down here to play anymore and if I go up there she's always playing with Joyce and the two of them play together and have fun, and I just stand there all by myself. I hate them both" (Gordon, 1970, p. 40).

What would you say? (The parents write down their responses.)

Individual responses can then be discussed on a volunteer basis. After discussing this situation, the group can repeat the process with another situation. Some counselors might prefer to have the participants write down their responses to several situations before opening the discussion.

Categorizing Responses   Utilizing another one of Gordon's Parent Effectiveness Training (PET) concepts (Gordon, 1970), the counselor can list the "Typical Twelve" categories of parental response and ask the parents to think along these lines.

COUNSELOR: Thinking back during the past week, did you find yourself falling into some of these categories? Maybe you can share some of the experiences that you had. (Long pause, no response.) How about today?

PARENT G: I think I did about every one of those today. I was visiting with a friend and sitting in an easy chair. My boy was up on the back of the chair. I ordered him to get down, and I commanded him. He said, "I don't have to." (Group laughs.) You're concerned about the pressure of others. The guy I was with said, "He's testing you." So I said, "O.K." "You sit there on the chair or get out of the room." I warned him, then threatened him. Then he sat down on the chair. So I guess I used the first two. (I.e., ordering-commanding and warning-threatening.)

There typically follows an exchange of examples and problems, attempts at classification of child-handling procedures, and possible solutions to the problems.

Didactic Approach   Another procedure is to present an idea to the group. This concept can be something like a communication model for active listening (Gordon, 1970, pp. 49–61). The model (i.e., the encoding-decoding process) can be presented and examples can be cited.

CHILD: Boy, do I have a lousy teacher this year. I don't like her. She's an old grouch.
PARENT: Sounds like you are really disappointed with your teacher.
CHILD: I sure am (Gordon, 1970, p. 53).

The primary goal, of course, is for the parents to practice active listening with their children.

The Parent Education Group

Parent education group meetings usually focus on a particular book (brochure) or procedure (e.g., play therapy training). Parent education in groups has been strongly supported by Hill and Luckey (1969). They state, "When a program of guidance becomes full fledged and more services are available to the child through the school, the demands and needs of parents are bound to increase to proportions that are impossible to meet except through some kind of organized group activity. These may be called group conferences, parent education, or family counseling; in any case the goal is the same: to help the parent learn to relate to and work with his own child so that the school will have less of it to do" (Hill & Luckey, 1969, p. 309). There seems to be some evidence (e.g., Larson, 1972; Price, 1971) that parent classes of a variety of kinds can affect family communications. Most parents are anxious to learn about their children.

One major type of parent education aims to help parents become familiar with basic concepts relevant to all normal children, including such topics as child growth and development and family patterns of interaction. Another type of parent group focuses primarily on learning such techniques as behavior modification.

In any event, there are many books one can use to structure the parent group, depending on one's theoretical orientation. The most fully documented area is probably behavior modification. The author has used books by Patterson and Gullion (1968), Smith and Smith (1964), and Wittes and Radin (1969). The latter book has been used by Gerba (1972) for her meetings with parents. Wittes' and Radin's book is divided into six lessons, which are appropriate to the closed type of group that has a fixed number of meetings. The group of parents Gerba (1972) describes reacted positively to Wittes' and Radin's book and experienced constructive outcomes with their children.

Among other books suitable for parents who are meeting in groups are those by Ginott (1965), Dreikurs and Soltz (1964), and Gordon (1970). The use of such structured materials allows for didactic input into the parent group meeting, which causes the parents to feel that they are gaining concrete knowledge that will help them cope more effectively with their children. It has the added benefit of helping to focus the group on the topics at hand. Irrelevant input can more easily be eliminated. The real test, of course, is the carryover of such new knowledge to the home situation. Open discussion of the parents' application of their reading can be encouraged during the group meetings.

The Filial Group   Another type of group session is the filial group meeting (Guerney, 1964). This procedure trains the parents (in groups of six to eight) of young children to conduct play sessions with their children from a client-centered frame of reference. After the training, the parents continue to meet with the counselor to discuss results, conclusions, and inferences about the children and themselves. The process includes an explanation of the theory of the client-centered approach to developing a relationship with children. The parent groups consist of mothers and fathers who are not spouses. Discussions generally focus on reading assignments from such sources as Axline (1947, 1964) and Gordon (1970). There is some support for the use of the filial approach in situations other than the home (Adronico & Guerney, 1967; Guerney, 1969). For example, the general principles of nondirective play can be taught to teachers.

The Play Therapy Group   Another approach to parent groups has been described by Smart (1970), who developed play therapy schools for parents. Nine or ten married couples meet three evenings a week. Two evenings are devoted to such play activities as finger painting, modeling with clay, and other arts and crafts. The primary task of the parents is to learn how children may feel while they are engaging in typical play activities. The third session is devoted to discussion of dominant themes that arose during the previous two sessions. The theoretical rationale for this approach is that when the parents recall and relive their own childhood experiences they can begin to understand themselves and their own children better. They can gain insight into how children respond to and enjoy particular kinds of activities. The parent who has shared such experiences should be more therapeutic in his interaction with his own children.

Family Counseling

Finally, counselors can undertake family counseling. A child's problems are often direct outgrowths of pervasive family problems. If the child is the identified patient (Satir, 1967), he is bound to suffer both at home and in school. When suffering affects his behavior or performance in school, it becomes the concern of the counselor. As in other types of approaches, there are a variety of theoretical orientations to family counseling.

One particularly interesting approach is that of Fulmer (1971).

Although his system is somewhat Adlerian, it avoids advice-giving and focuses primarily on clarifying communication in family transactions.

Another recent book, *Peoplemaking* (Satir, 1972, p. 197), is specifically addressed to parents. In her journey through the four most important aspects of family life (i.e., self-worth, communication, rules, system), Satir describes numerous experiments or exercises intended to change one's family functioning. An example from a chapter on communication is:

> Make what you believe to be a true statement to your partner. He is then to repeat it to you verbatim, mimicking your voice, tone, inflection, facial expression, body position, movement. Check him for accuracy, and if it fits, say so. If it doesn't, produce your evidence. Be explicit; don't make a guessing game out of this. Then reverse roles (Satir, 1972, p. 48).

LeBow (1972), who provides a theoretical framework more consistent with the work of the author, discusses the related stages in family therapy of assessment, intervention, and evaluation. Assessment involves interviewing the family, analyzing particular behaviors according to predetermined criteria, coding the behavior in order to record it efficiently, and gathering baseline information on the child. As in any form of counseling, the most important consideration is intervention. From a behavior modification framework, the counselor can select the appropriate technique, such as positive reinforcement, modeling, negative reinforcement, withdrawal of positive reinforcement, extinction, behavioral rehearsal, and systematic desensitization. Of course, generalization of the results of such procedures is extremely important. Generalization can be facilitated by training parents to manage their children, discussed above in connection with the filial approach, from a behavioral standpoint (e.g., Patterson, 1971). The behavior modification approach often has more input with parents due to the fact that there are particular types of procedures which can be suggested to parents in order to help them cope with the type of problem their child is experiencing.

Teacher Groups

Emphasis on Self-Development Groups

We shall focus in this section on two crucial areas, self and skills. There are only a few approaches to teacher groups that focus on the self of the teacher. Thoresen, Alper, Hannum, Barrick and Jacks (1970) have examined the sequential individual effects of systematic desensitization and behaviorally focused training on six elementary school teachers. They observed each teacher for nine days, categorizing and counting teacher and student behavior (such as talking out, being out of one's seat, commands, and the like) during academic work periods. Following this baseline behavioral count, each teacher participated in a program of systematic desensitization that focused on reducing internal stress to such situations as: "It is recess time, all the students are outside, you step back into the room and see two students fighting over a basketball." After the second period of classroom observation, each teacher participated in ten behaviorally oriented training sessions that focused on classroom behaviors. This training was followed by ten days of post phase observations. Two weeks later, during the last three weeks of the school year, nine more days of observations were made as follow-up. The incidence of children being out of their seats dropped sharply during the desensitization treatment, only to accelerate as sharply during the second baseline phase after the desensitization. The effects of behavioral training were evident in the abrupt reduction in out-of-seat responses, a reduction that was generally maintained during the post- and follow-up phases. Although desensitization (self-training) seemed to have an unstable effect, behavioral training (skill-training) revealed a more lasting effect on the teachers. Another study focused on desensitization with third- and fourth-grade teachers (Susskind, Franks, & Lonoff, 1971). This experiment was undertaken to explore methods for helping teachers to cope during the first year of teaching in order to lower or prevent the high attrition rate. The basic procedure was relaxation training, practiced at home and during free periods in school. Teachers set up their own hierarchies. The results of this study indicated that the experimental group benefited from the program and therefore were far less anxious and emotional than the control group. The authors conclude that the desensitization program did alleviate tensions and anxieties associated with teaching children in low socioeconomic areas and that it was more helpful to the teachers than the traditional group dynamics approach. The effects of desensitization were also found to be lasting. That is, it taught the teachers to cope better with the exigencies of their lives.

Another type of teacher group that focuses on self-development is described by Dinkmeyer (1971) and Dinkmeyer & Arciniega (1972). This approach is labelled the C-group (Dinkmeyer & Muro, 1971), its components being collaboration, clarification, confidentiality, confrontation, communication, concern, and commitment to change. The experimental C-groups were composed of five or six teachers, who sat in a circle and practiced group exercises, such as those described by Otto (1967), that encouraged them to get acquainted and talk about their formative experiences. They then shared descriptions of troubling situations or concerns involving the children they taught. The group would start with a common problem; the child behavior would be discussed and the teachers would respond in a feeling fashion. This type of group seems to combine the development of the self with particular kinds of skill enhancement.

The author uses a variety of procedures in working with teacher groups. The goal of the following exercises is greater self-understanding. Some exercises will be described in detail, and the sources of others will be cited. For example, a wealth of exercises is included in the three volumes by Pfeiffer and Jones (1969, 1970, 1971).

*Getting-Acquainted Exercise** The goal of this exercise is to provide you with an opportunity to practice a variety of interpersonal communication skills. It is designed to help you become more comfortable with self-disclosure in the early part of a relationship, give you an opportunity to check and sharpen your listening skills, to share your feelings in a "here and now" interpersonal situation, and to practice feedback techniques. Your learning can be enhanced if you carry out the exercise with people you do not already know, do not appear to share a lot in common with you, or whom you feel it would be difficult to get to know and accept easily. Allow approximately two hours to complete the exercise.

The following ground rules should be followed:

1. All of the personal data discussed should be considered confidential.

2. Each partner responds to each statement before continuing.

3. The statements should be completed in the order in which they appear.

4. You may decline to answer any question asked by your partner.

5. Stop the exercise if either partner becomes obviously uncomfortable or anxious. Try to talk over the source of such feelings, and continue if and when this seems appropriate.

   1. My name is . . .
   2. My home town is . . .
   3. I come from a family of . . .

*Adapted by permission from *A Handbook of Structured Experiences for Human Relations Training*, Volume I, J. W. Pfeiffer and J. E. Jones, eds. Iowa City, Iowa: University Associates (Box 615), 1969, pp. 97–107.

4. I am planning a career in . . .
   or
   My career is . . .

One of the most important skills in getting to know another person is listening. In order to get a check on your ability to understand what your partner is communicating, the two of you should go through the following steps *one at a time:* Decide which of you is to speak first in the next unit. The first speaker is to complete the following item in two or three sentences.

5. When I think about the future I see myself living a life . . .

The second speaker repeats *in his own words* what the first speaker has just said. The first speaker must be satisfied that he has been heard accurately.

The second speaker then completes the item himself in two or three sentences.

The first speaker paraphrases what the second speaker just said, to the satisfaction of the second speaker. This reflection can be of content (meaning), feelings, or behavior.

Share what you may have learned about yourself as a listener. The two of you may find yourselves later saying to each other, "What I hear you saying is . . ." to keep a check on the accuracy of your listening and understanding.

6. When I am just getting to know a new acquaintance I . . .
7. In a group situation, my typical style is . . .
8. One thing that people who know me well probably would say about me . . .

Listening check: "What I hear you saying is . . ."

9. Right now I'm feeling . . .
   (Look your partner in the eyes while you respond to this item.)
10. The thing that turns me off the most is . . .

Checkup:

Have a two- or three-minute discussion about this experience so far. Keep eye contact as much as you can, and try to cover the following points:

How well are you listening?
How open and honest have you been?
How eager are you to continue the interchange?
Do you feel that you are getting to know each other?

11. I tend to express anger . . .
12. Right now I'm responding most to . . .
13. I feel really free and spontaneous when . . .
14. The thing you said that surprised me the most was . . .
15. What I've learned about myself through this experience . . .

Building an Agenda   This procedure can be an important step in enhancing the counselor's accountability to the teacher group. That is, the teachers share in the planning of the meetings and therefore have responsibility for what is accomplished. The teachers can respond (in writing and orally) to such a question as the following: what do I want to gain from these group meetings? These goals should be evaluated in terms of the following guidelines:

1. Is the goal clear and specific enough to permit direct planning and action?
2. Is the goal useful and realistic?
3. How can others in the group help you to work on these goals?

At this stage in the process (the first or second meeting), the teachers may need to revise their goal descriptions. They should rewrite them on paper and hand them in when finished. These descriptions are then tabulated by the counselor and handed back at the next meeting; the goals' rank order of importance serves as the agenda.

Counseling-Communication Exercise   Three roles are assigned for this exercise. These roles can be labelled as counselor-counselee-observer or teacher-child-observer. It is essential that there be three persons; two interact while the third observes for purposes of feedback. The intent of the exercise is to give some insight into the variables involved in giving and receiving information in a relationship. The exercise should run 20–40 minutes in each role. Situations can be structured as deemed relevant; e.g., teacher-pupil; counselor-client; teacher-parent, and so on. Leaders may even want to coach the participants in their roles. The principles of feedback should be observed in this exercise (e.g., give participants the guidelines for giving and receiving feedback formulated by Dorn, Murdoch, and Scarborough, 1970).

Group Consensus Task   This task, which involves multiple techniques, can be carried out by almost any group. The list of debatable statements on page 144 was developed by John Bellanti for use with groups of classroom teachers, but appropriate statements can be generated for any group.

   A basic procedure to use with these statements is as follows:

1. Have each member of the group write down his first response to the item (5 minutes).
2. Group participants into pairs, take away the N category, and

Below are listed a number of statements which I would like for you to respond.

For each statement mark whether you strongly agree, are neutral, or strongly disagree.

SA   N   SD

____ ____ ____   1. The specific needs of each student should be accounted for in each teacher's lesson plan.

____ ____ ____   2. Students who are quiet need more attention than students who are too active.

____ ____ ____   3. It is better for the teacher not to show her feelings to her students because most of the time they will not be able to handle them.

____ ____ ____   4. Permitting students to behave in a manner that is really unacceptable to adults is a good and healthy practice.

____ ____ ____   5. The student's feelings are more important than the teacher's.

____ ____ ____   6. One should expect a teacher to behave calmly and coolly at all times.

____ ____ ____   7. The normal teacher is one who is a "middle of the roader."

____ ____ ____   8. Teachers should be consistent in the way(s) they teach all students.

____ ____ ____   9. If a teacher works hard, she can hide her feelings from her students.

____ ____ ____   10. Learning can take place only when there is a small amount of confusion and uncertainty.

____ ____ ____   11. The mature teacher should cope with life without stress, anxiety, and conflict.

____ ____ ____   12. More learning will take place in an unstructured classroom than a structured classroom.

____ ____ ____   13. Learning consists of the acquisition of new knowledge.

Figure 5-1   *Group Consensus Task*

tell them that they must agree on all items. (Allow enough time to finish.)

3. Group participants into fours, take away the N category, and tell them that they must agree on all items.

4. Group participants into eights, take away the N category, and tell them they must agree on all items. At this stage a "fishbowl" procedure can be used. The observers can be given guidelines (e.g., Pfeiffer and Jones, 1969, pp. 49–50) to observe the group as a whole (e.g., process, decisions, and so on) as well as the leader (e.g., choice, acceptance, kind of leadership role taken).

5. Re-form large group (the author has used this procedure with as many as 60 teachers). Discuss the dynamics of the exercise and the classroom applications of it.

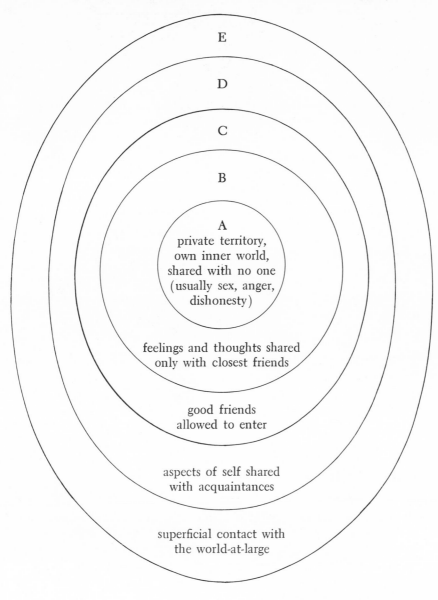

E

D

C

B

A
private territory,
own inner world,
shared with no one
(usually sex, anger,
dishonesty)

feelings and thoughts shared
only with closest friends

good friends
allowed to enter

aspects of self shared
with acquaintances

superficial contact with
the world-at-large

Figure 5–2   *Inner circle strategy.*

Inner Circle Strategy, Combined with Secret Pooling   The inner circle strategy, described by Lazarus (1969, 1971), is presented to the group by means of a chalkboard drawing or a large pad of paper. Figure 5.1 summarizes its conceptual framework, which is combined with the "grab bag" process (Rueveni, 1971). Each member writes down a secret characteristic of a personal zone (A, B, or C) on a piece of paper, folds or crumples it up, and throws it on the floor in the middle of the circle. The leader scrambles the papers (participants sometimes try to keep an eye on another person's secret), and then asks each group member to pick up a paper. The members take turns reading the secrets (not their own!) aloud and describing how they would feel about having such a secret. Other group members can comment on and share their feelings about the secrets. The anonymous discloser often realizes that his secret is not shameful or unique, and is thus encouraged to disclose more about himself in future meetings. Lazarus (1971) states that the most effective therapy affects personal zones A (sometimes shared with a very special person) and B.

Skill Training Groups

The second major kind of teacher group concentrates on skill training. Such structured activities are usually less threatening to teachers and easier to justify to school administrators (Foreman, Poppen, and Frost, 1967). Various skills and exercises will be discussed in connection with the Corl Street Project in the next section, which introduces administrators into the group.

Administrator Groups

With rare exceptions (Watson, 1969), administrators do not participate in groups. Thus, the procedures to be described are innovative. That is, the presence of parents, teachers, administrators and counselors in the same group can be seen as breaking the communication barriers that often occur when these persons function in isolation from each other. The situation is somewhat analogous to family counseling, in which all the vital parties are together simultaneously. More effective functioning is generally the result. In the following pages some of the training procedures are described and examples are given so that counselors may learn to implement such procedures with groups in their schools. After the training procedures are described, the final section will include some procedures for working with child guidance groups in the classroom.

The Corl Street Project: Parents, Teachers, Administrators and Counselors in the Same Group

During the initial phase of training for this project, the consultant visited with each teacher individually. Then each teacher was observed in the classroom for about 30 minutes. This all took place prior to the first group meeting.

At the adult group meetings, members heard lectures on theory and concepts, listened to and evaluated tapes made by group members, worked with partners (teacher and nonteacher) to set goals and evaluate classroom meetings, and role-played group meetings and processed the role-playing. These groups were composed of teachers, guidance counselors, parents, and administrators (usually principals). The purpose of the adult group meetings was to teach members how to listen reflectively (Rogers, 1951), own and share feelings, give and receive feedback, work in small groups, and use democratic procedures. The use of democratic procedures, which underlies much of the work of this project, is described by Guerney and Merriam (1972).

The initial skill to be developed was reflective listening (for its application to a school setting, see Randolph and Howe, 1966). Reflective listening involves attending to the words, gestures, tone of voice, posture, and eye movements of the speaker and responding to the speaker by synthesizing all these verbal and nonverbal cues into a restatement of what one perceives as the speaker's full meaning. Merriam (1971) has delineated at least four levels of reflective listening:

1. Reflection of content, in which the listener simply paraphrases the meanings of the words of the speaker.
2. Reflection of feeling, in which the listener reflects clearly spoken or obvious but unspoken feelings that accompany the speaker's words.
3. Reflection of behavioral implications, in which one synthesizes verbal and nonverbal cues and reflects what the speaker seems to be feeling, as well as its possible behavioral implications.
4. Reflection of underlying unspoken feelings, in which the listener reflects unspoken and nonobvious feeling and describes behavioral effects (if appropriate).

A variety of exercises were provided to allow the parents, teachers, and administrators to develop skill in reflective listening. One exercise involved the description of a situation, such as a child saying to a teacher during an art class, "I can't do this." The adults were given the following multiple-choice responses to choose among:

1. You have to do it. Just do the best you can.
2. Don't be ridiculous. Of course you can.
3. You feel you won't do it well enough.
4. Why not?

The purpose of this exercise was to help the participants to categorize their responses. The answers were checked with a key provided at the end of the exercise. In the example given, response A was ordering, supporting, and giving advice; B was shaming, disagreeing, supporting, reassuring and criticizing; C was reflective, and D, questioning.

In the second exercise, the participants responded to particular situations. For example, a stimulus situation might be a seven-year-old raising his hand excitedly volunteering, "Guess what? We're getting a puppy today, and he's going to be all mine to keep." The trainees wrote down their response to this situation. Then some examples of reflective responses were provided, such as, "You really seem excited about it. It's marvelous for you"; or "Getting a puppy all your .own makes it a very special day"; or "This feels like a really important day—it's almost like Christmas morning or something." Then space was provided for the adult's modified response (Merriam, 1971). Additional situations of this kind can be invented by the counselor. An illustration of a handout used in training teacher groups (to be discussed in Chapter Seven) is included in Appendix E. This handout includes both didactic material and some practice examples with modified responses.

Another skill that was developed was owning feelings and giving feedback about feelings, or, in other words clearly labelling one's own reactions to behavior. Feedback is the process of giving information to another person about one's perceptions of, and reactions to, their feelings or behavior. Giving feedback and owning feelings involves four steps (Merriam, 1971):

1. Correctly identifying for yourself the feelings you are experiencing in this situation.
2. Communicating clearly and accurately these feelings when they are in some way affecting the interaction you are having with another.
3. Identifying for yourself the sources of your feelings.
4. When the source of your feelings stems from the behavior of

another, clearly describing his behavior as you perceive it, following the principles of good feedback.

The *School Manual* (Merriam, 1971) provides some situations that the adult can respond to such as: "You are in a hurry to get home after a hard day. A student seems to be unnecessarily prolonging a conversation with you and does not respond to your many hints that you would like to stop talking and leave." The adult is to write down his response to this situation. On the next page (Merriam, 1971), an example is given of owning feelings, such as, "Look, I've got to tell you that I'm feeling frustrated right now. I want to keep talking about this, but I am in a hurry to get home because I'm beat. I'd like to pick up with you again on this the next time we get together. OK?" Then space is provided for one's modified response.

To develop effective listening skills, the group members worked in triads composed of a speaker, a listener, and an observer. The *School Manual* provides exercises for the participants to work on. In addition, a response-style Category Sheet (Merriam, 1972, Appendix 3) was used to help the participants identify their response styles.

Another useful exercise requires dividing the group in half and arranging both groups in circles. The instructions are as follows:

One person makes a statement. The person to his right is to repeat his statement word for word (verbatim) and identify the feeling behind it ("and you felt"). This is to be the most accurately perceived feeling that the listener can come up with. The process continues around the entire circle. This exercise teaches participants to actively listen, develop reflecting skills, and enlarge their feeling vocabularies. (For an illustration of this approach in action, see pages 155–156.)

A useful technique to enhance the generalization or carry-over of reflective listening skills into real-life situations is to keep a log of their applications. That is, one should record actual examples of the use of reflective listening, or describe situations in which one could have used reflective listening but failed.

An example of an application of reflective listening is as follows:

SPEAKER: I wish I didn't have to leave early.
LISTENER: You really want to stay?
SPEAKER: Yeah, I'm afraid I'll miss something.

One of the functions of the adult leader is didactic. This

means, among other things, giving the participants guidelines for classroom meetings. Two agendas follow. The application of such guidelines to a real-life situation is illustrated in the transcript of a second-grade classroom meeting that follows (pages 154–155).

Agenda for a decision-making meeting (Merriam, 1972):

1. Conduct a discussion. Face the issues.

2. Think about the possible implications, that is, what is and is not acceptable. The leader should state his own rules as well as those of the authorities (e.g., no picnic during school unless it can be justified as an educational activity).

3. Determine what information the group needs to know, where this information is available, and ways to get it.

4. Generate possible alternative decisions and write them on the board. With younger children, it is usually better to evaluate each alternative as it is presented. With older children (e.g., ages 7–8 and up), the evaluation can be held off until after all the alternatives are brainstormed.

5. Voting if you can't reach a consensus.

6. Schedule a re-evaluation of the solutions. That is, establish the time of the next classroom meeting. The purpose of this meeting is to look at the variables in classroom problems or the effects of decisions.

Agenda for a problem-solving session (Merriam, 1972):

1. Define the problem as behaviorally and specifically as possible.

2. Ask the children to describe their feelings and experiences about the problem. The purpose of this procedure is to help you find out how each child is experiencing the problem as a personal concern.

3. Brainstorm possible reasons why the problem is occurring.

4. Generate possible solutions.

5. Evaluate these solutions.

6. Reach a consensus regarding a solution or take a majority vote.

7. Set a time for the next class meeting in order to evaluate how well the selected solution is working.

These outlines for class meetings provide practical input for the counselor who wants to run adult groups. The focus is on problem-solving and decision-making procedures that allow the student to gain greater responsibility for behaviors through participation. The theory is that this will provide both adults and children with a permanent basis for functioning as a citizen in a democratic society. The philosophy behind democratic procedure is outlined by Guerney and Merriam (1972). The application of these procedures in child classroom meetings or child guidance groups will be covered in the next section.

—————— Child Guidance Groups: Classroom Group Meetings

The person who has done the most to popularize teacher-conducted group meetings is Glasser (1969), who discusses three kinds of classroom meetings:

1. Social-problem-solving meetings, concerned with the student's social behavior in school.

2. Open-ended meetings, focused on any thought-provoking question related to their lives.

3. Educational—diagnostic meetings, concerned with how well the students understand the concepts of the curriculum (Glasser, 1969).

Reading Glasser (1969), listening to him work on tape, and seeing him on film, it appears that he is the leader in charge of the classroom meeting. That is, he directs the interactions by questions and most exchanges are between Glasser and one child and then Glasser and another child.

The approach the author advocates is somewhat similar to Glasser's in that classroom meetings are conducted by the teacher and focus on reaching solutions to problems. The emphasis, however, is upon developing a more democratic situation. Group meetings in this democratic philosophy (Merriam, 1971) are of the following types:

1. Decision-making, in which the teacher systematically selects kinds of decisions the children can make themselves (with the teacher holding one vote). These decisions can range from the planning of parties and the use of free time to specific kinds of learning goals and their implementation.

2. Problem-solving, in which children and teachers can introduce personal and interpersonal problems each is experiencing as a result of the classroom interaction. All types of discipline and learning problems are included under this heading, for example, children hitting each other, talking while the teacher is talking, and recess. Although rules for classroom behavior can be set up *a priori*, it has been both Merriam's (1971) and the author's experience that it is better to create rules in response to actual problem situations (as described in Chapter Four) than in anticipation of problem situations. Such rules tend to set up the adult for limit-testing by the children.

3. Enlightenment, which includes all discussions of issues relevant to the teacher and children. Such discussions can focus either on social issues or on questions of value related to the subject matter being learned (Merriam, 1971). The major guidelines for classroom group discussions in the Corl Street project (Merriam, 1972) follow:

1. The teacher is the leader.

2. The teacher reflects as many comments as possible throughout the discussion, serving as a listening model for children and attempting to clarify the feelings of the students.

3. The teacher attempts to avoid praise and blame, or to evaluate any comment made. The teacher is nonjudgmental and accepts all ideas.

4. Any opinion expressed by the teacher is identified clearly as her own feeling.

5. The teacher frequently summarizes what has been said and asks for additions and corrections to the summary.

6. The teacher encourages children through her reflections to elaborate on their ideas and to support their ideas with evidence.

7. The leader encourages children, through reflection, to give differing opinions and fosters these differences of opinion.

8. The teacher does not arbitrarily impose direction on the discussion, but does keep the discussion on the track.

9. Parameters should be set so that children know the limits of their real power. Once the entire group has made a decision, it is binding on all until the group revokes or changes it.

10. Decisions are made by consensus when possible. When consensus is not possible, majority vote can be used.

11. Any member of the group, including the teacher, may introduce a concern for discussion in the group meeting. The topic of the meeting should be known in advance, if possible.

12. Periodically, the group should discuss how well it is doing and what needs to be done to make its meetings more successful. This is the process of feedback and this should be made available and carried out periodically. Taping and playing the tapes can be used occasionally for analyzing the group.

13. During group meetings, power lies with the children and not with the teacher. The teacher holds one vote and is guaranteed equal time with the other group members.

14. The teacher's main responsibility is to help create a climate

of interpersonal trust so that all group members feel free to express feelings and problems.

These types of classroom meetings can be, and have been, conducted at all levels from kindergarten through sixth grade (Merriam & Guerney, 1973; Guerney & Merriam, 1972). Of course, the range of subject matter and content differs with the grade, but the primary focus is on decision making and problem solving. The goal is to have the children experience real, as opposed to advisory, power. Among the concerns expressed by children at the kindergarten level are choosing activities for play time and recess, taking turns on the slide, voting on filmstrips, and voting on stories and games. In first grade, children have voted on what to study for a social studies unit, where to go on a field trip, how to arrange the seats in the classroom, and how to deal with name-calling. In the second grade, they have discussed seating arrangements, what to do during free time, and how to set up a new activity center. Third-grade discussions focused on the content and order of daily academic work in the classroom and ways to cope with a particular class member who was harassing the other children, and votes were taken on a field trip as a reward for learning multiplication tables, and classroom management (e.g., seating arrangements). During fourth-grade discussions, the children dealt with things to do on holidays, problems involving trips to the restroom, ways to cope with the traffic between the desks and the cloakroom, the difficulty of fighting in school and ways to deal with this problem by rearranging the classroom environment. Fifth-grade concerns involved playing records in the classroom, resolving conflicts with fourth graders who had knocked over a snow fort, lessen their harassment of kindergarten children by fifth-grade patrols by giving the kindergarteners rules to abide by, discussing feelings about a new teacher, planning a party, and of getting along with each other when playing games. These illustrative concerns from a variety of actual group interactions can serve as stimuli for dealing with the problems of children at different levels. The leader should begin by introducing topics the children feel comfortable with.

The following excerpts from actual group guidance sessions (classroom meetings) conducted by teachers in the Lock Haven (Pennsylvania) school district illustrate some of the concepts discussed above. The first illustrates reflective listening, problem solving, decision making, and voting in a second-grade classroom meeting. It should be noted that both sessions were conducted by teachers just beginning to learn these procedures. A useful exercise for the reader would be to evaluate the transcripts in the light of the content of this chapter. Another interesting procedure is to cover the teacher's responses and reply as you would to the children. Then compare your responses with the teacher's.

Second-grade Classroom Meeting— Problem-solving and Decision-making in the Democratic Model

TEACHER: This week our discussion is to be about a problem concerning the lunch program. This problem is what do children do with unwanted food? How do you feel about this problem?

CHILD P: My mother always told me that I'm supposed to finish everything on my plate.

TEACHER: Your mother says you're not supposed to waste it. And how do you feel about this?

CHILD P: I don't think you should waste it.

CHILD S: Even if I don't like it I eat some of it.

TEACHER: You eat some of it. You feel better if you don't waste all of it.

CHILD B: When I have something I don't like, we trade sometimes. Other times I just throw it away.

TEACHER: You find yourself trading even though you don't like to, so sometimes you throw it away. You feel others should do as you do and trade or do as you do and throw it down the garbage can.

CHILD B: Throw it down in the garbage can.

TEACHER: This is a possible solution—throw it in the garbage can. Now let's hear how some other people feel.

CHILD M: If you don't like it, then don't buy it.

TEACHER: Don't buy it if you don't like it. OK. That's another possible solution.

CHILD K: One time I saw something real horrible and I tasted it, and it tasted good. So I think you should taste it, because you might not have tasted it before, and if you taste it you might like it.

TEACHER: That's another possible solution. K says taste it, it looked horrible, but when you tasted it, you liked it.

CHILD T: If you don't like something you should give it away or you're just throwing away money.

TEACHER: Well, you don't like to throw away money. At least give it away. These are four possible solutions so far. Now here are the solutions so far. Someone says throw it in the garbage if it's something you don't like. Don't buy it if you don't like it. Taste it or at least give it away. Any others?

CHILD L: Try it.

CHILD R: You should eat it even if you don't like it.

TEACHER: Maybe we better vote about it.

CLASS: Yeah, yeah.

TEACHER: How many people think it is better to share food or give it away to someone else? How many people think that would be OK? ($N = 10$) How many people say throw it in the garbage can? ($N = 2$) How about don't buy it if you don't like it? ($N = 2$) How many people say taste it? ($N = 17$). Seventeen people say try it, maybe you'll like it.

The following transcript of a sixth-grade classroom meeting illustrates various procedures. The teacher predominately uses the technique of reflective listening, with the addition of a feeling sentence. (A beginner, his technique still needs improvement.) The mistake of making a problem too general *is* illustrated. After realizing his error, the teacher *personalizes* the problem. This draws the children into the discussion, and they subsequently work toward their own solutions.

Sixth-grade Classroom Meeting— Problem Solving

TEACHER: Now you decided today that you would talk about why some people pick on other people or what it feels like to be picked on, or why some kids do it. Anybody have anything to say?

CHILD M: I think that kids who pick on others, they just want to show off in front of their friends.

TEACHER: You feel they're being a big deal.

CHILD J: They think that they can beat them.

TEACHER: They think that they can beat them. They have a sense of power by doing this.

CHILD K: They want the other kid to chase them around.

TEACHER: They want the other kid to chase them around. It gives them a feeling of excitement.

CHILD R: They make fun of some retarded kids. But someday when they grow up one of their kids might be retarded.

TEACHER: They make fun of other slower kids and they may regret it later on. Anybody else? Any thoughts, emotions, feelings? (No responses for awhile. Teacher calls on a couple of children who don't respond. This beginning was, in retrospect, probably too generalized for the children to relate to. The next type of approach personalizes it more.)

TEACHER: O.K. What's one thing about school or other kids that bugs you . . . that really bugs you?

CHILD T: You may not like the way they act.

TEACHER: You might not like the way somebody acts.

CHILD S: They make up names for you.

TEACHER: They make up names for you. This doesn't feel too good with you, does it?

CHILD S: When kids come around and push you.

TEACHER: When kids push you around, this makes you angry.

CHILD J: Yeah, they call you names and stuff and you can't do nothing to them.

TEACHER: They call you names and you feel frustrated because you can't get back at them. Anything else that bugs you? (There follows a lively discussion about one teacher in the school.)

TEACHER: Like he doesn't understand how you feel.

CHILD J: Yeah, he always packs homework on top of us.

CHILD K: He's the only teacher that gives us a lot of homework.

CHILD L: Yeah, you're going on a trip on Saturday and he piles you down with homework on Friday and you can't go on Saturday. He almost always does that.

CHILD M: Why can't you go Saturday and do it Sunday?

CHILD L: I go to church on Sunday.

CHILD M: You don't stay there all day.

CHILD S: Not from 11 to 9.

CHILD Q: Take the books with you.

There follows an animated discussion of ways to cope with this problem. At this point, group interaction has increased and the teacher's activity has decreased. The children are attempting to solve their own problem.

Summary

This chapter has considered four types of groups the counselor can organize: parent, teacher, administrator, and child guidance groups. Initially, four types of parent groups were described: open, semi-structured, parent education, and family counseling. Then two kinds of teacher groups were described. Five exercises for the self-development type of teacher group were described and teacher skill training was briefly discussed. The concept of administrator groups was introduced. A training project in which parents, teachers, administrators, and counselors were all present in the same group was illustrated. Methods and guidelines for implementing this type of group were discussed and child guidance groups or democratic group meetings were described.

References

Adronico, M., & Guerney, B. The potential application of filial therapy to the school situation. *Journal of School Psychology*, 1967, 6, 2–7.

Axline, V. *Play therapy*. Cambridge, Mass.: Houghton Mifflin, 1947.

Axline, V. *Dibs: In search of self*. Boston: Houghton Mifflin, 1964.

Dinkmeyer, D. The C-group: Focus on self as instrument. *Phi Delta Kappan*, 1971, 52, 617–619.

Dinkmeyer, D., & Arciniega, M. Affecting the learning climate through "C" groups with teachers. *The School Counselor*, 1972, 19, 249–253.

Dinkmeyer, D., & Muro, J. *Group counseling theory and practice*. Itasca, Ill.: F. E. Peacock, 1971.

Dorn, R., Murdoch, P., & Scarborough, A. *Manual for self-development workshops*. Greensboro, N.C.: Center for Creative Leadership, 1970.

Dreikurs, R., & Chernoff, M. Parents and teachers: Friends or enemies? *Education*, 1970, 91, 147–154.

Dreikurs, R., & Goldman, M. *The ABC's of Guiding the Child*. Chicago: Alfred Adler Institute, 1964.

Dreikurs, D., & Soltz, V. *Children: The challenge*. New York: Hawthorn Books, 1964.

Faust, V. *The counselor-consultant in the elementary school*. Boston: Houghton Mifflin, 1968.

Foreman, M. E., Poppen, W. A., & Frost, J. M. Case groups: An inservice education technique. *Personnel and Guidance Journal*, 1967, 46, 388–92.

Frost, J. M. The elementary-school counselor and his work with groups. In N. Van Hoose, J. J. Pietrofesa, & J. Carlson (Eds.), *Elementary-School guidance counseling: a composite view*. Boston: Houghton Mifflin, 1973. Pp. 187–201.

Fulmer, D. *Counseling: Group theory and system*. Scranton, Penn.: International Textbook Company, 1971.

Gerba, J. The elementary counselor and his involvement with parent education groups. Unpublished master's thesis, Pennsylvania State University, 1972.

Ginott, H. *Between parent and child.* New York: Macmillan, 1965.

Glasser, W. *Schools without failure.* New York: Harper & Row, 1969.

Gordon, T. *Parent effectiveness training.* New York: Wyden, 1970.

Grams, A. *Facilitating learning and individual development.* St. Paul, Minn.: Minnesota Department of Education, 1966.

Guerney, B. Filial therapy: Description and rationale. *Journal of Consulting Psychology,* 1964, **28,** 304–310.

Guerney, B. G. (Ed.) *Psychotherapeutic agents: New roles for non-professionals, parents, and teachers.* New York: Holt, Rinehart & Winston, 1969.

Guerney, B. G., & Merriam, M. L. Toward a democratic elementary school classroom. *The Elementary School Journal,* 1972, **72,** 372–383.

Hill, G. E., & Luckey, E. B. *Guidance for children in elementary schools.* New York: Appleton-Century-Crofts, 1969.

Larson, R. Can parent classes affect family communications? *The School Counselor,* 1972, **19,** 261–270.

Lazarus, A. The "inner circle" strategy: Identifying crucial problems. In J. Krumboltz & C. Thoresen. *Behavioral counseling: cases & techniques.* New York: Holt, Rinehart & Winston, 1969. Pp. 19–24.

Lazarus, A. *Behavior therapy and beyond.* New York: McGraw-Hill, 1971.

LeBow, M. Behavior modification for the family. In G. Erickson & T. Hogan (Eds.), *Family therapy.* Belmont, Cal.: Wadsworth, 1972. Pp. 347–376.

Merriam, M. L. *School Manual.* Unpublished manuscript, Pennsylvania State University College of Human Development, 1971.

Merriam, M. L. *Corl Street School project: training in democracy.* Unpublished manuscript, Pennsylvania State University College of Human Development, 1972.

Merriam, M. L., & Guerney, B. G. Creating a democratic elementary school classroom: a pilot training program involving teachers, administrators and parents. *Journal of Contemporary Education,* 1973, in press.

Otto, H. *Group methods designed to actualize human potential.* Chicago: Stone-Brandel Center, 1967.

Patterson, G. R. *Families: Applications of social learning to family life.* Champaign, Ill.: Research Press, 1971.

Patterson, G. R., & Gullion, M. E. *Living with children: new methods for parents and teachers.* Champaign, Ill.: Research Press, 1968.

Pfeiffer, J., & Jones, J. *A handbook of structured experiences for human relations training: volumes I. III.* Iowa City, Iowa: University Associates Press, 1969–1971.

Price, E. Parent discussion groups. *Elementary School Guidance & Counseling,* 1971, 6, 92–97.

Randolph, N., & Howe, W. *Self-enhancing education.* Palo Alto, Cal.: Stanford University Press, 1966.

Rogers, C. *Client-centered therapy.* Boston: Houghton Mifflin, 1951.

Rueveni, V. Using sensitivity training with junior high school students. *Children*, 1971, **18**, 69–72.

Satir, V. *Conjoint family therapy*. Palo Alto, Cal.: Science & Behavior Books, 1967.

Satir, V. *Peoplemaking*. Palo Alto, Cal.: Science & Behavior Books, 1972.

Smart, A. Play therapy schools for parents. *Menninger Perspective*, 1970, **1**, 12–15.

Smith, J., & Smith, D. *Child management: A program for parents and teachers*. Ann Arbor, Mich.: Ann Arbor Publishers, 1964.

Susskind, D., Franks, C., & Lonoff, R. Desensitization program with third- and fourth-grade teachers: a new application and a controlled study. In R. Rubin, H. Fensteiheim, A. Lazarus, & C. Franks (Eds.), *Advances in behavior therapy*. New York: Academic Press, 1971. Pp. 171–182.

Thoresen, C. E., Alper, T., Hannum, J., Barrick, J., & Jacks, R. Comparison of systematic desensitization and behavior management training with elementary teachers. *Research Memorandum*. Stanford Center for Research and Development in Teaching, in press.

Watson, D. H. Group work with principals: implications for elementary counselors. *Elementary School Guidance and Counseling*, 1969, **3**, 234–241.

Wittes, G., & Radin, N. *Helping your child to learn: The reinforcement approach*. San Rafael, Cal.: Dimensions, 1969.

6

The term *collaboration* is preferred to *consultation* because it suggests a cooperative relationship. This type of joint work is necessary for the effective functioning of persons involved with and concerned about children. Dinkmeyer supports the use of this term, especially in working with teachers. As he says, "Consulting is a collaboration: The specialist does not provide ready answers. The teacher and the consultant work together to understand and resolve problems" (1968, p. 109). Hill and Luckey observe that "Consultative assistance to teachers, and close working relationships (collaboration) with teachers, is viewed, without exception by all the sources we were able to tap, as a significant function of the elementary school counselor" (1969, p. 142). Hansen and Stevic also state that "Consultation calls for a collaborative relationship in which the teachers, parents, and counselor work together in understanding the child and his environment" (1969, p. 127). Faust says, "The counselor-consultant is one who collaborates with the teacher in both classroom activities and curriculum development" (1968, p. 24).

The term consultant is, nevertheless, more often used. The process of consultation is generally regarded as one of the counselor's three main functions. The ACES-ASCA statement declares that "Consultation is the process of sharing with another person or group of persons information and ideas, of combining knowledge into new patterns, and of making mutually agreed upon decisions about the next steps needed" (Dinkmeyer, 1968, p. 103). Muro views the job of the consultant as "one of helping teachers and parents to restore or enhance their own confidence in working with children rather than one of dispensing computer punched

Collaboration-Consultation

cards chock full of wisdom with a magic prescription for a problem" (1970, p. 96).

Various authors have described formats of collaborative functions in the school. Some (e.g., Faust, 1968; Fullmer and Bernard, 1972) seem comprehensive and encompass topics covered in other chapters of this book. For example, Faust (1968, p. 34) discusses a hierarchy of consultative roles.

The collaborative relationship can be defined as a working relationship between two or more people. The somewhat ambiguous word "relationship" suggests the necessary condition for effecting constructive collaboration-consultation. As Muro states, "Consultation proceeds best in an atmosphere of mutual trust and confidence when the give and take of the interaction is on a somewhat informal basis" (Muro, 1970, p. 97). Other bases for defining the consultative relationship are that it is usually temporary, with a coprofessional, and usually voluntary for the purpose of discussing a third person (e.g., the child). Dinkmeyer and Caldwell (1970) have discussed several aspects of the consultative relationship. To summarize their points: the consultant is a person who cares and is capable of giving help while establishing a relationship of mutual confidence; the relationship focuses on helping the child to achieve educational objectives, and is a collaborative undertaking in which all concerned work to develop an atmosphere of cooperative problem solving; and, the responsibility for using or rejecting advice remains with the person being consulted.

Child Development Consultation

Although the primary focus of child development consultation is the elementary school child, it is also necessary that the counselor have some knowledge of preschool children and be able to supply reference sources for parents. That is, during the course of parent consultation the subject of other siblings in the family can arise, and references or sources of information for the counselor and or parents should be known. In addition, teachers and administrators often benefit from some information about child development.

A classic book in this area was written by Fraiberg (1959). The section of most relevance here covers ages three to six, and deals with such topics as the meaning of sex education, identification, and the education of conscience. Another useful book (especially the appendices) for parents who are concerned about preschool children is by Dodson. A source that deals with the preschool child, written by a pediatric psychiatrist (Spock, 1968), could be considered a parents' guide to living with children, especially where physical difficulties are concerned. Another especially informative source is provided by Smith (1969). He includes a map outlining the development of children from one month to five years of age. For a comprehensive discussion of childhood psychopathology, the interested reader should refer to Kessler (1966) or Engel (1972).

With regard to the school-age child, the approach advocated by the author centers around developmental expectations at various age levels. The work of Gesell and Ilg (1946) and the volume by Ilg and Ames (1964) are the underpinnings of this approach (discussed in Chapter Two). That is, one has particular expectations of children at various age levels in different areas of child functioning. For example, the child may be above age level in gross motor coordination but below age level in fine visual-motor coordination. Such a child might be expected to do fairly well in athletics but may have difficulty sitting down and concentrating. The two just-cited texts can provide a wealth of developmental information for the elementary school counselor concerned with expectations for particular age levels.

Another outline that has general applicability to child development for the elementary school counselor is provided by VanHoose, Peters and Leonard (1970). They consider the developmental needs of children in two age groups: ages 5 to 8, and ages 9 to 12. Their outline gives an analysis of the characteristics in each of four categories: (1) physical; (2) social, related to interactions with others; (3) emotional, having to do with internal feelings; and (4) learning, which has to do with cognitive growth. The reader is referred to the VanHoose, Peters, and Leonard's paperback (1970, pp. 18–32) for a detailed analysis of the outline.

To fill in the details of developmental processes, one can turn to several books, including those by Jersild (1960) and Stone and Church (1968). Stone and Church take the reader on a journey through middle years (ages 6 to 12) of "the society of children." Such things as childhood rituals, games and chants, stunts, and a variety of other childhood rites are discussed.

Perhaps the most important theorist to deal with developmental stages as they relate to children is Erik Erikson (1963). Of particular relevance here are the psychosocial dimensions that Erikson added to the original Freudian conception of psychosexual development. In this paradigm, a child is viewed as having achieved or failed to achieve certain basic equilibria. If he has not attained each by a particular age his personality development is deficient in some area. The first stage Erikson (1963) discusses is *trust vs. mistrust,* which corresponds to the oral stage in classic psychoanalytic theory and dominates the first year of life. It is important to note that the basic issue of trust versus mistrust arises again at successive stages of development. Elkind (1970) has said that the child who enters school with a sense of mistrust may come to trust a particular teacher who has taken the trouble to make himself trustworthy. Given such a second chance, the child can overcome his early mistrust. The psychosocial modalities that Erikson discusses (1959) are *to get* and *to give in return.* Erikson talks about drive and hope as necessary for life. With regard to counseling, the parent-child relationship needs remediation, by such processes as the filial approach (Guerney, 1964), if this is the dimension in which the child is lacking.

The second stage of Erikson's paradigm (1963) is *autonomy vs. shame and doubt.* This issue spans the second and third years of life, which Freudian theory calls the anal stage. Autonomy is an outgrowth of the motor and mental abilities the child develops at this age. When the persons responsible for the child are impatient and do for him what he can do himself, he can develop a strong sense of shame and doubt. This is especially true if the caretakers are consistently overprotective and critical of the child. Positive characteristics that Erikson associates with this period are self-control and will power. The attendant psychosocial modalities are *to hold on* and *to let go.* With regard to counseling, a closely related concept is positive reinforcement and its effect on a child during these years and later years when it might be necessary to undo damage inflicted during this period.

The third stage of development is *initiative vs. guilt.* This period corresponds to the genital stage in analytic theory and covers ages four to five. If the child is given considerable freedom and opportunity to undertake motor activity during this period, his sense of initiative is reinforced. Erikson talks about the importance of direction and purpose during this stage. The psychosocial modalities are *to make* or *go after things* and *to enjoy life* (playing). The treatment modality for the counselor concerned with a deficiency fostered during this period could be development of skills in decision making. In psychoanalytic treatment the major conflict to be dissolved through interpretation is oedipal.

The fourth stage is *industry vs. inferiority*. This period roughly covers the ages from 6 to 11 and is classically called the "latency" stage. This is the period when a child becomes capable of deductive reasoning and playing games by rules. He is very curious about how things are made and work. The striving for competence that is typical of this period has to do with the psychosocial modalities of *completing things* and *making things* together in a group. During this period relevant treatment would appear to be to allow children to finish their products, to give adequate praise, and to reward them for their efforts. This allows the child to experience the achievement of mastery and thus enhances industry. It is important that children have a sense of mastering some areas so that they can maintain or revitalize their interest in school. Although learning can provide its own rewards, certain children gain strength and positive feelings about themselves from a sense of achievement.

The fifth stage delineated by Erikson is *identity vs. role confusion*. Although this stage is not typically the concern of the elementary school counselor, some emotionally advanced children during the upper intermediate years, and certainly in the middle school, may have problems revolving around this issue. During this period the child moves into adolescence; it corresponds roughly to ages 12 or 13 to 18. Here the child is concerned about how he fits into the culture. During this stage the psychosocial modalities are *to be oneself* and *to share being oneself*. This represents an age of devotion and fidelity in which the child has to be faithful to something. The difficulty that can occur at this time, of course, is role confusion. Therefore, one counseling approach is to develop problem-solving skills and seek solutions to the problems the child confronts.

Almy (1955) discusses some "desirable guidance in the years from 6 to 12" (p. 384). During this age span the child expects "warm acceptance, faith in their potentiality for growth and learning, the protection that comes from reasonable limits, all this plus help in learning and achieving" (Almy, 1955, p. 384). A second issue is the ability to tolerate comparisons with others when they are made. Of course, this ability is related to one's self concept and the strength of one's feelings of self worth. Out of the home the child is questioning both the familiar and the new. A third phenomenon Almy discusses is the child's need for parents who are persons in their own right, with likes and dislikes. Children, nevertheless, need enough flexibility from their parents to allow them to seek their own models outside the home. This is a stage when the child goes away from the parents and looks to outside identification figures. The fourth desirable situation is that protection, when needed, should come from the parents. Parents should stand by their child when they are needed but should also practice "some loosening of rules and regulations, some increasing of both privileges and responsibilities" (Almy, 1955, p. 385). Education for responsibility is one of the primary subjects Glasser discusses in his books on reality therapy (Glasser, 1965) and schools (Glasser, 1969). The fifth thing Almy (1955) discusses is the child's need to feel that he is an accomplisher. The primary burden of fulfilling this need lies with the school, which is delegated the task of teaching the skills necessary for coping with the psychological, social, and physical world. Counseling can thus be seen as education to help the child cope with certain issues classroom education often neglects. These issues typically involve ways to deal with aggressive and sexual drives. Finally, during this stage it is important to look for signals of later difficulty; the prognosis for treatment and correction is much better during these years than during adolescence. This is one of the reasons for the prevention orientation of elementary school counseling.

Contingency Management in the Classroom

Classroom management is the observation, and subsequent remediation, of problematic classroom situations. That classroom management is of increasing importance in today's schools is evident in a recent issue of *Today's Education* devoted to mental health in the classroom. One of the articles (Center for Studies of Child and Family Mental Health, 1972) proposed eight basic principles of behavior modification applicable to classroom situation.

1. Behavior is learned when it is consistently reinforced;
2. Specific behavior that requires acceleration or deceleration must be identified and the child's strengths emphasized;
3. Behavior modification planning must initially anticipate small gains;
4. Consequences of behavior must be meaningful to the student;
5. Consequences, rewards, or punishments must follow the behavior immediately;

6. Reinforcement may be physical or social;

7. Purposes and goals should be clear;

8. The target behavior should be the best one for the particular student. The aim of behavior control should be self control.

Basic Procedures

1. Select a Behavior-change Target   The initial task of the behavior modifier is the selection of a behavior-change target (Neisworth, Deno and Jenkins, 1969). This goal can be an educational objective, instructional goal, or particular child behavior. It is important that these targets have two characteristics. One is countability; that is, the behavior must be stated in such a way that somebody else can count it. For example, parents and teachers sometimes say that a child acts in a particular way a lot. When asked to quantify it during the next week, they return to report that it did not occur; the author has even known instances in which a behavior described as happening a lot did not occur once in an entire month. The behavior may, nevertheless, be magnified in the mind of the perceiver. The second important aspect of selecting a behavior-target is to indicate the direction of the change. That is, do you want to increase, decrease, maintain and stabilize the frequency of behavior, or teach new behaviors?

2. Keeping Records   The second important variable in procedurally carrying out behavior modification is keeping records. Data collection is important in order to determine both the current extent of a behavior and the success in attempts to change it. Although subjective impressions can be useful, change can be documented more reliably if one makes data collection on a quantitative basis. This is generally called the collection of baseline data. There are various formats for this process. In addition to Wherry and Quay's (1969) method, discussed in Chapter Two, another has been developed by Becker, Madsen, Arnold, and Thomas (1967). Their classroom behavioral rating schedule measures motor behavior at the seat, gross motor behaviors not at the desk (e.g., running), aggression, deviant talking, non-attending and disobeying, sucking (thumb, pencil, etc.), relevant behaviors (e.g., listening), hand-raising behaviors, teacher attention, positive comments, general reprimands, and negative comments.

Another consultative device that the author has found useful for teachers is the framework developed by Amidon and Flanders (1967). In order to help teachers change their behavior, Amidon and Flanders devised an interaction analysis feedback system. The first four observation categories in this paradigm comprise indirect teacher influences:

1. accepting feelings
2. praising or encouraging
3. accepting or using the ideas of the students
4. asking questions about content or procedure

Direct teacher behaviors are:

5. lecturing
6. giving directions
7. criticizing or justifying authority

The classifications of student talk are:

8. student talk-response
9. student talk-initiation
10. silence or confusion

One may also use an interaction analysis, which lists specific problem areas in which the teacher might consider substituting alternative behaviors in interaction with the student. For example, if the teacher exhibits few behaviors in categories one or two, then he might want to attempt consciously to increase these kinds of facilitative behaviors.

3. *Changing Behavioral Consequences* The third basic procedure is changing the consequences of the behavior. If one wishes to increase the frequency of a behavior, one should reinforce it immediately and consistently. Only after a behavior has been established should one consider a more random presentation of consequences or reinforcers.

There are a variety of ways of teaching new behaviors. Sulzer and Mayer (1972) have described many, one of which is *response differentiation*. One rewards behaviors that fall within the limits and meet the requirements set on behavioral dimensions (e.g., writing, basketball shooting). In the fine visual-motor area, one would reinforce appropriate writing, starting with a scribble. In the gross motor coordination area of basketball, one can reinforce approximations as the child gradually develops the skill to get the ball into the basket. A second method of teaching a behavior is *shaping* by successive approximations to the goal behavior. An example is the speech of children who say "fee" and are gradually reinforced until they can say the word "free." A third approach is *chaining*, in which the counselor takes simple behaviors already in the repertoire of the individual and combines them into more complex behaviors. An example is writing letters first and eventually combining them into one's name or other words. Another way of teaching behavior is *fading*, by gradually removing prompts and cues. An example is to teach a sentence and gradually drop out parts of the cues in the sentence. For example, one might teach a child a sentence by first having him repeat the whole thing (i.e., "This is a ball."), then gradually fade out the cues (e.g., "This is a b____"). Then say, "This is a ____." The teacher gradually eliminates cues, with reinforcement contingent upon a correct response, until the child can repeat the whole sentence.

If one wishes to decrease the frequency of behavior, one should employ a weakening consequence or negative reinforcer immediately and consistently. Another approach is to increase the frequency of a behavior incompatible with the unwanted behavior. For example, one cannot fight while cooperating with another person, or attend in class while sleeping.

If he wishes to maintain the frequency of a behavior and make it persistent, the counselor should employ a strengthening consequence or reinforcer immediately but inconsistently. Occasional rewards tend to stabilize behavior. For example, gambling has inconsistent rewards, which tend to maintain the chance-taking behavior.

4. Changing Behavior   The fourth major consideration is the shaping of a behavior in the process of encouraging or eliminating it. The principle of successive approximations states that one should strengthen behaviors that are closer and closer approximations of the target-behavior. Target-behaviors can be either academic or social-personal. The counselor is traditionally more concerned with social-personal, and the teacher with academic, goals. There are three questions one should ask about changing behavior: When will the behavior happen, or what are the circumstances of the behavior? What should one look for in observing its performance (i.e., what is the target)? Can its occurrence be counted, or by what criteria is the behavior judged? An example of a social target for a child would be working quietly at his desk. The circumstance would be a particular assignment. The target would be sitting at the desk. The criterion could be to remain quietly in his seat for ten minutes.

These behavior modification procedures are reviewed to help the counselor in aiding the child to develop in a behavioral-humanistic sense, i.e., the synthesis of behavioral techniques with humanistic goals (Thoresen, 1972). In the end, the goal is to help the child help himself develop responsible self-control. Certain writers have devised plans for utopian worlds (Skinner, 1948, 1971). Spock (1968, 1971) recommends restricting television watching for children and not giving them toy guns to play with.

Nevertheless, children also laugh harder at "boob-tube" programs the more violent they are. Some programs use behavior modification principles: unconditional positive regard is applied on *Misteroger's Neighborhood*; principles relevant to preschoolers are observed on *Sesame Street*; life concerns and coping styles are handled on *Ripples*; and the *Electric Company* applies learning principles to teach nonreaders.

The behavioral modification program for preschool or early elementary school-age children presented in the following outline has been implemented by the author with some success. The result indicated (Keat, 1973) that while behavioral changes as measured by the Operation Headstart Behavior Inventory and the Cooperation-Aggression Scale (Keat, 1970), completed by teachers' aides, were nonsignificant, the cooperation level after the behavior modification training program was significantly higher than before it (as measured on behavioral observation scales completed by the investigator and case worker). Although these results are inconsistent, they seem to lend some support, at least on an intuitive level, to such a program as the following one.

A Behavior Modification Program

I. Introduction
    This behavior modification program involves the systematic use of the learning principles of reinforcement (rewards) as applied to children's behavior. The method involves selecting a specific behavior one wants to influence or modify, and then developing a plan of reinforcement (reward) for changing it.

II. Target Behavior
    The target behavior for this particular program is cooperation. This behavior is in contrast to competitive or aggressive behavior, which is usually incompatible with it. Cooperative behavior has two main areas: a. *with peers or children of approximately the same age*; and b. *with the teacher, parent, or other authority figure*.
    The initial phase of the program involves observing the child for a selected period of time engaging in a certain activity. Since the behavior to be observed is cooperation, the child is to be observed for two periods of fifteen minutes each (during the morning) and the number of times he cooperates with peers or adults will be counted (baseline data). The situation should be structured as follows: have two children remain in the block play area for fifteen min-

utes. This will allow for adult-child and child-child interaction in a standardized setting, the results of which will
serve as a baseline of cooperative behavior that can be compared to the observations made over the next few months.

III. Goals of Program
      The goals of this program are essentially twofold:
      A. To strengthen the desirable behavior of cooperation,
          which will compete with the less desirable one of ag-
          gression.
      B. To weaken the undesirable behavior of aggression to
          peers and adults.

IV. Procedures
     In view of these goals, the following procedures are to be
     followed daily for each specific aim:
     A. To strengthen the cooperative behavior: One should
         reinforce cooperative behavior as often as possible,
         whenever it occurs. This reinforcement should initially
         be continuous, although later it can be intermittent.
         Rewards can be of the following basic kinds:
         1. Social
             Social rewards are interpersonal reinforcements. Ex-
             amples are interest, attention-listening, praise, ap-
             proval, talking to the child, smiling, shaking hands,
             hugging, kissing, and expressions of love.
         2. Nonsocial or Material
             Nonsocial rewards are material gifts, of such things
             as candy (e.g., m&m's), ice cream, various other
             foods, tokens, money, tickets, toys, games.
         3. Point (Token) System
             In addition, a system can be established in which a
             child earns points or tokens and later trades them
             for something important to him (e.g., food, a trip
             to the circus, a movie, and so on).

     Social and nonsocial reinforcements are usually used at
the same time; e.g., the child is praised for being cooperative
and simultaneously given a piece of candy.
     B. To weaken the aggressive behavior: One manipulates
         various reinforcement contingencies.
         1. Withdrawing of Positive Reinforcement
             This procedure primarily involves pairing the unde-
             sirable behavior with words that make clear that
             the child is not eligible for a reward as a conse-
             quence of his behavior. It often involves deprivation

of privileges, in which the maladaptive behavior is given as the reason the child cannot do something desirable.

2. Ignoring the Behavior
   Lack of attention provides the child with no payoff for his behavior. The unpleasant consequence is that he is not reinforced in any way.

3. Providing Alternatives to Aggressive Behavior
   One should offer the child something else in place of what is being denied him. For example, if he starts a fight with another child it would be possible to give him a choice between getting along with the child or deciding to do something else entirely (e.g., leave the game). Decision-making skills are thus enhanced. At times one should redirect the child's activity into another channel. For example, hitting a pillow or kicking a ball sublimates aggressive feelings.

4. Timeout Procedures
   One may remove the child from the classroom or central play area if he is engaging in inappropriate behavior, such as aggression or refusal to comply with the teacher's instructions. He could be given the choice of abandoning the inappropriate behavior or being isolated. Thus, timeout from positive reinforcement would usually be imposed when the child:
   a. is behaving aggressively toward another pupil, teacher, or visitor. This procedure weakens behavior associated with hitting, actual hitting, and preludes to aggressive acts (e.g., shoving, pushing, threats).
   b. refuses to cooperate with the teacher's instructions. In this situation, one should concentrate on strengthening cooperative behavior. One should begin by requesting that the child do something that he does habitually. Gradually and systematically introduce new behaviors. One effective procedure is behavior rehearsal. Initially, choose for practice situations in which the child often cooperates. Make a request and reinforce cooperation with immediate social and nonsocial reinforcements. Gradually work up to situations in which he almost never cooperates.

By the use of such role-playing situations, the child can become more aware of his negative effects on others, practice more cooperative behavior, and thus behave more appropriately.

Some Other Applications to the Classroom

There are various other applications of contingency management to the classroom that can be utilized by the counselor. For example, the child may refuse to complete a homework assignment. A reward might entice him to do so. The child could be given the opportunity to choose his reward from among several activities on a reinforcement survey (Keat, 1972). With these extraneous reinforcements, the less preferred behaviors (e.g., spelling) may be carried out in order to obtain the rewards and gradually (as skills increase) doing the schoolwork itself may become rewarding.

Chronic misbehavior is amenable to modification by the use of timeout procedures. Kubany, Wiess, and Sloggett (1971) combined timeout with reinforcement. Token reinforcement and timeout from rewards were used to reduce the disruptive behavior of a child in first grade. A fifteen-minute electric timer with a false face was set up, and for each two minutes of displayed running time, the boy earned a treat for the class (group reinforcement). The clock ran only when the child was quiet and in his seat. When he misbehaved, the teacher turned the clock off. This particular six-year-old child's conditioning was generalized, which is evidence of the effectiveness of behavioral approaches.

Another approach is contingency contracting (Homme, Csanyi, Gonzales & Rechs, 1970). A contract is an agreement in which the child promises to do something in order to win certain rewards. Although it is more easily limited to the individual child, a contract can also be made with an entire class.

Another procedure applicable to the classroom is curriculum manipulation. The affective curriculum will be covered in Chapter Seven, but it should be mentioned here that the teacher can set up centers for such things as perceptual motor training in the area of fine and gross motor activities. Daily tasks can be specified to correspond to the task objectives.

O'Leary and Becker (1970) placed a small booklet with a rating scale on each child's desk. Points on the 1–10 scale reflected the extent to which the child followed instructions. Points or ratings were then exchanged for such rewards as candy, comics, and kites. Group points (also on a 1–10 scale) reflected the extent to which the children were quiet while ratings were being recorded in the booklets. In the same study deviant behavior was extinguished by ignoring it while responding to the child's appropriate behaviors.

Axelrod (1972) has written about the use of recess, special privileges, and weekly grades as reinforcement with a learning disabled class. Also, the allowance a child received from his parents was determined by his weekly grades. The desired behavior change can thus be coordinated between the home and the school in the form of gaining behaviors which the teachers and parents find desirable. This gets the parents involved. B. F. Skinner suggested on television that one could pay children for certain behaviors, giving part of the reward to the child and part to the parents. This gives both concerned persons—parent and child— a stake in acceptable behavior. Axelrod also makes the point that it is important to employ reinforcers already available in the school classroom. For example, play time, field trips, and games are rewards readily available in the classroom. These procedures allow the counselor to diverge from the "m&m stereotype" some administrators have of behavioral modification, and may cause the counselor's work to be held in higher esteem by all concerned persons. Other reinforcers already available in the school can be such things as small classroom responsibilities, feeding classroom animals, being chauffered home after school in the teacher's car, extra dessert, and the like. The author has had clients who like to do such things as cleaning blackboards, moving the television set, and helping the teacher clean up. Of course, each individual's reinforcement schedule should be determined on the basis on the child's reward system (Keat, 1972).

If one wants to investigate the use of specific procedures (e.g., timeout) in particular settings (e.g., adjustment classes) on particular problems (e.g., stuttering), one may consult a rapidly growing literature. Some examples are Neisworth and Smith (1973), Harris (1972), Sulzer and Mayer (1972), Ackerman (1972), Vernon (1972), Buckley and Walker (1970), Homme *et al.* (1970), Ulrich, Stachnik and Mabry (1966, 1970), and Neisworth *et al.* (1969).

Inservice Education

It is commonly agreed that the counselor should work with teachers. The counselor should be able to affect the behavior of the persons who control the classroom environment. Elementary school counselors can bring about changes in the classroom through inservice teacher training sessions. Orlando believes that for inservice training one should use more specialized and highly skilled special education teachers as teacher trainers (Orlando, 1972). Peterson and Sanborn (1972) state that inservice sessions should be characterized by small group settings, a high degree of structure, and emphasis on specific teaching practices.

A major contribution to inservice education for practitioners is a book by Harris, Bessent, and McIntyre (1969), who define inservice education as "planned activities for the instructional improvement of professional staff members" (p. 2). The major approach these authors support—one the author also adheres to—is the laboratory approach. The characteristic design of this approach is that the participant is actively involved, problem situations are simulated as realistically as possible, feedback is provided and the problem situations are related to the actual classroom life-space of the teachers. The bulk of the Harris *et al.* book discusses procedures the counselor can use in inservice programs. Although many of the procedures are educational in orientation, some have to do with styles of interviewing, group communication, and the effects of feedback.

It has been the author's experience that the most effective way of launching a new program, such as an affective curriculum, is to meet with teachers in an inservice situation (see Chapter Seven). During this training period (e.g., two days), teachers can become familiar with the materials, observe demonstrations of their use with children (modeling), gain skill in interpersonal processes, and learn some of the basic principles of group communication necessary to run classroom meetings. A series of half- or whole-day sessions is preferable. For the collaborator-consultant, these days can focus on such things as child development, classroom management procedures, affective education, and the like. The group should ideally be limited to 20 participants per leader, although groups of from 30 to 50 are sometimes necessary. In this situation, it is best to divide the group into smaller groups and circulate among them while they carry out group discussions, demonstrations, or role-playing. If possible, of course, one should solicit the aid of a colleague or other person trained in group procedures.

Staff Case Conferences

The case conference can be viewed as a case study in action. It is a meeting during which concerned persons can pool their understandings and make joint decisions with regard to a child. Some persons view the case conference as an excellent form of inservice training because understanding of human behavior and cooperative education are illustrated. A more valuable aspect of the case conference is that the participants pool the knowledge of the child they have gained from their contacts with him. It is expected that their joint efforts can yield a deeper understanding of the child than could be achieved by one individual. At times one conference is sufficient; sometimes a series of consultations is necessary (Newman, 1967).

The relevance of case analysis for elementary counselors is highlighted by a regular column on the subject in the *Elementary School Guidance and Counseling Journal*. The title of this section is "Case analysis: consultation and counseling." Some representative references from this column are Hagens (1971, 1972, 1973), McGehearty and Webb (1970), and McGehearty (1969).

The most widely used form of consultation is client-centered case consultation (Caplan, 1970). In this process, a consultee who is having difficulty dealing with one of his clients calls in the specialist—the counselor—to investigate the situation and advise him on the case. The primary goal of this type of consultation is to develop a plan that will help the client.

Combining Caplan's (1970) outline of steps in the consultation process with cases of the author, the following is presented as a general guideline to the case conference.

Consultation Request

A request for consultation in the elementary school typically comes from an adult in the environment of the child—a teacher, administrator, or parent—and rarely from the child himself. Counselors can make a form available for teachers or parents to fill out to initiate the request. This form should include important information about the situation in question. The information might resemble that given in the case history discussed in Chapter Two, or the counselor may wish to operate on a more informal basis and take referrals by word-of-mouth.

Assessment of the Problem

Assessment involves two processes. The first is assessment of the identified client by the trained persons (e.g., counselor, psychologist, teacher) in the school. This assessment could involve an individual intelligence evaluation and personality appraisal by the school psychologist, a neurological evaluation by the school's physician, a hearing checkup by the school nurse, and appraisal of the child's educational skills by the learning disability specialist. In addition, the child's learning environment needs to be assessed.

The classroom teacher and special education teachers, if this type of placement is under consideration, are involved in this appraisal. Therefore, the counselor's role in assessment involves coordinating personalities as well as developing his own input or data. These data are derived from the assessment procedures discussed in Chapter Two, as well as from the interview and counseling sessions discussed in Chapter Three.

Case Conference

The case conference draws together all of the personnel involved in the situation in question, potentially including teachers, the psychologist, the learning disabilities specialist, the nurse, the physician, the counselor, the custodian, and anyone else who is relevant. With regard to possible recommendations, the counselor might wish to refer to such sources as Madsen and Madsen (1972), Ullmann and Krasner (1965), Ulrich *et al.* (1966, 1970), and Krumboltz and Thoresen (1969). In addition, the author likes to include the child at some point during this conference. This is especially valuable when one reaches the point of recommending solutions to the child's problems. (See Dreikurs, Grunwald & Pepper, 1971.) Although the child should realize that his recommendations may not be able to be implemented, he should nevertheless have some voice in the planning of his program. This procedure gives him some investment in it. If this is impossible at a particular conference, this type of approach should be strongly recommended to the parents in working with their child. That is, they should be encouraged to share with the child responsibility for solving a problem.

Implementation of Recommendations

Once recommendations have been made, it is the primary function of the counselor to see that they are carried out. The recommendations, of course, should be realistic so that they can actually be implemented. It is usually important at the start of the conference to enumerate the available alternatives.

Follow-up

Follow-up is often neglected for lack of time, but it can be important for a variety of reasons. Follow-up can serve as a rough method of evaluating the efficacy of consultation, and it attests to personal involvement on the part of the consultant or counselor and can have a beneficial effect on the situation and on future collaboration-consultation. In practice, follow-up involves such things as visiting the child's classroom. In the process, one can talk to the teacher about the child's progress as well as having individual contact with the child. A case study will be discussed in Chapter Ten in order to illustrate the contributions of various persons on the "team" devoted to a particular child. The next section is an illustration of counselor-teacher collaboration on a case.

--------------------------------- **The Collaboration-Consultation Process**

The following transcript illustrates some of the procedures discussed above. The basic steps in the process are referral, establishment of a relationship(s) with the involved person(s), assessment of the problem, and the development of helping strategies.

One must first receive a referral. The source can be parents, teachers, or some other adult in the child's life, or the child himself. For situations in which a standardized form (e.g., Dinkmeyer & Caldwell, 1970, p. 203) would be facilitative, one should have copies available.

The relationship has been discussed as of utmost importance in collaboration. The quality of this relationship quite often determines the success one has in helping a child (Mayer, 1972).

Assessment of the problem is a prelude to developing helping strategies. The referral problem in this case was a rather typical one: a seven-year-old child who had difficulty controlling himself in the classroom. This dialogue is between the teacher and counselor, although contacts were made with the parents, child, and school administrator.

TEACHER: Well, I guess you know why we're here today.

COUNSELOR: I have some general idea. It's about Jay. He seems to be having some troubles. Could you fill me in on what he is doing?

TEACHER: Why, yes. He just can't sit still. He's all over the place—bugging other kids, you know. And he gets to me after a while.

COUNSELOR: What specifically does he do?

TEACHER: Well, you know. He kind of, well . . . he just, you know, is always into something.

COUNSELOR: Like . . .

TEACHER: Like he will get up from his seat and crawl under the table. And he also shouts out sometimes. But it's mostly that he just is into something or somebody—like throwing something, spitting, or hitting other kids.

COUNSELOR: I see. He seems to be bothering the other children a lot and it's making things difficult for you in the classroom.

TEACHER: Oh yes.

COUNSELOR: Let's see. Could you tell me something about his family situation?

TEACHER: Yes. He's got an older brother. His father is a salesman and is gone quite a bit. His mother works as a hairdresser. Basically, I hear that he's a pretty neglected kid. And I see him wandering around by himself quite a bit. He also has gotten into trouble for beating up some younger kids last year on their way home from school.

COUNSELOR: So his parents don't seem to have much time for him.

TEACHER: That's probably it. And he has special difficulty in spelling. Some words, like "sometimes" and "kittens," he just can't get. The other day I gave him a —5 for his spelling test. And he said he would be scared to go home.

COUNSELOR: It seems as though Jay is having lots of trouble with spelling, getting attention from his parents, and concentrating on what he's doing, and getting along with other children. Let me look into this a little bit. I'd like to observe him in the classroom for a while and then I'll have a better feel for him. With regard to the spelling, it does seem that those two words you mentioned are a bit difficult for a boy on his level [actually they are several grades above his level]. Perhaps easier ones would be more appropriate for him. Also, how many did he get right on his spelling test?

TEACHER: Twenty.

COUNSELOR: Then he got twenty right and only five wrong. Remember the old song "Accentuate the positive, eliminate the negative?" Well, it might be better to give him a +20 rather than a —5. Then he also might not be afraid to go home and see his parents if he can think positively about what he had done correctly. This would also be more encouraging for him. How does that sound?

TEACHER: O.K. But I'm sure about the marking. It's easier for me to just mark the ones wrong and count them up.

COUNSELOR: That's right. But by subtraction you could quickly figure out how many he had gotten right by taking away the number wrong from the total number given.

TEACHER: O.K. What else can we do now?

COUNSELOR: I'll observe Jay the next day I'm in this building.

That'll be a Friday. And then next week we'll get together and then schedule a conference with his parents. Then we might be able to get them involved and make plans for helping Jay.

Summary of Contact

This teacher-counselor dialogue illustrates numerous points. First there is a behavioral delineation of the problem. By attempting to understand what the teacher is confronted with, the counselor has started to establish a working relationship. Secondly, the family background is of relevance not only for understanding the child but also for planning helping strategies. Thirdly, the counselor's comments on spelling problems and developmental expectations would probably have been more appropriate coming from another source—that is, the curriculum supervisor or principal. Or his point could have been made in a child development consultation or an inservice education program. It should, nevertheless, be gotten across in some fashion because children (almost the whole class, in this case) can become frustrated and give up if they cannot cope with the work they are given. Fourthly, the exchange on positive reinforcement could also have been covered in a teacher group or inservice session. This case was discussed in a behavior modification workshop about a month after this consultation took place. The teacher, despite the resistance evident in the transcript, was open and concerned enough to make the situation public in a small group. Finally, a plan of action and time sequence was mapped out with the teacher.

The next step was to observe Jay in the classroom. During a 20-minute observation, he did most of the things the teacher had reported. He crawled under the table, hollered, and hit another child. It is noteworthy that he did all this with a devilish smile on his face.

COUNSELOR: I see what you mean about Jay. He'd really bother me after awhile.

TEACHER: Yeah. Sometimes I feel like tearing my hair out.

COUNSELOR: Well, it seems as though he is an emotionally deprived child from what you say about his family. Much of his classroom behavior would seem to be active-destructive attention-getting. These are his nuisance and pest behaviors in the classroom. Some of his other behaviors are also active-destructive. I mean his revenge-seeking viciousness in hitting and spitting on other children. It is positive that he hasn't given up yet. But he is disturbing others, so we need to do something about it.

TEACHER: Such as?

COUNSELOR: Well, what have you tried so far?

TEACHER: I've told him 20 times to stop, but he only does, when he does, for awhile. Then I sometimes switch the lights on and off. This stops the others, but not him. I've put him out in the hall, too. (pause) I guess that's about it.

COUNSELOR: Well, you certainly have done quite a bit. He is a tough child. It seems that we have at least two concerns here. One is to attempt to meet some of his deprivation needs for attention. For this we'll have to get in his parents and we'll all try to figure out what we can do. The second area is that of self-control. We need to attempt to motivate him to want to behave better. For this I'll have to get together with Jay so that we can figure out something which he likes (Keat, 1972). Then we can use this as a payoff for better behavior on his part.

Summary of Contact and Plans for the Future

Initially, the counselor attempted to align himself with the teacher (e.g., "He'd really bother me after awhile"). Then the counselor initiated some Dreikurian (Dreikurs, Grunwald & Pepper, 1971) consultation to explain Jay's behavior. The teacher's question about what to do was quickly reversed to explore what had already been done. This step is usually necessary in working with both teachers and parents. Finally, two main areas of concern are outlined: Jay's need for attention and lack of self-control.

The next step was to meet with the child and then his parents in order to develop his "reinforcement menu" (Keat, 1972). An individual contact was made with Jay, and then a conference was held with the parents.

The helping strategies focused on the two areas of concern. The teacher was to pay attention to Jay when he was engaged in appropriate behaviors and use one of the four behavior modification strategies outlined in this chapter when he behaved inappropriately. In addition, the encouragement process was discussed (Dreikurs & Soltz, 1964). With the parents, the importance of time spent with the child (both quantity and quality) was emphasized. Second, classroom target behaviors were delineated (e.g., Jay must sit in his seat appropriately unless given permission to get up) and rewards were established (praise for appropriate behavior and a record of his points on a behavior report card—a 3x5 card that he kept). These points could be traded in for special such privileges as being first in line for lunch (3 points) and extra recess time (5 points). An attempt was made to coordinate in-school behavior with rewards at home. The parents were giving him an allowance of several dollars a week. Under this program the money reward was made contingent upon appropriate behavior in school; such behaviors were rewarded with stars on a chart kept on the refrigerator at home. At the end of the week, the stars were added up (i.e., 1 star = $.25) and Jay was given his allowance. Follow-up after several weeks revealed fewer attention-getting behaviors in the classroom and better self-control.

--- **Summary**

This chapter has focused on the collaboration-consultation function of the elementary school counselor. The collaborative relationship is of the utmost importance. It is important that the elementary counselor develop expertise in the area of child development, so that he can focus on children's developmental needs and convey his understanding to significant others in the child's life environment. Contingency management in the classroom was discussed. After the delineation of the four basic procedures of behavior modification (selecting a behavior change-target, keeping records, changing the consequences of behavior, and making behavioral changes), a behavior modification program was outlined and some explicit applications of learning theory approaches were discussed. Inservice education was discussed as an important way of influencing the education of all children and thus of enacting the developmental approach to elementary school counseling. The five components of staff case conferences—consultation requests, assessment of the problem, the case conference, implementation of recommendations, and follow-up—were outlined, and the collaboration-consultation process was illustrated with a dialogue between a counselor and teacher.

--- **References**

Ackerman, J. M. *Operant conditioning techniques for the classroom teacher*. Glenview, Ill.: Scott, Foresman, 1972.

Almy, M. *Child development*. New York: Holt, 1955.

Amidon, E. J., & Flanders, N. A. *The role of the teacher in the classroom*. Minneapolis: Association for Productive Teaching, 1967.

Axelrod, S. Token reinforcement programs in special classes. In M. B. Harris (Ed.), *Classroom uses of behavior modification*. Columbus, Ohio: Charles E. Merrill, 1972, pp. 245–259.

Becker, W. C., Madsen, C. H., Arnold, C., & Thomas, D. R. The contingent use of teacher attention and praise in reducing classroom behavior problems. *Journal of Special Education*, 1967, 1, 287–307.

Buckley, N. K., & Walker, H. M. *Modifying classroom behavior.* Champaign, Ill.: Research Press, 1970.

Caplan, G. *The theory and practice of mental health consultation.* New York: Basic Books, 1970.

Center for Studies of Child and Family Mental Health. Behavior modification. *Today's Education,* 1972, **61,** 54–55.

Dinkmeyer, D. (Ed.) *Guidance and counseling in the elementary school.* New York: Holt, Rinehart & Winston, 1968.

Dinkmeyer, D., & Caldwell, E. *Developmental counseling and guidance: A comprehensive school approach.* New York: McGraw-Hill, 1970.

Dinkmeyer, D., & Muro, J. *Group counseling theory and practice.* Itasca, Ill.: F. E. Peacock, 1971.

Dodson, F. *How to parent.* New York: Signet, 1971.

Dreikurs, D., & Soltz, V. *Children: the challenge.* New York: Hawthorn Books, 1964.

Dreikurs, R., Grunwald, B., & Pepper, F. *Maintaining sanity in the classroom: Illustrated teaching techniques.* New York: Harper & Row, 1971.

Elkind, D., Erik Erikson's eight ages of man. *New York Times Magazine,* 5 April 1970, 25–119.

Engel, M. *Psychopathology in childhood: social, diagnostic and therapeutic aspects.* New York: Harcourt Brace Jovanovich, 1972.

Erikson, E. H. *Childhood and society.* New York: Morton, 1963.

Erikson, E. H. Identity and the life cycle. *Psychological Issues,* 1959, monograph 1.

Faust, V. *The counselor-consultant in the elementary school.* Boston: Houghton Mifflin, 1968.

Fraiberg, S. *The magic years.* New York: Charles Scribner's Sons, 1959.

Fullmer, D., & Bernard, H. *The school counselor-consultant.* Boston: Houghton Mifflin, 1972.

Gesell, A., & Ilg, F. *The child from five to ten.* New York: Harper & Row, 1946.

Glasser, W. *Reality therapy.* New York: Harper & Row, 1965.

Glasser, W. *Schools without failure.* New York: Harper & Row, 1969.

Guerney, B. G. Filial therapy: Description and rationale. *Journal of Consulting Psychology,* 1964, **28,** 304–310.

Hagens, L. M. Case analysis: Consultation and counseling. *Elementary School Guidance and Counseling,* 1971, 6, 112–115.

Hagens, L. M. Case analysis: Consultation and counseling. *Elementary School Guidance and Counseling,* 1972, 6, 190–194.

Hagens, L. M. Case analysis: The case of Mrs. Cook. *Elementary School Guidance and Counseling,* 1973, 7, 300–304.

Hansen, J. C., & Stevic, R. R. *Elementary school guidance.* New York: Macmillan, 1969.

Harris, B. M., Bessent, W., & McIntyre, K. E. *In-service education.* Englewood Cliffs, N.J.: Prentice-Hall, 1969.

Harris, M. B. (Ed.) *Classroom uses of behavior modification*. Columbus, Ohio: Charles E. Merrill, 1972.

Hill, G. E., & Luckey, E. B. *Guidance for children in elementary schools*. New York: Appleton-Century-Crofts, 1969.

Homme, L., Csanyi, A., Gonzales, M., Rechs, J. *How to use contingency contracting in the classroom*. Champaign, Ill.: Research Press, 1970.

Ilg, F. L., & Ames, L. B. *School readiness*. New York: Harper & Row, 1964.

Jersild, A. *Child psychology*, 5th ed. Englewood Cliffs, N.J. Prentice-Hall, 1960.

Keat, D. B. *Cooperation-aggression behavior scale*. University Park, Penn.: Author, 1970.

Keat, D. B. A reinforcement survey schedule for children. University Park, Penn.: Author, 1972.

Keat, D. B. A behavior modification program for pre-school children: Snags, pitfalls and some behavioral changes. Unpublished manuscript, Pennsylvania State University, 1973.

Kessler, J. *Psychopathology of childhood*. Englewood Cliffs, N.J.: Prentice-Hall, 1966.

Krumboltz, J. D., & Thoreson, C. E. *Behavioral counseling: Cases and techniques*. New York: Holt, Rinehart & Winston, 1969.

Kubany, E. S., Weiss, L. E., & Sloggett, B. B. The good behavior clock: A reinforcement time-out procedure for reducing disruptive classroom behavior. *Journal of Behavior Therapy and Experimental Psychiatry*, 1971, **2**, 173–179.

Madsen, C. K., & Madsen, C. H. *Parents/Children/Discipline*. Boston: Allyn & Bacon, 1972.

Mayer, G. R. Behavioral consulting: Using behavior modification procedures in the consulting relationship. *Elementary School Guidance and Counseling*, 1972, 7, 114–119.

McGehearty, L. Case analysis: Consultation and counseling. *Elementary School Guidance and Counseling*, 1969, **3**, 289–293.

McGehearty, L., & Webb, D. Case analysis: Consultation and counseling. *Elementary School Guidance and Counseling*, 1970, **4**, 245–252.

Muro, J. J. *The counselor's work in the elementary school*. Scranton, Penn.: International Textbook Company, 1970.

Neisworth, J., Deno, S., & Jenkins, J. *Student motivation and classroom management: A behavioristic approach*. Lemont, Penn.: Behavior Technics, 1969.

Neisworth, J., & Smith, R. *Modifying retarded behavior*. Boston: Houghton Mifflin, 1973.

Newman, R. G. (Ed.) Psychological consultation in the schools. New York: Basic Books, 1967.

O'Leary, K. D., & Becker, W. C. Behavior modification of an adjustment class; A token reinforcement program. *Exceptional Children*, 1967, **33**, 637–642.

Orlando, C. A problem or opportunity for change? *Pennsylvania Education*, 1972, **3**, 15–16.

Peterson, T. L., & Sanborn, M. P. Counselor conducted in-service training sessions for teachers. *Journal of Counseling Psychology*, 1972, **19**, 156–160.

Skinner, B. F. *Beyond freedom and dignity.* New York: Alfred A. Knopf, 1971.

Skinner, B. F. *Walden Two.* New York: Macmillan, 1948.

Smith, L. *The children's doctor.* Englewood Cliffs, N.J.: Prentice-Hall, 1969.

Spock, B. *Decent and indecent.* New York: Fawcett World Library, 1971.

Spock, B. *Baby and child care.* New York: Pocket Books, 1968.

Stone, L. J., & Church, J. *Childhood and adolescence.* New York: Random House, 1968.

Sulzer, B., & Mayer, G. R. *Behavior modification procedures for school personnel.* Hinsdale, Ill.: Dryden Press, 1972.

Thoresen, C. *Behavioral humanism.* Research and Development Memorandum No. 88. Stanford, Cal.: Stanford Center for Research and Development in Teaching, 1972.

Ullmann, L. P., & Krasner, L. *Case studies in behavior modification.* New York: Holt, Rinehart & Winston, 1965.

Ulrich, R., Stachnik, T., & Mabry, J. Control of human behavior, vols. 1 and 2. Glenview, Ill.: Scott, Foresman, 1966, 1970.

VanHoose, W., Peters, M., & Leonard, G. *The elementary school counselor.* Detroit: Wayne State University Press, 1970.

Vernon, W. M. *Motivating Children: Behavior modification in the classroom.* New York: Holt, Rinehart & Winston, 1972.

Wherry, J. S., & Quay, H. C. Observing the classroom behavior of elementary school children. *Exceptional Children*, 1969, **35**, 461–470.

7

One of the major functions of the elementary school counselor is to work cooperatively with other members of the school staff to plan and implement a curriculum that allows the child to grow in cognitive knowledge as well as in the personal values and affective skills that contribute to maturity. It has been stated that "curriculum development is, in reality, probably the counselor's major focus, inasmuch as it is the total curriculum world of the child that the counselor works to influence" (Faust, 1968, p. 63). Zudick asserts that "current conceptualizations of guidance cast it as being inseparable from instruction." The same author also says that we should "appreciate guidance as an intimate corollary of instruction in the educational process (Zudick, 1971, p. 57). Knapp (1959) has stated that

> The curriculum provides the experiences that the child needs: guidance functions to help the pupil succeed in those experiences. Guidance and teaching, which puts the curriculum into operation, cannot be separated. They are part of the same process; both are necessary to the fulfillment of the objectives of elementary education which are the development of self-sufficient, cooperative, and sharing members of our society. Guidance and curriculum must be fully integrated and recognized as being of equal importance in effective education (p. 179).

Keat, Logan, McDuffy, Malecki and Selkowitz (1973) have proposed that an affective curriculum is necessary for the actualization of twenty-first century man. The federal government has also manifested an interest in today's children, who will be the leaders and decision makers of tomorrow. The report to the White House Conference on Children says:

> We ask first, then, not what kind of education we want to pro-

Curriculum Development:
Focus on the Affective Domain

vide but what kind of human being we want to emerge. What would we have twenty-first century man be? We would have him be a man with a strong sense of himself and his own humanness, with awareness of his thoughts and feelings, with the capacity to feel and express love and joy and to recognize tragedy and feel grief. We would have him be a man who, with a strong realistic sense of his own worth, is able to relate openly with others, to cooperate effectively with them toward common ends, and to view mankind as one while respecting diversity and differences. We would want him to be a being who, even while very young, somehow senses that he has it within himself to become more than he now is, that he has a capacity for lifelong spiritual and intellectual growth. We would want him to cherish that vision of the man he is capable of becoming and to cherish the development of the same potentiality in others (1970, p. 75).

Curriculum Theory

Curriculum: What Is It?

In order to understand curriculum theory, it is necessary to define curriculum. Shane, Shane, Gibson, and Munger have attempted to synthesize the various definitions of curriculum in the following statement:

> The curriculum is a written document (a necessity if it is to be consulted, planned, or revised) . . . suggesting the educational experiences of students (it is meaningless without significant content) and often proposing aims, materials, and procedures (lest each teacher, without references to what his colleagues are doing and at incongruous effort, be obliged to determine and select them for himself).

In some form the curriculum indicates a faculty consensus as to the breadth and often the general sequence of what is to be learned (to diminish overlapping and the problem of professional anarchy) . . . and it includes, directly or indirectly, ventures that instruct the learner in those values of his culture which schooling can communicate (since the curriculum is inevitably shaped by the cultural values of the adults who support it).

The success of a particular curriculum design is determined by the nature of changes in the behavior desired of the learner (hence, the teachers' and counselors' evaluative functions, as they gauge the intellectual, social, and psychological changes in children, and the effectiveness of the curriculum)" (Shane, Shane, Gibson, and Munger, 1971, pp. 128–129).

Chasnoff (1964) defines curriculum more generally as the pupils' cognitive, affective, and social experiences. This definition encompasses just about everything that happens to the child at school. In support of this definition, Dinkmeyer and Caldwell define curriculum as "primarily concerned with all of the learning experiences of the child under the direction of the school" (1970, p. 75). "Guidance and good teaching are not identical, but they are interdependent" (Dinkmeyer and Owens, 1969).

This trend to broaden curricular offerings by including the whole life of the child in the program of the school is in congruence with the theory of the author. Ragan's (1966, p. 5) comments on this broad concept of the curriculum are noteworthy:

1. The curriculum exists only in the experience of children; it does not exist in textbooks, in the courses of study, or in the plans and intentions of teachers.

2. The curriculum includes more than content to be learned. . . . The human relations in the classroom, the methods of teaching, and the evaluation procedures used are as much a part of the curriculum as the content to be learned.

3. The school curriculum is an enterprise in guided living. Instead of being as broad as life itself, the school curriculum represents a special environment which has been systematized, edited, and simplified for a special purpose.

4. The curriculum is a specialized learning environment deliberately arranged for directing the interests and abilities of children toward effective participation in the life of the community and nation. It is concerned with helping children to enrich their own lives and to contribute to the improvement of society through the acquisition of useful information, skills, and attitudes.

Confluent Education

Brown (1971a) defines confluent education as "the integration or flowing together of the affective and cognitive elements in individual and group learning—sometimes called humanistic or psychological education" (Brown, 1971a, p. 3).

"Affective" refers to the feeling or emotional aspect of experience and learning. How a child or adult feels about wanting to learn, how he feels as he learns, and what he feels after he has learned are included in the affective domain. "Cognitive" refers to the activity of the mind in knowing an object, to intellectual functioning. What an individual learns and the intellectual process of learning it would fall within the cognitive domain (Brown, 1971a, p. 4).

To these two domains, many educators add the psychomotor domain (Krathwohl, Bloom & Masia, 1964). This area has to do with the development of motor skills. Psychomotor activities are divided into two areas, the fine perceptual-motor coordination required for handwriting, and the gross motor coordination used in physical education.

Brown says that "If we add an emotional dimension to learning, the learner will become personally involved and, as a consequence, there will be a change in the learner's behavior" (1971b, p. 10). Krathwohl and others state that:

> The affective domain contains the forces that determine the nature of an individual's life and ultimately the life of an entire people. To keep the "box" (Pandora's) closed is to deny the existence of the powerful motivational forces that shape the life of each of us. To look the other way is to avoid coming to terms with the real (Krathwohl *et al.*, 1964, p. 91).

Can the Affective Curriculum Be Taught?

Although many educators would recognize the importance of affective objectives in the school setting, not very many would accept their fulfillment through a planned program in which affective factors are as much a part of the content as cognitive factors. Williams (1969) supports affect as content by commenting that "recognizing and meeting the intellectual as well as emotional needs of children, leading towards uncovering their creative potential, have become respectable goals or purposes of education" (Williams, 1969, p. 7). After reviewing research on affective content, Krathwohl and others (1964) concluded that the evidence suggests that desirable affective behaviors develop when appropriate learning experiences are provided for students in much the same way as cognitive behaviors result from appropriate learning experiences. Weinstein and Fantini (1970) also concluded from their efforts that pupils' concerns can be legitimate content in their own right. Finally, a recent empirical study measuring the effects of affective activities on the behavior and attitudes of the participating students revealed that "giving deliberate attention to social and emotional development in the classroom can have an important positive effect on students" (Stanford, 1972, p. 591).

If one concludes that affective material can be content in itself, one must ask what is necessary to establish it as an aspect of a functioning and effective curriculum. Krathwohl *et al.* (1964) provide the following guidelines. First, affective objectives can only be achieved by the schools if their attainment is regarded as sufficiently important by teachers and administrators. Second, if affective objectives are to be achieved with the students, learning experiences must be of a two-way nature in which the students and the teacher interact, rather than expecting one to present material to be "learned" by the other. Third, if affective objectives are to be realized, they must be clearly defined. Fourth, learning experiences to help the student develop in the desired direction must be systematically provided. And fifth, there must be some organized method for appraising the extent to which the students grow in the desired ways.

Jones (1968) has stated a fundamental rule of relevance here. This rule states that the "cultivation of emotional issues in classrooms, whether by design or in response to the unpredictable, should be means to the ends of instructing the children in the subject matter" (Jones, 1968, p. 160). In discussing the progress of emotional growth, Jones (1968) draws heavily on Erikson's theory (covered in Chapter Six) to provide a theoretical framework for considering emotional growth. In the process he modifies Erikson's epigenetic chart and adds the concepts of imagery and fantasy. He views Erikson's conception as relevant to coordinating developmental and curricular issues, cognitive skills with emotional and imaginal ones, and classroom management with instruction. Herr states that "it can be concluded that they [elementary school children] learn about such phenomena [information about work, occupational differences, personal preferences] in ways similar to the concept learning that transpires in other affective and cognitive domains" (p. 209). Herr also cites research (Tiedeman and O'Hara, 1963) that verifies the psychological crises defined by Erikson (1963). In addition, Herr also discusses some support for Piaget's ego centrism theory (Gunn, 1964).

Affective curricula are being developed by local school districts and universities throughout the country. For example, "Project Insight" of the Cleveland, Ohio public schools has been initiated for the purpose of getting children to know and talk about themselves and their relationships to other persons (Enterline, 1970).

Through Ford Foundation grants, the University of California at Santa Barbara has established the Laboratory for Confluent Education (Brown, 1971a). The purpose of the California center is to modify conventional curricula by incorporating affective elements. The University of Massachusetts at Amherst has established a Center for Humanistic Education, where entirely new curricula are being developed to engage students' feelings and attitudes in the learning process (Emotional Emphasis in Education, 1971; Ivey & Alschuler, 1973). The elementary school teaching project (Weinstein and Fantini, 1970) has produced a model for developing affective curricula, while the Human Relations Education Project organized by several western New York school districts is seeking to improve human relations teaching through curriculum adaptation. Finally, the Philadelphia school district is attempting to give districtwide emphasis to affective education in its Affective Development Program (Stanford, 1972).

These affective curriculum projects represent an approach to the problem of content relevance. They are intended to redress an imbalance in our school system by addressing a vital area (i.e., the affective) that the traditional educational system has largely ignored. In the process of integrating the cognitive and affective domains, the goals of these two areas can at times be achieved simultaneously. In view of the need for a systematic approach to affective education, most of the rest of this chapter is presented as a means of implementing emotional education in the schools.

The intermingling of the cognitive and affective areas must be stressed because of the important relationship between school success and the development of a positive self-concept. What follows is not meant to deprecate the importance of the acquisition of skills in such areas as language arts and arithmetic, but to attempt to achieve a balance between the domains.

Content and Materials

Much of what is presented here involves the implementation of a tailor-made curriculum so that the teacher can personalize classroom offerings for his students. There are some excellent materials available commercially for this purpose (e.g., Dinkmeyer, 1970; Limbacher, 1969; Bessell & Palomares, 1970), some of which were used to develop the program described in the final section of this chapter. The materials described in this section can be purchased and used with a minimal financial expenditure. Many of these are described in the volume by Keat *et al.* (1972). The following brief descriptions of materials for flexible and personalistic use are organized into seven broad areas (Keat *et al.*, 1972).

A Guide to Affective Curriculum Materials

1. *Literature*   Literature is perhaps the broadest and most far-reaching of the language arts. Reading is an activity that goes on both at home and in school. Recommended books, within this volume, listed with their grade levels, publishers, and authors, are categorized along the following abridged alphabetical lines: accepting self and understanding others, adoption, bedtime, boy-girl relationships, child-adult relationships, cooperation, fear of darkness, death, etiquette, family relationships, fantasy, forgiving others, foster parents, generosity, helping others, initiative, jealousy, knowledge acquisition, leadership, maturing, neatness, obedience, personal adjustment (school, teasing), responsibility, sex education, twins, and the world of work.

For example, in most classrooms there is a tendency for children to be unable to admit their faults. That is, they want to maintain an idealized image of selves who have no failings. If this is the situation, the teacher might introduce a story by Hall (1960) appropriate for grades 3 to 5. After reading this story, the children can discuss the content and be encouraged to express and admit to their own human failings. On a similar theme, a story called "The Hundred-Dollar Lie" (Gardner, 1972) illustrates how a child can be pushed into lying and how the teacher can help with a solution. As other children were telling stories about the fun they had had during the summer, a child who had only watched television made up a story about winning $100 betting in Las Vegas. He later wasted a lot of emotional energy trying to defend his lie. The teacher helped by assigning a class composition on "How I learned from something I did wrong." The child learned the two lessons that when you lie you are afraid people will find out and that you also feel bad about yourself.

2. *Arts and Crafts*   Properly used, arts and crafts can aid the child in the development of an adequate self concept, the acquisition of gross and fine motor skills, and the enhancement of his sense of creativity. The child can gain a sense of cooperation by working with peers in a group atmosphere. Arts and crafts are not only applicable in the school setting but also generalize to activities outside the school. Because they promote peer acceptance, children often feel better about themselves. This section of the guide contains references to books, journal articles, and pamphlets that can be used by teachers, parents, and counselors. For example, if the teacher desires to introduce puppetry he can refer to Scott and May's book (1971). Once skill is gained in making

puppets, they may be used therapeutically by the children (Wolt-mann, 1964; 1972).

3. *Games and Physical Activities* "Carefully planned and su-pervised games and activities can be good sources of affective ex-periences for children in the classroom, on the playground, or even in the home. They can easily be integrated into the child's daily educational routine" (Keat *et al.*, 1972, p. 31) and are a part of most educational systems. For some children this is the most positive part of their daily experiences. This section of the guide is prefaced by developmental descriptions (by grade) of elementary school children's characteristics, achievements, atti-tudes, rhythm skills, and game skills. The bulk of the section is devoted to an annotated listing of 65 games. For each game there is listed its purpose, necessary equipment, number of children, the appropriate grade level, and procedure. For example, the game "Who Is It?" has the dual purposes of practicing communi-cation skills in a group and learning about each other; two chairs are needed, 20–40 can play, and it is appropriate for grades 1 to 4. The procedures are explained in the final paragraph under each game heading.

4. *Audiovisual Materials* The materials in this section of the guide are classified according to the eight guidance learnings de-lineated by Hill and Luckey (1969): understanding of self, re-sponsibility for self, understanding education and work, ability to make decisions, solving one's problems, understanding human be-havior, adjusting to life's demands, and maturing in sense of values and high ideals. The actual materials include films, film strips, film loops, transparencies, and audio tapes. Sources for the materials are given. Although the primary emphasis is on materi-als for children's use, there is also a section on audiovisual ma-terials for use with counselors, teachers, and parents.

5. *Dramatics and Music* The "affective curriculum in the schools can be enhanced through the media of drama, music, role-playing, puppetry, sociodrama, and psychodrama" (Keat *et al.*, 1972, p. 101). This section of the guide lists resource and idea materials to be used by teachers and counselors in order to become familiar with the various forms of affective expression. Within each of the sections, relevant materials are listed in an alphabetical order by author. In particular, Bettie McComb, a creative and innovative counselor in the Nova elementary school

in Fort Lauderdale, Florida, has developed learning activity packages (LAPS) for use in group guidance. For example, the Friends LAP (McComb, 1969) was written to meet the developmental needs of 10-, 11-, and 12-year-olds in the area of social interaction. The sessions focus on different kinds of activities: e.g., role-playing, group counseling and discussion, games and creative activities. The Friends LAP is divided into seven sessions. The first meeting is devoted to a game called "Checkerboard Friends" (to get acquainted with other children in the group), the second to a group discussion of "what I like about my friends," the third to role-playing based on a short story, the fourth to a game called "the friendly maze," the fifth to group counseling focusing on "how I feel when someone is unfriendly to me and what can I do about it," the sixth to collages, and the seventh to evaluation of the projects, involving writing positive comments about children in the group and listing three ways that have been learned to show friendliness.

McComb has developed several other LAPS, for use in an open classroom school including a timely one on drug use prevention (McComb, 1971).

In the area of music there are numerous books. Fred Rogers (1970) ties in a Freudian influence with his song writing. Some of his songs deal with such topics as identification ("I'd like to be like mom," "I'd like to be like dad"), the Oedipal situation ("I'm going to marry mom"), castration anxiety ("everybody's fancy"), and sibling rivalry ("when a baby comes"). These materials are also available on records and in a songbook for piano or guitar (Rogers, 1970).

6. *Multi-ethnic Curriculum Materials*   This section of the guide lists children's literature and audiovisual media. The largest portion presents children's literature categorized under the rubrics of 32 affective growth understandings (e.g., encouraging sensitivity to the needs of others). The literature section is divided into three ethnic subdivisions: Negro, Puerto Rican, and American Indian. The audiovisual media listing includes books with accompanying records, sound filmstrips, records with accompanying filmstrips, and teacher's guides. These materials are intended to make children in a multiracial society capable of understanding, appreciating, and accepting cultural diversity and various ethnic backgrounds.

7. *Additional Resource Materials*   This section of the guide lists materials that can be used to supplement the guide. Books and

commercial kits are grouped according to topics. The entries include annotated books in human relations, music, and poetry. In addition, books on sex education for parents are listed.

_____ **Procedures and Process**

The counselor plays the major role in implementing the coordination of the affective and cognitive curricula. Yawkey and Aronin (1972) discuss ways in which the counselor can help to integrate language experience and self-awareness into the curriculum. Although the variety of grouping plans in effect in schools today—self-contained, homogeneous team teaching, or nongraded (continuous progress)—influence the applicability of these kinds of approaches, they can be utilized in any situation with some adjustments (Hansen and Stevic, 1969).

Teacher Training for Classroom Guidance

One of the primary methods of implementing an affective curriculum in the classroom is by staging a somewhat structured classroom meeting such as is described in Chapter Five. In this approach a structure is provided by the story, role-playing, or other activity around which the teacher organizes the situation. This provides a stimulus to which the children can respond and focuses the discussion in an open atmosphere.

Of course, teachers need to be prepared to introduce new materials by means of inservice training. It would typically require a half day (see Table 7-1 on p. 198) to introduce the theory of the approach and to sell the teachers on the idea of integrating affective materials with the cognitive ones they ordinarily use in language arts and social studies. In addition, some teachers have applied problem-solving and decision-making skills to mathematical concepts. After the half day devoted to explaining theory and winning cooperation, the counselor is ready to introduce the teachers to the actual content materials. The use of these materials can best be illustrated by having the counselor demonstrate a lesson with some children. Another half day of inservice training should be arranged for the teachers themselves to try out the materials in a demonstration practice session for the counselor(s) and other trainers to observe. Training can be concluded with some practice in classroom process techniques. Finally, there should be an extended period of continuous consultation with the teachers as they integrate the new materials into their curricula. The final section of this chapter is a detailed description of such a program.

Faust (1968) advocates the use of "feelings classes" in the schools. He suggests that all the members of such classes bring pictures from magazines and newspapers that illustrate such emotions as happiness, anger, fear, loneliness, and the like. Other suggested activities are to draw one's own picture and to write stories about personal feelings. During these activities the teacher can use "timely teaching"—that is, can interrupt an activity to examine feelings, ideas, and interpersonal relationships at the moment they are occurring. The four objectives Faust (1968, p. 70) lists for "feelings classes" are:

1. To make the children aware that feelings exist.

2. To make the children aware that almost all people possess, at times, all kinds of feelings.

3. To make the children aware that feelings are not bad, naughty, or immoral.

4. To introduce socially approved ways of expressing feelings that, in general, are unacceptable to society. This involves such sublimation activities as pounding nails into wood to release pent-up anger and the "hostile pillow" (i.e., "a pillow on which children express all kinds of feelings—most often those of anger," Faust, 1968, p. 67), and cathartic activity termed "directed muscular activity" by Lazarus (1971). These types of activities can make the feelings (emotions) of the child an inseparable part of the learning situation.

The Emotional Resource Center

An emotional resource center is a special room in the school containing affective materials, set aside for children to use to deal with their feelings. In a conducive social climate, a variety of media can be made available for this purpose. The materials can include the books, movies, and other resources discussed in *Helping Children to Feel*, a guide to affective materials (Keat *et al.*, 1972). Such equipment as a tape recorder for playing and listening (e.g., relaxation tapes, Lazarus, 1970), film loops and audiovisual materials, and record players for listening to relevant kinds of things (e.g., appropriate music). The school counselor or a counseling aide could coordinate these materials and be available to help direct children's activities in an appropriate fashion.

If such a room or center is not available (which may be the situation in most schools), teachers can arrange centers in their classrooms (Hewett, 1968). Although Hewett suggests several centers focusing on order, mastery, and exploration and are primarily academic in orientation, a teacher could also organize an emotional learning center in the classroom. Specialized emotional centers might be (1) an area for speaking and releasing feelings (with tape recorders available for children to vent feelings into), (2) a see-and-hear center for guidance filmstrips, and (3) a manipulative area for special projects (e.g., crafts). Visits to these centers should be conceived of as rewards for a child who has completed his other tasks.

A Program in Action

The purpose of this final section is to describe a program the author uses in one school district to train teachers in the use of content materials and process techniques. Although the program is limited to two days by external constraints a longer initial training period would be ideal. If it is more practical, one may wish to schedule the training for four half-days (e.g., 3–5:30 P.M. after school). The time segments suggested (see Table 7–1) are those the author uses when teachers are freed from classroom commitments by substitutes or aides.

Day One

The first half of day one is spent as follows: The first hour is devoted to an open meeting of the group (the number of members has varied from 9 to 24). This initial hour has three purposes (see Table 7–1). The first goal is to get acquainted with the group. To initiate talk, the group conductor can share some facts about himself (e.g., "I'm from the university and have been working in the schools and with children in some professional capacity for about 12 years now") and some feelings ("I'm feeling a bit tense about how you will react to these materials today. I mean, whether or not you will like them and get involved with them in your classes"). It is hoped that the teachers will imitate this model and talk about themselves and their feelings. Factual information is usually forthcoming (e.g., "I'm Jane Smith, I've been teaching for five years and right now I'm working with a third-grade class") but personal feelings other than physical ones ("I'm sleepy, I'm hungry, it's hard to sit in these low seats") are often not initially shared with the group. It is important to note this difficulty and to confront the group with it because expressing feelings is the very thing the teachers are to encourage children to do. Almost everyone needs to develop a feeling vocabulary to be comfortable labeling and expressing emotions. Some teachers have found it useful for the class to identify feeling words and post them in the room so that everyone can become more familiar with them.

Table 7–1   *A Two-day Program in Action*

	HOURS	EVENTS
DAY ONE	9–10 a.m.	Open Meeting with Teachers getting acquainted outlining program personal concerns
	10–11 a.m.	Didactic Input confluent education guidance learnings character education
	11–12 a.m.	The Materials hands-on exposure and explanation
	1–1:30 p.m.	The Lesson familiarity with lesson
	1:30–2:15 p.m.	Presentation demonstration
	2:15–3 p.m.	Discussion of Lesson plans for the next session
DAY TWO	9–9:30 a.m.	General Questions Room preparation
	9:30–12 a.m.	Individual One-Half Hour Practice Sessions Presented by Teachers
	1–2 p.m.	Appraisal of Guidance Learnings analysis of measuring instrument item by item
	2–3 p.m.	Classroom Process reflective listening handouts and practice exercises guidelines for classroom group discussions decision-making meetings problem-solving sessions

The second purpose of the first hour is to outline the two-day program. It can help to dispel some of the teachers' concern if they know what is going to happen. Of course, knowing they have to perform for the group the second day can also increase their tensions. Most of these anxieties can be resolved. In training ten groups involving hundreds of teachers, the attrition rate on the second day has been only two: one had a jury duty commitment and the other was ill.

The third objective of the first hour is to deal with questions or concerns about the program. These inquiries usually have to do with such things as the availability of materials, the amount of additional time this program will involve, number of classroom meetings per week, and so on. It is important to deal with these concerns early in order to "clear the air" for what is to follow.

The second hour is usually devoted to three major activities. The first is a presentation on "confluent education." This talk focuses on the terms "cognitive" and "affective" and emphasizes the integration of the two. For illustrative purposes, a table developed by Brown (Brown, 1971a, p. 4; or 1971b, Table 1) is reproduced on the board and discussed with the group. The content of this table has to do with Columbus's discovery of America (e.g., straight cognitive: Columbus visited the New World in 1492; straight affective: What have I discovered about myself?) Personal illustrations can be developed by the counselor. For example, the author usually adapts a brief story from the Stanford-Binet test ("The Wet Fall," Terman & Merrill, 1960), which is followed by cognitive intelligence test questions (e.g., What is the name of the story? What did the pony do?). Instead of asking cognitive questions that tap rote memory, one should try to elicit affective thoughts by questions such as "How did Dick feel when the pony ran away with him on it? How did he feel as he got out of the ditch into which he had fallen?" With regard to confluent education, the counselor reviewed existing curricular materials and identified areas that would lend themselves to both cognitive and affective learnings, prior to meeting with the teachers. By thus helping the teachers to see that it is not entirely foreign to them, and encouraging them to offer their own ideas about eliciting expressions of emotion, the teachers are more likely to be won over to the cause of affective education.

The second third of the second hour is devoted to presentation of "guidance learnings" in a form similar to that of Chapter One. To reiterate, these learnings have to do with understanding and accepting oneself (developing a positive self concept), becoming aware of and understanding feelings (appropriate labeling and expression of emotions), understanding human behavior (emotional maturity), developing responsibility for oneself, participating positively in social groups, understanding choices and practicing problem solving, learning coping skills, and developing a sense of values and ideals.

The final third of the second hour is spent in discussing the final guidance learning, moral and value-oriented education. This subject is introduced by showing a filmstrip entitled "First Things: A Strategy for Teaching Values," distributed by Guidance Associates of Pleasantville, N.Y. The filmstrip (and accompanying record) includes theoretical background and a model lesson called Debbie's Dilemma ("The Trouble With Truth"). Six distinct stages or orientations of moral thinking are identified: punishment and obedience (conformity to what the child thinks adults want); instrumental relativism (equal exchange); interpersonal concordance, or "good boy-nice girl" (empathy for the feelings of others); "law and order" (responsibility to society); social-contract legalism; and the universal ethical principle ("personal conscience"). Discussion of these stages follows the film. The group conductor's knowledge about moral development can be enhanced by reading Kohlberg and Whitten (1972). For more information on the values clarification approach, see Raths, Harin and Simon (1966), Simon, Howe and Kirschenbaum (1972) and Goodman, Simon and Witort (1973).

The final hour of the first half day is spent becoming familiar with materials. After a general orientation about "personalizing" the materials for one's own classroom through the use of a guide (Keat *et al.*, 1972), the teachers are given some concrete materials. For example, the primary teachers become familiar with a program like DUSO (Dinkmeyer, 1970), and the intermediate teachers peruse materials from *Dimensions of Personality* (Limbacher, 1969), which provides a different book for each grade (i.e., grade 4, "Here I Am"; grade 5, "I'm Not Alone"; grade 6, "Becoming Myself"). It is advisable to train primary and intermediate teachers in separate groups at different times. If this is not possible, then co-conductors should be engaged to deal with different materials with different grade levels.

The second half day begins with the arrangement of the physical environment in a suitable fashion. If the primary group has more than 6 to 8 members, it is advisable to divide into two groups for the demonstration. For the intermediate teachers, there should be separate demonstrations for each grade level. These smaller groups can be conducted by other counselors in the district, counseling interns, teachers experienced with these materials, or administrators from the district. The main purpose of presenting the lesson to a class or smaller group of children (the author usually uses 6 to 9 children) is to provide the teachers a model of one way to use the materials. The post-demonstration discussion deals with the materials and methods used. The final portion of the second half day is spent making arrangements for the next meeting. It is necessary to arrange for rooms (the library, an all-purpose room, or a boiler room is usually free) and to schedule entire classes or selected children for the teacher practice sessions.

The second day starts with a general question period and anxiety alleviation session. Then the rooms and materials are prepared. The teacher presentations usually take 20 to 25 minutes. This leaves 5 to 10 minutes for discussion of the lesson. By running two groups simultaneously in different rooms, ten teachers could present and discuss their lessons during the designated time block (9:30–12 A.M.).

The second half of the second day begins with an explanation of the importance of measuring affective learning despite the inherent difficulties (Keat, 1973). The Guidance Learning Rating Scale (see Appendix F) is gone over item by item. During this time the author attempts to lead the teachers toward a common understanding of each item on the scale.

The final portion of the last teacher meeting is devoted to classroom process. Although day(s) could be devoted to this subject, time dictates limitations. Therefore, the following four types of materials are meant to serve as an introduction to the concepts to be developed in the follow-up phase of the program. The first subject covered is reflective listening, the theory behind which was presented in Chapter Five. Selective reflective listening-responding seems to be useful for moving teachers from a content-based inquiry style to one that is more facilitative of the expression of emotions. The forms the author uses (adapted from Merriam, 1971) are included in Appendix E. The first three pages are scanned by the participants and summarized by the conductor. Then the teachers are asked to respond to Statement 1. After about 15 seconds (one doesn't have very long to formulate a reply to a child), responses are shared. Consideration is given to some of the reflective responses illustrated on the final page of the handout, and teachers can then consider modifying their responses.

The final three handouts given to the teacher group, all included in Chapter Five, are the 14 guidelines for classroom group discussions, the agenda for a decision-making meeting, and the meeting structure for a problem-solving session. The materials provide concrete suggestions for the teachers to follow in implementing classroom meetings. To illustrate, the group conductor can draw upon excerpts such as those included in Chapter Five, play tape-recorded examples, or conduct an actual session with the group in which the leader attempts to work through a decision or solve a problem (e.g., Where should we eat lunch?).

Following this training period, the collaboration with teachers should continue on a weekly basis. During these contacts one can work through initial problems, increase the teacher's facility with the materials, and process questions. The number of contacts can gradually be reduced as the teacher comes to feel more comfortable and capable with the materials. It has been the author's experience that the reactions of teacher and children are interdependent: as the children and teacher(s) get turned on to the materials, there is an increase in the amount of classroom time devoted to emotional learning.

Summary

This chapter on the affective curriculum was divided into four major sections. The first, on curriculum theory, discussed the affective curriculum and confluent education, followed by a discussion of whether a curriculum of affect could be taught. The second section had to do with materials for implementing an affective program. A guide to affective curriculum materials that help children to feel was described. Next, the procedures and processes necessary to implement these kinds of ideas in the classroom were delineated. After a model for conducting training programs for teachers was presented, the concept of "feelings classes" was described. The development of an emotional resource center, either within or outside the classroom, was outlined. The fourth section provided the reader with a detailed model for launching an affective education program.

References

Bessell, H., & Palomares, U. *Methods in human development.* San Diego, Cal.: Human Development Institute, 1970.

Brown, G. I. *Human teaching for human learning: An introduction to confluent education.* New York: Viking Press, 1971a.

————. Confluent education: Exploring the affective domain. *College Board Review,* 1971b, 80, 5–10.

Chasnoff, R. (Ed.). *Elementary curriculum: A book of readings.* New York: Pitman, 1964.

Dinkmeyer, D. *Developing understanding of self and others* (DUSO). Circle Pines, Minn.: American Guidance Service, 1970.

Dinkmeyer, D., & Caldwell, E. *Developmental counseling and guidance: A comprehensive school approach.* New York: McGraw-Hill, 1970.

Dinkmeyer, D., & Owens, K. Guidance and instruction: Complementary for the educative process. *Elementary School Guidance and Counseling,* 1969, 3, 260–268.

Emotional emphasis in education. *School and Society*, 1971, **99**, 78.

Enterline, J. S. Project insight. *Grade Teacher*, 1970, **88**, 32–36.

Erikson, E. H. *Childhood and society*. New York: Norton, 1963.

Faust, V. *The counselor-consultant in the elementary school*. Boston: Houghton Mifflin, 1968.

Gardner, R. A. *Dr. Gardner's stories about the real world*. Englewood Cliffs, N.J.: Prentice-Hall, 1972.

Goodman, J., Simon, S., & Witort, R. Tackling racism by clarifying values. *Today's Education*, 1973, **62**, 37–38.

Gunn, B. Children's conceptions of occupational prestige. *Personnel and Guidance Journal*, 1964, **42**, 558–663.

Hall, N. *The world in a city block*. New York: Viking, 1960.

Hansen, J. C., & Stevic, R. R. *Elementary school guidance*. New York: Macmillan, 1969.

Hewett, F. *The emotionally disturbed child in the classroom: A developmental strategy for educating children with maladaptive behavior*. Boston: Allyn & Bacon, 1968.

Hill, G. E., & Luckey, E. B. *Guidance for children in elementary schools*. New York: Appleton-Century-Crofts, 1969.

Ivey, A. E., & Alschuler, A. S. (Eds.). Psychological education: A prime function of the counselor. *Personnel and Guidance Journal*, 1973, **51**, 586–691.

Jones, R. M. *Fantasy and feeling in education*. New York: Harper & Row, 1968.

Keat, D. B. The appraisal of guidance learning outcomes resulting from confluent education curriculum interventions. *Elementary School Guidance and Counseling*, 1973, 8, in press.

Keat, D. M., Logan, W. L., Malecki, D., McDuffy, I., & Selkowitz, L. The making of the twenty-first century person: His need for an affective curriculum. Unpublished manuscript, Pennsylvania State University, 1973.

Keat, D. B., Anderson, S., Conklin, N., Elias, R., Faber, D., Felty, S., Gerba, J., Kochenash, J., Logan, W., Malecki, D., Martino, P., McDuffy, I., Schmerling, G., Schuh, C., & Selkowitz, L. *Helping children to feel: A guide to affective curriculum materials for the elementary school*. State College, Penn.: Counselor Education Press, 1972.

Knapp, R. H. *Guidance in the elementary school*. Boston: Allyn & Bacon, 1959.

Kohlberg, L., & Whitten, P. Understanding the hidden curriculum. *Learning*, 1972, **1**, 10–14.

Krathwohl, D. R., Bloom, B. S., & Masia, B. B. *Taxonomy of educational objectives: Affective domain*. New York: David McKay, 1964.

Lazarus, A. A. *Behavior therapy and beyond*. New York, McGraw-Hill, 1971.

Lazarus, A. A. *Daily Living: Coping with tensions and anxieties*. Chicago: Instructional Dynamics, 1970.

Limbacher, W. J. *Dimensions of Personality*. Dayton: Geo. A. Pflaum, 1969.

McComb, B. Y. *Friends: A guidance learning activity package for intermediate children*. Unpublished manuscript, Nova Elementary School, Fort Lauderdale, Florida, 1969.

————. *Drug detectives: A drug prevention LAP for intermediate students*. Unpublished manuscript, Nova Elementary School, Fort Lauderdale, Florida, 1971.

Merriam, M. L. *School manual*. Unpublished manuscript, Pennsylvania State University College of Human Development, 1971.

Ragan, W. *Modern elementary curriculum*. New York: Holt, Rinehart & Winston, 1966.

Raths, L., Harin, M., & Simon, S. *Values and Teaching*. Columbus, Ohio: Charles E. Merrill, 1966.

Rogers, F. *Misterogers' songbook*. New York: Random House, 1970.

Scott, L. B., & May, M. E. *Puppets for all grades*. Dansville, N.Y.: Instructor Publications, 1966.

Shane, J. G., Shane, H. G., Gibson, R. L., & Munger, P. F. *Guiding human development: The counselor and the teacher in the elementary school*. Belmont, Cal.: Wadsworth Publishing Company, 1971.

Simon, S., Howe, L., & Kirschenbaum, H. *Values clarification*. New York: Hart, 1972.

Stanford, G. Psychological education in the classroom. *Personnel and Guidance Journal*, 1972, 50, 585–592.

Terman, L. M., & Merrill, M. A. *Stanford-Binet Intelligence Scale: Manual for the third revision Form L-M*. Boston: Houghton Mifflin, 1960.

Tiedeman, D. V., & O'Hara, R. P. *Career development: Choice and adjustment*. New York: College Entrance Examination Board, 1963.

Weinstein, G., & Fantini, M. D. *Toward humanistic education: A curriculum of affect*. New York: Praeger, 1970.

White House Conference on Children. *Report to the President*. 1970. ERIC document No. ED 052 828.

Williams, F. E. Models for encouraging creativity in the classroom by integrating cognitive-affective behaviors. *Educational Technology*, 1969, 9, 7–13.

Woltmann, A. G. Psychological rationale of puppetry. In M. Haworth (Ed.), *Child psychotherapy*. New York: Basic Books, 1964, pp. 395–399.

Woltmann, A. G. Puppetry as a tool in child psychotherapy. *International Journal of Child Psychotherapy*, 1972, 1, 84–96.

Yawkey, T. D., & Aronin, E. L. The curriculum, the counselor, and the language experience. *Elementary School Guidance and Counseling*, 1972, 6, 263–268.

Zudick, L. *Implementing guidance in the elementary school*. Itasca, Ill.: F. E. Peacock, 1971.

8

Over the past two decades, there has been an acceleration of concern that elementary schools increase their commitment to assisting children to acquire self-knowledge, knowledge of their future educational and occupational alternatives, and the rudiments of effective choice-making behavior. This impetus is not a dramatic reversal of former elementary school foci; such matters have always been considered important in elementary school philosophy and practices. However, the typical response has been fragmented provision of information deemed pertinent to such goals. What is new is the priority being placed on career orientation and the comprehensiveness with which responses to it are pervading elementary curricula, teacher attitudes, and the role of the elementary school counselor.

The growth of career orientation in the elementary schools has many antecedents: a rising awareness that styles of choice behavior in adolescence and adulthood are presaged by the types of developmental experiences that occur in childhood; expanding knowledge about the interrelationships between personality development and what has come to be labeled "career development"; evidence that many of the materials and readers used in the elementary school portray the world of work inaccurately and abet unnecessary sex-typing of occupations; and acknowledgment that feelings of personal competence to cope with the future grow with knowledge of one's strengths, ways to modify one's weaknesses, the goals from which one might choose, and alternatives available in occupation and in education. The following sections will examine the validity of some of these positions prior to an examination of models by which counselors might facilitate career orientation in elementary school children.

Career Orientation
in the Elementary School

by Edwin L Herr
The Pennsylvania State University

Characteristics of Readers and Materials

At a very basic and perhaps negative level, several studies have examined the portrayal of work in readers and other materials to which elementary school children are typically exposed. If accuracy or comprehensiveness of coverage are valid criteria, these materials do not measure up. For example, Tennyson and Monnens (1963) reported after reviewing 54 elementary readers that the presentation of the world of work in these books (1) was limited in scope; (2) emphasized primarily professional, managerial, and service occupations; and (3) gave only minor emphasis to skilled, clerical, and sales occupations. Clyse (1959) found a similarly biased picture in basal readers. Lifton (1959–1960) and Kowitz and Kowitz (1959), among others, have deplored the fact that much of the reading material available for elementary school use ignores the existence of large numbers of jobs that do not require professional preparation, employ large numbers of workers, offer a diversity of gratifications, and are growing in demand. Stefflre (1969), in a report that supports many of the assertions of the women's rights movement, describes the vast discrepancy between the portrayal of women workers in elementary readers and present reality. Lyon (1966) has argued that:

> The lack of material and the lack of logic of deferring concern until a more "appropriate age" have produced a situation in which it is easier to learn about the historical, geographical and natural world in the elementary school than it is to understand the economic, sociological, and psychological aspects of the world of work . . .

Knowledge of and Interest in Work ————————————————

The inaccuracy and incompleteness of information about work and other aspects of life beyond the school may seem of little consequence to some readers. If children were unconcerned about such things and formed no opinions about them until senior high school or adulthood, there would be no issue. However, the accumulated weight of evidence is that children's opinions about life, work, and themselves are shaped in infancy and that by the time they have completed elementary school such perspectives may be well-formed.

Nelson (1963) has reported research data indicating that interest in occupations is an important factor in third grade. Remmers and Bauernfeind (1951) indicated that their data of twenty years ago showed that many children express interest or concern about occupations by grade 4. Davis, Hagan and Strouf (1962) found in a study of twelve-year-old children in a Detroit suburb that 60 percent of the 116 in the sample made more tentative than fantasy choices, with more mature choices correlating with intelligence and feminine sex. O'Hara (1962) reported that in his sample of 829 boys and 750 girls from elementary schools in suburban Boston, girls in grades 4, 5, and 6 made choices primarily on the basis of values, with interests of secondary importance. Boys made choices based principally on interests, although values were also important. Parker (1970) reported that fewer than 10 percent of 29,000 students in the seventh grade in Oklahoma described themselves as having no vocational goals. Creason and Schilson (1970) indicated that of a sample of 121 sixth graders who were asked about their vocational plans, none indicated that they were without vocational preferences, and only eight indicated a lack of knowledge about the reasons for their choices.

Thompson and Parker (1971) have reported data showing that fifth-grade students can learn about the world of work and relate it to their own environment. Wellington and Olechowski (1965) described the eight-year-olds in their study as able to:

1. Develop a respect for other people, the work they do, and the contributions made by providing production and services for everyone.

2. Understand that occupations have advantages and disadvantages for the worker.

3. Understand some of the interdependent relationships of workers.

Thus children in the elementary school not only formulate

perceptions of the gross dimensions of occupations and of their own relationships to these perspectives, but also focus on more subtle dimensions. For example, Simmons (1962) reports that the elementary school children in his study exhibited a high degree of awareness of occupational prestige. Gunn's (1964) study suggests that the child begins in the third grade to notice a status hierarchy in jobs; at that time "it is no longer a matter of simply doing 'daddy's job' or picking out the thing that is most fun." It is in grades 4, 5, and 6, according to this study, that the ability to rank jobs is learned. DeFleur's (1963) study indicates that knowledge of roles and status increases as a linear function of age from six through thirteen. However, even young children acquire a basic sense of prestige ranking and have considerable information about the labor force. Hansen and Caulfield (1969) asked 210 boys and their fathers (70 in each grade from 4 to 6) to rank 11 jobs in order of prestige. The rank order correlations show that boys and fathers were quite similar in their rankings and that in support of DeFleur's findings, the correlations for sixth graders and their fathers were slightly higher than for the other two groups. The authors concluded that the boys in this study exhibited a high degree of awareness of occupational prestige and were as knowledgeable about the occupations ranked as were their fathers.

In sum, these studies, while not exhaustive, suggest that elementary school children are interested in and acquire a large amount of information about work, differences in occupations, personal preferences, and status rankings of occupations. Thus, it can be concluded that they learn about such phenomena in ways similar to the concept learning that transpires in other affective and cognitive domains. However, if the findings cited earlier about the degree and accuracy with which such information is presented in elementary schools is indeed generalizable, many children are formulating concepts about the world of work and their place in it without the benefit of accurate or systematic experiences comparable to those typical of other domains of learning.

Theoretical Perspectives on Career Orientation

One of the characteristics of the last decade or more is the development of a body of research and theory about the elementary school child. Some of these insights are drawn from developmental psychology; others come from the various groups devoted to "career development."

Among the best-known theoretical approaches to understanding how children learn is that of Piaget (1926). Fundamentally, the premise of Piaget's work is that children go through stages—concrete operational, formal operational—that are reflected in the way concepts are learned: e.g., five- and six-year-olds are likely to be egocentric in their approach to learning and expression of preferences; seven- to ten-year-olds are likely to engage in cooperative behavior and group learning, and so on. Gunn (1964) applied this model of learning to the ways in which children develop status hierarchies of occupations, reasoning that if children differentiate between jobs on the basis of prestige, they must use some criteria or value system. In order to test this hypothesis, she compared the reasons given by children of various ages (20 boys from each grade, 1–12) for their rankings. In essence, she found that boys in grades 1 and 2 described the occupational world very largely in terms of what it meant to them personally, thus supporting Piaget's concept of egocentrism. Most of them knew what they wanted to be and simply picked the job they wanted. The preferences these children expressed were not influenced by questions about their own capacities or society's values; it was sufficient for them to want a particular job. By third grade, however, the boys began entering a new stage characterized by widening horizons and a tendency to look at jobs in terms of their importance to the community. By grades 4, 5, and 6, the criteria by which they ranked jobs and their understanding of the occupational differences had sharpened considerably. These findings suggest, at least to some degree, that as the boys' social radius expanded and their interaction with other boys increased, they learned a variety of information that increased the complexity with which they viewed such phenomena. In general, such findings support Piaget's concepts.

While Piaget is a valuable resource for understanding how children learn, there is a whole series of perspectives in the literature on career development that helps to clarify to the formulation of preferences, occupational identity, and the development of choice-making behavior. Several of the major theorists and their emphases will be discussed in the next sections.

Ginzberg, Ginzburg, Axelrad and Herma

The work of these theorists is notable for several reasons, not the least of which is the timing of the publication of their first theoretical speculations in 1951. At that time, they asserted:

> Occupational choice is a developmental process; it is not a single decision but a series of decisions made over a period of years. Each step in the process has a meaningful relation to those which

precede and follow it (Ginzberg, Ginsburg, Axelrad & Herma, 1951, p. 185).

A central axiom in the theoretical rationale for this assertion is their view that the choice process is defined by life stages in which preadolescents and adolescents are faced by decision tasks that vary with institutional and other demands at different chronological points. As the individual interacts with the tasks confronting him, a process of compromise between wishes and possibilities serves to define the field of alternatives among which choices are considered. Ginzberg *et al.* have labeled the developmental stages of the choice process as *fantasy* (ages 0–11), *tentative* (11–17) and *realistic* (beyond 17). Each of these periods, with the exception of the fantasy period, is again divided into substages. The tentative period is subdivided into the *interest, capacity, value,* and *transition* stages. The realistic period is composed of *exploration* and *crystallization* substages.

Ginzberg and his colleagues have clearly located the roots of the career development process in the early life of the child. They have indicated, particularly in the fantasy and tentative periods, that as the child matures factors such as interests, capacities, and values surface as sequentially dominant filters through which choice possibilities are screened. In essence, the undifferentiated preference response of characteristic of the child converges into the increasing specificity and reality orientation of the adolescent.

The rate at which young people move through the various developmental stages is, of course, variable. Some will tend to maintain a fantasy mode well into adolescence; others will begin serious consideration of certain tentative choices before leaving adolescence. Regardless of pace, however, children cannot consider, even in fantasy, jobs or educational alternatives about which they are ignorant. Bugg (1969) has suggested that

> if fantasy choices influence later choices and if fantasy choices are influenced by knowledge and attitudes available to the child, providing occupational information to the young child might broaden his horizons and experiences in play and otherwise enhance his chances of vocational selection . . . A well-planned and well-executed occupational service during the elementary school year would broaden the range of possible choices during all stages (p. 166).

Super and Associates

More than any other perspective on career development, the work of Super and his associates (Super, 1957; Super, Starishevsky, Matlin, Jordaan, 1963; Super, 1969b) has sharpened the awareness of the intimate relationship between career development and personal development. Within such a context the process of career development is viewed as primarily the developing and implementing of the self-concept; it consists, in fact, of a developmental psychology of the emerging self. Thus, the individual is seen as choosing occupations or life styles which will permit him to function in a role consonant with his self-concept. The latter is seen as a function of one's developmental history.

Super's approach, in some ways similar to Ginzberg's, gives importance to the individual mastery of career development tasks which become increasingly complex as the individual moves through different chronological periods. The stages identified by Super's structure occur throughout the total life span: growth (childhood), exploration (adolescence), establishment (young adulthood), maintenance (maturity) and decline (old age). However, his major emphasis has been placed on the exploratory and establishment stages which he divided further into substages. For example, the exploratory stage is broken down into the tentative, transition, and trial (with little commitment) substages; the establishment stage includes the trial (with more commitment), stabilization, and advancement substages. Gross developmental tasks in the exploratory stage include crystallizing a vocational preference and specifying it while those of the establishment stage include implementing it, stabilizing in the chosen vocation, consolidating one's status, and advancing in the occupation.

While not placing a major emphasis on the growth stage (birth to about eight or ten), Super's concern for developmental tasks and the evolution of behavior clearly emphasize the importance of this period. It is seen as a period when psychological and physical growth are interrelated. It is a time when behavioral mechanisms and attitudes that have implications for self-concept development are being formed. At the same time, the individual's experiential background is growing in such a way as to yield background knowledge of work differences that serves as the foundation for future tentative choices. The exploratory period of preadolescence and adolescence is, in this view, given over to

> . . . formulating ideas as to fields and levels of work which are appropriate for him, self and occupational concepts which will enable him, if necessary, to make tentative choices, that is, to commit himself to a type of education or training which will lead him toward some partially specified occupation (Super, Starishevsky, Matlin, & Jordaan, 1963, p. 82).

Specifically, Super *et al.* have declared that the behaviors and attitudes that foster effective coping with the exploratory period include:

1. Awareness of the need to crystallize.
2. Use of resources.
3. Awareness of factors to consider in formulating a vocational preference.
4. Awareness of contingencies which may affect vocational goals.
5. Differentiation of interests and values.
6. Awareness of present-future relationships.
7. Formulation of a generalized preference.
8. Consistency of preference.
9. Possession of information on the preferred occupation.
10. Planning for the preferred occupation.
11. Wisdom of the vocational preference.
12. Specification (Super, Starishevsky, Matlin, & Jordaan, 1963, pp. 84–87).

While these behaviors are characteristic of persons able to cope effectively with expectations defined by the exploratory process, they, in combination with the tasks that precede or succeed them, represent dimensions of vocational maturity. Thus, they represent points on a time line beginning in early childhood and leading to some form of vocational maturity in late adolescence or adulthood. Simultaneously, they serve as a pool of themes or emphases that can be used to plan programs at different points on the time line to facilitate the acquisition of vocationally mature behavior. Super's recent research suggests strongly that these behaviors can be facilitated and learned. For example, he has reported (1969b) that the boys in the ninth grade and later who were able to make the best career choices in view of their personal abilities and opportunities were those who earlier had had the greatest exposure to valid experiences and information about the world of work.

Tiedeman and O'Hara

Tiedeman and O'Hara (1963), separately and together, have also considered stages in the development of vocational/career behavior, which they have associated with a continuing process of differentiating ego identity dependent upon: (1) early childhood experiences with the family unit; (2) the psychological crises, defined by Erikson's (1963) constructs, encountered at various developmental stages; and (3) the agreement between society's and the individual's meaning system.

While they do not advocate the concept of developmental tasks as actively as Super and his associates, Tiedeman and O'Hara clearly suggest that behavior evolves from the individual resolution of the crises identified by Erikson (1963). Within this context, they indicate that vocational development can be divided into gross stages of anticipation and induction. Anticipation includes the substages of exploration, crystallization, choice, and clarification. Implementation includes such substages as social induction, reformation, and integration.

Of particular interest is the observation of Tiedeman and O'Hara that individual identity and preference are shaped by perceptions of career choices as well as by the norms and values of the members of different vocations. There is, then, an interplay between career and personality development; thus, the career is a significant influence. The process of choice is characterized by the differentiation of occupational concerns followed by the integration of the differentiated response into the total life pattern. According to this approach, the school should provide a wide range of programs and activities that enable the student to test himself and achieve an identity. Complementing these programmatic concerns, the ultimate attainment of a personal identity requires a comprehensive program of pertinent information during the early school years designed to increase the child's awareness of his own characteristics and of the future alternatives available to him.

Roe

Anne Roe's (1956) work has not emphasized a developmental approach, as has that of Ginzberg, Super, or Tiedeman and O'Hara. However, she has speculated about and emphasized the effect of the child's early experiences on his later choice-making styles and preference orientations. In this regard she has suggested a connection between child-rearing practices—e.g., democratic, overprotecting, rejecting—and the child's later orientations toward or away from people. While research findings pertinent to this theory have been inconsistent, her other contributions to understanding career development have yielded a considerable number of insights. Among them, she has classified by field and level major occupations' degree of intimacy with people or with things. In addition, the levels she identifies within each field represent various degrees of education, responsibility, and intelligence.

Roe has also emphasized the role of acquired or unmet needs as unconscious motivators of vocational behavior. Of particular import to this area of her work has been the use of Maslow's (1954) Theory of Prepotent Needs. Fundamentally, this approach suggests that one can arrange human needs into a hierarchy in which the emergence of higher-order needs is contingent upon the relative satisfaction of lower-order, more primitive needs. Beginning with the most primitive and potent, the needs identified by Maslow are:

1. Physiological needs
2. Safety needs
3. Needs for belongingness and love
4. Needs for importance, self-esteem, respect, and independence
5. Need for information
6. Need for understanding
7. Need for beauty
8. Need for self-actualization

Basically, Roe proposes that those needs that are lowest in the hierarchy and inconsistently or tenuously met act to define the level and character of the occupational choices to which an individual will aspire. Thus, in essence, occupations are perceived as channels for achieving the satisfaction of needs, the beginnings of which are generated in early childhood.

Holland

Like Roe, Holland (1966) has addressed himself to level hierarchies within occupational environments. More importantly, he has classified work environments into six categories corresponding to or reflecting six major personality types: realistic, investigative, social, conventional, enterprising, and artistic. A major assumption of his approach is that each individual develops a hierarchy of habitual or preferred methods for dealing with environmental tasks as a result of the early and continuing influences of his genetic structure and the kinds of interaction he has experienced with his environment. Thus, the personal orientation or behavioral style that comes to characterize the individual causes him to gravitate toward those environmental settings—occupational, educational, and personal—that will satisfy his personal orientation.

Holland views occupational and educational environments as ways of life that differ because they are chosen by persons of different behavioral styles and personality types. He contends, then, that one can speak of people and situations in the same terms in reference to differences in gratifications, abilities, identifications, values, and attitudes. Finally, this approach suggests that interests are expressions of personality and, that a person's vocational stereotypes have important psychological and sociological implications.

Bordin and Associates

Bordin and his colleagues Nachman and Segal (1963) have more clearly than the other theorists discussed here related psychoanalytic theory to vocational behavior. They have attempted to correlate the gratifications that various types of work offer to differences in individual impulses. They replace interests and abilities as key constructs in explaining vocational development or choice behavior with modes of impulse gratification, the status of one's psychosexual development, and anxiety levels. Fundamentally, these researchers contend that relationships exist between the early development of coping mechanisms and later adult behavior. In particular, they argue that adult vocations are sought as sources of instinctual gratification for needs developed in early childhood and that an individual's particular needs and patterns of satisfying them are established by age six.

Career Development

Implications

Each of the career development theories discussed here views vocational behavior and choice making as processes of self-classification. Each, with greater or lesser emphasis, sees vocational behavior and identity, as well as personal decision-making in adolescence or adulthood, as engendered in early childhood. It is evident that the opportunities and information available to the individual for exploration and reality-testing have much to do with the acquisition of self-knowledge and coping mechanisms.

Lyon, in drawing implications from the work of Holland, Roe, Ginzberg and Super, has suggested that

> . . . from the start vocational development is part and parcel of the growing child's self-concept, his identifications in the adult world, his expectations concerning the rewards of work, and even the clarity of his perception of American society . . . It is possible that children who become vocationally mature through earlier contacts with occupational exploration would approach education with a greater commitment, even in the grade schools (Lyon, 1966, p. 369).

Thompson's analysis of the meaning of career development in the elementary school suggests that it

> . . . focuses upon the importance of providing adequate exposure and experience for children from the time they enter school, which in turn will enable them to make more adequate decisions regarding their work roles at points of actual decision-making. This concept does not (imply) placing pressure upon children

to make earlier vocational choices . . . The rationale for career development is that it is a developmental process which should begin in elementary school and continue throughout a person's lifetime (Thompson, 1969, p. 208).

After reviewing most of the theories briefly summarized here, Bugg concluded that, from an action standpoint,

> . . . the job of the grade school is to focus the attention of children on the general meaning of work in our society and to assist them in gaining information about the total range of occupational opportunities. Considerable attention should be given to the individual differences of both workers and jobs and to the varying rewards (intrinsic and extrinsic), social and physical characteristics, and general training requirements of different occupational fields. The elementary school program should attempt to communicate to children why people work; why all honest work is important; the fact that someday they too, will work; and the impact that a job is likely to have on them personally (Bugg, 1969, p. 180).

Current Models

Until the Vocational Education Act Amendments of 1968 specified the need to develop exemplary programs and projects with a prevocational dimension, vocational guidance and career development activities in the elementary school were limited in availability as well as scope. From 1968 to 1971, however, models of career development for elementary schools began to appear with increasing rapidity.

In January 1971, Commissioner Marland, United States Commissioner of Education, launched a program, relevant to all levels of American education, termed "Career Education." Field tests of models designed to implement programs of career education are now underway at six national sites and in every state. These models are intended to operationalize many of the career development concepts discussed above (Herr, 1972). Like the earlier models spawned by the Vocational Education Act Amendments of 1968, the more recent Career Education models have a strong elementary school component. The next several sections will examine some of these models.

The Comprehensive Career Education Model (CCEM)

The school-based Comprehensive Career Education Model is a federally funded model being studied and developed at the Ohio State University Center for Vocational and Technical Education. Components are now being field tested at Mesa, Arizona; Hackensack, New Jersey; Los Angeles, California; Atlanta, Georgia; Pontiac, Michigan; and Denver, Colorado. In this model, Career Education is defined as a comprehensive educational program focused on careers, beginning with the entry of the child into a formal school program and continuing into the adult years. Thus, the program is addressed to a systematic approach spanning grades K–12. It is intended to affect all students at all educational levels and to use a variety of materials, activities, and experiences to accomplish its objectives.

The CCEM has identified a series of elements and outcomes of which career education is comprised. They include (Miller, 1972, p. 3):

Element	Outcome
Career Awareness ⟶	Career Identity
Self-Awareness ⟶	Self-Identity
Appreciations, Attitudes ⟶	Self-Social Fulfillment
Decision-making Skills ⟶	Career Decisions
Economic Awareness ⟶	Economic Understanding
Skill Awareness and Beginning Competence ⟶	Employment Skills
Employability Skills ⟶	Career Placement
Educational Awareness ⟶	Educational Identity

The assumption is that each of these elements can be converted into performance objectives that extend across all grade levels. However, some of the elements are more appropriate at certain grade levels or, are prerequisites to activities at higher grade levels. Thus, the total K–12 continuum is divided into three gross stages as follows (Reinhart, 1972):

	6	9	
K	Career Awareness	Exploration	Preparation 12

In turn, these stages are composed of themes from which goal statements and performance objectives can be derived. For example, one of the themes of career awareness at grade 5 is the following:

> The student will understand that "career" involves progression through stages of preparation for and the performance of occupational roles and may involve a change in basic vocational direction (Reinhart, 1972, p. 9).

This theme in turn leads to such goal statements and performance objectives as:

Goal Statement	Performance Objective
The student will recognize that some jobs have unique specific requirements for success.	Given a list of skills required for success in some jobs, and a list of personal interests, skills, aptitudes, etc., the student will list in writing one or more examples of match or mismatch of job success requirements and individual variables.
	or
	Given instruction, the student will classify specific job requirements into job clusters on the basis of unique or similar requirements or types of requirements.
The student will understand the relationships between present job experience and those of the future.	Given a class interview with a worker, the student will compare the things that the class is studying with the skills the worker had to learn before he could perform his job and thus understand the relationship of present experiences to future goals.
	or
	Given a list of jobs and school activities, the student will match jobs with school activities necessary for the job and understand their relationships.

This very brief example illustrates the attempt of the CCEM to move from the level of theory to specific goals and then to student performance objectives that can be monitored and individualized. This approach accords with the national concern for accountability and the need to identify the specific kinds of educational change necessary.

Another interesting dimension of the CCEM is its use of a clustering for career groupings. The creation of such a structure was necessary to supply the student with information about the world of work, to help him relate available career choices to his interests and abilities, and to provide for the shaping of instructional objectives and learning experiences. The clusters that

emerged for the elementary and junior high school included the
following (Reinhart, 1972):

CCEM Clusters for K–9

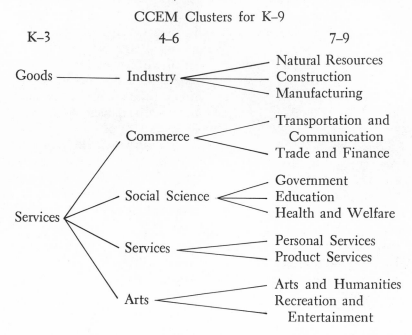

| K–3 | 4–6 | 7–9 |

In this model, then, activities to generate career awareness in
grades K–3 simply divide the world of work into occupations that
produce goods and those that produce services. This division can
be elaborated in grades 4–6 to five clusters and in grades 7–9 to
twelve clusters for career exploration and later career preparation.
Each of these clusters can be related to the industries and occupations included in the *Dictionary of Occupational Titles* (DOT)
(United States Department of Labor, 1965).

The State of Ohio Model

The model used by the State of Ohio Department of Public Instruction is unrelated to the Comprehensive Career Education
Model. Spatial limitations prohibit discussing it in depth. However, it also begins with career development inputs from which
evolving emphases develop at different educational levels. Basically, it uses a framework such as the following (Weaver, 1971):

K–6	7–8	9–10	11–12
World of work	Career Orientation	Career Exploration	Vocational Education or College Preparation

Career Development Education in Georgia

Bottoms (1972) has described the Career Development Education Program in Georgia, which encompasses kindergarten through post-secondary and adult levels, as composed of eight elements:

1. *Orientation*—assisting individuals to learn about their own characteristics and environment in terms of a career set.

2. *Exploration*—providing opportunities for students to test themselves in terms of their career self-concept through "hands-on experiences" in simulated or direct work settings.

3. *Interdisciplinary Education*—"unifying the natural relationship between the academic and career curriculum so that selected concepts and skills of general and academic courses are required through career oriented activities, problems and tasks" (Bottoms, 1972, p. 24).

4. *Career Curriculum*—courses focusing upon specific job preparation skills related to the career area as well as on math, science, communication skills, and social science in the context of the career area.

5. *Intensive Short-term Specialized Courses*—a specialized training course preparing a student for employment in a single skilled occupation over a period of less than a year.

6. *Outreach*—reaching through personal contact unemployed youth and adults for the purpose of returning them to an appropriate learning situation or to part-time training and related employment.

7. *Job Placement and Follow-through*—assisting youth and adults to enter, adjust to, and satisfactorily progress in a job.

8. *Guidance and Counseling*—helping students personalize the meaning of their career experiences at each educational level, assisting them at key decision-making points, and helping prescribe their educational treatment.

Obviously, not all these tasks are appropriate to the elementary school. However, orientation, exploration, interdisciplinary education, and guidance and counseling have program implications for grades K–6.

The Jones County School System, Mississippi Model

This model views the students' total school experience as preparation for life, and focuses on earning a living. The career-centered concept on which this program is based assumes that people need three types of skills to be successful in life: (1) sociological skills, to adjust to and participate in changes in the community, state, nation, and world; (2) psychological skills, to achieve self-awareness and develop desirable personal characteristics; and (3) occupational skills, to earn a living and grow and advance in a career.

This program begins in the elementary school by introducing students to a realistic picture of the world of work through the systematic use of information and the provision of counseling to clarify their interests and abilities (Goldhammer & Taylor, 1972a).

The Pikeville, Kentucky Universe Model

This program also embraces all students in grades 1–12. At the elementary school level, a major goal is to establish curricula focused on grades 1–3 and 4–6. Occupational orientation is the principal vehicle for the teaching of basic education. It is intended that, by the end of the sixth grade, students exposed to this program will have attained the following attitudes and behaviors:

1. An appreciation of work as a means of achieving self-satisfaction in a full and fruitful life.
2. An understanding of the social and economic importance of a number of easily identifiable occupations and occupational groups.
3. Acquisition of basic education skills to a degree equal to, if not greater than, that which is otherwise possible.
4. A degree of self-realization and awareness that will lead students to seek careers commensurate with their abilities and aptitudes.
5. An understanding of the impact of technology on the world of work and of the importance of a career strategy that will enable students to cope with a changing labor market.

A second major goal of this program is to provide guidance and educational opportunities in which students in grades 1–6 can see positive relationships between school and the world of work. Of particular interest in this regard are the development of positive concepts of self, work, interest, and skills (Goldhammer & Taylor, 1972b).

The Wisconsin Model for Integrating
Career Development into Local Curriculum

This model (Drier, 1971) is extremely comprehensive, in terms both of the systematic K–12 approach and of coverage within educational levels. Rather than dealing exclusively with concepts relevant to the world of work or some other single dimension, this career development model addresses itself to the self, the work world, career planning and preparation, and the decision-making interaction among them occasioned by the continuing emergence of self and vocational identity. Thus, the self and vocational identity are treated as dynamic rather than static. This means that each educational level—K–3, 4–6, 7–9, 10–12—has contributions to make to the student's acquisition of the behaviors, knowledge, attitudes, and skills that comprise the self, work world, and career planning and preparation components.

Fourteen concepts have been identified that need to be introduced and/or developed in middle childhood (K–3), late childhood (4–6), or both:

1. An understanding and acceptance of self is important throughout life.

2. Persons need to be recognized as having dignity and worth.

3. Occupations exist for a purpose.

4. There is a wide variety of careers that may be classified in several ways.

5. Work means different things to different people.

6. Education and work are interrelated.

7. Individuals differ in their interests, abilities, attitudes and values.

8. Occupational supply and demand have an impact on career planning.

9. Job specialization creates interdependency.

10. Environment and individual potential interact to influence career development.

11. Occupations and life styles are interrelated.

12. Individuals can learn to perform adequately in a variety of occupations.

13. Career development requires a continuous and sequential series of choices.

14. Various groups and institutions influence the nature and structure of work.

The first seven concepts are introduced in K–3 and developed in 4–6, and the last seven are introduced in grades 4–6 and developed in grades 7–9. Other concepts are introduced in grades 7–9 and developed later. These concepts are, in turn, translated into student behaviors that should occur at different educational levels if the student is acquiring the behaviors associated with each concept. Thus, concept 1, *an understanding and acceptance of self is important throughout life,* suggests at grades K–3 and 4–6 respectively that the student should, among other behaviors:

1.1 begin to recognize the need for continuous self appraisal in a diversified society. . . .
1.3 understand the importance of examining one's strengths and limitations (Bottoms, 1972, p. 24).

This concept suggests other behaviors in the Work Component and still others in the Career Planning and Preparation Component. In addition, this model identifies resources and materials appropriate to the accomplishment of the different student outcomes.

The Elementary School Counselor and Career Development

Many other models that attempt to implement career development in the elementary school could be identified (Hansen, 1970), but those cited are sufficient to indicate that there are many ways to accomplish such a goal. Some approaches attempt only to expose students to information about the characteristics of alternative kinds of work; others tie together the development of student knowledge relating educational and occupational alternatives; an increasing number attempt to integrate student development in the areas of the self-concept and awareness of environmental options (personal, educational, and occupational) with decision making and planning skill acquisition. Some of the models are limited supplements to current practices in the elementary school; others are integrated into curricula and other components of the elementary school structure in dramatically different and massive ways. Some approaches are tailored to local resources and student needs; others are designed for statewide or national adoption.

Regardless of the focus or limitations of any given career orientation program, its existence will have implications for the role of the elementary school counselor. At a gross level, the question it poses can be summarized as whether the counselor will discharge his responsibilities in a treatment- or stimulus-oriented mode (Herr & Cramer, 1972).

In a treatment mode, the elementary school counselor would not intervene until a student is having difficulty with some aspect of career orientation—e.g., poor self-concept, deficient or inaccurate information about opportunities, inability to plan. In such instances, the elementary school counselor would probably operate remedially after a problem had developed of sufficient affective concern either to the child or to an agent of referral to require attention. Given such conditions, the counselor is unlikely to be able to influence large numbers of students in a developmental fashion.

A different role for the elementary counselor is suggested by a stimulus mode. Rather than waiting for problems to occur, the counselor anticipates the need for pertinent attitudes, knowledge, and skills among elementary children and develops ways by which they can be systematically acquired. Such a stance is active rather than reactive in responding to student needs. It is future-oriented and anticipatory rather than *ex post facto* and problem-oriented. In a word, such an elementary school counselor role is *developmental*.

A stimulus-oriented elementary school counselor must act on several assumptions:

1. The elementary school counselor cannot do the job of career orientation or career development alone. To accomplish the objectives of such a program, he will have to work closely with teachers and representatives of different aspects of the community.

2. The elementary school counselor must see himself as a contributor to the total educational mission of the elementary school, not simply as a professional housed in an elementary school to proffer treatment to the rejects or misfits.

3. The elementary school counselor must know career development theory and research thoroughly and must know different ways by which such knowledge can be put to use on behalf of all students.

4. The elementary school counselor will function as a consultant, resource person, counselor, coordinator and in a wide range of other roles.

Regardless how an elementary school counselor attempts to translate career development concepts into practice, it is necessary to consider the characteristics of the elementary school child. In a basic sense, whatever is done should emphasize concreteness rather than abstraction, at least in the primary grades; action, involvement, and activity are preferable to verbalization; multimedia, rather than unidimensional approaches, are desirable (Herr & Cramer, 1972).

O'Hara (1968), for example, has suggested that in working with elementary school children it is necessary to establish readiness for vocational development. One way to do so is to provide reinforcement, through social approval from teachers, counselors, and parents, for behaviors oriented to consideration of choices, information-seeking, and participation in exploratory activities. In addition, since many of the alternatives, decision points, and behaviors for which the elementary school lays a foundation are remote in time or distance, it is necessary to provide direct or simulated experiences that allow for information delivery or reality-testing. As an outcome of these activities, the child must be helped to develop means by which he can differentiate himself from the environment and from others and begin to distinguish concepts and ideas that are important to him from those that are not. Finally, the elementary school child needs to be helped to develop a vocabulary appropriate to these goals. Without such a vocabulary, his characteristics and those of the world around him are abstract and susceptible to a great deal of distortion. With it, he has the rudimentary tools to manipulate and symbolize the world as it is available and pertinent to him.

Obviously, the curriculum of the elementary school is a vehicle that can be infused with the attitudes, knowledge, concepts, and opportunities of career orientation. Whether the specific content is language arts, arithmetic, science, health, or physical education, it can be related to educational and occupational differences, problem solving, work options, and personal interests and values. These learnings can be conveyed, reinforced, or emphasized through field trips, resource people, observations, student dramatizations, role-playing, movies, slides, projects, reading, games, or simulations. The range of possibilities is limited only by the ingenuity of the teacher or counselor. The elementary school counselor might serve as a consultant to teachers about the inclusion of career development concepts in the curriculum, a resource person for planning programs, a coordinator of role models or resource persons; or he might teach some units himself as part of a group guidance program or of the regular curriculum. Readers may get some ideas from the approaches reported in the following sections.

Descriptions of approaches to career development are becoming more widely available. For example, Leonard (1972a) reports on an effective way to build career guidance experiences into a self-contained classroom situation and curriculum. The creation of a Popcorn Factory enabled the teacher to make spelling, reading, writing, and arithmetic more interesting and meaningful and simultaneously to expand each student's perspective on work and on himself. Students played the roles of various workers in the factory. They also played the board of directors, sold shares in the company, and voted their personal shares of stock to elect board officers, company supervisors, and foremen. They contacted a representative of a popcorn manufacturer, who donated a bagging machine.

The student foremen selected their employees from job applications made by students in the class. Every student was involved in the production process, and different jobs were identified by uniforms, badges, and work caps. Students who worked well were given "coffee breaks" at specific periods during the school day, but students who came to work with dirty hands or manifested other ineffective behaviors risked being fired by their foreman.

Throughout this experience, students were helped to recognize the relevance of spelling, reading, writing, and arithmetic to the various work processes. They also learned about the importance of attitudes and responsibility and the interdependence of various work activities.

In the Louisville, Kentucky, Public Schools, the K–6 elementary program focuses on (1) creating an awareness of work, self, family, school, and community, and of their interrelationships; (2) sequentially developing skills necessary to critical thinking, problem solving, decision making, and inquiry; (3) developing basic academic skills; and (4) emphasizing the aesthetic qualities of life.

At each grade level from kindergarten through grade 6 there is an area for exploration, to which is tied accomplishment of the aforementioned objectives (Preli, 1972):

Grade Level	Emphasis
Kindergarten	School, Family, Neighborhood
1	Agriculture
2	Industry
3	Professions
4	City
5	State
6	World

Each of these grade level emphases is then related to appropriate clusters of work activity so that students can understand their differences and their academic requirements. In the process it is expected that self-awareness, as well as awareness of work, academic relevance, and social skills, will be enhanced.

Bank (1969) has suggested a modification of this approach focusing on vocational role models representative of particular emphases. For example, role models for the first two grades include:

| Kindergarten | School role models | Principal, teacher school secretary, University professor |
| First Grade | Community role models who help feed us | Grocer, milkman, waitress |

Other community role models are people who protect our health (second grade), provide shelter and protect us (third grade), provide transportation (fourth grade), provide communication (fifth grade), and conduct business (sixth grade). Obviously, these two approaches attempt to relate, in a developmental way, the roles and emphases to which children are exposed as a function of their expanding experience in the community.

Another project with a systematic approach to career development is the Developmental Career Guidance Projects in inner-city Detroit (Leonard, 1968). In kindergarten, the focus is on developing readiness for knowledge of workers that children encounter daily. Coloring, drawing, cutting, and pasting are related to different types of workers. Some role-playing and resource persons are used. In first grade, knowledge of workers in the community is extended by means of walking tours and field trips. Children discuss aspects of work, the work their parents do, and parental views about their jobs. In the second grade, pertinent vocabulary is developed and the study of job families (e.g., people who work with animals, people who work in transportation) is initiated. These are integrated with appropriate school units, and role-playing sessions are conducted. In the third grade, children are helped to look at themselves and others. They gain self-knowledge and begin to formulate an understanding of social interaction. In the fourth grade, attention is focused on attitudes, feelings, and values related to different types of occupations. Hobbies and after-school activities are discussed in terms of their similarity to job activities. In the fifth grade, children discuss work habits, rewards, and the shared characteristics of good students and good workers. In the sixth grade, children consider requirements for success in various occupations in terms of such personalized questions as "Do I have the strength to be _____?" Throughout these years additional job families are introduced, field trips conducted and resource people used.

Dodson (1971) has described the need of inner-city elementary pupils for occupational exploration programs and outlined the characteristics of one such program conducted in Norfolk, Virginia. On the assumption that inner-city children, especially black children, need successful identity models in the vocational world to stimulate their dreams about the future, an occupational program is presented to the pupils each month. Sponsored by the Guidance Club, it includes (1) a ten-minute broadcast over the public address system, (2) a luncheon for invited occupational speakers, and (3) informal talks by speakers. The occupations presented are chosen by the children by means of surveys in grades K–7. Children in kindergarten through grade 3 participate in a taped interview program focusing on the theme, "What will I Be?" Pupils in grades 4 through 7 give talks about different kinds of work, using the *Dictionary of Occupational Titles* (U.S. Department of Labor, 1965) and the *I Want to Be* series as primary references. The pupils in grades 4 through 7 also interview and get to know young blacks from disadvantaged backgrounds who have attained success and respect in various types of work.

Teachers are encouraged to provide preparatory and follow-up activities. For example, pupils in one third-grade class combined language arts and art lessons to produce pictures of what they wanted to be. These were displayed on bulletin boards in the corridors.

In another project in Detroit, an elementary school employment service has been developed to give children the opportunity to learn about the rules of work and to have work experiences in and after school (Leonard, 1972b). Corollary goals are for children to learn how to fill out job applications, develop positive attitudes toward work and a sense of responsibility toward a job, and understand the relationship between their school life and the world of work. Procedures are developed by which students can apply for, consider the requirements of, interview for, and be hired for such jobs as safety patrol member, service squad member, future teacher, lunchroom helper, room helper, audiovisual aide, office helper, custodian's helper, and library staff member.

At the American Institutes for Research in Palo Alto, California, a newly developed system of individualized education, Project PLAN, has integrated current information about occupations into each student's regular social studies and language arts programs (Hamilton & Webster, 1971). In the primary grades, this information is interwoven with the study of economics and contemporary problems. In grades 1 to 4, there are approximately 20 instructional objectives that emphasize:

(a) the nature and variety of work in some of the specific occupations usually visible to young students, such as community and personal services; (b) patterns of interaction with other persons in job settings that differentiate work from other social roles; (c) roles that various occupations play in fulfilling social and economic needs; and (d) general ways that people prepare for occupations (Hamilton & Webster, 1971, p. 216).

In grades 5 through 8, a set of 12 groups of occupations is presented to students as representing a range of educational and training requirements. Students are exposed to planning and decision-making exercises using case studies in which measurement profiles of fictionalized goals are discrepant. The skills acquired are used to help PLAN students choose their own tentative primary and secondary long-range educational-vocational goals from among the 12 occupational families. These individualized goals, in turn, are used to determine the kinds and emphases of individualized learning units to which students are exposed.

Decision Making

Decision making has been identified as a goal of career development in the elementary school. Yet this should not be taken to mean that the goal of such decision making is an early closure of options about what the student "will become" after his formal education is complete. What is sought is an increase in the openness of choice making and its ultimate effectiveness as students are helped to develop both the elements of decision-making prowess and the ability to process the vast amount of information with which they are constantly deluged. Nelson (1962) points out that the process of choosing is as important as the choice itself. He contends that:

> . . . The process is an evolving one of choice rather than one made easily and then reconciled to one's way of life. The early choice pattern reflects a closed system of looking at oneself. It entertains plans for the future in terms of an already made decision. The developmental choices pattern selects plans in terms of possibilities for exploring the meaning of tentative choices with their feasibility for change, if needed (Nelson, 1962, p. 25).

Nelson's observations are echoed by Arbuckle, who concludes that:

> Choosing is not finding the right thing, but is rather the ability to move within restrictions, modifying and changing them . . . It is a belief in the inability to have any choice that makes the lack of choice real . . . (Arbuckle, 1963–1964, p. 84).

These observations suggest that what is meant by decision making is the development of a conviction among elementary school students that they have a future and a vast number of alternatives among which they can choose, that present behavior will affect the future choices they can make, that they have the personal competence to plan and consider, and that their evolving self-knowledge is an appropriate domain in which to shape preferences and plans.

–––––––––––––––––––––––––––––––– **Information on Career Orientation**

The importance of information is a pervasive, though implicit, assumption of this chapter. For example, Hoppock (1957) over a decade and a half ago identified eight reasons for providing occupational information in the elementary schools. The vitality and importance of the insights they convey seem to increase with the current complexities faced by children. They are:

1. To increase the child's feelings of security.
2. To encourage the natural curiosity of young children.
3. To extend the occupational horizons of the child.
4. To encourage wholesome attitudes toward all useful work.
5. To begin developing a desirable approach to the process of occupational choice.
6. To help students who are dropping out of school and going to work.
7. To help students who face a choice between different high schools or high school programs.
8. To show children who really need money how they can get it without stealing (Hoppock, 1957, pp. 344–346).

The substitution of words like *self, personal, social,* and *educational* for *occupational* in the eight reasons for the use of information cited by Hoppock makes the point that children need to develop knowledge not only about work but also about other aspects of life related to it. Grell (1961), among others, has suggested that information is needed on such matters as work habits, attitudes toward work, the relation of self to work, and the establishment of a tolerance and understanding for the work that various people perform, as well as on factual data. In this regard, Miller (1961) has pointed out that while a child is achieving selfhood, he is also formulating a concept of an ideal self. He is experiencing a preview of his future and the opportunity to rehearse in a protected context the preparation and behaviors necessary to the goals he is beginning to formulate. Occupation is an aspect of this ideal self, but not the whole of it. Thus, an array of informational foci must be available to provide the fuel for comprehensive career development.

Information is delivered in many ways: in curriculum content, through experience and in the attitudes of teachers, counselors, parents, and peers toward work and life. Thus, there are human and nonhuman information delivery systems, the former often more powerful than the latter (Herr, 1972). Specifically, activities and techniques such as the following represent some media for information presentation:

Word games	Simulations (e.g., The Popcorn
Decision-making games	Factory)
Biographies	Audiovisual materials
Role-playing	Career logs
Resource people	Hobbies
"Hands on" activities with	Counseling
tools	Group work
Dramatization	Test interpretation
Field trips	Interviews with adults
Special units	Reinforcement modeling
Observation	

As a result of a study of the type of occupational information used in vocational decision making by 294 boys in grades 4, 6, 8, 10, and 12, Biggers (1971) concluded that "less effort might be devoted to novel ways of disseminating information and more effort given to helping students learn to use the information." He further maintains that "the guidance program beginning in the elementary grades must recognize the need and plan appropriate experiences to increase the student's ability to use information in vocational decision-making, which is the reason for disseminating vocational information in the first place." This is a caution well worth noting. To be useful in the elementary school, information must be available in a wide range of reading levels and other sensory modes.

Role of the Elementary School Counselor

Very little emphasis has been given in the programs cited to the role of the elementary school counselor in individual or group counseling relative to career orientation. This is not to suggest that counseling is inappropriate in this context but to emphasize other roles likely to extend the counselor's influence to larger numbers of students.

Obviously, some students do not achieve the behaviors identified throughout this chapter as necessary to career development by means of curricular or other group modes. Problems involving personal relationships, decision making and problem solving, adjustment to one's failures and successes, and meeting the demands of everyday living (Gibson, 1972) are best handled in an individually tailored counseling mode rather than in a stimulus mode. Even so, counseling can be developmentally focused and integrated with the latter. Pertinent here is Blocher's observations that

> . . . facilitating the development of human effectiveness thus involves two rather basic functions: (a) designing learning situations in which appropriate patterns of coping and mastery behavior can be achieved; and (b) designing social systems which maximize opportunities for all members to develop as effective human beings. The first aspect of this program is the domain of developmental counseling. The second, which is essentially a social engineering function, is, in the educational setting at least, the province of the developmental guidance program (Blocher, 1968, p. 172).

Such an approach to counseling in the elementary school is compatible with what has come to be known as Reality Therapy (Hawes, 1969), the goals of which include helping the child to become more self responsible (worthwhile) and socially responsible (capable of love). These goals are accomplished by facilitating the child's personal involvement, accentuating present time, concentrating on behavior rather than causes of behavior, reflecting upon and making a value judgment about his personal behavior, and encouraging him to make a plan and commit himself to its realization. Punishment is not used to attain these ends, nor are excuses for ineffective or irresponsible behavior reinforced.

"Vocational counseling" is too limited a concept to be viable in the elementary school. However, individual counseling can be related to knowledge, attitudes, and skills pertinent either directly or indirectly to vocational and educational behavior and to the child's developing self awareness.

Summary

This chapter has considered the current status of career orientation in the elementary school and the counselor's roles in it. The role emphasized here is active and developmental rather than passive and treatment-oriented. The relationship between selected theoretical approaches to career development and examples of current elementary school "Career Education" models has been identified. Specific attention has been given to the integration of career development concepts into the curriculum, the use of information in this context, and some of the implications of career development for the elementary school counselor as a consultant, a resource person, and counselor.

References

Arbuckle, D. Occupational information in the elementary school. *Vocational Guidance Quarterly*, 1963–64, **12**, 77–84.

Bank, I. M. Children explore careerland through vocational role models. *Vocational Guidance Quarterly*, 1969, **17**, 284–289.

Biggers, J. L. The use of information in vocational decision-making. *Vocational Guidance Quarterly*, 1971, **19**, 171–176.

Blocher, D. H. Developmental counseling: A rationale for counseling in the elementary school. *Elementary School Guidance and Counseling*, 1968, **2**, 163–172.

Bordin, E. S., Nachman, B., & Segal, S. J. An articulated framework for vocational development. *Journal of Counseling Psychology*, 1963, **10**, 107–116.

Bottoms, G. *Career development education kindergarten through post-secondary and adult levels.* Atlanta: Georgia Department of Education, Division of Adult and Vocational Education, 1972.

Bugg, C. A. Implications of some major theories of career choice for elementary school guidance programs. *Elementary School Guidance and Counseling*, 1969, **3**, 173–180.

Clyse, J. What do readers teach about jobs? *Elementary School Journal*, 1959, **59**, 456–460.

Creason, F., & Schilson, D. L. Occupational concerns of sixth grade children. *Vocational Guidance Quarterly*, 1970, **18**, 219–224.

Davis, D. A., Hagan, N., & Strouf, J. Occupational choice of twelve year olds. *Personnel and Guidance Journal*, 1962, **40**, 628–629.

DeFleur, M. L. Children's knowledge of occupational roles and prestige: Preliminary report. *Psychological Reports*, 1963, **13**, 760.

Dodson, A. G. An occupational exploration program for inner city elementary pupils. *Vocational Guidance Quarterly*, 1971, **20**, 59–60.

Drier, H. N., Jr. (Ed.) *K-12 guide for integrating career development into local curriculum.* Madison: Wisconsin Department of Public Instruction, December 1971.

Erikson, E. H. *Childhood and society,* 2nd ed. New York: W. W. Norton, 1963.

Gibson, R. L. *Career development in the elementary school.* Columbus, Ohio: Charles E. Merrill, 1972.

Ginzberg, E., Ginsburg, S. W., Axelrad, S., & Herma, J. R. *Occupational choice: An approach to a general theory.* New York: Columbia University Press, 1951.

Goldhammer, K. & Taylor, R. E. Career-centered curriculum for vocational complexes in Mississippi: An exemplary program. *Career education: Perspective and promise.* Columbus, Ohio: Charles E. Merrill Publishing Company, 1972a, pp. 247–251.

———. A universe model of occupational education for Pikeville, Kentucky. *Career education: Perspective and promise.* Columbus, Ohio: Charles E. Merrill, 1972b, pp. 253–272.

Grell, L. A. How much occupational information in the elementary school? *Vocational Guidance Quarterly*, 1961, **9**, 48–55.

Gunn, B. Children's conceptions of occupational prestige. *Personnel and Guidance Journal*, 1964, **42**, 558–663.

Hamilton, J. A., & Webster, W. J. Occupational information and the school curriculum. *Vocational Guidance Quarterly*, 1971, **19**, 215–219.

Hansen, J. C., & Caulfield, T. J. Parent-child occupational concepts. *Elementary School Guidance and Counseling*, 1969, **3**, 269–275.

Hansen, L. *Career guidance practices in school and community*. Washington: National Vocational Guidance Association, 1970.

Hawes, R. M. Reality therapy: An approach to encourage individual and social responsibility in the elementary school. *Elementary School Guidance and Counseling*, 1969, **4**, 120–127.

Herr, E. L. *Review and synthesis of foundations for career education*. Washington: Government Printing Office, 1972.

Herr, E. L., & Cramer, S. H. *Vocational guidance and career development in the schools: Toward a systems approach*. Boston: Houghton Mifflin, 1972.

Holland, J. L. *The psychology of vocational choice*. Waltham, Mass.: Blaisdell, 1966.

Hoppock, R. E. *Occupational information*. New York: McGraw-Hill, 1957.

Kowitz, G. T., & Kowitz, N. *Guidance in the elementary classroom*. New York: McGraw-Hill, 1959.

Leonard, G. E. *Developmental career guidance in action: An interm report*. Detroit: Wayne State University, 1968.

———. Career guidance in the elementary school. *Elementary School Guidance and Counseling*, 1972a, **6**, 198–201.

———. Career guidance in the elementary school. *Elementary School Guidance and Counseling*, 1972b, **6**, 283–286.

Lifton, W. M. Vocational guidance in the elementary school. *Vocational Guidance Quarterly*, 1959, **60**, 79–81.

Lyon, R. Vocational development and the elementary school. *Elementary School Journal*, 1966, **66**, 368–376.

Maslow, A. H. *Motivation and personality*. New York: Harper & Row, 1954.

Miller, A. J. Strategies for implementing career education: A school based model. Paper presented at the 1972 annual meeting of the American Educational Research Association, Chicago, April 1972.

Nelson, R. C. Knowledge and interests concerning sixteen occupations among elementary and secondary school students. *Educational and Psychological Measurement*, 1963, **23**, 741–754.

Nelson, R. C. Early versus developmental vocational choice. *Vocational Guidance Quarterly*, 1962, **2**, 23–26.

O'Hara, R. P. The roots of careers. *Elementary School Journal*, 1962, **62**, 277–280.

O'Hara, R. P. Theoretical foundation for the use of occupational information in guidance. *Personnel and Guidance Journal*, 1968, 46, 636–640.

Parker, H. J. 29,000 seventh graders have made occupational choices. *Vocational Guidance Quarterly*, 1970, 18, 219–224.

Piaget, J. *The language and thought of the child*. New York: Harcourt Brace, 1926.

Preli, B. *Overview of elementary model*. Louisville, Kentucky, Public Schools, September 1972.

Reinhart, B. A comprehensive career education model: A bridge between school and work. Paper presented to the Southside Research Coordinating Council, Clearwater, Florida, May 1972.

Remmers, H. H., & Bauernfeind, R. H. *Examiners Manual for the S.R.A. Junior Inventory*. Chicago: Science Research Associates, 1951.

Roe, A. *The psychology of occupations*. New York: John Wiley and Sons, 1956.

Simmons, D. Children's ranking of occupational prestige. *Personnel and Guidance Journal*, 1962, 41, 332–336.

Stefflre, B. Run, mama, run: Women workers in elementary readers. *Vocational Guidance Quarterly*, 1969, 18, 99–102. 102.

Super, D. E. *The psychology of careers*. New York: Harper & Row, 1957.

Super, D. E. Vocational development theory: Persons, positions, and processes. *The Counseling Psychologist*, 1969a, 1, 2–9.

Super, D. E. The natural history of a study of lives and vocations. *Perspectives on Education*, 1969b, 2, 13–22.

Super, D. E., Starishevsky, R., Matlin, N., & Jordaan, J. P. *Career development: Self-concept theory*. New York: College Entrance Examination Board, 1963.

Tennyson, W. W., & Monnens, L. P. The world of work through elementary readers. *Vocational Guidance Quarterly*, 1963–64, 12, 85–88.

Thompson, C. L., & Parker, J. L. Fifth graders view the work world scene. *Elementary School Guidance and Counseling*, 1971, 5, 280–288.

Thompson, J. M. Career development in the elementary school: Rationale and implications for elementary school counselors. *The School Counselor*, 1969, 16, 208–210.

Tiedeman, D. V., & O'Hara, R. P. *Career development: Choice and adjustment*. New York: College Entrance Examination Board, 1963.

United States Department of Labor. *The dictionary of occupational titles*, vol. 1–3, 3rd ed. Washington: The Department, 1965.

Weaver, C. *The Ohio model*. Paper presented at the American

Vocational Association Annual Convention, Portland, Oregon, 1971.

Wellington, J., & Olechowski, V. Attitudes toward the world of work in elementary schools. *Vocational Guidance Quarterly*, 1965, **14**, 160–162.

9

The ecology of childhood is "the transactional relationships that exist between the young learner and certain social and cultural aspects of his environment" (Shane, Shane, Gibson, & Munger, 1971, p. 289). These writers also define the challenges of educational ecology as "helping a child, over a period of time, to build defenses against the contamination caused by repeated socioculturally damaging exposures, to learn how to respect and to understand his own subculture and the subcultures of others, to improve his interpersonal and intercultural relations, and to learn how to exploit his environment for worthy purposes of personal-social improvement" (Shane et al., 1971, p. 292).

The ecological emphasis of this chapter reflects a primary concern for certain key interlocking psychosocial systems and component subsystems, rather than individuals per se (Auerswald, 1968). The stress upon prevention indicates that efforts should be directed toward effecting desirable modifications of the key target systems of school, home, and community (Carroll, Bell, Brecher, & Minor, 1970). Therefore, the following sections will be devoted to these major target systems of school, home, and community.

An additional theoretical consideration of interest here is the concept of prevention. A useful analogy is that putting one's finger in the dike is less satisfactory than dealing with the water near its source so that it does not become voluminous enough to leak through or break the dam. Another analogy is that it is better to build a fence at the end of a cliff than a hospital at the bottom of it. Prevention is an important component of developmental guidance and counseling. There will, of course, always be crisis situations that must be handled.

Environmental Considerations
and Action Plans

Caplan and Grunebaum (1967) provide the theoretical basis for thinking about prevention and identify three types of prevention. Primary prevention aims at reducing the incidence of new cases of mental disorder and disability in the population. Efforts can be made to modify the environment (active community involvement) and strengthen individual capacities to cope with situations (crisis intervention, anticipatory guidance, and consultation) (Bloom, 1971). Caplan considers such approaches as modifying community-wide practices by changing laws, regulations, administrative patterns, and values and attitudes. Primary prevention is concerned with three types of resources: (1) physical—food and living space; (2) psychosocial—personal interactions at school, work, and church; (3) sociocultural—the social structure of the community and culture in which the child is living. In discussing primary prevention, the training of "teachers to differentiate between the use of healthy and pathological mechanisms to cope with life's stresses" (Visosky, 1967) is of importance. He feels that inservice training should be provided in these areas with the goal of sensitizing teachers to emotional conflict in children before symptoms appear. In addition, Visosky (1967) explores the expansion of the teacher's capacity to deal effectively with children under stress and to help other children to learn to cope more adequately with the stresses of our society. The two major areas of relevance for primary prevention in the schools are curriculum (see Chapter Seven) and the teacher (see Chapters Five and Six); "The teacher makes or breaks the material she handles" (Kessler, 1966, p. 493).

Bolman and Westman (1967) state that "it is clear that much of the knowledge on primary prevention suggests that we must change institutions, not only individuals." The complementary approaches used should be child-centered efforts dealing with the child in the school, home, family, and community.

Kelly (1971) discusses three preventive interventions: (1) mental health consultation as a process radiating from the consultant (counselor) to the consultee (teacher) to the consultee's clients (i.e., children); (2) organizational change as environmental restructuring in order to facilitate the school's effectiveness in dealing with crises (e.g., inservice training for staff to redistribute decision-making functions); (3) the development of a community as an evolutionary process in which the community plans for its own change (i.e., mobilizing citizens to participate in change).

Secondary Prevention

The next level of concern is secondary prevention, which aims at reducing the duration of cases of mental disorder that will occur despite programs of primary prevention. By shortening the duration of existing cases, the prevalence of mental disorder in the community is reduced. This may be accomplished by organizing case-finding, diagnostic, and remedial services so that mental disorders are detected early and dealt with effectively and efficiently. Berlin (1967) discusses the early identification of disorders and also talks about helping parents make decisions about such matters as when to administer medication to children (e.g., asthmatics). With the school-age child, various kinds of emotional disturbance (e.g., extreme aggressiveness; withdrawal; apathy) can seriously interfere with learning (Berlin, 1967).

The special kind of consistent relationship necessary for foster children is similar to that which should be provided for socially and culturally deprived youngsters (Arsenian, 1961). Carroll, Cunningham, Keat, Sherman, and Paguaga (1969) have noted similar characteristics of deprivation in adoptive children.

Tertiary Prevention

Tertiary prevention aims at reducing the community rate of residual defect, which is often a sequel to acute mental illness. Rehabilitation services are the primary *modus operandi* in this area (Freedman, 1967). In particular, such alternatives to hospitalization as keeping the disturbed child in the community through home care and organizing dropout clubs for children and parents should be considered.

Three major helping strategies are discussed by Herr and Cramer (1972): individual counseling, group work, and environmental treatment. He identifies the goals of environmental treatment as twofold:

1. to change individual behavior, and
2. to provide optimal conditions for educational and personal experiences for all students (Herr and Cramer, 1972, p. 242).

The first goal involves altering a given student's reality situation. The second goal has to do with insuring that negative psychonomic factors are either eliminated or prevented from occurring.

With regard to intervention strategies for school, home, and community to be discussed in this chapter, it is unrealistic for a counselor to become involved in all of these programs. The counselor must order his priorities in order to have the greatest impact.

School Interventions

The school is the child's major life environment in which the counselor has his main input. It is in this particular setting that the helper has contact not only with the children themselves, but one can also exert some control over the learning environment in which the child is called upon to function. The school situation, therefore, is the most important setting for the counselor to consider in making interventions which can have a positive influence on the life of the child.

> The school counselor can and should operate within the total school environment to insure that the learning and behavior of students are viewed in psychological and sociological rather than moralistic terms (Herr, 1971, p. 68).

> The counselor of the future will likely serve as a facilitator of the environmental and human conditions which are known to promote the counselee's total psychological development, including his vocational development, as well as a strong sense of self identity with which he can cope with change. Thus, the conference participants expect the counselor to be active, to assume a positive offense, to be more committed and willing to fight for what he considers correct (Herr, 1972, pp. 244–245).

The same author goes on to state that "counselors must be oriented to get out of their offices and to the places where the action is" (Herr, 1972, p. 245). After strongly supporting environmental manipulation Herr discusses some strategies that can be used in order to have an impact on teachers and administrators in the schools. Most of these strategies involve social-learning theory.

Some School Considerations

Such learning theory approaches can develop and enhance the environments for learning and thus affect the entire school environment. For example, some of the ideas of Bandura and Walters (1963) could be put into effect to influence the whole system. These include the scheduling of reinforcement (e.g., withholding of positive reinforcers to discipline a child), awareness of vicarious reinforcement by models (i.e., student behavior is modified in response to reinforcement administered by a model), generalization (e.g., "intermittently reinforced aggressive responses not only are more persistent but also tend to generalize to new situations," Bandura and Walters, 1963, p. 123), and discrimination (e.g., "punishment by an authority figure seems to inhibit direct aggression in the presence of the punitive agent, but to be associated with high aggression toward other possible targets," Bandura and Walters, 1963, pp. 129–130). By gaining some control over these aspects of the life environment of the child, the counselor can influence the environment for learning of the school.

> It can be expected that such a consultative or change agent role by the school counselor will have cumulative effect on the nomothetic structure, the outer-limiting and outer-directing elements, to make it more sensitive to what is known about student learning, developmental processes, and the environmental conditions in which they operate most effectively (Herr, 1971, p. 67).

Organizational Development Approach   Another technology the counselor should be aware of is organizational development (O.D.). A group experiencing an O.D. problem undertakes the following process:

1. Identification of problems.
2. Setting problem priorities.
3. Development and sharing of data concerning these problems.
4. Joint action planning emphasizing alternatives.
5. Implementation and testing of selected alternatives.
6. Periodic review and further action (NTL, 1968, pp. 1–2).

Miles, Calder, Hornstein, Callahan, and Schiavo (1970) have discussed the application of this kind of approach to the school system. They conceive of the school system as existing in an environment from which it receives various inputs (primarily the children's learning and socialization). Internally, the system consists of four basic components: (1) goal perceptions, to which are connected a series of (2) role specifications and performances, regulated primarily through the application of (3) rewards and sanctions and (4) norms controlling the style in which interactions take place. By the process of O.D., members of the organization collaboratively gather, analyze, and interpret the data they have gleaned from various aspects of the organization. These data are then presented at meetings of the various groups involved and, finally, the staff and consultants analyze their interactions. As a result of analysis and feedback, the organization ideally becomes a more healthy one with appropriate goals, open communication, equality of power utilization, appropriate resource use, a reasonable degree of cohesiveness, an adequate level of morale, innovativeness, some sense of autonomy, adaptiveness to environmental considerations, and problem-solving adequacy (Miles *et al.*, 1970).

The physical environment's influence on behavior is often overlooked. A wide range of assumptions can be made about the influence of the physical environment on behavior. For example, one is that "although the participant remains largely unaware of his surroundings in the environmental process, these surroundings continue to exert considerable influence on his behavior" (Proshansky, Ittelson, and Rivlin, 1970, p. 37). Studer (1970), discussing physical systems from a behavioral standpoint, views the designed environment as capable of being programed as a learning system, "a system in which the energy matter variables are arranged to bring about the requisite state of behavioral affairs" (Studer, 1970, p. 64).

Interpersonal Relationships One of the most important initial concerns of the school counselor needs to be interpersonal relationships of children. For example, in order to facilitate cooperation and reduce aggression, one could deal with children in talk- or simulation-oriented situations (as described in Chapters Four and Five).

Various persons have been attempting to teach behavioral theory to children in the elementary schools. Farris, Kent, and Henderson (1970) attempted to teach children in the 8–12 age range to conduct laboratory exercises as a major component of instruction. The exercises included demonstration and simple experiments à la experimental psychology. The authors considered the performance of their elementary school students comparable to that of college freshmen. The work of Long (1970), however, is more in line with the author's image of an ideal model for elementary school behavioral science. Long describes the socioeducational program as a rehearsal for real life. Utilized with 18 children from the fourth and sixth grades, it initially emphasized action, later supplemented by theory. This approach is based on the educational truism that children (and adults, too) must *do* in order for something to be meaningful for them. Long (1970) views her program as an approach to primary prevention.

Vocational Perspectives   Another important consideration of the elementary counselor in the school is the development of vocational perspectives (see Chapter Eight of this text), whose applications are limited only by the ingenuity and the time of the counselor. Some school districts (following a recommendation from the Report of the Joint Commission on Mental Health of Children to "utilize community talent resources to enrich the educational experiences of children," 1969, p. 84) invite every parent to visit classes to describe their occupations. This not only provides occupational information, but makes children aware of various attitudes to life and work, and other important factors quite often overlooked in the vocational orientation sphere.

The Disadvantaged Child   The disadvantaged child is also of concern to the elementary school counselor. Although this subject could take up an entire chapter (e.g., Muro, 1970), we will briefly discuss some of the relevant variables here. Goldin and Margolin speak of disadvantaged individuals as "those persons who for social, emotional, physical, economic and educational reasons cannot satisfactorily adjust to the stresses and demands of life" (Goldin & Margolin, 1966, p. 1).

The author (Keat, 1973) has discussed a behavioral modification program for disadvantaged preschool children. The children (four blacks, four whites, and two Puerto Ricans) were from Head Start child development classes. The issue of fair assessment, which has been debated now for over a decade, should be addressed with great delicacy. There are, nevertheless, a variety of procedures that can be used to assess children's physical status, intellectual skill, language ability, and social-emotional development. Among the procedures used were a developmental map invented especially for the program (Keat, 1973), Gesell Copy Forms (Ilg & Ames, 1964), the Draw-a-Person Test, the Peabody Picture Vocabulary Test (translated into Spanish by one of the social workers so as not to penalize Spanish-speaking children for lack of verbal understanding), an articulation and language test previously used with Head Start children, the Head Start behavioral inventory, a cooperation-aggression behavior scale (Keat, 1970), and a cooperation behavior count scale. After the assessment phase was completed, the behavioral modification program outlined in Chapter Six was instituted. Since the major goal of this work was to increase cooperative behavior and decrease aggressive behavior, the emphasis was on behavioral rating scales. The results indicated that while behavioral changes as measured by the Head Start behavior inventory and the cooperation-aggression scale were nonsignificant, the cooperation level after was significantly higher than before behavior modification training (as assessed by the behavioral observation scales). These behavioral observations were carried out by the investigator and the case worker with the Head Start program. In addition, the teachers were trained in behavior modification procedures.

The author has run inservice education programs for teachers who work with the disadvantaged. In order to point out the unfairness of most assessment, the author began the session by giving the teachers a completely inappropriate and irrelevant test. This test was administered in all seriousness, and some of the teachers became quite upset (some almost withdrew from the program). After allowing them about 10 or 15 minutes to attempt to cope with their feelings about the difficult and inappropriate test, their reactions were discussed. This experience gave them some insight into how children can feel when subjected to irrelevant evaluations. Another exercise used in this inservice training program was a list of statements to which the teachers were to respond (see Figure 9–1 on page 246). The statements aroused heated discussion, revealed some prejudices prevalent among teachers working with disadvantaged children. People can be made aware of their prejudices and one can attempt to cope with them by keeping them under rational control or by changing them.

Inservice programs to train people to work with the disadvantaged should address themselves to such counseling considerations as awareness of one's language, classroom management procedures that involve behavioral modification, and curriculum integration. A developmental approach would seem especially useful in helping to understand and treat disadvantaged children.

Legal and Ethical Considerations The counselor as change agent must also confront legal and ethical considerations. Keat (1972) has stated that "one must conclude from the paucity of writing and lack of counselor involvement in the legal and ethical area that there is a dire need for further relevant literature and greater concern." Perhaps the most viable approaches for activist counselors are to make recommendations as a professional group to state legislatures and to bring test cases before the courts. Only through these kinds of actions can the counselor attempt

```
Below are listed a number of statements which I would like for you to respond.

For each statement mark whether you strongly agree, are neutral, or strongly
  disagree.


SA    N    SD

___   ___  ___   1.  Middle-class teachers cannot adequately cope with the
                      disadvantaged child.

___   ___  ___   2.  Disadvantaged children tend to be biologically and mentally
                      inferior to middle class children.

___   ___  ___   3.  The values of disadvantaged children are inappropriate for
                      the larger society.

___   ___  ___   4.  In counseling with disadvantaged children, the counselor
                      must be careful not to let his own values intrude.

___   ___  ___   5.  Disadvantaged children often lack the necessary motivation
                      to do well in school.

___   ___  ___   6.  Counselors often provide low levels of relationships to
                      clients who hold different values.

___   ___  ___   7.  Permitting students to behave in a manner that is really
                      unacceptable to adults is a good and healthy practice.

___   ___  ___   8.  The student's feelings are as important as the teacher's.

___   ___  ___   9.  Learning can take place only when there is a small
                      amount of confusion and uncertainty.

___   ___  ___  10.  More learning will take place in an unstructured class-
                      room than a structured classroom.

___   ___  ___  11.  Students are capable of selecting the goals for a class.
```

Figure 9–1 *Teacher-Response Statements*

to influence the legal environment. With regard to one's daily functioning, such principles as the confidentiality of communications—as a general rule, secure permission before communicating any privileged information—are important and have recently been spelled out for helping persons working in Pennsylvania:

Confidentiality of Student Communications—No *guidance counselor,* school nurse or school psychologist in the public schools or in private or parochial schools or other educational institutions providing elementary or secondary education, including any clerical worker of such schools and institutions, who, while in the course of his professional duties for a guidance counselor, school nurse or school psychologist, has acquired information from a student in *confidence* shall be compelled or allowed without the consent of the student, if the student is eighteen (18) years of age or over, or, if the student is under the age of eighteen (18) years, without the consent of his or her parent or legal guardian, to disclose that information in any legal proceeding civil or criminal, trial, investigation before any grand, traverse or petit jury, or any officer thereof, before the General Assembly or any committee thereof, or before any commission, department or bureau of this commonwealth, or municipal body, officer or committee thereof" (Senate Bill No. 209, Section 1319, June 12, 1972).

The legal and ethical considerations in counseling are complex, and at least a full-term course is necessary to treat adequately such issues as privileged communication (absolute and qualified), immunity, libel and slander, rights of privacy, malpractice, criminal liability, and the various ethical responsibilities of the counselor (e.g., competence level, referrals, confidentiality, recording sessions, and so on). For further information on these issues, the reader should consult such sources as Adams (1965), Schmidt (1962), Christiansen (1972), APGA (1965) and APA (1967) casebooks, Huckins (1968), Flowers and Bolmeier (1964), Ware (1964), London (1964), Nolte (1969 & 1971), and Long and Impellitteri (1971).

The teacher's primary task might be viewed as "character education," or a values-oriented approach. Goble (1967) argues that the teaching of values can be effective in preventing lawlessness and delinquency. His report viewed early lack of responsibility as the root cause of the deterioration of our society, as does Glasser. Therefore, education for character should be one of our basic goals. It is the task of the school to offer systematic teaching of character and human relations. Such courses could also be made available to parents; efforts might also be made to work with churches for the development of responsibility. There are numerous audiovisual aids the counselor or teacher can use to help implement a values orientation approach. The appropriately trained teacher can also integrate these materials into the existing curriculum.

One further general comment should be made, on competition in schools. The goal of organized sports in the schools can be seen as fostering and enhancing the development of a nation of lethargic and passive individuals who prefer to sit in the stands and watch the "stars." The author feels that an attempt should be made to involve as many children as possible in sports through age-appropriate activities as determined by teachers trained in movement education. The development of programs for everyone (e.g., intramurals) can help to reduce the emphasis on school-wide team sports in which only a few participate while hundreds or thousands watch. (For an ecological analysis of a basketball game, see Barker, 1968, pp. 94–99.) Although playground programs and organized teams (e.g., Little League) are not mutually exclusive in theory, in practice they seem to undermine one another.

School Action Programs

Orientation programs One of the major activities of the counselor in the school is to plan and provide orientation for children at important transition points. The first of these points is entry into kindergarten or first grade; the second is the transition to junior high or middle school. The child needs, first, some knowledge of the new physical environment he will encounter. This can be imparted by arranging school tours.

Psychological orientation is, of course, more complex because of the variety of possible attitudes and feelings toward change and toward the new situation. Psychological orientation might be accomplished by talking with groups of children or arranging for older children to help younger children get acquainted with the new school and the types of experiences they may encounter there. Shane *et al.* (1971) provide a schedule for orienting the child who is leaving elementary school. This schedule begins in February and extends to the end of the year. Initially, weekly visits are made to the elementary classrooms by former pupils in order to share their experiences and discuss selected (by the elementary children) topics. Visits by teachers in March are followed in April by visits of special personnel service people (e.g., counselor, principal, coaches) to the elementary school. Finally, in May, the elementary children make several visits to the new school, followed by discussions to plan for the coming year. This type of systematic approach can ease the anxiety of children about to encounter a new experience. Stamm and Nissman (1971) describe two informational handbooks useful in such transitions. The first is a kindergarten handbook that discusses such topics as what kindergartens are for, what do kindergarteners do, and what can parents do to help (Stamm & Nissman, 1971, pp. 153–163). The second guidebook, for the middle or junior high school, is generally formulated by the individual school in response to the questions of sixth graders about such things as lunch periods and changing classes. Examples from one school are contained in Stamm and Nissman's book (1971, pp. 147–152).

P.T.A./P.T.O. The counselor is also involved in school action programs with the Parent-Teacher Organization (P.T.O.) or Parent-Teacher Association (P.T.A.). This task involves relations with the community and parents, and can be conceived of primarily as a public relations job for the counselor. The actual functioning of the P.T.O. will be covered later in this chapter. The counselor can help develop and serve as a consultant to committees on such matters as cultural arts, buildings and grounds, and the like. Another public relations function of the counselor is to provide a handbook for parents. A practical type of handbook illustrated in Stamm and Nissman's book (1971, pp. 46–84) covers such topics as how to prepare a child for school, how to help a child develop a stable personality, how to satisfy a child's curiosity about sex, homework, and so on. Some elementary principals feel that public relations is the principal's and counselor's most important function. Community involvement should be continually encouraged. Parents can serve on committees dealing with such things as crafts activities, and parent aides can be introduced into the classroom.

Paraprofessionals in the Schools   The use of paraprofessionals in the schools can be helpful for both teachers and counselors (Guerney, 1969). The counselor's role is to train paraprofessionals (Riessman, 1967). A counselor-initiated program for adult volunteer counselors has been outlined by Muro (1973):

1. The school requests assistance from community agencies in finding adult volunteers to provide assistance to elementary-school children. The counselor interviews, screens and compiles a file on each adult (e.g., hobbies, time available, and so on).

2. Using these files, the counselor attempts to match the children referred with volunteers. The counselor then arranges a conference with the volunteer to discuss the child and a teacher-volunteer consultation conference time is established.

3. "Volunteer activities with the children include discussing mutual interests and listening to each other, reading stories, playing games, reviewing assignments engaging in arts and crafts and other related projects" (Muro 1973, p. 249). The emphasis is on the interpersonal relationship.

4. The role of the counselor is to provide consultation and supervisory help for the volunteer and to arrange for appropriate inservice training.

Warner (1971a) has reported on the use of adult paraprofessionals to implement a comprehensive vocational guidance program. Two aides were assigned to each level (elementary, junior, and senior high school). Before beginning work in the schools, the paraprofessionals participated in a six-week training session covering vocational development, test information, child and adolescent development, information resources, information delivery, guidance objectives, communication skills and a seminar on the structure of the school. Throughout the school year weekly meetings were held for continued training. Warner (1971b) reports the following major tasks of the aides: developing of two mini-career resource centers (incorporated into the regular school library), implementing vocational units for the fifth and sixth grades, contacting and bringing in workers from the community, developing and implementing units on self-understanding and interpersonal relationships.

Referral   Counselors involved in helping relationships with other people must occasionally consider referral. As Ramsey has pointed out, "Referral is an old, recognized and frequently used aspect of counseling. A survey of the literature shows that it is a much neglected topic" (Ramsey, 1962, p. 443). Baker (1973) has surveyed the literature of the decade following Ramsey's observation and concluded that "it is difficult to locate suggestions from which one can operate while making his own decisions concerning the minutiae of administrative details" (Baker, 1973, p. 19).

Peters, Shertzer, and Van Hoose (1965) discuss numerous aspects of the decision to make a referral. Among the points they make are that there should be administrative support for the use of the process; that the counselor refers when he believes that another agency's staff is competent to assist the pupil; that the referral should be made to appropriate available agencies; that the purpose of the referral should be clear; and that there is a need for follow-through to determine the effectiveness of the referral process. A further point is that the school counselor has the responsibility of surveying community agencies available for guidance referrals. Baker (1973) discusses the who, when, where, and how of the referral process. If the helper evaluates his own competencies and limitations, he is in a position to know *who* to refer. If, after assessing his own skills and the client's needs, the counselor feels that he cannot service the client, he seeks specialized assistance *when* the help needed by the client is not available from the counselor and is available somewhere else. *Where* does one refer a client for the help he needs? A satisfactory answer to this question requires the identification of possible referral sources, a working knowledge of the services they offer, implementation of their services, and the development of a reciprocal partnership in the referral process. One approach to the final question, *how?*, is to follow Brammer and Shostrom's (1968) suggestion of instructing referral sources about the client. Another is to help the client make the arrangements (of course, some clients can do so for themselves). If the referral is rejected, the helping person may need new information about the client. In the case of partial referrals, the counselor continues to provide services that are within the realm of his own expertise.

Counselor's Self Development   Although there are varying opinions (e.g., Hutson, 1971; Morgan, 1972) about how and how much the counselor should pursue his own self development, it can be valuable for the counselor to join a group focused on self growth (ideally, one composed of other helping professionals). Everyone experiences problems, crises, and conflicts in the normal process of life. One can use such a group as a buffer for crises or a vehicle for self actualization, depending upon one's circumstances and needs at the moment. A group encounter can provide the counselor with a sense of human belongingness, a mode of communication, and the therapeutic release that can result from talking about one's concerns with a group of helping persons. This experience can be a kind of oasis in life to which one turns in time of need. It affords the counselor a chance to become more intimate with other human beings than is possible in the ordinary course of life. Such experiences can thus be growth-enhancing in and of themselves. The basic encounter group emphasizes personal growth and development and the improvement of interpersonal relationships through an experiential process. Writings such as those of Rogers (1970) and O'Banion and O'Connell (1970) describe this type of group experience. But the only way one can actually know what it is like is to join such a group.

Home Interventions

One extremely important factor in considering home intervention is the physical space available—that is, the nature of the home, the play areas available for children, and the neighborhood in which the family lives. Only by visiting can the counselor reliably determine the home situation and thereby gain some insight into the child's life in this environment. The accessibility of a playground is another relevant consideration. Another important consideration, one parents can easily overlook, is the availability of peer playmates in the neighborhood.

Some Home Considerations

Caplan (1961) discusses the life history of the family unit. In the initial stage, the relation of the man and woman who become husband and wife is basically a closed system. "In the second phase of the history of a family the marital system becomes distant. As the parent-child system appears in the family, the marital system loosens, and this facilitates a close relationship between each of the parents and the children" (Caplan, 1961, p. 135). After the children grow up and leave the family, the marital system closes again.

Work with Parents   The use of parents as behavioral managers has been discussed in previous chapters, especially under the rubric of family counseling. Patterson, McNeal, Hawkins, and Phelps (1967) discuss the realignment of the child's social environment by training parents to use behavior modification procedures. The stance of Patterson and his coworkers is that the behavior modifier should focus his efforts on altering the child's social environment, rather than working directly with the deviant child. This topic is covered more thoroughly in Chapter Three.

Another approach is to have the husband and wife stage conferences in their own home (Rutledge, 1962). Rutledge reproduces a home conference plan in which couples arrange two conference periods a week, of approximately an hour each. During each conference the wife speaks for 20 minutes and then the husband talks for 20 minutes. Each then has 10 minutes for questions to clarify feelings. Rutledge's (1962) approach is basically an exercise in communication and the sharing of feelings in an attempt to understand one another. This approach puts the couple in the position of accepting responsibility for their own adjustment process.

Influence of Television   Television is a major influence in the home. The following poignant exchange from hearings before the Subcommittee on Communications of the U.S. Senate Committee on Commerce (1972) illustrates its current status:

SENATOR JOHN O. PASTORE: And you are convinced, like the Surgeon General, that we have enough data now [about the effects of television on children] to take action?

DR. ELI RUBENSTEIN (vice chairman, Surgeon General's Scientific Advisory Commitee on Television and Social Behavior):   I am, Sir.

SENATOR PASTORE: Without a re-review. It will only substantiate the facts that we already know. Irrespective of how one or another individual feels, the fact still remains that you are convinced, as the Surgeon General is convinced, that there is a causal relationship between television and social behavior on the part of children?

DR. RUBENSTEIN: I am, Sir.

SENATOR PASTORE: I think we ought to take it from there.

The evidence seems to be in. As quoted in Chapter Two, four authors reported that "it was demonstrated that there is a probable causative influence of watching violent television programs in early formative years on later aggression" (Eron, Huesmann, Lefkowitz and Walder, 1972). Approximately 80 percent of all programs surveyed contained some violence, and the frequency of violent acts in cartoons was 22.5 per hour. Preschool children averaged at least four hours a day and ten-year-olds averaged four to six hours a day of television-watching! "Observation of aggressive behavior produces increased aggression whether the model is live, on film, in commercial cartoons, or in a story" (Stein, 1972, p. 188). There is a "clear need for a reduction in the level of violence portrayed on television" (Murray, 1973, p. 477).

"At the same time it is equally important to encourage broadcasters to modify the balance of programming in favor of prosocial content" (Murray, 1973, p. 477). Stein and Friedrich (1972) report that children who watched prosocial programs (*Misterogers' Neighborhood*) were significantly more self-controlled in all three areas of measurement (obedience to rules, tolerance of delay, and persistence at frustrating tasks) than were children who watched aggressive (*Batman* and *Superman*) programs.

Some other programs also seem to be having positive effects. Doan (1972) reports that *The Electric Company* seems to be achieving its goal of having a positive impact on second-graders who are experiencing failure in their reading programs. "The Electric Company has the single narrow purpose of teaching 7-year-olds to read" (Mayer, 1973, p. 15). Figures from 1972 indicated that *The Electric Company* was being viewed in 29 percent of all primary schools and that more than 50 percent of the schools with television sets in the classroom were using the show (Mayer, 1973). Another new program called *Multiplication Rock* (available on Capitol Records SJA-11174, *Multiplication Rock*, music and lyrics by Bob Dorough) combines short rock songs (e.g., "Three is the magic number") with animated cartoons to teach children the multiplication tables. These programs, used in the school, have the same effect on primary-school children as does *Sesame Street* on the cognitive life of preschoolers watching at home. The programs just cited concentrate, as do the schools, primarily on the cognitive domain.

There seems to be a need for more concern with such issues as cooperation, positive ways of coping with frustration, appropriate morals, and helping others (as in *Misterogers' Neighborhood*). A question remains about the capacity of parents and other important adults to control television and to point the socialization of our children in more positive directions.

Liebert and Poulos (1972) suggest some action programs. Their sample of children overcame their fears of dogs and dentists by being shown model children fearlessly coping with both. After the children had seen brief ten-minute films, eight out of nine willingly approached a German Shepherd and the other group expressed more positive attitudes toward dentists. Another of Liebert and Poulos' suggestions is that future counselors make available videotape cassettes for home use by problem children.

Home Action Programs

P.T.A./P.T.O. One of the primary ways of involving parents in school and community action is through parent-teacher organizations. A variety of types of parental input can be encouraged. One example is an attempt to learn how much parents know about the schools. In one instance, a group met at lunchtime for several weeks to devise a parent questionnaire dealing with philosophy of education, the parents' participation in various activities of the school, and including concrete informational items to which the parents could respond in a feeling fashion. An example of this type of questionnaire is included in Appendix G (for a briefer 16-question survey, see Phillips, 1972).

The results from a selected sample ($N = 25$) of female respondents who had lived in the district from one to three years, typical in a mobile university community, were as follows (on a 5-point scale in which 1—no help, 2—of little help, 3—helpful, 4—very helpful, 5—extremely helpful): Elementary counselor conferences are (Sum = 60, Mean = 2.4); elementary counselor conferences could be (Sum = 95, Mean = 3.8). The t-test for related measures was applied and a value ($t = 6.36$) significant at the .01 level was obtained. It seems that mothers hoped for much more than they were receiving from the elementary conferences. In addition, 20 persons from this sample were not included in the tabulation because they had never had any contact with a counselor ($N = 4$), only ranked "could be" and did not attach a numerical value (i.e., 1 to 5) to "are" ($N = 10$), or gave no response ($N = 6$). As a consequence, at the next parent-teacher organization meeting the elementary counselor spent half the program describing his work and fielding questions from the parents.

Companions The use of self-enhancing and therapeutic companions is pertinent when significant figures are literally or emotionally absent from the home. The main question for the counselor is the identity of such companions. Goodman (1967, 1972) matched college students with boys ("quiets" and "outgoings") needing big brothers. The benefits of such a "buddy" relationship include the enhancement of the child's self-esteem, the partial filling of a gap in one-parent families, and the fulfillment of developmental needs stemming from economic and/or social deprivation (Leubuscher & Davis, 1972).

There are at least two other populations that can potentially serve as companions for children in the elementary schools—high school and intermediate elementary students. The use of high-school students in one-to-one relationships with elementary school children has been discussed by Winters and Arent (1969). Leaman (1972) developed a volunteer "buddy" program in which high-school students related to children in the elementary school on a one-to-one basis. Recruitment was undertaken through the local Future Teachers of America club. An outline of the proposed "buddy" program was presented at one of the FTA's meetings, and applications were subsequently distributed to all interested students. Twenty applications were received from the 35 members. Eighteen students were interviewed individually. The number of students considered eligible for the program was finally reduced to 15 (12 girls and 3 boys). Elementary-school teachers submitted the names of children they thought could benefit from this kind of one-to-one relationship. The volunteers and children were matched according to the two criteria of sex and geographical proximity. One difficulty, of course, is that boys in elementary school tend to have more problems than girls; there were only three male volunteers and referrals for boys predominated. From among all the volunteers and children, seven pairs were matched (3 pairs of boys and 4 pairs of girls). The seven volunteers met for a general orientation period and were asked to spend a minimum of two hours each week with their child, under the supervision of the elementary counselor. Although the primary impact of the program is on the children, learning is occurring for the high-school volunteers. The enthusiasm on both sides was apparent. It was felt that the program was a start toward developing a bigger one in this rural community. The counselor's function in the "buddy" program was that of initiator, consultant, and coordinator.

Another program (McWilliams & Finkel, 1973) used underachieving high-school students as aides to work with teacher-referred withdrawn children in the primary grades. Contacts lasted about one-half hour and occurred once or twice a week. Activities included conversation, walking, painting and drawing, crafts, reading, and indoor and outdoor games. The primary-grade children exposed to the aides were perceived as more trusting, warm, attentive, and less withdrawn, sad, and frightened than they had previously been. For the aides, engaging in human service activities led to a more functional and rewarding high-school experience.

Another type of companionship program is the use of volunteers from the intermediate elementary grades to work with primary-grade children. Cook (1971) used sixth-grade volunteers as big brothers for fatherless boys. The goal of these big brothers was to lessen disordered behaviors and meet the emotional needs of the children. Some schools have the upper-grade children work with younger children in a tutorial fashion (Prentice & Sperry, 1965). This kind of program focuses primarily on the cognitive development of the child.

Parent Orientation Groups   Parent orientation groups can be useful in the schools. A family outreach plan in the community mental health center has been described by Joelson (1972). These parent orientation groups ordinarily met three times and included from 12 to 16 parents. Their goal was to orient parents to the clinic and to give them an opportunity to get to know one another, have their questions answered, and discuss their own children. This type of *in vivo* experience enabled parents to learn what the experience of treatment is like. The results seemed to be favorable and there were some indications that these groups could be continued as counseling groups. This concept might be applied with disadvantaged groups, who are often alienated from the schools. Parents could be introduced to some of the roles and functions of the school, enabling them to feel closer to their children's situation. In the work of Carroll *et al.* (1970) with an inner-city population, parent and child were asked to come to school together and remain together throughout a one-day orientation program. Kindergarten and first-grade teachers (optional for second-grade teachers) divided their classes into six small groups. During the first three days of the new school year, each group was invited to spend one half day in school participating in the parent-child orientation program. Teachers usually worked with six to ten children and their parents during each half day session. The four goals of this parent-child orientation (Carroll *et al.*, 1970) program were:

1. To familiarize the children with their teacher and her expectations in a friendly atmosphere in order to facilitate their adjustment to school.

2. To enable the teacher to obtain a much clearer and personal knowledge of each child and his parents.

3. To enable the teacher and parents to begin the school year by getting to know one another on a more personal basis.

4. To provide the parents with information and skills (e.g., games to play with their children at home complementing the teacher's work in school) which would enable them to better assist the child at home in developing his learning potentials (p. 10).

Community Interventions

Community interventions in which the school counselor might become involved are, theoretically, quite numerous. Some can be engaged in as a function of one's job; others are restricted to counselors who become involved as parents on behalf of their own children. Some community activities that counselors have been known to engage in are involvement in outdoor recreation programs, perceptual motor training programs for children on Saturdays and during summers, Lion's Club vision programs, Cubs and Brownies, Boy and Girl Scout organizations, Kiwanis, and the like. These are just some of the ways the counselor can become involved in community life; the possibilities are limited basically by the counselor's compassion, available time, investment in his job, and involvement in his own family. Compassion grows out of the recognition of community. "Compassion is the awareness that we are all in the same boat and that we all shall either sink or swim together" (May, 1972, p. 251).

The communications media are making awareness of the world beyond one's immediate community unavoidable. With regard to the counselor's job, state and federal governments directly affect his day-to-day functioning. That is, the outlook of the incumbent administration influences funding of projects implemented in the community. For example, during certain administrations, the war on poverty was given priority and projects dealing with disadvantaged children were funded. More recently, emphasis has been placed on correction of criminal conduct, e.g., drugs or antisocial behaviors. Funding, therefore, has been primarily concentrated in the areas of detention and drug programs. Faced with this reality, the counselor may be lured to where the money is in order to implement programs that need financial support.

Assessment of Community Needs

Evaluation of school and community needs is a necessary prerequisite to action. Stamm and Nissman (1971) suggest that such an evaluation should be characterized by goal clarification, records of community programs, involvement of community representatives, numerous modes of evaluation, competent consultation on the experimental design, acting upon and publicizing the results of the evaluation, and presentation of the results to the community in an understandable fashion. This community survey should assess vocations and industry, recreational facilities, community government, and community services (e.g., fire department, police, local guidance agencies, and the like).

Carkhuff (1971, pp. 118–124) provides a useful guide for studying community organization. Among the recommendations of this outline are an analysis of the top man in the community (e.g., mayor), assessment of city departments and agencies, reorganization within the organization which is based on making effective whatever is ineffective by shifting personnel and reassigning duties, orientation and training of all personnel in such areas as sociology of the city and human relations, utilization of the community's existing resources, and the use of small groups to solve problems.

Community Action Programs

Preschool Programs   The elementary counselor should be concerned with preschool programs in the community. For example, the counselor may be a consultant to such a program as Head Start. This could involve collaboration with teachers to set up programs to be implemented in the preschool setting. In certain school districts, the program is coordinated by a person from the elementary counseling staff. It is supplemented by a follow-through program once the children are in school. Thus, the counselor can aid in coordinating and sustaining the gains made during the preschool programs.

Community Education   A community education program should be broadly influential. "Community education is the process by which the educational needs of the individual and of the society are met" (Weaver, 1972, p. 155). Fourteen strategies for establishing such a program are outlined by Carrillo and Heaton (1972) and include activities like the scheduling of meetings (e.g., of interested school and community persons), development of committees, establishment of a pilot community school, and implementation of the community school program. A community school program initiated in Flint, Michigan, in 1935 now includes adult education classes, a broad range of recreational activities, support for "big brothers," and home-school counselors. "Counselors are chosen because of the nobility and humanity they exemplify more than for any other reason. Because they have warmhearted, kindly personalities, they have been able to establish empathy with patrons of the neighborhood school quickly" (Campbell, 1972, p. 196). Some activities and topics that can serve to enliven the community school curriculum are outdoor education, career awareness, values clarification, adjusting to others, sharing in citizenship, and asserting personal identity (Olsen, 1972). These concerns are often among the goals of elementary school counseling. The counselor may serve as a coordinator and/or collaborator in community education programs.

Scouting Groups Another way in which the counselor can become involved in the community is by working with Scouting groups. This can be done either as a parent or as an interested adult in the community. A particularly interesting scouting program was reported by Hogle (1972). The children involved in this program were mentally retarded and educable. The den "dads" were inmates of a medium security prison for first adult felony offenders under the age of 27. This correctional institution emphasizes retraining and resocialization. (For a report of a project that focuses on self rehabilitation for inmates, see Byrd & Goines, 1973.) The boys meet these men once a week for two hours. This program has been in operation for three years and seems to be fairly successful.

Outdoor Recreation Programs Elementary counselors can coordinate recreational programs in school and community facilities. The goal of an outdoor program could be the social-emotional development of children living together with adults in a resident outdoor school camp setting. The process of children and adults living together for some days and nights can lead to an appreciation of self and others, fruitful and responsible attitudes of citizenship, and the resolution of difficulties in small-group problem-solving settings. Stephan (1963) has described experiences designed to develop social and emotional competencies in a program of outdoor education for the elementary school years. These experiences are directed toward such goals as learning to get along with agemates with the objective of social development. At grade one, the experiences designed to enhance this type of development are learning to walk single-file as partners or as a group, discussing ways to be considerate of others, taking turns at being guides, sharing findings on excursions with classmates, and the like. At the fifth and sixth grade levels, the same objective can be met by selecting classmates other than one's best friend to share responsibility for a project, volunteering for responsibilities that may not be one's first choice, and so on. Faber (1972) has outlined a proposal for an elementary-school outdoor program focusing on group problem-solving meetings and the establishment of optimum learning environments in the outdoor camp setting. Elementary-school counselors can coordinate and participate in such programs.

Establishment of Substitute Homes Another project that the elementary counselor can help to coordinate is the establishment of homes for children who either do not have a place to live or are rejected in their current living situations. Such a residential "learning house" (Mahoney & Mahoney, 1973) is patterned loosely on "achievement place" (Phillips, 1968). The goal of the Mahoney and Mahoney (1973) model was to provide a community-centered foster home for problem children aged from 3 to 12 years. Six children resided in the house with an adult couple. Behavioral management was the preferred mode of treatment. Academic, social, and self care skills received particular attention. Children attended classes in the regular schools. Some of the techniques described in the paper were a token economy, socialization and timeout, "cooling it" (having the children sit quietly to await a delayed gratification), the "hot seat" (one child sits in a chair with the task of keeping cool while all the other children try to make him angry), modeling, and self-reinforcement. The cases discussed in the Mahoney and Mahoney (1973) paper seemed to evidence quite favorable outcomes and indicate the viability of a family-style behavior modification program centered in the community.

Summary

This chapter has considered a variety of environmental considerations and action plans. The topics were divided into three key target systems—school, home, and community. After the initial discussion of levels (i.e., primary, secondary, tertiary) of prevention, school interventions were described. Approaches involved counselors as change agents, organizational development, space arrangements, enhancing interpersonal relationships, vocational perspectives, programs for the disadvantaged, legal and ethical considerations, orientation programs, P.T.O.'s, paraprofessionals in the schools, referral, and the counselor's self development. Under the rubric of home intervention, physical space, work with parents, the influence of television, P.T.O.'s, companionship programs, and parent-orientation groups were discussed. Finally, community strategies included community education programs, preschool education, Scouting groups, outdoor recreation programs, and the establishment of homes for needy children.

References

Adams, J. F. Ethical responsibilities of the counselor. In J. F. Adams (Ed.), *Counseling and guidance: A summary view.* New York: Macmillan, 1965, pp. 376–385.

American Personnel and Guidance Association. *Ethical standards casebook.* Washington: the Association, 1965.

American Psychological Association. *Casebook on ethical standards of psychologists.* Washington: the Association, 1967.

Arsenian, J. Situational factors contributing to mental illness in the United States. *Mental Hygiene,* 1961, **45**, 194–196.

Auerswald, E. H. Interdisciplinary versus ecological approach. *Family Process,* 1968, 7, 202–215.

Baker, S. B. Referrals: who? when? where? and how? *Pennsylvania Personnel and Guidance Association Journal,* 1973, 1, 19–23.

Bandura, A., & Walters, R. H. *Social learning and personality development.* New York: Holt, Rinehart & Winston, 1963.

Barker, R. G. *Ecological psychology.* Stanford, Cal.: Stanford University Press, 1968.

Berlin, I. N. Secondary prevention. In A. M. Freedman & H. I. Kaplan (Eds.), *Comprehensive textbook of psychiatry.* Baltimore: Williams & Wilkins, 1967, pp. 1541–1548.

Bloom, B. L. Strategies for the prevention of mental disorders. In G. Rosenblum (Ed.), *Issues in community psychology and preventive mental health.* New York: Behavioral Publications, 1971, pp. 1–20.

Bolman, W. W., & Westman, J. C. Prevention of mental disorder: An overview of current programs. *American Journal of Psychiatry,* 1967, **128**, 1058–1068.

Brammer, L., & Shostrom, E. *Therapeutic psychology.* Englewood Cliffs, N.J.: Prentice-Hall, 1968.

Byrd, D., & Goines, L. The Lorton Project. *Downbeat,* 1973, **40**, 13.

Campbell, C. M. Contributions of the Mott Foundation to the community education movement. *Phi Delta Kappan,* 1972, **54**, 195–197.

Caplan, G. *An approach to community mental health.* New York: Grune and Stratton, 1961.

Caplan, G., & Grunebaum, H. Perspectives on primary prevention:

A review. *Archives of General Psychiatry,* 1967, **17**, 331–346.

Carkhuff, R. R. *The development of human resources.* New York: Holt, Rinehart & Winston, 1971.

Carrillo, T. S., & Heaton, I. C. Strategies for establishing a community education program. *Phi Delta Kappan,* 1972, **54**, 165–167.

Carroll, J. F. X., Keat, D. B., Sherman, F., Cunningham, J., & Paguaga, C. Theoretical model for the analysis of adoptive parenthood. *Catholic Charities Review,* 1969, **53**, 12–20.

Carroll, J. F. X., Bell, A. A., Brecher, H., & Minor, M. W. An ecological, preventive program of psychosocial services for elementary schools—A breakthrough for tradition-bound school psychologists and counselors. Unpublished manuscript, Philadelphia nonpublic school project, 1970.

Christiansen, H. D. *Ethics in counseling: Problem situations.* Tucson: University of Arizona Press, 1972.

Cook, H. Big brother for the fatherless. *Elementary School guidance and counseling,* 1971, 6, 142–143.

Doan, R. K. Is the Electric Company turning children on? *TV Guide,* 1972, **20**, 14–17.

Eron, L. D., Huesmann, L. R., Lefkowitz, M. M., & Walder, L. O. Does television violence cause aggression? *American Psychologist,* 1972, **27**, 253–263.

Faber, D. A. An outdoor elementary school guidance program to facilitate the social-emotional development of children. Unpublished masters thesis, Pennsylvania State University, 1972.

Farris, H. E., Kent, N. D., & Henderson, D. E. Teaching behavioral science in the elementary and junior high school. In R. Ulrich, T. Stachnik, & J. Mabry (Eds.), *Control of human behavior,* vol. II. Glenview, Ill.: Scott, Foresman, 1970, pp. 309–314.

Flowers, A., & Bolmeier, E. C. *Law and pupil control.* Cincinnati: W. H. Anderson, 1964.

Freedman, A. M. Tertiary prevention. In A. M. Freedman & H. I. Kaplan (Eds.), *Comprehensive textbook of psychiatry.* Baltimore: Williams & Wilkins, 1967, pp. 1548–1551.

Goble, F. *Character education as a means of reducing crime and delinquency.* Pasadena, Cal.: Thomas Jefferson Research Center, 1967.

Goldin, G. J., & Margolin, R. J. Motivation and the disadvantaged. Paper presented at the APGA Convention, Washington, D.C., April 1966.

Goodman, G. An experiment with companionship therapy: College students and troubled boys—assumptions, selection and design. *American Journal of Public Health,* 1967, **57**, 1172–1777.

Goodman, G. *Companionship therapy.* San Francisco: Jossey-Bass, 1972.

Guerney, B. G. (Ed.) *Psychotherapeutic agents: New roles for nonprofessionals, parents, and teachers.* New York: Holt, Rinehart &

Winston, 1969.

Hearings before the Subcommittee on Communications of the Committee on Commerce, United States Senate, 92nd Congress, 1972, p. 152.

Herr, E. L. The school counselor and the school as a social system: Some elements of a change agent role. In J. C. Hansen & S. Cramer (Eds.), *Group guidance and counseling in the schools.* New York: Appleton-Century-Crofts, 1971, pp. 59–69.

Herr, E. L., & Cramer, S. H. *Vocational guidance and career development in the schools: Toward a systems approach.* Boston: Houghton Mifflin, 1972.

Hogle, C. A. "Lean on Me": A unique scouting program. *Children Today,* 1972, 1, 7–10.

Huckins, W. *Ethical and legal considerations in guidance.* Boston: Houghton Mifflin, 1968.

Hutson, P. W. Sensitivity training. *Pennsylvania Keynotes,* 1971, 6, 3.

Ilg, F. L., & Ames, L. B. *School readiness.* New York: Harper & Row, 1964.

Joelson, R. B. Family outreach in a community mental health center. *Children Today,* 1972, 1, 11–12.

Keat, D. B. Cooperation-aggression behavior scale. University Park, Penn.: Author, 1970.

Keat, D. B. Legal and ethical concerns of counseling psychologists. A review of books supporting a case of uninvolvement. *The Journal of Forensic Psychology,* 1972, in press.

Keat, D. B. A behavior modification program for pre-school children: Snags, pitfalls, and some behavioral changes. Unpublished manuscript, Pennsylvania State University, 1973.

Kelly, J. G. The quest for valid preventive interventions. In G. Rosenblum (Ed.), *Issues in community psychology and preventive mental health.* New York: Behavioral Publications, 1971, pp. 109–139.

Kessler, J. *Psychopathology of childhood.* Englewood Cliffs, N.J.: Prentice-Hall, 1966.

Leaman, L. J. Initiating a "Be a Buddy" program in the Tyrone Area School District. Unpublished masters thesis, Pennsylvania State University, 1972.

Leubuscher, F., & Davis, D. The "Buddy" program as a significant contribution to student personnel services. Unpublished manuscript, Pennsylvania State University, 1972.

Liebert, R. M., & Poulos, R. W. TV for kiddies: Truth, goodness, beauty and a little bit of brainwash. *Psychology Today,* 1972, 6, 123–128.

London, P. *The modes and morals of psychotherapy.* New York: Holt, Rinehart & Winston, 1964.

Long, B. E. A model for elementary school behavioral science as an agent of primary prevention. *American Psychologist,* 1970, 25, 571–574.

Long, T. E., & Impellitteri, J. T. Ethical practice: Preserving human *dignity. The Personnel and Guidance Journal,* 1971, **50**, 245–330.

Mahoney, M. J., & Mahoney, F. E. A residential program in behavior modification. In R. D. Rubin, J. P. Brady & J. D. Henderson (Eds.), *Advances in behavior therapy,* Vol. 4. New York: Academic Press, 1973, 93–102.

May, R. *Power and innocence.* New York: Norton, 1972.

Mayer, M. The Electric Company: Easy reader and a lot of other hip teachers. *The New York Times Magazine,* 28 January 1973, 14–29.

McWilliams, S. A., & Finkel, N. J. High school students as mental health aides in the elementary school setting. *Journal of Consulting and Clinical Psychology,* 1973, **40**, 39–42.

Miles, M., Calder, P., Hornstein, H., Callahan, D., & Schiavo, R. Data feedback and organizational change in a school system. In R. T. Golembiewski & A. Blumberg (Eds.), *Sensitivity training and the laboratory approach.* Itasca, Ill.: F. E. Peacock, 1970, pp. 352–361.

Morgan, L. B. Sensitivity training: Another side of the issue. *Pennsylvania Keynotes,* 1972, **6**, 3–4.

Muro, J. J. *The counselors work in the elementary school.* Scranton, Penn.: International Textbook Company, 1970.

Muro, J. Elementary-school guidance—Quo Vadis? In W. H. Van Hoose, J. J. Pietrofesa, & J. Carlson *Elementary School guidance and counseling: A composite view.* Boston: Houghton Mifflin, 1973, pp. 240–254.

Murray, J. P. Television and violence. *American Psychologist,* 1973, **28**, 472–478.

Nolte, M. C. *Guide to school law.* West Nyack, N.Y.: Parker, 1969.

Nolte, M. C. *School law inaction.* West Nyack, N.Y.: Parker, 1971.

NTL Institute. What is OD? *NTL Institute: News and Reports,* 1968, **2**, 1–2.

O'Banion, T., & O'Connell, A. *The shared journey.* Englewood Cliffs, N.J.: Prentice-Hall, 1970.

Olsen, E. G. Enlivening the community school curriculum. *Phi Delta Kappan,* 1972, **54**, 176–178.

Patterson, G. R., McNeal, S., Hawkins, N., & Phelps, R. Reprogramming the social environment. *Journal of Child Psychology and Psychiatry,* 1967, **8**, 181–195.

Peters, H. J., Shertzer, B., & Van Hoose, W. H. *Guidance in elementary schools.* Chicago: Rand McNally, 1965.

Phillips, E. L. Achievement place: Token reinforcement procedures in a homestyle rehabilitation setting for "pre-delinquent" boys. *Journal of Applied Behavior Analysis,* 1968, **1**, 213–223.

Phillips, J. D. A survey can increase school-community interaction. *Pennsylvania Education,* 1972, **3**, 8–10.

Prentice, N. M., & Sperry, B. M. Therapeutically oriented tutoring of children with primary learning inhibitions. *American Journal of Orthopsychiatry,* 1965, **35**, 521–530.

Proshansky, H. M., Ittelson, W. H., & Rivlin, L. G. The influence of the physical environment on behavior: Some basic assumptions. In H. M. Proshansky, W. H. Ittelson, & L. G. Rivlin (Eds.), *En-*

vironmental psychology: Man and his physical setting. New York: Holt, Rinehart & Winston, 1970, pp. 27–37.

Ramsey, G. V. The referral task in counseling. *Personnel and Guidance Journal,* 1962, **40,** 443–447.

Report of the Joint Commission on Mental Health of Children. *Crisis in child mental health: Challenge for the 1970's.* New York: Harper & Row, 1969.

Riessman, F. Strategies and suggestions for training nonprofessionals. *Community Mental Health Journal,* 1967, **3,** 103–110.

Rogers, C. *Carl Rogers on encounter groups.* New York: Harper & Row, 1970.

Rutledge, A. L. Husband-wife conferences in the home. *Marriage and Family Living,* 1962, **24,** 151–154.

Schmidt, L. D. Some legal considerations for counseling and clinical psychologists. *Journal of Counseling Psychology,* 1962, **9,** 35–44.

Shane, J. G., Shane, H. G., Gibson, R. L., & Munger, P. F. *Guiding human development: The counselor and the teacher in the elementary school.* Belmont, Cal.: Wadsworth, 1971.

Stamm, M. L., & Nissman, B. S. *New Dimensions in elementary guidance: Practical procedures for teachers, counselors and administrators.* New York: Richards Rosen, 1971.

Stein, A. H. Mass media and young children's development. In *Early Childhood Education Seventy-First Yearbook,* 1972, 181–202.

Stein, A. H., & Friedrich, L. K. The influence of aggressive and prosocial television programs on the naturalistic behavior of preschool children. Unpublished manuscript, Pennsylvania State University, 1972.

Stephan, S. J. A program of outdoor education for the elementary school, grades one through six. Unpublished masters thesis, State University of Iowa, 1963.

Studer, R. G. The dynamics of behavior contingent physical systems. In H. M. Proshansky, W. H. Ittelson & L. G. Rivlin (Eds.), *Environmental psychology: Man and his physical setting.* New York: Holt, Rinehart & Winston, 1970, pp. 56–76.

Visosky, H. M. Primary prevention. In A. M. Freedman & H. I. Kaplan (Eds.), *Comprehensive textbook of psychiatry.* Baltimore: Williams & Wilkins, 1967, pp. 1537–1541.

Ware, M. L. (Ed.) *Law of guidance and counseling.* Cincinnati: W. H. Anderson, 1964.

Warner, R. Paraprofessionals I: Rationale and training. *Pennsylvania Keynotes,* 1971, **6,** 3.

Warner, R. Paraprofessionals II: Uses and evaluation. *Pennsylvania Keynotes,* 1971, **6,** 1–4.

Weaver, D. C. A case for theory development in community education. *Phi Delta Kappan,* 1972, **54,** 154–157.

Winters, W. A., & Arent, R. The use of high school students to enrich an elementary guidance and counseling program. *Elementary School Guidance and Counseling,* 1969, **3,** 198–205.

While the practicing counselor may not directly organize or manage an elementary guidance program, some knowledge of management and coordination principles will enable him to understand what he is doing in the broader context of a school system. The counselor will occasionally be called upon for substantial input into the system, and there may be times when the counselor will manage a particular program.

Dinkmeyer (1968) states that

> the philosophy and basic concepts of guidance only become meaningful as they are applied in the guidance program. The crucial step from philosophy to action involves administration and organization, focusing on objectives, role definitions of various professionals within the program, and the interrelationship of the pupil personnel services (Dinkmeyer, 1968, p. 40).

Dinkmeyer and Caldwell (1970) talk about the crucial area of administration and coordination as focusing

> on providing effective communication of the philosophy, principles, and techniques of the guidance program to administration, teachers, parents, and other pupil personnel workers. It is concerned with developing a meaningful pattern of child services. (Dinkmeyer & Caldwell, 1970, p. 75).

Hill and Luckey (1969) discuss the effective guidance program in the elementary school as characterized by the acronym "PLEA": Planned (it is not a hit-or-miss affair); Led (it demands constant and well-organized management); Executed (responsibilities are assigned and carried out); and Assessed (it is evaluated, its impact upon children is appraised).

In the final analysis, the task of the elementary counselor is to

Organization, Implementation, Management and Coordination of Elementary School Guidance Services

develop a counseling program unique to the particular elementary school or schools in which he functions. Dimick and Huff (1970) consider some of the basic elements of the counseling program to be a warm, honest, and mutually respectful environment, the total climate of the school, and the evident competence of the counselor. The "showing of wares" on the part of the counselor involves advertising his services and behaving in a way that is worth modeling.

The following topics will be discussed in this chapter: the organization and implementation of new programs, the management of existing ones, and the coordination of a variety of services that are potentially available in the schools. In each of these areas, it may be necessary for the reader to personalize the information offered to make it more pertinent to his situations.

Organization

Certain principles of organization should be followed in guidance programs. Humphreys, Traxler, and North (1960) discuss such matters as preparing clear-cut statements of the objectives of the guidance service, assigning specific duties to those in the program, defining the working relationships among the people in the program, and keeping the organization plan as simple as possible. Hill and Luckey (1969) talk about the involvement of the staff in organization. Implementation can be enhanced when those involved participate in planning. Such involvement requires starting where the staff is, encouraging staff leadership, insisting upon factual studies of matters that concern the staff, screening recommendations from the staff to see if they can be put into effect, and reiterating the school's chief concern—meeting children's needs.

A Systems Approach to Counselor Functions

The systems approach "involves the application of the methods of science to problems of the engineering and development of practical programs" (Cooley & Hummel, 1969, p. 252). With the current emphasis on accountability (e.g., Sullivan & O'Hare, 1971), the development of systems applicable to guidance programs appears to be a promising approach. The formulation of behavioral objectives was delineated in Chapter One. With regard to inaugurating a systems approach, Herr and Cramer (1972) have noted two methods that have been utilized. One involves changes in work practices, such as the implementation of a new curriculum, new grouping practices, and the like. The second approach is aimed at improving problem-solving capabilities. Herr and Cramer declare that "it appears that thing technologies hold greater likelihood for change than do people technologies" (p. 340), and go on to delineate a seven-step program to implement the systems approach (pp. 341–343):

1. The change agent first thoroughly grounds himself in the precepts, concepts, and methodologies of the systems approach.
2. All involved persons should participate in the formulation of goals and subscribe to these objectives.
3. Each group (i.e., teachers, administrators, students, community persons) should be represented on a steering or advisory committee, responsible for overseeing the inauguration, implementation, and evaluation of the new approach.
4. The advisory committee should have as its initial task the production of environmental conditions that will enhance the possibility of successfully implementing the systems approach.
5. The committee should see that the resources essential to goal achievement are available and mobilized.
6. The program is now ready for implementation. The head counselor or pupil personnel director should bear general responsibility for the coordination of the program.
7. Finally, it is necessary to carefully evaluate what has happened in relation to the goals of the program.

Ryan and Zeran (1972) have attempted to apply the systems approach to guidance management. Their rather comprehensive system involves ten elements in the management of guidance services: (1) conceptualization of the system; (2) establishment of the system's philosophy and assessment of needs; (3) definition of goals and objectives (this step involves the formulation of behavioral objectives, which many state and national organizations are currently soliciting); (4) processing of the information; (5) development of plans; (6) the pilot test study; (7) introduction of the system into the guidance program; (8) operation of the system, which requires the logistic support of staff as well as the inclusion of the learner population; (9) evaluation of the system and the individuals involved in it; (10) elimination of the system. Ryan and Zeran (1972) have applied this system to a variety of guidance programs, including individual analysis services, information services, career development and decision-making education, placement and work experience, and counseling services. Three other authors have applied the systems approach to the "three major components of the guidance program" which they identify as the "relationship system," the "communications system," and the "information system" (Blocher, Dustin, & Dugan, 1971).

The Counselor's Calendar

The elementary counselor typically works according to identifiable formats. That is, he approaches each day in the work week in predictable ways. In addition, there is an overall format for each year. Finally, there seem to be life cycles that affect the workings of the counselor (both environmental and self originating demands).

Daily Schedules   The counselor's typical work day will vary according to the person. There are, nevertheless, some typical patterns that counselors seem to abide by. Kaczkowski (1971) has identified patterns in the daily records kept by selected counselors. The first professional contact was normally made with a teacher before the pupils arrived at school. Small-group work with teachers was also done before school hours. These were either cognitively oriented or counseling groups that focused on the intrapersonal concerns of the participants. The third task normally engaged in before the children arrived at school was to work on such ancillary procedures as scheduling appointments, making telephone calls, or reading correspondence. After the start of classroom instruction, the counselor tended to have a brief contact with a principal, parent, or another pupil personnel worker. The first pupil contact was likely to be an individual counseling interview. The logs indicated that 65 percent of the counselor's morning was spent working with individuals. Another important work period that is quite often overlooked is the lunch hour. During this time, the counselor makes contact with adults and other pupil personnel workers. Some counselors spend up to three periods in the lunchroom meeting with teachers. In some schools the lunch period is the most accessible time for consultation. Professional activity after lunch was primarily devoted to group work with children; more classroom guidance sessions are conducted in the afternoon than in the morning. After the pupils were dismissed, the counselor's work centered on adults, such as teachers, administrators, and parents. The counselor's evening activities which are often overlooked (except by practicing counselors), included Board of Education meetings, community interest group meetings, PTA meetings, home visitations, and group work with parents.

Seasonal Cycles There also seem to be seasonal emphases in the counselor's job. Although most of the activities mentioned in this paragraph go on throughout the year, they are emphasized at certain times of the year more than at others. For example, curriculum consultation is most appropriate during the summer, when the curriculum committee meets to plan the program for the coming year. There also might be more time available for contacts with community agencies during the summer. Orientation activities typically take place in the fall, and again in the spring to prepare children about to make transitions. Testing typically takes place during the fall, with follow-up evaluations in the spring. Counselors' involvement in report cards can vary. If report cards are a new phenomenon, a great deal of activity may be stimulated during the fall when the grading system needs to be introduced. Both parents' and teachers' attitudes need to be considered and worked through. Counseling and consultation functions sometimes take a couple of months to establish each year. This is the feeling-out period, when teachers begin working with their new charges. Evaluation and research quite often take place during the fall and spring terms. Changes are evaluated by comparing initial and subsequent measurements.

The frequency of referrals varies during the school year. Several weeks after school opens, referrals start to pour in. These involve initial crises that teachers have been unable to resolve, and call for evaluation, consultation, or counseling. Although Christmas is normally a happy time for people with intact and accessible families, it can become a season of depression for many others; there is a syndrome called the "Christmas Blues" (Gunther, 1971). That is, if they do not have appropriate emotional attachments within the family, if there has been a loss in the family, if a conflict exists, or if they are deprived in some other way, Christ-

mas can be a very sad time for both children and adults. Therefore, there may be a flurry of referrals just before Christmas or
after the New Year. The latter situation could also be a function
of the New Year's resolution syndrome, in which adults vow to
make a fresh start with their children and therefore attempt to
remedy their failings of the past year. During March and April
referrals seem to come out of the woodwork, and the counselor
can be deluged with numerous types of crises. One of the major
precipitating factors is probably the issue of whether or not to
promote a child to the next grade, change levels, or place him
in some other kind of classroom situation.

_____ **Implementation**

The eight steps suggested by Peters and Shertzer (1969, p. 335)
can provide a useful framework for building an elementary school
guidance program where none has existed before.

1. The guidance committee (counselors, teachers, and administrative staff) should determine the emphasis to be given to the
program (e.g. developmental, remedial, therapeutic).

2. Study the needs of the students to determine the focus and
limitations of the program.

3. Relate the social-personal phase of the guidance program to
the learning effectiveness of the pupils, as well as their total
development.

4. Given an adequate number of certified school counselors,
allow ample counseling time for development of positive relationships as well as remediation.

5. Include the social-personal phase of the counseling program
in the guidance budget.

6. If there is more than one counselor, designate one to be
chiefly responsible for social-personal guidance.

7. Decide on procedures for handling confidential data.

8. Evaluate the program.

Planning the Elementary Guidance Program

There should be some assessment of current needs, as well as
cooperative planning by all persons to be involved in the program.
Peters *et al.* (1965) feel that guidance should focus on the developmental needs of the children. A necessary step in organizing
the guidance program is to appraise the existing guidance services.
Although these may not be in the bailiwick of the elementary
counselor, services may be provided by someone in the school,
whether it be teachers, the psychologist, special remedial teachers,

or others. It is important to examine the role that teachers currently play in guidance and to determine what their role might be in the future. Other tasks are reviewing the types of information filed, delineating the philosophy of the school system, determining what the function of guidance will be, and staffing the guidance program. Logan (1971) has stated that the elementary counselor should service approximately 700–800 students. He also states that there should be one counselor for each elementary school building. This may be a desirable future goal, but for now it seems unrealistic in most school systems.

Starting the Elementary Guidance Program

Dinkmeyer and Caldwell (1970) state that

> it is important in initiating a guidance program that each school system analyze its own situation, guidance needs, and services already available, and then develop a program which fits a unique locale (Dinkmeyer & Caldwell, 1970, p. 64).

Johnston (1968) delineates the steps involved in initiating an elementary guidance program in a school district. The first activity of Johnston's committee on guidance was the exploration of published materials dealing with guidance at the elementary school level. The second was visits to schools that have or are contemplating the introduction of guidance programs. The third phase of the committee's work was an analysis of the guidance needs of elementary pupils in the school district and consideration of an appropriate design of service to meet these needs more adequately.

Stamm and Nissman (1971, pp. 24–25), the Pennsylvania Department of Education (1972, pp. 111–113), and Miller, Gum and Bender (1972, p. 297) all provide forms to evaluate the faculty's stand on the value of an elementary school guidance program. This information can serve as a bridge between the counselor and the faculty members of a particular school, and can also highlight the value of elementary counseling in districts considering budget trimming or staff expansion.

Hill and Luckey (1969) discuss five steps in the initiation of a guidance program. The first is the identification of dissatisfactions in the school and the organization of the staff to discuss these issues in order to stimulate data necessary for sound decision making. This process may point up the need for more individualized help for certain pupils. The third step involves adding to the school staff a person(s) who provides the needed services, whether they be diagnostic, remedial, or corrective; and a person who will be a ready and knowledgeable referral source for studying individual children as well as consulting with teachers and developing preventative methods of aiding children (i.e., the elementary school counselor). The fourth step is to develop a productive program to enhance the school staff's understanding of the children with whom they must deal. This can involve such matters as the need for better records, adequate testing, and more relevant home information. The fifth step is to address the issues of educational goals and the limits of the school's responsibility for the child. This subject relates to the "guidance learnings" discussed in Chapter One.

A final consideration—and one that is commonly overlooked —is the necessity of establishing an appropriate relationship with the staff. One way to initiate such a relationship is for the counselor to be introduced to the staff at a faculty meeting. At this time the counselor can describe his educational background, previous experience with children, and role in the school. He should assure the teachers that guidance already exists informally in the school, and that a guidance-oriented point of view is already held by many teachers for whom the optimum development of children is a crucial concern (Muro, 1970). The counselor can also familiarize himself with the faculty by visiting classrooms during the first several weeks of school. The counselor should be generally available to the staff whenever he is needed. Roeber (1968) discusses various strategies for interpreting guidance programs to school personnel. These include large-group meetings, small-group procedures, departmental meetings, the pupil-study conference as an interpretive strategy, counselor-teacher consultations, the public media, and functioning with the guidance committee— which includes other members of the educational team.

The counselor's relationship with the student body as a whole needs to be established and enhanced throughout the school year. It is important for the counselor to establish his role as somewhat different from that of the other adults in the child's life. This can be accomplished by explaining to children what one does as an elementary counselor. An effective way of introducing oneself to the children is to run an affective or democratic classroom meeting (discussed in Chapters Seven and Five respectively). At the end of the session, the availability of the counselor can be announced and sign-up sheets can be made available. Students may be told they can come either individually or, preferably, in small groups. Many children like to visit the counselor in the company of some friends. Hill and Luckey have stated that "the new counselor will spend a good deal of time going from room to room to be introduced to the boys and girls and to tell them what his work is to be, where he can be found, what kinds of assistance he is expected to provide for them" (1969, p. 407). Anderson (1972) has suggested that the counselor have lunch with the students in the cafeteria. She believes that this approach will cause the counselor to be perceived more as a friend than as a supervisor. In this more relaxed setting, the children may bring up matters which they are reticent about discussing during more formal sessions with the counselor. Anderson also suggests interacting with the children on the playground. She emphasizes that the counselor should become actively involved with children, rather than being a passive observer.

McClary (1968) has suggested six major types of group sessions for introducing the guidance program to the pupils: orientation sessions for new pupils, school-wide or grade-level assembly programs, homeroom meetings, subject-matter classes, club meetings, and special interest groups. Other suggestions are to prepare pupil handbooks and bulletin boards.

Management

Once a program is functioning, what principles are important in its management?

The Leadership Process

Good leadership is necessary for effective work to take place. Peters and Shertzer have identified eight factors in the leadership process: "In guidance, this requires organization with respect to (1) goal determination, (2) planning, (3) decision making, (4) mobilizing resources, (5) directing, (6) developing, (7) evaluating, and (8) taking the next steps" (1969, p. 18). These steps can be "modifications of old ones, or new ones, or a combination of modified and new steps" (Peters & Shertzer, 1969, p. 23). Hatch and Stefflre (1965) have analyzed the administrative function in education more succinctly as divisible into the four processes of planning, organizing, staffing, and directing. In Hill's earlier writing, he discusses seven bases for administrative decisions in guidance. Of special interest is his statement that "the administrator must be a counselor, a mediator of difference of opinion, an expert in human relations" (1965, p. 82). More recently Hill and Luckey have discussed five basic aspects of effective leadership. The effective leader is a "personnel officer who practices the fine art of selecting and placing staff members with perception and skill"; he has a single goal, the fulfillment of the best interests of each child in the school; he "has a passion for purpose"; he knows the various roles and functions of each staff member; and he is "a skillful mediator of differences, an expert in effective interpersonal relations" (1969, pp. 394-395). More recently Shane, Shane, Gibson, and Munger (1971) have discussed twelve leadership principles, among them a focus on goals, flexibility, coordination, good interpersonal relations, and recognition of the importance of the quality of the people working for the best interest of the child.

School Board Contacts

Malcolm and Hays (1969), as co-chairmen of an ACES-ASCA committee, prepared a statement about the school counselor directed toward the superintendent and school board. Many observers claim that school board members really run the schools (in collaboration with the superintendent). Therefore, contacts with the school board are often necessary. The ACES-ASCA policy statement is prefaced by the declaration that "the superintendent of schools and the school board have a right to expect: The work of the school counselor to contribute to the purposes of the school; the counselor to be the protective guardian of individuality and of the individual; the work of the counselor to be centered on sound rationale; the counselor to have a commitment to school counseling as a profession." In addition, the statement defines the commitments of administrators: "The superintendent and the school board should make a commitment to: View counseling as a professional career position; view counseling as a staff, not a line, position; provide the counselor with sufficient time and facilities for effective performance of his duties; hire only well qualified, fully trained professionals and then to give them the freedom and responsibility commensurate with their level of specialized preparation" (Malcolm & Hays, 1969).

If the counselor wants, for example, to institute a peer counseling program in the school, he must draw up an outline of the program and present it to the school board. If the board approved the proposal, it would be up to the counselor to coordinate the screening and training of the peer counselors (e.g., children in the intermediate grades). The school board's approval is a necessary prerequisite to many new programs. Therefore, the counselor should be prepared to make a meaningful case before them.

Budget

Effective administration of any program requires a knowledge of its cost. It is generally difficult to compare costs from school to school because of disagreement about what is chargeable to guidance. It is recognized, however, that expenditures vary geographically and within states, counties, and even cities. Among the major categories in any budget are the following:

1. Staff.   The salaries of pupil personnel staff members.

2. Materials and supplies.   Tests, paper, paints, handbooks, record forms, and the like.

3. Equipment and maintenance.   Telephone equipment, light, maintenance of the physical plant, audiovisual materials necessary for classroom guidance programs.

4. Travel.   Travel expenses for counselors and the use of referral services that charge a fee.

5. Research and evaluation.   Staff and aides for the analysis of research data collected in the schools.

6. Administrative overhead.   Sometimes estimated as 25 percent of the first five items listed above (Mathewson, 1962, p. 336).

7. Play media.   Items included in the "playbag," described in Chapter Three: easels, puppets, clay, paints, crayons, paper, blackboards and chalk, dollhouses, classroom items, and miscellaneous toys and games.

Coordination

Coordination means working together as a team. Topics to be discussed under this rubric are the conducting of a staff meeting, the organization and functioning of the guidance council, the team approach to working with cases, guidance functions of the school staff, and an application to a case.

Staff Meetings

Staff meetings are devoted to coordination. In many school districts, there are several elementary school counselors. Therefore, the frequency, composition, and structure of the meeting, as well as its leadership, should be considered. It seems to be workable for the group to meet once a week for a period of about two hours. Friday afternoons are not an ideal time to meet because many people are phasing out from the school situation in preparation for the weekend. The morning, an extended lunch hour, or an afternoon other than Friday are frequently found to be most practical.

In addition to the elementary counselor, the meetings may be attended by the elementary superviser, curriculum coordinator, learning disabilities specialist, school psychologist, assistant superintendent, a consultant from a university, and/or anyone else who is suitable.

A major goal of these meetings can be professional development. Topics can be selected, movies shown, and discussions held to contribute to professional development. It is especially appropriate for school supervisors working with interns to keep abreast of what is going on in the university classes. The supervisors should be at least as well informed as university students. Of course the supervisors' practical background gives them an experiential edge over their interns. Part of the meeting should be devoted to internship supervision and feedback to the university supervisor.

The author believes that the leadership of the meeting should be determined by the structure of the group session. It should be a basically leaderless group, which different members direct when the subject of discussion is within their special province.

The Guidance Council

In an early book on elementary guidance, three authors discuss the concept of "the guidance council." As they state,

> In the elementary schools, much impetus to the program of guidance services can be given through an active guidance council. Only through the active cooperation and participation of all can a program of guidance services succeed. Thus, the formation of a guidance council can well serve the focal point of the program of guidance services (Bernard, James, & Zeran, 1954, pp. 297–298).

Another author (Ohlsen, 1964) sees the main function of the guidance council as the coordination of services. The guidance council, in his view, should be composed of representatives from each of the school's "guidance committees" (small committees composed of about three teachers, the principal, and others having guidance duties) and have not more than 15 to 20 members. Its primary areas of functioning should be

> to develop school policies and make recommendations on such issues as the evaluation of the cumulative record, methods for transferring a pupil's cumulative record from school to school, testing programs, promotion policies, adequacy of course offerings and the extra-class activities program, use of community guidance services, sources and use of occupational information and reports to parents" (Ohlsen, 1964, p. 436).

Peters *et al.* (1965) view the major functions of such a council as threefold: to establish guidance policies, to make recommendations on guidance to the director of guidance and the school administration, and to assist in evaluation of the guidance program.

The composition of this council is an important issue. Teachers, principals, elementary and junior high school counselors, and other specialists should be included. The goal of this system-wide staff group is to provide leadership in the area of guidance services. More recently, Ryan and Zeran (1972) have suggested that students be on the guidance committee.

The Team Approach to Case Staffing

The concept of teamwork implies working together toward a common goal. Kowitz and Kowitz (1968) suggest two interesting analogies, sports and music, that can be used to introduce the concept of teamwork. Another music analogy could go something like this: Musicians (counselors) have a common language and aspire to a common goal. The participants must identify the composition they are going to play. The composition will itself determine the rules by which it is played. Even free-form jazz composition normally has some limits and structures that dictate the modes or chord sequences the performers must follow. The players rehearse the skills necessary to play the composition, both individually and as a group. The final goal is a public performance, and the resulting positive feedback that can ensue if the performance is adequate. Most human beings seem to need end goals in order to stimulate them. A delineation follows of the guidance functions of the personnel on the school team.

The Counselor   The counselor can be conceived of as a collaborator and coordinator who also performs the functions of other professionals unavailable to the school district. One author has stated that "a primary role of the counselor is to help personalize the educational experience for the student, and to interpret to the school community the changing needs of students which necessitate changes in the services provided by the school" (Logan, 1971, p. 5). The counselor's role has been thoroughly described elsewhere in this book.

The Teacher   The teacher is generally considered to play the most important role in the implementation of classroom guidance. The teacher's role can be to provide support, of which teaching well is the primary component. In addition, he should be able to interpret the guidance program to the pupils. The teacher could be a member of the guidance council and a participant in case conferences, and can conduct personal conferences with parents. Another function of the teacher is referral. In addition, the teacher may want to introduce to the counselor colleagues who may need help or a parent who could benefit from counseling. The teacher has individual conferences with students from time to time. During these conferences, he can listen to and accept what the child has to say. He should also implement classroom meetings and discussions of understanding oneself and others.

The School Administrators   The support of the school administrators is extremely important in sustaining a guidance program. Meeks (1968) has included among the superintendent's responsibilities giving direction and structure to the guidance program through harmonious policy, evaluating the administrative leadership in the school to determine the extent and quality of concern for effective guidance services, providing opportunities for administrators to participate in conferences and workshops devoted to guidance-oriented issues, and evaluating the use of specialist's time. A school administrator can do much to aid the guidance program through budget support, staff selection, staff meetings. Administrators can also serve a consultative function with parents and district committees, as well as representing guidance favorably to the school board. The administrator can refer individual children to counselors. The principal is, of course, the administrator with whom the counselor has the most day-to-day contact. The principal's primary responsibilities to the guidance program include: providing support and encouragement, securing well-trained staff, introducing the counselor to people who can use his services, providing time for inservice education for the entire school staff, encouraging the use of class time for group guidance, "retaining primary responsibility for disciplinary action and utilizing the counselor not as a disciplinarian, but as a specialist in understanding misbehavior and discipline situations" (Dinkmeyer and Caldwell, 1970, p. 59).

The School Psychologist   Logan (1971) has stated that "psychologists bring consultation and evaluation to the professional staff in order to help diagnose the learning difficulties of students as well as to help understand the dynamics existing in a student, class, or school" (Logan, 1971, p. 9). In most school systems, the psychologist acts primarily as an evaluator. This situation has been fostered by the requirement in certain states that an individual psychological evaluation be made in order for a child to be placed in a special educational situation. In a sense, the psychologist has painted himself into a diagnostic corner, and in most school districts, he is looked to primarily for evaluation. Muro (1970) feels that the school psychologist should concentrate more on assisting counselors and teachers to work with severely troubled children, and on the preventative and consultative aspects of work with severely disturbed children. Another author has predicted that school psychology will probably remain child-crisis-centered (Faust, 1968).

The School Nurse   The school nurse often knows more children better than anyone else in the school (with the possible exception of the principal). She is generally viewed as a substitute mother, supporter, and health expert. Although nurses generally concentrate on the physical health of the child, there has been an effort on the part of many nursing groups to increase their knowledge in the area of mental health. Nurses are increasingly becoming involved in the treatment of the child's emotional life.

The Librarian   The librarian can contribute to guidance by providing for guidance materials in the library budget, organizing exhibits on the guidance process, observing the behavior of children in the library, talking to the children, and perhaps organizing classroom meetings in which guidance materials are discussed with children.

The Custodian   The custodian can be of help in two ways. He can provide available facilities for a counselor who moves from building to building and needs a place in the school to call home-for-a-day. And he can interact with children. Many school custodians are looked upon as loving and nurturing people who not only take care of the school but also provide an adult male relationship for children—a rarity in most elementary schools.

Learning Disability Specialists   Increasingly, schools have on their staffs a specialist who diagnoses weaknesses and prescribes remedial learning programs for children with learning difficulties.

The Social Worker   The school social worker's primary purpose is to provide a liaison between the school and the home. Some social workers can also consult on classroom contingency management.

The Attendance Officers   Attendance officers' primary function is to create a smooth relationship between home and school, if children are deficient in school attendance.

The Curriculum Director The curriculum director is an expert on how children learn; the materials of the curriculum are his specialty. Ideally, he cooperates with the elementary guidance counselor on curriculum coordination and the implementation of affective education.

The Psychiatrist Certain school districts have availed themselves of a child psychiatrist. When available, psychiatrists can be of benefit to the school system. The author has worked with child psychiatrists who have been able to provide classroom consultation services, individual therapy for children, consultation with teachers, as well as medication.

The Speech Therapist His estimates are that speech defects are present in up to 10 percent of the school population (Peters *et al.*, 1965). The speech therapist can diagnose and implement corrective procedures for speech disorders.

The Special Area Staff Other teachers can be of aid to guidance. For example, physical education teachers can train children in motor coordination. Art and music teachers can encourage self-expression and help enhance children's self-images.

The Paraprofessionals The role and training of paraprofessionals has been discussed in Chapter Nine.

The Parents Parents serve a variety of functions, such as supporting the election of a good board of education, becoming involved in community organizations, and meeting the needs of their children. They can serve a consultative function by working in the PTA or serving on the guidance council. Parents can also refer their children to a counselor. As a prelude to the referral, they can give pertinent information about the child to the counselor.

A Case Illustration

A child was referred for the purpose of determining the best learning situation (i.e., placement) for him. He was having difficulty learning to read, and having trouble with his peers. A little less than half of the persons discussed above were involved in consultation on this case. Figure 10-1 illustrates the relative involvement of various persons. The center circle represents the child, and the circles radiating around it represent the next persons to intervene (i.e., from child to parent to counselor). The arrows represent the primary direction of the relationships between the various involved persons and to point from the person who initiates the interaction. The parents contacted the counselor in response to their interactions with their child and his reported experiences with teachers in the past. The counselor had the child come to his office, and subsequently consulted with the special education supervisor and called upon other specialists (learning disability specialist, school psychologist, and psychiatrist) to see the child. Finally, the principal had administrative input regarding the placement of the child at the time of the case conference, at which all of the involved persons were present. It can be seen that the counselor is highly involved in coordinating the process.

The elementary counselor assessed the child by administering the Binet word list (a quick estimate of verbal intelligence), the Peabody Picture Vocabulary Test (Dunn, 1965), perceptual-motor drawings, the *Lifestyle Inventory* (Shulman, 1971), A Reinforcement Survey Schedule (Keat, 1972), neurological evaluation based on the Gesell commands (Ilg & Ames, 1964) and the Purdue Perceptual Motor Survey (Roach & Kephart, 1966), the Benton Visual Retention Test (Benton, 1963), projective questions, and incomplete sentences. These scales are described in Chapter Two. In addition, the counselor observed the child in the classroom, talked to the teachers, and commented on the various classroom environments in which the child might be placed.

The school psychologist's primary function was diagnostic. She administered the *Wechsler Intelligence Scale for Children* (Wechsler, 1949), and the Bender-Gestalt test (Bender, 1946). She also had considerable knowledge of the various special classes available.

The learning disability specialist carried out an evaluation in the areas of fine motor integration, perceptual-motor skills, mathematical concepts, and language arts functioning skills. She also provided input on the classroom environments available.

Psychiatric consultation was arranged primarily because of the state's requirement of a psychiatric opinion for special placement. In addition, the question of medication was evaluated and a recommendation was made.

A few teachers were involved in this case. The special education supervisor commented on the teachers the child would have in various placements. The class composition was reviewed and goals for the specific learning environments were considered. Another teacher commented on the child's functioning during the past year. The elementary counselor commented on the skills, strengths, and weaknesses of the teacher with whom the child would be placed in the regular classroom. The principal made recommendations about administrative arrangements for various

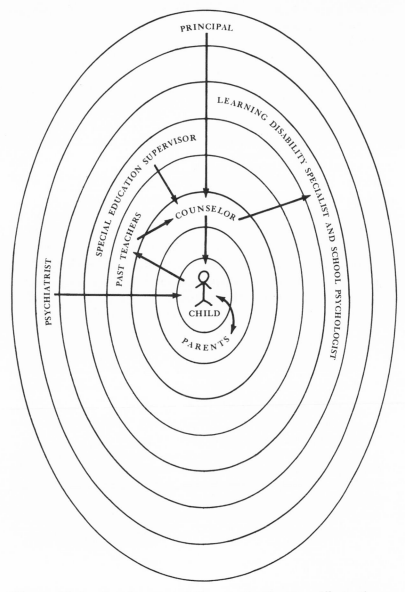

Figure 10–1 *Involvement of Persons in the Case Illustration.*

placements; special arrangements would have to be made for the parents to drive the child to an "open-classroom" building.

The parents were called on to comment upon the child's behavior at home, his reactions to school, and his feelings about various potential placements for the next year. After the opinions of all the involved persons had been stated, the parents deliberated for a week. It was decided to place the child in a special education class for one year, with the understanding that he would probably rejoin the regular class at the end of the year. For the first several months of the school year, the child responded favorably and was so anxious to begin working in the morning that he would not even take off his jacket before launching into the day's activities.

Summary

This chapter has reviewed a broad range of topics related to the administration of elementary-school guidance services. Discussion of the organization of programs addressed a systems approach, the counselor's daily schedule, and referral seasons during the school year. The implementation of a new program was outlined in detail, and the management of already existing programs was examined. Topics covered under this rubric were leadership, administrator and school board policies, and budget considerations. The final major topic was the coordination of programs, including the conduct of staff meetings, the guidance council, the team approach to cases, the guidance functions of a variety of school staff, and an illustrative application of those functions to a case.

References

Anderson, S. L. Implementing a preliminary and integrative guidance program into an elementary school system. Unpublished masters thesis, Pennsylvania State University, 1972.

Bender, L. *Bender Motor Gestalt Test.* New York: American Orthopsychiatric Association, 1946.

Benton, A. *The revised visual retention test.* New York: Psychological Corporation, 1963.

Bernard, H. W., James, C. E., & Zeran, F. R. *Guidance services in elementary schools.* New York: Chartwell House, 1954.

Blocher, D. H., Dustin, E. P., & Dugan, W. E. *Guidance systems: An introduction to student personnel work.* New York: Ronald Press, 1971.

Cooley, W. W., & Hummel, R. C. Systems approaches in guidance. *Review of Educational Research,* 1969, 30, 251–262.

Dimick, K. M., & Huff, V. E. *Child counseling.* Dubuque, Iowa: Wm. C. Brown, 1970.

Dinkmeyer, D. (Ed.) *Guidance and counseling in the elementary school.* New York: Holt, Rinehart & Winston, 1968.

Dinkmeyer, D., & Caldwell, E. *Developmental counseling and guidance: A comprehensive school approach.* New York: McGraw-Hill, 1970.

Dunn, L. M. *The Peabody Picture Vocabulary Test*. Circle Pines, Minn.: American Guidance Service, 1965.

Faust, V. *The counselor-consultant in the elementary school*. Boston: Houghton Mifflin, 1968.

Gunther, M. Christmas blues. *Family Health*, 1971, **3**, 22–24.

Hatch, R., & Stefflre, B. *Administration of guidance services*. Englewood Cliffs, N.J.: Prentice-Hall, 1965.

Herr, E. L., & Cramer, S. H. *Vocational guidance and career development in the schools: Toward a systems approach*. Boston: Houghton Mifflin, 1972.

Hill, G. *Management and improvement of guidance*. New York: Appleton-Century-Crofts, 1965.

Hill, G. E., & Luckey, E. B. *Guidance for children in elementary schools*. New York: Appleton-Century Crofts, 1969.

Humphreys, A., Traxler, A., & North, R. *Guidance services*. Chicago: Science Research Associates, 1960.

Ilg, F. L., & Ames, L. B. *School readiness*. New York: Harper & Row, 1964.

Johnston, E. G. Waterford studies elementary guidance. In D. Dinkmeyer (Ed.), *Guidance and counseling in the elementary school*. New York: Holt, Rinehart & Winston, 1968, pp. 71–74.

Kaczkowski, H. R. An appraisal of role behavior of an elementary school counselor: Summary of a project report. *Elementary School Guidance and Counseling*, 1971, **6**, 5–12.

Keat, D. B. A reinforcement survey schedule for children. University Park, Penn.: Author, 1972.

Kowitz, G., & Kowitz, N. *Operating guidance services for the modern school*. New York: Holt, Rinehart & Winston, 1968.

Logan, R. *Pupil personnel services in Pennsylvania*. Harrisburg, Penn.: Pennsylvania Department of Education, 1971.

Malcolm, D., & Hays, D. What administrators should expect of and do for counselors. *Idaho Guidance and Views*, 1969, **10**, 1–4.

Mathewson, R. H. *Guidance policy and practice*. New York: Harper & Row, 1962.

McClary, G. O. *Interpreting guidance programs to pupils*. Boston: Houghton Mifflin, 1968.

Meeks, A. *Guidance in elementary education*. New York: Ronald Press, 1968.

Miller, G. D., Gum, M. F., & Bender, D. *Elementary school guidance: Demonstration and evaluation*. St. Paul, Minn.: Minnesota Department of Education, 1972.

Muro, J. J. *The counselors work in the elementary school*. Scranton, Penn.: International Textbook Company, 1970.

Ohlsen, M. E. *Guidance services in the modern school*. New York: Harcourt, Brace & World, 1964.

Pennsylvania Department of Education. *Guidelines for self-study of a school district guidance program*. Harrisburg: Division of Guidance Services, 1972.

Peters, H. J., & Shertzer, B. *Guidance: program development and management*, 2nd ed. Columbus, Ohio: Charles E. Merrill, 1969.

Peters, H. J., Shertzer, B., & VanHoose, W. H. *Guidance in elementary schools*. Chicago: Rand McNally, 1965.

Roach, E. G., & Kephart, N. C. *The Purdue perceptual-motor survey*. Columbus, Ohio: Charles E. Merrill, 1966.

Roeber, E. C. *Interpreting guidance programs to school personnel*. Boston: Houghton Mifflin, 1968.

Ryan, T. A., & Zeran, F. R. *Organization and administration of guidance services*. Danville, Ill.: Interstate, 1972.

Shane, J. G., Shane, H. G., Gibson, R. L., & Munger, P. F. *Guiding human development: the counselor and the teacher in the elementary school*. Belmont, Cal.: Wadsworth, 1971.

Shulman, B. M. *The life style inventory*. Chicago: Alfred Adler Institute, 1971.

Stamm, M. L., & Nissman, B. S. *New dimensions in elementary guidance. Practical procedures for teachers, counselors and administrators*. New York: Richards Rosen, 1971.

Sullivan, H. J., & O'Hare, R. W. *Accountability in pupil personnel services: A process guide for the development of objectives*. Fullerton, Cal.: California Personnel and Guidance Association, 1971.

Wechsler, D. *Wechsler Intelligence Scale for Children*. New York: Psychological Corporation, 1949.

11

One can view research as a basic attitude toward and way of evaluating what one is currently doing in counseling, an attitude of searching for and trying out appropriate techniques with one's clients. Wrenn has said that "research is more than a method; it must become a way of thinking for every counselor" (1970, p. ix). Other authors take the position

> that many questions arising naturally in the work of the counselor are better answered by data than by supposition; that such data are often already available or easily made available; and that modest skills in the collection, organization, and interpretation of such data can be acquired quite easily (Cramer, Herr, Morris, & Frantz, 1970, p. 2).

Two other authors state emphatically that "today's school counselor must spend a part of his time in research" (Peters & Hansen, 1964, p. 170).

The following seven procedural steps gleaned from such sources as Cramer *et al.* (1970), Hansen and Stevic (1969), and Dinkmeyer (1968), should be followed in the conduct of research.

1. Behavioral objectives. Initially the problems should be defined and behavioral objectives chosen. Peters, Shertzer, and Van-Hoose (1965) identify such guidance objectives as early identification of each pupil's learning capacities, an analysis of the child's responses to others, collection of data on the child's concept of himself, a portrait of the child's habits of study and behavior at school, and interpretation of the child's developmental progress.

2. Criteria. Objectives must be translated into criterion measures if they are to be measured. Goals stated in behavioral terms,

Research on Elementary Guidance

are more easily verified than are vague constructs (e.g., self concept).

3. Research design. One must decide on the type of research to be considered and the appropriate population for the study, and must control for as many external variables as possible with minimal disruption of service to the student.

4. Initial collection of the data. Prior to initiating the study, data should be collected to determine the baseline behavior the counselor or teacher is attempting to change. Sociometric devices, checklists, questionnaires, interviews, and standardized tests can be used to accumulate data.

5. Implementation of services. The program implemented may be individual counseling, group counseling, curriculum change, inservice training for teachers, behavioral management in the classroom, and the like. The choice of program, of course, is influenced by the objectives stated in step 1.

6. Testing the effects of the program. Analysis and interpretation of the data must be thorough. Many studies seem to focus on analysis to the exclusion of interpretation. Interpretation is needed in order to make the data meaningful for parents and school personnel. Therefore, clear presentation of the data is of the utmost importance.

7. Program changes. The foregoing steps may reveal some improvements or deletions that should be made in ongoing programs. Peters *et al.* (1965) say of research that "its major purpose is to indicate what should be done in the future" (p. 237). In-

deed, recommendations for change or for the maintenance of the *status quo* are the most important outcomes of any research study.

A variety of evaluation methods is available to the researcher. Action research—research that collects data on and evaluates local school situations—is probably the most relevant type for the counselor to consider. Applied research which yields information about ways to alleviate problems in an interventionistic fashion, can also be valuable. The rest of this chapter will concern itself with the test development aspect of research, individual case studies, description of students, the development of materials (particularly affective materials), environmental assessment, program evaluation, and follow-up studies.

The Literature

There is a variety of journals and books from which counselors can glean information about developments in their profession. Initially, one must survey the literature for research relevant to one's own concerns. Of course, one must be able to understand this research, which occasionally requires various levels of statistical sophistication.

Survey of the Literature

It is the counselor's responsibility to be aware of developments in his profession. Shane, Shane, Gibson, and Munger (1971) have listed eight important sources of information on research for the counselor, six of which will be covered herein.

1. Bibliographic Tools. *Cumulative Book Index, A World List of Books in the English Language, Education Index, Monthly Catalogue of U.S. Government Publications, Textbooks in Print.*

2. Research in Education. *Dissertation Abstracts, Encyclopedia of Educational Research, Handbook of Research on Teaching* (Gage, 1963), *Masters Theses in Education* (Lamke & Silvey, 1953 to date).

3. Miscellaneous Publications Dealing with Research. *American Foundations and Their Fields* (Rich, 1955), *Mental Measurements Yearbook* (Buros, 1972), *Sociological Abstracts, Psychological Abstracts, Tests in Print* (Buros, 1961).

4. Continuing Publications. The classic example is *Review of Educational Research.* Among the most important journals (pri-

marily quarterlies) for the elementary school counselor are *Elementary School Guidance and Counseling, Counselor Education and Supervision, Measurement and Evaluation in Guidance, Personnel and Guidance Journal, The School Counselor, Journal of Counseling Psychology, Psychology in the Schools, Journal of Educational Psychology, Educational and Psychological Measurement, Teachers College Record, American Psychologist, Childhood Education, Elementary School Journal, Behavior Therapy, Behavior Research and Therapy, Journal of Behavior Therapy and Experimental Psychiatry, Journal of Clinical Psychology, Journal of Educational Research, Journal of Psychology, School and Society, Today's Education.*

The growing importance of research to the elementary counselor can be traced in the development of the *Elementary School Guidance and Counseling* (ESGC) journal. Although case analyses, idea exchange and "issues and dialogues" have had a place in this journal almost since its inception, a column on research did not appear until December 1971 (Muro, 1971). Muro is editing a column directed to the practitioner and consumer, as well as the conductor, of research. This column is a vehicle for disseminating the results of investigations related to elementary school guidance and counseling and reports of new and innovative practices in the field (e.g., Keat, 1973, in Muro's column).

5. Fugitive Materials. These materials, designated fugitive because they can be elusive, generally emanate from state and federal governmental agencies, foundations, universities, and professional groups.

6. Leads other than the usual sources. *Saturday Review of Education, New Republic, Harper's Magazine, Scientific American, Daedalus, American Scholar, Trans-Action, Psychology Today, Human Relations, New York Times Sunday Magazine.*

Understanding Research Reports

One needs to evaluate the results of studies on various levels, e.g., relevance, practicality (usability), implications, and overall treatment. One should scan the table of contents of a journal for titles that appear to be related to one's work. By scanning the section of the article entitled "Methodology," the counselor can determine whether it is applicable to his own work. If it appears to be so, he can quickly read the discussion and/or summary to see if the outcome supported further use of the procedures tested. If the outcome was positive, the counselor can check into the procedures in more detail. One should ask, "Are the techniques delineated clearly enough?" The reader may have to consult other references in order to define the terms and procedures used in a particular study.

With regard to the overall treatment of the study, the reader can choose to trust the writers and editors to guarantee validity or, for oneself, check the methodology (including procedures, measuring instruments, groups used, and statistics) in more detail. In the latter case, it is helpful for the counselor to understand what the statistical data means. To this end, there are certain resources with which the counselor could familiarize himself. Most readers of this book will have had a fundamental statistics course. Statistical concepts are beyond the scope of this text; therefore basic sources are listed below. Among the better introductory statistical sources are books by Cramer *et al.* (1970), Guilford (1965), McNemar (1966), Walker and Lev (1958), Bruning and Kintz (1968), and Games and Klare (1967). For more advanced statistical treatments, the counselor may wish to refer to Kerlinger (1964), Campbell and Stanley (1963), Edwards (1967), Baggley (1964), Tryon and Bailey (1970), Borg (1963), and Winer (1962). These books deal with more sophisticated topics, e.g., analysis of variance and factor analysis.

Areas of Research in Guidance and Counseling

Seven areas of research in guidance and counseling will be discussed in this section and examples of studies will be described.

Test Development

Counselors are often called upon to use tests or to develop tests for their own purposes. The example of MARK II (Kinsbourne, 1972) was cited in Chapter Two. The data available on this test for kindergarten and first grade are simple descriptive statistics on such matters as the range, mean, and standard deviation. For example, on the retention-of-form subtest in the MARK II, the mean for kindergarten children was 5.25; mean for first-grade males was 5.60; for females it was 5.84. The standard deviation on the subtest for each of these groups respectively was 1.89, 2.62, and 2.63. Such simple descriptive statistics provide one with the average, as well as some measure of the variability, for each subtest or test scale.

The author has developed a scale to measure cooperation and aggression, entitled *Cooperation-Aggression Behavior Scale.* In a study to be discussed later in this chapter, the child's score reflected how cooperative he was; the higher the score the more coopera-tion. The changes measured by the scale were not significant (Keat, 1973); the range of children's scores on first evaluation was from 52 to 93, and upon retesting was 48 to 94.

A study by Mayer, Beggs, Fjellstedt, Forhetz, Nighswander, and Richards (1970) utilized six instruments. The more sophisti-cated statistics they used were correlation coefficients and analysis of variance. Correlation coefficients indicate the degree of rela-tionship between two sets of scores. For example, a significant relationship was found between understanding responses, mea-sured by the *Counselor Verbal Response Scale* (CVRS) (Kagan & Krathwohl, 1967), and reduction in school anxiety, measured by the *Test Anxiety Scale for Children* (TASC) (Sarason, Hill, & Zimbardo, 1964). The analysis of variance is much more com-plicated, but basically involves determining the significance of the differences between two variances (F-test). In this example, the results of a nonsignificant F-test indicated that anxiety change scores (TASC) were not different among the five treatment groups (Mayer *et al.*, 1970).

The validity of Caldwell's cooperative pre-school inventory (1970) was evaluated by Drummond (1972) by analyzing subtest correlations on the *Cooperative Preschool Inventory* (CPSI) and the *Metropolitan Readiness Test* (MRT). In addition, a factor analysis was run on the CPSI and MRT. In this particular study, it was found that the Cooperative Preschool Inventory is a rele-vant test for children of this age. Factor and cluster analysis are important procedures in the sphere of test development (Tryon & Bailey, 1970). Factor analysis is "a method of analyzing this set of observations from their intercorrelations to determine whether the variations represented can be accounted for adequately by a number of basic categories smaller than that with which the investigation was started" (Fruchter, 1954, p. 1). For example, one might begin with 160 test items and factor them into 14 scales (Keat & Hackman, 1972). Cluster analysis is the process whereby similar phenomena, whether items or persons, are grouped together by virtue of some common characteristic. For example, 500 in-dividuals can be grouped into 11 types ("person-clusters") on the basis of the similarity of their test profiles (Keat & Hackman, 1972).

Table 11-1 is a summary of some tests useful in guidance re-search. All of these tests are mentioned and/or discussed in this book. They are grouped into ten categories. The address of a publisher for whom a catalogue is not at hand can be found in Anastasi (1968, Appendix B, pp. 636–637).

Table 11-1   *Summary of Tests for Use in Guidance Research*

TITLE	PUBLISHER (YEAR)
INTELLIGENCE	
Wechsler Intelligence Scale for Children	Psychological Corporation (1949)
Wechsler Pre-School and Primary Scale of Intelligence	Psychological Corporation (1967)
Stanford-Binet Intelligence Scale	Houghton Mifflin (1960)
Slosson Intelligence Test	Slosson Educational Publications (1963)
Peabody Picture Vocabulary Test	American Guidance Service (1965)
Quick Test	Psychological Test Specialists (1962)
California Short Form Test of Mental Maturity	California Test Bureau (1963)
Otis-Lennon Mental Ability Test	Harcourt, Brace & World (1967–1968)
Lorge-Thorndike Intelligence Tests	Houghton Mifflin (1959)
Primary Mental Abilities Test	Science Research Associates (1958)
Kuhlmann-Anderson Intelligence Tests	Personnel Press (1952)
ACHIEVEMENT	
Wide Range Achievement Test	Guidance Associates (1965)
Stanford Achievement Test	Harcourt, Brace & World (1953)
Iowa Tests of Basic Skills	Houghton Mifflin (1956)
Metropolitan Achievement Tests	Harcourt, Brace & World (1960)
California Achievement Tests	California Test Bureau (1959)
Sequential Tests of Educational Progress	Educational Testing Service (1959)
READING	
Gray Oral Reading Test	Bobbs-Merrill (1963)
MARK II	Kinsbourne (Author, Duke University, 1972)
Gates-MacGinitie Reading Tests	Teachers College Press (1965)
SRA Achievement Series	Science Research Associates (1954–58)
LEARNING DISABILITIES	
The Pupil Rating Scale	Grune & Stratton (1971)
Illinois Test of Psycholinguistic Abilities	University of Illinois Press (1968)
A Psychoeducational Inventory of Basic Learning Abilities	Fearon (1968)

TITLE	PUBLISHER (YEAR)
SPEECH AND HEARING	
Riley Articulation and Language Test	Western Psychological Services (1966)
Templin-Darley Tests of Articulation	State University of Iowa (1960)
Kindergarten Auditory Screening Test	Follett (1971)
COORDINATION	
Bender Motor Gestalt Test	Psychological Corporation (1946)
Benton Visual Retention Test	Psychological Corporation (1963)
Frostig Developmental Test of Visual Perception	Consulting Psychologists Press (1963)
Goodenough—Harris Draw-a-man Test	Harcourt, Brace & World (1963)
Purdue Perceptual-Motor Survey	Charles E. Merrill (1966)
PERSONALITY	
Children's Apperception Test—Human Figures	C.P.S. (1965)
Self-Esteem Inventory	W.H. Freeman (Coopersmith, 1967, reference on p. 53).
Piers-Harris Children's Self-concept Scale	Counselor Recordings and Tests (1969)
Early School Personality Questionnaire	Institute for Personality and Ability Testing (1966)
Childrens' Personality Questionnaire	Institute for Personality and Ability Testing (1968)
The Forer Structured Sentence Completion Test	Western Psychological Services (1957)
MOTIVATION AND INTERESTS	
A Reinforcement Survey Schedule for Children	Author: Keat, Pennsylvania State University (1972)
What I Like To Do	Science Research Associates (1958)
SOCIAL	
Pre-School Attainment Record	American Guidance Service (1966)
Vineland Social Maturity Scale	American Guidance Service (1965)
The Guidance Learning Rating Scale	Keat (Author, Pennsylvania State University, 1971)
ENVIRONMENTAL ASSESSMENT	
Barclay Classroom Climate Inventory	Educational Skills Development (1972)
Organizational Climate Index	Wiley (in Stern, 1970)

Individual Case Study

Although the individual case study has not been considered by some to be a valid source of research, it is hoped that its usefulness can be demonstrated here. That is, some counselors have been developing ways to utilize the case study in a more scientific fashion and thus to make it more acceptable to proponents of strict quantitative procedures. Some examples of elementary school counseling interviews are cited by Hawkins (1967) and Leventhal and Kranzler (1968).

Lazarus and Davison (1971) have done much to advance the case study. They state that "when a creative clinician learns new things from patients and invents new procedures to resolve difficult problems, he is conducting a form of research" (Lazarus & Davison, 1971, p. 200). According to them, the individual client can be studied in two ways. The first way, he is used as "his own control." In the second, "the truly intensive individual clinical design, the subject becomes his own laboratory, and hypotheses that arise are tested solely with reference to that particular individual" (Lazarus & Davison, 1971, p. 209). A case study can provide a valuable prelude to subsequent controlled research. An illustration is a study of the effects of tranquilizers on children. Davison and Valins (1969) proposed that it would be beneficial to tell a child after withdrawing a placebo that he had not in fact received an active tranquilizer. The idea to be tested was that a child deprived of the explanation that his improvement had been drug-induced might be more likely to continue his improved behavior. The placebo subjects maintained their "drug-induced" improvement to a significantly greater degree than did the drug subjects. Another unique characteristic of the case study is that it can provide the opportunity to apply principles and test notions in entirely new ways. Although Lazarus and Davison (1971) support the imaginal stimulus situations, with children *in vivo* seems to be a much more useful procedure (Keat, 1972). Lazarus and Davison also say that a case study can help put "meat" on the theoretical skeleton. They also suggest that unusual procedures can be tried out in place of accepted ones; in systematic desensitization, for example, emotive imagery might be used in place of relaxation (Lazarus & Abramovitz, 1962). The use of emotive imagery with a ten-year-old boy who was afraid to travel in the family car entailed a series of imagined scenes in which the boy and his father proudly showed the automobile to the boy's favorite cartoon characters, e.g., "And imagine that Yogi Bear is very excited and is asking your daddy to take him for a drive" (Lazarus & Davison, 1971, p. 210). The final image used with this child was an exciting chase in which the boy and his father drove "Green Lantern" in pursuit of some bank robbers. After only two sessions, the boy willingly went on a family outing in the car and displayed no further anxiety. These examples may suggest new techniques for the counselor's repertoire.

Thoresen (1972) recently presented a paper on the intensive case design, or the experimental study of the individual case. In this paper Thoresen states, "research in counseling must go back to the basics: direct observation, careful description and systematic planned interventions with individual subjects" (p. 4). "Intensive designs offer excellent experimental control in having the subject serve as his own control for all kinds of past events prior to the actual investigation" (p. 10); "Causal relationships can be established by replication (reproducibility) of the specific results by means of certain intervention techniques across individuals" (p. 13). He then goes on to discuss particular intensive designs. The first to be discussed is the "time series" (A) design (A represents the baseline phase; A' represents return to baseline; B, C, etc. represent treatment phases) in which successive observations are made over a relatively long period of time (e.g., self monitoring behavior). The next approaches discussed are AB and B designs (uncontrolled baseline) in which the subject's behavior is observed in a natural setting (classroom or family). In the ABA design, a second baseline or nontreatment phase is added. The ABAB design uses a treatment reversal by replicating both baseline and treatment phases (e.g., Barlow, Leitenberg & Agras, 1969). Thoresen, Alper, Hannum, Barrick, and Jacks (1973, in press) present a variation on the ABAB design that can be labeled ABACAF. Two different treatments were used; B represents group systematic desensitization with elementary school teachers, and C represents behavioral classroom management training. F represents the follow-up phase employed after the third baseline. Thoresen (1972) contends that these intensive designs permit more rigorous experimental approaches and will foster more intimate research focused on the actions of the particular individual the counselor is working with.

Another source of strong support for the use of the individual case study is the work of Browning and Stover (1971), who attempt to wed scientific and counseling ("experimental-clinical") practice. These authors report on their work with children using a same-subject experimental design: Among the topics they discuss are the B design, which is simply the administration of a treatment technique for which no baseline was obtained (analagous to a counselor's observations on what happened during counseling); the BC design, which involves two successively administered treatment techniques; the AB design, in which a baseline is obtained and then a treatment procedure is instituted; the ABC design, which involves two treatment techniques following the baseline; the ABA design, involving a baseline-treatment-baseline procedure; the ABAB design, which involves baseline (A) treatment (B) baseline (A) and then the reinstitution of treatment (B); the ABACD design, which involves two baselines and three treatment procedures of differing types; and the ABACA design, which includes three baselines and two separate types of treatments. Browning and Stover present examples of the use of each type of design with children.

Description of Students

Tests are, of course, one means of describing students. A systematic compilation of data from various tests of personality and achievement, such as those discussed in Chapter Two, should be made available.

Class rank and average in academics can be of concern to the counselor. Cramer *et al.* (1970) discuss such matters as converting scales to grade point averages, weighting averages, and putting the results to use. The same source also contains a relevant discussion of expectancy tables. These types of data are useful in decisions about academic placement and predictions of success in the attainment of particular goals.

In particular, the counselor has a need for local norms. Stefflre (1968) has supported local and descriptive research. For example, some student populations are well above or below national norms. The construction of local norms is well covered by Cramer *et al.*

Finally, description of students has been undertaken in research pertaining to groups (the topic of Chapter Four). Crow (1971) compared three group counseling techniques utilized with sixth graders: a structured aural approach, a structured visual approach, and an unstructured group approach that used no initial external stimulus. The combined groups of experimental subjects made greater mean gains than the control subjects on all of the seven variables except grades. These results have an important implication for practicing counselors: that is, it is generally preferable to provide a group of children with some structure initially, in order to acclimate the children to the group process. The unstructured approach will subsequently have greater effect.

Another study, by Callao (1972), did not obtain significant results but suggested that group counseling can help children to become more accepted by their peers. Drowne (1972) found the use of play media in group counseling superior to the classroom meeting approach with regard to changes in self concept. This finding appears especially relevant to work with primary school children (Thombs & Muro, 1973).

Development of Materials

The development of materials is related to the topics covered in Chapters Seven and Eight. Examples of the elementary counselor involvement in this area are the development of affective curriculum materials (Keat *et al.*, 1972) and the implementation of a model for career education such as that cited by Herr (see Chapter Eight).

The largest federally funded center for the development of materials for use in the schools is Research for Better Schools (RBS), which currently has six component programs (Scanlon, 1972): early childhood, individualizing learning (e.g., Scanlon & Brown, 1971), humanizing learning, curriculum development, administering for change, and career education. Of particular interest to the counselor is the Humanizing Learning Program (HLP). The topics included in this rubric are affective interpersonal skills and the higher-order cognitive skills (e.g., problem solving). Research procedures typically involve a review of the literature, development of materials for children, pilot testing with two to four classes, modification of the materials, and finally field-testing on a larger scale. Only after this final testing process (often several years after initiation) do the materials become available for commercial distribution. A unit on feelings is projected to be ready for public distribution by Autumn, 1973. Awareness of the availability of this kind of material can enlarge the elementary school counselor's repertoire.

Environmental Assessment

Cramer *et al.* (1970) suggest steps, similar to those outlined earlier in this chapter, for assessing environments. A rather comprehensive demonstration and evaluation program has recently been completed and published. This study involved a review of the literature, a well-conceived design, computer analysis of the data, and a meaningful summary including implications and recommendations (see Miller, Gum, & Bender, 1972). Some other examples of the application of environmental assessment in the schools follow.

Stern has contributed considerably to the assessment of environments (e.g., 1970). Although much of his work has focused on the evaluation of high-school or college environments, the development of the Organizational Climate Index (OCI) partially fills the gap at the elementary-school level. The OCI (Stern, 1970) was prepared with the student environment as the frame of reference. Results of the school study can be perused in Steinhoff (1965) who found elementary-school teachers to be much more dependent and conformist and secondary-school teachers more independent and achievement-oriented. An OCI factor score profile (Stern, 1970, p. 273) indicated that elementary school practices are significantly higher than senior high schools in practicality (F significant at .05 level) and orderliness (.001 level), and higher than both junior and senior highs in supportiveness (.001 level).

The Barclay Classroom Climate Inventory (BCCI), based on ten years of research, is designed for grades 3–6 (Barclay, 1972). It includes 42 short scales for measuring self competence skills, peer judgments, vocational awareness, behavioral expectations, and teacher expectations. It takes approximately an hour and a quarter to administer, but the scoring must be done by machine and analyzed by computer (which takes about two weeks). The feasibility of this inventory will depend upon the funds available (computer-scoring costs over $1.00 per pupil for a 25–35 student classroom).

Bedrosian, Sara and Pearlman (1970) conducted a study to determine the effectiveness of guidance classes in developing self understanding in children. Its main purpose was to develop an instructional program in guidance that would meet the needs of fourth-grade elementary-school children. The t-test, the main statistic used, indicated that the experimental group taught by teachers utilizing 30 guidance lessons showed significant changes between the pre- and the posttest. The experimental group, taught by counselors, did not show a significant change, but their experience did help prevent the accumulation of pressure that seems to cause emotional stresses and therefore was of benefit in a prophylactic sense. The control group did not show any significant change. This study nevertheless supports the contention made in Chapters Six and Seven that regular classroom teachers can be trained in the techniques of guidance to conduct affective classes.

Krantz and Risley (1972) recently presented an article on classroom environments. The statistical approach utilized was a mean percent of on-task behavior; *on-task* was defined as sitting cross-legged, visually attending to the teacher as materials were presented, and not engaging in any disruptive behaviors. The mean percent on-task during crowded conditions was 60 percent; during uncrowded conditions it averaged 87 percent. In another situation, mean percent on-task behavior under crowded conditions was 51 percent, whereas the mean percent on-task behavior under uncrowded conditions was 90 percent. These data tend to demonstrate a clear relationship between spatial arrangements of children and on-task behaviors exhibited during teaching sessions in the classroom. The second part of this study had to do with the sequence of scheduled activities, which has implications for both the classroom and group counseling situations. In the experimental situation, the active sessions that preceded story period were devoted to dancing, musical chairs, and outdoor play. The inactive sessions that preceded story time involved resting with heads on desks. The mean number of seconds required for transition was 35 when the story was preceded by an active session, and only 21 when the story was preceded by an inactive session. This relates to a point made in Chapter Four about the desirability of groups talking first and playing later. To remediate some of these situations, the authors suggest making praise and classroom privileges contingent on attentive nondisruptive behaviors. With these contingencies, the mean percent on-task behavior during teacher demonstration increased from 51 percent during the baseline observation to 93 percent with reinforcement. Mean percent on-task behavior during the story increased from 60 percent during baseline to 92 percent with the use of praise and classroom privileges.

Program Evaluation

Evaluation is "a process of determining the value of an activity or object" (Cramer *et al.*, 1970, p. 87). There is, of course, a variety of procedures to use in program evaluation.

The initial procedure to be considered is the survey. Peters and Shertzer (1969) define the survey method as follows: it (1) "uses predetermined criteria or standards for a guidance program, (2) collects evidence of the guidance services being offered, and (3) takes stock of how these existing services compare with the predetermined standards" (Peters & Shertzer, 1969, p. 531).

The Pennsylvania Department of Education Guidelines (1972) suggest three steps (i.e., A, B, C) for a self study. Phase A of the self study process is data collection. It is recommended that the data come from the following sources: (1) former students, (2) present students, (3) teachers, (4) administrators, (5) parents, and (6) relevant segments of the community. Several scales which relate to the first five of these areas are reproduced in the appendices (State College Area School District, 1973): These include a follow-up survey of former elementary students (Appendix I), present students awareness of services (Appendix J), a teacher survey (Appendix K), an administrator survey (Appendix L), and a parent survey (Appendix M). In addition, but perhaps something which logically should be done initially, the counselors should evaluate their own functioning (Appendix N). The second part of the Phase A is the analysis of data, whose purpose is to determine the effectiveness of the present program and to evaluate the implications of the data for the school. For example, question d of the elementary student guidance awareness survey (Appendix J) asks "Has _____ ever talked to your class?" The results indicated that 1036 (55%) students said yes and 846 (45%) said no. The implications of this finding could be that the counselor(s) should be getting into the classrooms more.

Phase B is preparation of the appropriate objectives, strategies, and assessment methods. It should be noted that this sequence of phases is out of keeping with the author's, presented earlier in this chapter, in which the choice of objectives comes first. The primary steps in Phase B are interpretation of the information that has been gathered, development of a statement on the goals and objectives for the guidance program, and specification of activities designed to achieve these objectives. With regard to the example cited in the last paragraph, the interpretation was that the counselor should be in the classroom more. Therefore, the goal would be to gain more effective exposure time in the classroom. The specification of activities could include a procedure such as conducting democratic classroom meetings.

Phase C, the final phase, is implementation. The school district is given the opportunity to respond to the findings and recommendations of the study and to convert them to meaningful program revisions. This represents the transition from thought to action. The following is an example of action based on the results of a parent survey.

The results of a parent questionnaire (Appendix G) were presented in Chapter Nine. Actual figures for the tabulation are included here in Table 11-2, which illustrates the use of the t-test for related measures (Bruning & Kintz, 1968, pp. 12–15). The parents were responding to the item "elementary counselor conferences are . . . could be . . ." and using a five-point scale (e.g., $1 =$ of no help; $5 =$ very helpful).

Adhering to the steps outlined by Bruning and Kintz (1968), the resulting t-value of 6.36 was significant at the .01 level. As

Table 11-2 *Parent Questionnaire* $(N = 25)$: *Elementary
counselor conferences*

ARE	COULD BE	DIFFERENCE	SQUARE
3	3	0	0
3	5	−2	4
1	5	−4	16
2	3	−1	1
2	5	−3	9
1	4	−3	9
3	4	−1	1
3	4	−1	1
3	4	−1	1
5	5	0	0
2	4	−2	4
2	3	−1	1
3	4	−1	1
1	4	−3	9
2	3	−1	1
3	3	0	
4	4	0	
2	2	0	
2	4	−2	4
3	3	0	
3	5	−2	4
3	4	−1	1
1	3	−2	4
1	3	−2	4
2	4	−2	4
Sum = 60	Sum = 95	Sum = −35	Sum = 79
(Mean = 2.4)	(Mean = 3.8)		

noted previously, a direct outcome of this survey was a presentation to the next PTO meeting by the elementary school counselor.
The other gap, failure to meet parental expectations, can only be
bridged by enhancing the counselor's day-to-day competence.

A major approach to program evaluation is the experimental
method, in which research is applied to groups of people and a
determination is made as to its effect on their behavioral processes. An experimental behavior modification program was discussed in Chapter Six and the development of instruments for
the measurement of a disadvantaged population was outlined in
Chapter Nine. The results of the study (Keat, 1973) were taken
basically from the three relevant measures pertaining to the major
behavioral change goal of the program, i.e., cooperation. Table
11-3 presents data from behavioral observations of ten individuals.

In this analysis the statistic of choice was the Wilcoxon matched pairs signed-ranks test (Siegel, 1956; Bruning & Kintz, 1968). A nonparametric procedure was chosen for the following reasons: the observations were dependent (i.e. related: same-subject); this was not a normally distributed population; and an ordinal-scale measurement was utilized for the measurement of variables. In addition, because it was predicted that children who were exposed to the behavioral modification program would be more cooperative, a one-tailed statistical test was called for.

The results of the behavioral observations (baseline) charted by the investigator and a caseworker are presented in Table 11-3. Reference to the critical values table for the Wilcoxon Test (Bruning & Kintz, 1968, p. 242) indicated that a tabled value of 8 or less is significant at the .025 level for a one-tailed test. There is a significant difference between these two behavioral observations, which involved counting of cooperative behaviors. Therefore, one can conclude (based on the behavioral observation scales utilized in this study) that the cooperation level was significantly higher after the behavior modification training program than that before it.

The final major type of research evaluation to be considered is action research, in which data is collected to evaluate the local situation. Frost and Frost (1967) attempted to evaluate both the elementary-school guidance program and on-going research projects in this system. They investigated two methods of interpreting achievement-test scores to fourth- and sixth-grade elementary pupils. One group received group interpretation and the other

Table 11-3 *Results of the Wilcoxon Test on the Behavioral Observation Data*

CHILD	BEHAVIOR OBSERVATION ONE	BEHAVIOR OBSERVATION TWO	DIFFERENCE	RANK
I	12	14	2	3
II	13	21	8	8
III	4	7	3	4.5
IV	6	10	4	6.5
V	6	15	9	9.5
VI	8	12	4	6.5
VII	6	15	9	9.5
VIII	10	9	−1	1.5
IX	10	9	−1	1.5
X	13	10	−3	4.5

Sum + = 47.5; Sum − = 7.5

individual interpretation. Findings indicated that the fourth graders gained a better understanding of achievement test scores when they were interpreted by the group method. Neither method was superior to the other in interpreting test scores to sixth graders. Another study had to do with the self concept of fourth and sixth graders and was analyzed by the chi-square technique (a nonparametric procedure). Fourth graders seemed to be relatively consistent in their patterns of self concept from pre- to post-test administration. The sixth graders showed no significant difference in patterns. An analysis of items, however, sometimes leads one to discover data not immediately apparent. One item, concerning how the child felt about the way he got along in school, produced a significant difference. This finding led the authors to "the conclusion that children change their self-concept with regard to how well they are doing in school when knowledge of their test results is presented to them" (Frost & Frost, 1967, p. 125). Thus, counselors should not overlook the components of test scores when analyzing for significance, even though overall statistical significance may not be found.

Another example of action research was conducted by Daldrup, Hubbert, and Hamilton (1968). This study attempted to assess the reactions of teachers, parents, and children to the school situation by the use of questionnaires. The "results indicated that students found counseling to be helpful and preferred to talk with the school counselors regarding personal problems, to discuss schoolwork difficulties with their teachers, and family problems with their parents" (Daldrup *et al.*, 1968, pp. 124–125).

Gordon (1958) has developed a model that includes the child for all or part of the parent-teacher conference. Gordon (1958) also commented that the children he contacted liked to be included in these conferences.

Follow-up Studies

Follow-up studies can help to determine the effectiveness of a particular program, curriculum, or guidance approach. Again, the survey method is one of the major procedures utilized. This can involve the collection and analysis of opinions, attitudes, information, or any other data on the effects of particular guidance procedures on the behavior of children. Peters *et al.* (1965) have stated that the majority of all research studies on guidance evaluation are follow-up surveys. An example of a follow-up study the author was recently engaged in is included here.

Hill and Luckey (1969) discuss product criteria and methods in their chapter on research and evaluation. "Guidance learnings"

Table 11-4 *Means and Within Subject Anovar for Pre-Post Tests*

GRADE LEVEL	PRE M.	POST M.	WITHIN SUBJECT 2 OF SQUARES		MEAN SQUARES	DF	F	PR. IF ASSUMPTIONS ARE MET
Kdt (N)								
1 (44)	128.6	135.6	J =	3924.13	3924.13	1	16.428*	0.000
2 (54)	128.2	138.7	AJ =	144.668	144.668	1	0.606*	.438
			error =	22931.7	238.872	96		
1								
A1 (27)	121.7	105.5	J =	3568.91	3568.91	1	35.449*	0.000
			error =	2617.59	100.677	26		
2								
A1 (25)	145.4	153.5	J =	2401.25	2401.25	1	53.89*	0.000
A2 (25)	119.7	135.8	AJ =	2156.62	718.872	3	16.107*	0.000
A3 (25)	113.8	119.6	error =	4284.64	44.6317	96		
A4 (25)	115.4	113.0						
3								
A1 (26)	127.0	135.2	J =	2721.38	2721.38	1	52.551*	0.000
A2 (26)	115.2	127.6	AJ =	116.346	116.346	1	2.247*	0.140
			error =	2589.27	51.7854	50		

GRADE LEVEL	PRE M.	POST M.	WITHIN SUBJECT 2 OF SQUARES		MEAN SQUARES	DF	F	PR. IF ASSUMPTIONS ARE MET
4								
A1 (28)	101.5	106.2	J =	1950.54	1950.54	1	21.158*	0.000
A2 (28)	109.8	137.4	AJ =	13668.5	4556.16	3	49.422*	0.000
A3 (28)	141.9	125.5	error =	9956.48	92.1896	108		
A4 (28)	142.0	149.7						
5								
A1 (26)	122.1	118.1	J =	1655.74	1655.74	1	14.041*	0.000
A2 (24)	101.9	111.8	AJ =	4686.51	1171.63	4	9.935*	0.000
A3 (21)	116.2	137.9	error =	13679.3	117.925	116		
A4 (21)	110.2	109.8						
A5 (29)	124.1	125.9						
6								
A1 (31)	127.5	130.9	J =	1643.80	1643.80	1	7.895*	0.006
A2 (28)	121.7	126.6	AJ =	1859.80	464.950	1	2.233	0.069
A3 (27)	112.6	121.4	error =	27901.4	208.219	134		
A4 (29)	118.8	129.4						
A5 (24)	119.5	114.8						

* = significance at .05 level
J = columns AJ = rows

are viewed as objectives and a variety of methods are suggested for achieving these objectives. An initial attempt to develop a teacher rating checklist to evaluate "guidance learnings" proceeded as follows: the scale included in appendix E was administered to the children in the program by teachers. Table 11-4 illustrates the application of analysis of variance (F-test) to data of this type to assess the significance of pre- and posttest changes for children in grades K–6. Table 11-4 represents a summary of a computer printout based on a program by Games and Klare (1967, pp. 540–547). Computer analyses of data seem to be necessary if one wants to analyze large quantities of data (see Cramer *et al.*, 1970, ch. 12). The counselor can consult a statistician, explore the desired topics in a book, or simply visit the computation center and explain one's data to a technician.

Inspection of Table 11-4 reveals that significant changes in the expected positive direction (i.e., increased means scores from pre- to posttest) were found in 17 of the 23 groups. Overall F-tests were also significant, with two exceptions. The first of these deviances was an inverse finding for grade 1 (i.e. a significant decrease in scores). This was probably due to the fact that only one class was available at this level. If a larger sample had been available at this level, this singular loss might have been balanced by other gains (as was the case in grades 2, 4, 5, and 6). The other nonsignificant result was in the sixth-grade (.069 level) and had to do with the lack of overall intra-individual change. This was probably due primarily to the loss in group A5 (about five points). It should be noted, nevertheless, that the overall gains were promising. These improvements took place after only three months (March, April, and May) in the program; the results encouraged the program directors to continue the "guidance learning" approach but to start it at the beginning of the school year (Keat, 1973).

Summary

This chapter has explored elementary guidance research. After delineating some procedural steps, a variety of sources were listed in which one could survey the literature. In order to understand the literature and research reports, an approach was suggested for reading journals. A variety of types of counselor research was discussed and demonstrated, with examples from the author's research efforts and from the literature. The areas covered were test development; utilization of individual case studies in an intensive analysis of the person; descriptive studies of students, including development of local norms and group evaluations; development of classroom materials; environmental assessment procedures; program evaluations (including surveys, experimental methods, and action research approaches); and finally follow-up studies, with an application to the "guidance learnings" discussed in Chapters One and Seven. These procedures were discussed in the hope of stimulating counselors to adopt a research orientation.

————————————————————————— **References**

Anastasi, A. *Psychological testing*, 3rd ed. New York: Macmillan, 1968.

Baggaley, A. R. *Intermediate correlational methods*. New York: Wiley, 1964.

Barclay, J. R. The Barclay classroom climate inventory. *Elementary School Guidance and Counseling*, 1972, 6, 298–99.

Barlow, D. H., Leitenberg, H., & Agras, W. S. Experimental control of sexual deviation through manipulation of the noxious scene in covert sensitization. *Journal of Abnormal Psychology*, 1969, 74, 596–601.

Bedrosian, O., Sara, N., & Pearlman, J. A pilot study to determine the effectiveness of guidance classes in developing self-understanding in elementary school children. *Elementary School Guidance and Counseling*, 1970, 5, 124–134.

Borg, W. R. *Educational research: An introduction*. New York: David McKay, 1963.

Browning, R. M., & Stover, D. O. *Behavior modification in child treatment*. Chicago: Aldine-Atherton, 1971.

Bruning, J. L., & Kintz, B. L. *Computational handbook of statistics*. Glenview, Ill.: Scott, Foresman, 1968.

Buros, O. K. (Ed.) *Tests in print*. Highland Park, N.J.: Gryphon Press, 1961.

Buros, O. K. (Ed.) *Mental measurements yearbook*. Highland Park, N.J.: Gryphon Press, 1972.

Caldwell, B. M. *Cooperative preschool inventory*. Princeton, N.J.: Educational Testing Service, 1970.

Callao, M. J. Sociometric change among elementary school children involved in a shared goals model of group counseling. *Elementary School Guidance and Counseling*, 1972, 6, 208–210.

Campbell, D. T., & Stanley, J. C. *Experimental and quasi-experimental designs for research*. Chicago: Rand McNally, 1963.

Cramer, S. H., Herr, E. L., Morris, C. N., & Frantz, T. T. *Research and the school counselor*. Boston: Houghton Mifflin, 1970.

Crow, M. L. A comparison of three group counseling techniques with sixth graders. *Elementary School Guidance and Counseling*, 1971, 6, 37–42.

Daldrop, R. J., Hubbert, A., & Hamilton, J. Evaluation of an initial elementary school counseling program. *Elementary School Guidance and Counseling*, 1968, 3, 118–125.

Davison, G. C., & Valins, S. Maintenance of self-attributed and drug-attributed behavior change. *Journal of Personality and Social Psychology*, 1969, 11, 25–33.

Dinkmeyer, D. (Ed.) *Guidance and counseling in the elementary school*. New York: Holt, Rinehart & Winston, 1968.

Drowne, J. L. Three group counseling approaches. *Elementary School Guidance and Counseling*, 1972, 6, 291–293.

Drummond, R. J. Concurrent and predictive validity of the cooperative preschool inventory. *Elementary School Guidance and Counseling*, 1972, 7, 60–61.

Edwards, A. L. *Statistical methods*. New York: Holt, Rinehart & Winston, 1967.

Frost, J. A., & Frost, J. M. An evolving elementary school guidance program and ongoing research projects. *Elementary School Guidance and Counseling*, 1967, 2, 121–126.

Fruchter, B. *Introduction to factor analysis*. Princeton, N.J.: D. Van Nostrand, 1954.

Gage, N. L. (Ed.) *Handbook of research on teaching*. Chicago: Rand McNally, 1963.

Games, P. A., & Klare, G. R. *Elementary statistics: Data analysis for the behavioral sciences*. New York: McGraw-Hill, 1967.

Gordon, I. J. Action research improves an aspect of elementary school guidance. *Personnel and Guidance Journal*, 1958, 37, 65–67.

Guilford, J. P. *Fundamental statistics in psychology and education*. New York: McGraw-Hill, 1965.

Hansen, J. C., & Stevic, R. R. *Elementary school guidance*. New York: Macmillan, 1969.

Hawkins, S. The content of elementary counseling interviews. *Elementary School Guidance and Counseling*, 1967, 2, 114–120.

Hill, G. E., & Luckey, E. B. *Guidance for children in elementary schools*. New York: Appleton-Century-Crofts, 1969.

Kagan, N., & Krathwohl, D. R. *Studies in human interaction*; Project No. 5-0800. U.S. Department of Health, Education and Welfare, Office of Education, Bureau of Research, 1967.

Keat, D. B. *Cooperation-Aggression Behavior Scale*. University Park, Penn.: Author, 1970.

Keat, D. B. Broad-spectrum behavior therapy with children: A case presentation. *Behavior Therapy*, 1972, 3, 454–459.

Keat, D. B. A behavior modification program for pre-school children: snags, pitfalls, and some behavioral changes. Unpublished manuscript, Pennsylvania State University, 1973.

Keat, D. B., Anderson, S., Conklin, N., Elias, R., Faber, D., Felty, S., Gerba, J., Kochenash, J., Logan, W., Malecki, D., Martino, P., McDuffy, I., Schmerling, G., Schuh, C., & Selkowitz, L. *Helping children to feel: A guide to affective curriculum materials for the elementary school.* State College, Penn.: Counselor Education Press, 1972.

Keat, D. B., & Hackman, R. B. A method of clustering persons' profiles for counseling. *Measurement and Evaluation in Guidance,* 1972, **5**, 373–378.

Keat, D. B. The appraisal of guidance learning outcomes resulting from confluent education curriculum interventions. *Elementary School Guidance and Counseling,* 1973, 8, in press.

Kerlinger, F. N. *Foundations of behavioral research.* New York: Holt, Rinehart & Winston, 1964.

Kinsbourne, M. *Mark II.* Durham, N.C.: Author, 1972.

Krantz, P. J., & Risley, T. R. The organization of group care environments: Behavioral ecology in the classroom. Paper presented at the meeting of the American Psychological Association, Honolulu, September 1972.

Lamke, T. A., & Silvey, H. M. *Master's theses in education.* Cedar Falls: Iowa State Teachers College, 1953 to date.

Lazarus, A. A., & Abramovitz, A. The use of "emotive imagery" in the treatment of children's phobias. *Journal of Mental Science,* 1962, **108,** 191–195.

Lazarus, A. A., & Davison, G. C. Clinical innovation in research and practice. In A. E. Bergin and S. L. Garfield (Eds.), *Handbook of psychotherapy and behavior change.* New York: Wiley, 1971, pp. 196–213.

Leventhal, R. B., & Kranzler, G. D. The relationship between the depth of intrapersonal exploration and constructive personality change in elementary school children: An exploratory study. *Elementary School Guidance and Counseling,* 1968, **3,** 12–19.

Mayer, G. R., Beggs, D. L., Fjellstedt, N., Forhetz, J., Nighswander, J. K., & Richards, R. The use of public commitment and counseling with elementary school children: An evaluation. *Elementary School Guidance and Counseling,* 1970, **5,** 22–34.

McNemar, Q. *Psychological statistics.* New York: Wiley, 1966.

Miller, G. D., Gum, M. F., & Bender, D. *Elementary school guidance: Demonstration and evaluation.* St. Paul: Minnesota Department of Education, 1972.

Muro, J. Research related to elementary school guidance and counseling. *Elementary School Guidance and Counseling,* 1971, 6, 134–136.

Pennsylvania Department of Education. *Guidelines for self-study of a school district guidance program.* Harrisburg: Division of Guidance Services, 1972.

Peters, H. J., & Hansen, J. C. The school counselor as a researcher. *School Counselor,* 1964, **11,** 165–170.

Peters, H. J., & Shertzer, B. *Guidance: Program development and management.* 2nd ed. Columbus, Ohio: Charles E. Merrill, 1969.

Peters, H. J., Shertzer, B., & VanHoose, W. H. *Guidance in elementary schools*. Chicago: Rand McNally, 1965.

Rich, W. S. *American foundations and their fields*. New York: American Foundations Information Service, 1955.

Sarason, S. B., Hill, K. T., & Zimbardo, P. G. A longitudinal study of the relation of test anxiety to performance on intelligence and achievement tests. *Monographs of the society for research in child development*, No. 98, 1964, 29, 1–51.

Scanlon, R. G. *Research for Better Schools: Progress Report*. Philadelphia: Research for Better Schools, 1972.

Scanlon, R. G., & Brown, M. V. Individualizing instruction. In O. S. Bushnell & D. Rappaport (Eds.), *Planned change in education: A systems approach*. New York: Harcourt Brace Jovanovich, 1971, pp. 93–106.

Shane, J. G., Shane, H. G., Gibson, R. L., & Munger, P. F. *Guiding human development: the counselor and the teacher in the elementary school*. Belmont, Cal.: Wadsworth, 1971.

Siegel, S. *Nonparametric statistics for the behavioral sciences*. New York: McGraw-Hill, 1956.

State College Area School District. *A self-study of the counseling and guidance department of pupil personnel services*. State College, Pennsylvania, 1973.

Stefflre, B. Research in guidance: Horizons for the future. In D. Dinkmeyer (Ed.), *Guidance and counseling in the elementary school*. New York: Holt, Rinehart & Winston, 1968, pp. 385–390.

Steinhoff, C. R. *Organizational climate in a public school system*. Unpublished Ed.D. dissertation, Syracuse University, 1965.

Stern, G. G. *People in context*. New York: Wiley, 1970.

Thombs, M. R., & Muro, J. J. Group counseling and the sociometric status of second grade children. *Elementary School Guidance and Counseling*, 1973, 7, 194–197.

Thoresen, C. E. The intensive design. An intimate approach to counseling research. Paper presented at the meeting of the American Educational Research Association, Chicago, April 1972.

Thoresen, C. E., Alper, T., Hannum, J., Barrick, J., & Jacks, R. Comparison of systematic desensitization and behavior management training with elementary teachers. *Research Memorandum*, Stanford Center for Research and Development in Teachers, 1973, in press.

Tryon, R. C., & Bailey, D. E. *Cluster Analysis*. New York: McGraw-Hill, 1970.

Walker, H. A., & Lev, J. *Elementary statistical methods*. New York: Henry Holt, 1958.

Winer, B. J. *Statistical principles in experimental design*. New York: McGraw-Hill, 1962.

Wrenn, G. G. Editor's introduction. In S. H. Cramer, E. L. Herr, C. N. Morris, & T. T. Frantz. *Research and the school counselor*. Boston: Houghton Mifflin, 1970, p. ix.

The Pennsylvania State University
Elementary Counseling Program

Selection

The university graduate school has certain minimum selective admissions requirements. A junior-senior grade-point average (GPA) of at least 2.5 on a 4.0 scale is expected as a minimum graduate school requirement. Because competition for available openings in the counselor education program is keen, it can be assumed that those chosen will usually possess higher undergraduate GPA's than the minimum. Another requirement is a minimum of 27 credits in related areas such as education, psychology, economics, sociology, and so forth. Grades of B or better are expected in these courses. The importance of elementary school teaching experience has been a much debated subject. There exists great variability among states with 33 (of 49 reporting) requiring teaching experience and accepting no alternatives. In Pennsylvania and 16 other states, alternative experience is acceptable if all other requirements are met; at Penn State applicants with adequate preparation but no teaching experience have been admitted and placed in school internships which enhance their classroom experience as well as lengthen their graduate programs.

Another criterion for admission is the quality of writing and level of self-disclosure as evidenced on an autobiographical sketch discussing influences on personal goals, anticipated vocational goals, and related plans for achievement. For certain individuals, letters of recommendation are also solicited.

When he or she has filed the appropriate forms and passed through the screening process, the potential counselor trainee spends several hours on campus. There the prospective counselor undergoes a series of experiences, scheduled randomly according to the criteria of feasibility and practicality. One is an interview with the coordinator of the counseling program. During this interview the coordinator typically asks such questions as "Tell me about yourself." "How would your best friend describe you?" What are some of your strengths and weaknesses?" "What changes would you like to see in schools and how would you go about making these changes?" "Why do you want to become an elementary school counselor?" "What do you hope to gain from being an elementary school counselor?" "How did you resolve a recent problem?" "What types of counselees would be difficult for you to work with?" and "What do you think elementary counseling is?"

Another phase of the screening process is a child interview play session. The applicant is taken into a playroom, introduced to a child (first name only), ambiguously told that he will be spending some time with this child, and left alone. The applicant is then observed through a one-way mirror by the coordinator and several people currently enrolled in the elementary counseling program. The observers are told to look for how the prospective counselor initially makes contact with the child, how communication takes place, the extent and direction of limit structure, how the child seems to be enjoying himself, and the general overall effectiveness of the person's ability to relate to a primary-age child. The ratings of the observers are then totaled. Ratings are made on a five-point scale, with one meaning poor, two below average, three average, four above average, and five excellent. Accepted applicants usually average between three and four in their ratings. Most people with teaching backgrounds tend to structure the session too much, initiating didactic experiences such as naming colors, teaching numbers, or directing the composition of a drawing.

The third main component of the screening process is a group interview. The applicant spends a half hour with four or five persons currently enrolled in the elementary school counseling program, who typically ask such questions as "What were your most important undergraduate courses?" "What are your past experiences with children?" "What has prompted your interest in this elementary counseling program?" and "What would you like to do as an elementary counselor?" These people are then asked to rank the person on a three-point scale with − (minus) representing a negative reaction to the person, zero meaning indifference, and + (plus) representing conviction that the applicant would be a good elementary counselor.

The applicant spends the final portion of the screening process responding to some kind of structured stimuli. Two forms of situations have been used in recent years. One is the 16 helping stimulus expressions developed by Carkhuff. If the applicant is accepted, his scores prior to entering the program can be compared with those recorded at the end of the program to measure changes in his development of particular skills as represented by the Carkhuff scales. Another scale was developed as a 20-item multiple-choice scale (School Counselor Attitude Inventory) that locates the counselor's preferred behaviors on a continuum from *status quo* through counselor model to change agent. This scale, as well as the scoring key, is reprinted in part in Appendix B.

Selective Progressive Retention

All students begin the elementary school counseling program in the summer term. Group meetings are held weekly to allow them to get acquainted, deal with concerns, become familiar with requirements, develop communication skills, and grow in the understanding of self and others. This is their initial group experience with persons they will be meeting on a weekly basis for the duration of the year.

All students are exposed to a group process experience blending didactic material on group dynamics and group processes with sensitivity training and self understanding foci. This experience gives the staff an opportunity to know each candidate intensively, assess his flexibility and personal characteristics, and help him come to terms with whether or not this preparation program and subsequent professional role are suitable for him. In addition, it is assumed that self selection will operate to convince certain candidates of their lack of compatibility with the program's requirements in sufficient time to leave the program prior to the Fall term, when they can secure employment or enter another program.

Because students are block-scheduled, a staffing conference with participating faculty is conducted each term, or whenever appropriate, to assess the degree to which each trainee is attaining program goals. This evaluation can involve both the candidate's perception of his competencies and those of staff working intimately with him.

Since Cn. Ed. 503, 506, and 507 and 515 involve field work with elementary school students under university supervision, the individual trainee's progress will be continuously monitored. These group and one-to-one contacts enable the coordinator to facilitate the student's development toward the goal of being an effective elementary school counselor.

In a less formal fashion, the staff interacts regarding the individuals in the program. This interaction can take various forms. Ordinarily, during (1) staff meetings and/or (2) informal conversations faculty members explore perceptions of students and consult individual(s) enrolled in the program.

Program Description of Courses

First term
Foundations of Guidance and Counseling Processes   (3 credits)
Group Procedures in Guidance and Counseling   (2 credits)
Basic Statistics   (2 credits)
Advanced Child Development   (3 credits)

Second term
Counseling Theory and Method   (3 credits)
Guidance Services in Elementary Education   (3 credits)
Use of Tests in Counseling   (3 credits)
Seminar placing observation in appropriate frames of reference about significant others and the school as a social system   (1 credit)

Third term
Foundation of Counseling Information   (3 credits)
Individual Analysis and Counseling Procedures   (3 credits)
Filial Modification Program   (3 credits)
Seminar examining the contribution of other disciplines to the understanding of elementary school children   (1 credit)

Fourth term
Counseling Practicum   (3 credits)
Seminar on organization, administration, and evaluation of elementary

school guidance programs   (1 credit)
Filial Modification Program   (2 or 3 credits)

Program Evaluation

Evaluation of the programs will be continuous. The instructional staff
will regularly seek feedback from students as to how their skills, understandings, and competencies might be improved through program
activities. At the end of each experience students will respond to
questionnaires asking for suggestions about how activities and experiences could be made more effective.

An example of this type of questionnaire is reprinted in Appendix C.
It should be noted that, after checking the responses of a group of 11
interns, the suggested changes were implemented for the next year's
group. Probably the most significant of these was increased time in the
school, i.e., 1 to 1½ days per week the second term; 2 to 2½ days
days the third term; 3 to 3½ days during the final term of the program.

Appendix B

School Counselor's Attitude Inventory (SCAI)*
by S. Baker

Directions: Choose that response which best suits your style as a
counselor. Please place the letter signifying that response in the proper
blank on the answer sheet.

   3. You have found out that one of your counselees is failing most
      of his subjects because of a severe reading deficiency. Your
      school has no remedial reading program and none of the faculty
      members can actually teach people how to read.

      a. Attempt to give the student some leads concerning persons
         or organizations that might help him to attack this problem.
      b. Go to the administration and seek help or else go to outside-
         of-the-school sources and seek help.
      c. Sympathize with the student's problem and encourage him
         to try his best.
      d. Through counseling, attempt to help the student to adjust
         to the school's conditions and to attempt to make the most
         of the situation.
      e. Inform the student that he will have to take whatever he can
         get in the way of grades.

Selected items reproduced by permission. For complete copies of inventory
and scale contact S. Baker at The Pennsylvania State University.

    f. Counsel the student with the goal in mind of helping to discover ways to attack the problem and to find a possible solution.

7. A fifth grader has revealed to you his consternation with his parents because they will not let him stay outside after dark. He argues that he should be able to stay out after dark because all of his friends are allowed to do so.
    a. Try to help the boy to think through this situation so that he can accept the parents' rules and live with them.
    b. After informing the boy that his parents know best, talk to him about the reasons behind curfews and the problems and responsibilities of parenthood.
    c. Go to the parents and see if you can successfully present the boy's point of view to them.
    d. Suggest that he have his parents talk to other parents and offer to arrange the details of a meeting for him.
    e. Tell the boy that he should obey his parents.
    f. Try to help the boy to think through this situation in order to figure out ways of approaching his parents successfully for new hours.

8. You are approached by a fifth grade girl who is in tears because the teacher has threatened the class members with additional homework if they did not return the administrative materials that were sent home for parental signatures earlier in the week. She has lost hers and the parents are working.
    a. Send the girl to the principal, or to her parents, who might be able to influence the teacher so that she can avoid the punishing assignment.
    b. Support the teacher and tell the student that she will have to do the homework.
    c. Support the teacher and help the student to see the value in doing extra homework.
    d. Through counseling, attempt to help the girl to figure out a way to handle this situation satisfactorily and avoid the homework.
    e. Go to the teacher and see what you can do about getting him to change his punishing rule.
    f. Through counseling, help the student to adjust to the teacher's ways.

10. A teacher in the elementary school has sent a 7-year-old boy to the office for discipline because of his continual disruptive behavior in school. The principal at your school sees discipline as a function of the counselor's role.
    a. Discipline the boy according to the standards of the school.
    b. Offer to work with the boy as a counselor and speak to the principal concerning his viewpoint on counselors and discipline.

    c. Mete out the necessary discipline and talk to the boy about the need to avoid preventing the other students from getting their education.

    d. Through counseling, attempt to help the boy to explore his behavior concerning the causes and the results.

    e. Through counseling, attempt to help the boy to see the need to adjust his behavior to the classroom norms.

    f. Take a firm stand against counselors as disciplinarians.

12. One of your counselees has asked to be dropped from elementary school orchestra but the teacher has refused. The teacher has asked you to intervene with the child and the parent, if necessary, because it would be a shame to let such a talented child quit.

    a. Support the teacher and talk to the child about the teacher's interest in making the most of one's talents.

    b. Support the teacher completely.

    c. Inform the teacher that such a decision should be made by the child and the parents rather than the school personnel.

    d. Try to help the child through this matter in order to be able to adjust to the situation.

    e. Offer to arrange for a meeting between the teacher, the parents, and possibly the child, in order to settle this matter in the best interests of the child.

    f. Try to help the child think through this matter in order to be able to decide which is the best course of action to take.

14. A member of the faculty has come to you for advice and, possibly, for support. The faculty member feels that the school should openly advocate the discussion of all points of view on such matters as sex education, drug usage, civil rights, political conservatism vs. political radicalism, and religion.

    a. Help the faculty member to think through his ideas in order that he can come up with the best possible plan of action for him.

    b. Join with the faculty member in his efforts to introduce these ideas and change existing regulations if they need to be changed.

    c. Hold to the school policy line but respect the faculty member for his beliefs and concern.

    d. Stand by whatever the school policy is.

    e. Help the faculty member to think through his ideas as they relate to the existing school policies with hope that whatever he does will not violate the policies.

    f. Offer to arrange for the faculty member to meet with people with whom he might have a meaningful dialogue about incorporating his ideas into the curriculum.

SCAI Answer Sheet

Directions: Each item in the SCAI presents a client problem for you to consider. From the responses offered to you, choose that one which you most prefer and place the corresponding letter in the proper space provided on the answer sheet for that item.

Category Totals:

3. _____	10. _____	Sum up the number of answers	1. _____
7. _____	12. _____	above which fall into each of the	2. _____
8. _____	14. _____	six categories. Each integer of	3. _____
	18. _____	one (1) represents 5 percentile	4. _____
Total:		points on the accompanying	5. _____
		profile sheet.	6. _____

SCAI Scoring Key

	CATEGORY					
QUESTION	1	2	3	4	5	6
3	e	c	d	f	a	b
7	e	b	a	f	d	c
8	b	c	f	d	a	e
10	a	c	e	d	b	f
12	b	a	d	f	e	c
14	d	c	e	a	f	b
18	b	f	d	c	a	e

1. Strong status quo advocate.
2. Status quo advocate with secondary interest in the counselee.
3. Status quo oriented counselor.
4. Change oriented counselor.
5. Semi-active change advocate.
6. Strong change advocate.

SCAI Profile Form

```
    ............................................................
90  ............................................................
    ............................................................
80  ............................................................
    ............................................................
70  ............................................................
    ............................................................
60  ............................................................
    ............................................................
50  ............................................................
    ............................................................
40  ............................................................
    ............................................................
30  ............................................................
    ............................................................
20  ............................................................
    ............................................................
10  ............................................................
    ............................................................
 0  ............................................................
    ────────────────────────────────────────────────────────────
        1       2       2       3       4       5       6
```

1. Strong status quo advocate: the counselor is unwilling to change the status quo.
2. Status quo advocate with secondary interest in the counselee: the counselor is willing to be of some help but is not interested in change.
3. Status quo oriented counselor: the counselor is not interested in changing the status quo but is desirous to help the counselee adjust through counseling.
4. Change oriented counselor: the counselor is interested in change, if need be, but wishes to help the counselee to become a self-directed change agent through counseling him.
5. Semi-active change advocate: the counselor is interested in change, if need be, and desires to assist the client in finding sources of help.
6. Strong change advocate: the counselor is interested in change, if need be, and desires to take an active personal role in changing conditions and helping the counselee.

Program Evaluation Questionnaire
by S. Baker

Part One

Directions: After you have read each of the statements below, circle one of the numbers which follow. The numbers represent the degree to which you are satisfied that your internship experience fulfilled your needs and expectations with regard to the content of that statement. The higher the number, the greater the degree of satisfaction on your part. Conversely, the lower the number, the lower is the degree of satisfaction on your part. For example, circling number 4 will indicate the highest level of satisfaction while circling number 1 will indicate the lowest level of satisfaction on your part.

1. My satisfaction with the location of my internship is   1 2 3 4

2. My satisfaction with the physical facilities of the school where my internship took place is   1 2 3 4

3. My satisfaction with the relationship between me and my field supervisor, supervising counselor, or school administrator is   1 2 3 4

4. My satisfaction with the level of competence displayed by my field supervisor, supervising counselor or school administrator is   1 2 3 4

5. My satisfaction with the treatment and acceptance of me by the staff (counseling and other) where I interned is   1 2 3 4

6. My satisfaction with the treatment and acceptance of me by the students where I interned is   1 2 3 4

7. My satisfaction with my relationship with my University supervisor is   1 2 3 4

8. My satisfaction with my experience in the University 597 seminar is   1 2 3 4

9. My satisfaction with my relationship with the 597 seminar leader is   1 2 3 4

10. My satisfaction with my total internship experience is   1 2 3 4

11. My satisfaction with my output and effort with regard to the internship experience is   1 2 3 4

Part Two

Directions: The purpose of the following statements is to allow you to express any important feelings you have in relation to the internship that were not covered by the structured questions above. Please respond to the stimulus presented in the statement.

12. If I could have my way, I would have the internship changed in the following manner:
13. Those conditions of the internship which I strongly feel should be maintained for future use are:
14. I would like to make the following statement because no other item in this questionnaire allowed me to express these feelings:

Appendix D

A Reinforcement Survey Schedule
for Children
by D. B. Keat

Part One

The items in this questionnaire refer to things and experiences that may give you joy or other pleasurable feelings of attraction, or be of interest to you. Check each item, in the column that describes how much you like it now. Answer beside each item by checking under the heading which shows how you feel. That is: not at all, a little, a fair amount, or very much.

RATING	NOT AT ALL	A LITTLE	A FAIR AMOUNT	VERY MUCH
1. *Foods*				
a) Ice cream	___	___	___	___
b) Candy	___	___	___	___
c) Fruit	___	___	___	___
d) Nuts	___	___	___	___
e) Pastry	___	___	___	___
f) Cookies	___	___	___	___
g) Sandwiches	___	___	___	___
h) Pie	___	___	___	___
i) Gum	___	___	___	___
j) Popcorn	___	___	___	___
k) Seeds (e.g. sunflower)	___	___	___	___
l) Other ___	___	___	___	___

	RATING	NOT AT ALL	A LITTLE	A FAIR AMOUNT	VERY MUCH

2. *Beverages*
   a) Water
   b) Milk
   c) Soda
   d) Cocoa
   e) Juices
   f) Other

3. *Animals*
   a) Dogs
   b) Cats
   c) Horses
   d) Birds
   e) Fish
   f) Turtles
   g) Other

4. *Playing Sports*
   a) Football
   b) Baseball
   c) Basketball
   d) Golf
   e) Swimming
   f) Pool
   g) Running
   h) Tennis
   i) Boxing
   j) Fishing
   k) Hunting
   l) Skiing
   m) Other _____

5. *Reading*
   a) Comic book
   b) Sports
   c) Newspapers
   d) Adventure
   e) Famous people
   f) Travel
   g) Humor
   h) Science

6. *Music*
   a) Play instrument
   b) Listen to records
      1) Classical
      2) Jazz
      3) Rock
      4) Folk

RATING	NOT AT ALL	A LITTLE	A FAIR AMOUNT	VERY MUCH
5) Pop	____	____	____	____
6) Shows	____	____	____	____
7. *Like to dance*				
a) With boys	____	____	____	____
b) With girls	____	____	____	____
c) Ballet	____	____	____	____
d) Square dancing	____	____	____	____
e) Folk dancing	____	____	____	____
f) Modern dancing	____	____	____	____
8. *Shopping*				
a) Clothes	____	____	____	____
b) Toys	____	____	____	____
c) Food	____	____	____	____
d) Sports equipment	____	____	____	____
e) Records	____	____	____	____
9. *Television*	____	____	____	____
10. *Movies*	____	____	____	____
11. *Hiking or walking*	____	____	____	____
12. *Camping*	____	____	____	____
13. *Sleeping*	____	____	____	____
14. *Taking a bath-shower*	____	____	____	____
15. *Being praised*				
a) About appearance	____	____	____	____
b) About work	____	____	____	____
c) About strength	____	____	____	____
d) About athletic ability	____	____	____	____
e) About your mind	____	____	____	____
16. *Old men and women*	____	____	____	____
17. *Watching other people*	____	____	____	____
18. *Talking to friends*	____	____	____	____
19. *Saying prayers*	____	____	____	____
20. *Peace and quiet*	____	____	____	____
21. *Games*				
a) Chess	____	____	____	____
b) Checkers	____	____	____	____
c) Puzzle	____	____	____	____
d) Cards	____	____	____	____
e) Dominoes	____	____	____	____
f) Tic Tac Toe	____	____	____	____
g) Ball	____	____	____	____
h) Marbles	____	____	____	____
i) Jacks	____	____	____	____
j) Pick-up stix	____	____	____	____

RATING	NOT AT ALL	A LITTLE	A FAIR AMOUNT	VERY MUCH
k) Scrabble	_____	_____	_____	_____
l) Sorry	_____	_____	_____	_____
m) Other	_____	_____	_____	_____

22. *Play*

	NOT AT ALL	A LITTLE	A FAIR AMOUNT	VERY MUCH
a) Cut and paste	_____	_____	_____	_____
b) Clay	_____	_____	_____	_____
c) Painting	_____	_____	_____	_____
d) Drawing (crayons)	_____	_____	_____	_____
e) Tinker toys	_____	_____	_____	_____
f) Dolls, puppets	_____	_____	_____	_____
g) Cars	_____	_____	_____	_____
h) Lego	_____	_____	_____	_____
i) Other	_____	_____	_____	_____

23. *Talking*

	NOT AT ALL	A LITTLE	A FAIR AMOUNT	VERY MUCH
a) With a friend	_____	_____	_____	_____
b) With mother	_____	_____	_____	_____
c) With father	_____	_____	_____	_____
d) With brothers, sisters	_____	_____	_____	_____
e) With adults	_____	_____	_____	_____
f) Into a tape recorder	_____	_____	_____	_____

24. *Material objects*

	NOT AT ALL	A LITTLE	A FAIR AMOUNT	VERY MUCH
a) Note pads	_____	_____	_____	_____
b) Pencils	_____	_____	_____	_____
c) Crayons	_____	_____	_____	_____
d) Paper	_____	_____	_____	_____
e) Coloring book	_____	_____	_____	_____
f) Eraser	_____	_____	_____	_____
g) Felt pens	_____	_____	_____	_____
h) Combs	_____	_____	_____	_____
i) Flowers	_____	_____	_____	_____
j) Stamps	_____	_____	_____	_____
k) Coins	_____	_____	_____	_____
l) Sports cards (e.g. football)	_____	_____	_____	_____
m) Other	_____	_____	_____	_____

25. List the things you like best of all in life.

26. If you could buy 3 games that you would like, what would they be?

27. What are the 3 jobs that you like to do most in the classroom?

28. What do you like to do with your parents?

29. What do you like to do with your friends?

Appendix E

Reflective Listening
by M. L. Merriam

Reflective listening is a term given to the type of active listening which involves *attending* to the words, gestures, tone of voice, posture and eye movements of the speaker and then *responding* to the speaker by synthesizing or putting together all of these verbal and nonverbal cues into a statement of what you perceived the speaker's full meaning was. There are at least four methods involved in reflective listening:

1. Reflection of Content

In this the listener simply paraphrases the meaning of the words of the speaker. You reflect at this level to indicate basic understanding.

CHILD: "The Little League is no good. They make you play in the rain, you can't miss practices, and you can't be on the same team as your friends are."

ADULT: "In the Little League you have to play when the weather is bad, you can't miss practices and you can't be with your friends. . ."

2. Reflection of Feeling

On this level the listener reflects feelings which are accompanying the words of the speaker. Your reflection indicates your acceptance of these feelings.

CHILD: "The Little League is no good. They make you play in the rain, you can't miss practices, and you can't be on the same team as your friends are."

ADULT: "You really don't like the Little League. . ."

3. Reflection of Behavioral Implication

This level is much more complicated since the listener must synthesize verbal and nonverbal cues and reflect what he perceives the speaker is feeling as well as what might be the implication of the speaker's.

CHILD: "The Little League is no good. They make you play in the rain, you can't miss practices, and you can't be on the same team as your friends are."

ADULT: "You don't feel you want to join the Little League. . ."

4. Reflection of Both Content Implications and Feelings

This is the most difficult reflection that can be made. The listener reflects the unspoken and not so obvious feeling accompanied by a statement of behavioral effects, if appropriate.

CHILD: "The Little League is no good. They make you play in the rain, you can't miss practices, and you can't be on the same team as your friends are."

ADULT: "You are afraid that you are going to be pressured into joining the Little League and you don't feel you want to join. . ."

The implications of reflective listening are:

a. I want to understand how you are feeling and what you are thinking.
b. I want to share with you MY perceptions of what you have told me.
c. I do not want to give you a solution to your problem. I want to explore those problems with you and help you clarify them in your own mind.
d. I want to suspend my value judgments of your feelings and fully accept your feelings. I will not agree or disagree with what you say. I will tell you only how I perceive what you are saying.
e. I want to accept and respect your feelings and I want you to be able to accept and respect them also. I see you as a worthwhile person.

All reflections should be made on the basis of verbal and nonverbal messages given by the speaker. Reflections are NOT interpretations you, as listener, bring to the speaker out of your own experience. Rather, they come from your ability to "listen" to all of the verbal and nonverbal cues, to synthesize these cues into a meaningful statement of what you perceive the speaker to be saying. At the highest level, reflections put the listener in the shoes of the speaker. Using all of the available data in the communicative situation, the listener reflects his perceptions of the total situation.

In all cases reflections should be given in a tone of voice that suggests tentativeness and openly invites a response on the part of the speaker to confirm, reject or elaborate on what has been reflected. Part of the intent of reflecting is to allow the speaker to be heard more completely before the listener gives his ideas and feelings.

Reflections *differ* from questions in that:

a. Syntactically they are NOT stated as questions although in tone of voice they are questioning.
b. You are sharing *your* perceptions of the situation rather than *asking* the person for his perceptions.

The intent of reflections include:

a. If there is a problem, being able to gather more information so that the problem can be correctly identified.
b. Letting a person fully explore his feelings and accept these feelings.
c. Hearing a person more completely and understanding him more thoroughly.
d. NOT blaming others.

e. Letting the other person find his own solution to his problem.

f. Checking out the validity of your own perceptions.

Reflective Listening Worksheet

Directions: On this sheet you will find statements *made* by children. Read the statement and form a reflective response. Then turn to the next page and read the sample reflective responses we have made. Compare your response with ours and make any necessary revisions on your response with regard to its style.

Statement 1.
"Why don't we ever do that like all the other kids do?"
Response: _____
_____
_____

Statement 2.
"Nobody wants to play with me."
Response: _____
_____
_____

Statement 3.
"She took my book and won't give it back to me."
Response: _____
_____
_____

Reflective responses for statement #1:
"You're unhappy because we don't do the things you'd really like to do."
"You'd like to be able to do the same things your friends do."
Your modified response: _____
_____
_____

Reflective responses for statement #2:
"You're feeling lonesome since you have no one to play with."
"You're feeling out of things."
"You'd like me to play with you."
Your modified response: _____
_____
_____

Reflective responses for statement #3:
"You want your book back and you don't know how you're going to get it."
"You think she's being mean to you."
Your modified response: _____
_____
_____

Appendix F

The Guidance Learning Rating Scale
by D. B. Keat

Student Name _____

Date _____Grade Level _____Age _____

Teacher's Name (rater) _____

Directions: For each item (each behavior) circle the number of the rating descriptions which is most appropriate. Base your rating on your observation of and experience with the student up to this time.

Rating Descriptions

1. Never	if the behavior never occurs
2. Rarely	if the behavior occurs at wide intervals (e.g., once a month)
3. Occasionally	if the behavior occurs more often than *rarely* (e.g., once a week)
4. Often	if the behavior occurs more often than *occasionally* (e.g., once a day)
5. Very frequently	if the behavior occurs more than *often* (e.g., several times daily)

	NEVER	RARELY	OCC.	OFTEN	VERY FRE-QUENTLY
Understanding of Self					
1. Makes appropriate expression of felt emotions.	1	2	3	4	5
2. Is aware of and expresses concerns with clarity.	1	2	3	4	5
3. Engages in activities in which he will succeed.	1	2	3	4	5
4. Avoids belittling self for failures.	1	2	3	4	5
5. Accepts his personal uniqueness.	1	2	3	4	5

329

	NEVER	RARELY	OCC.	OFTEN	VERY FRE-QUENTLY

Understanding Feelings and Emotions

	NEVER	RARELY	OCC.	OFTEN	VERY FRE-QUENTLY
6. Is aware of her emotions.	1	2	3	4	5
7. Is able to express positive and negative feelings.	1	2	3	4	5
8. Acts on appropriate emotions non-verbally (e.g. crying).	1	2	3	4	5
9. Accepts feelings without shame or guilt.	1	2	3	4	5
10. Understands how others feel.	1	2	3	4	5

Understanding Human Behavior: Emotional Maturity

	NEVER	RARELY	OCC.	OFTEN	VERY FRE-QUENTLY
11. Can handle stressful situations.	1	2	3	4	5
12. Responds well (e.g. not nervous when teacher calls upon him).	1	2	3	4	5
13. Failure is handled appropriately.	1	2	3	4	5
14. Utilizes appropriate outlets for his worries and anxieties.	1	2	3	4	5
15. Changes of activity are handled well.	1	2	3	4	5

Assumes Self Responsibility

	NEVER	RARELY	OCC.	OFTEN	VERY FRE-QUENTLY
16. Accepts results of his own action.	1	2	3	4	5
17. Completes school assignments promptly.	1	2	3	4	5
18. Carries out assigned room responsibilities.	1	2	3	4	5
19. Takes his part in completing activities.	1	2	3	4	5
20. Confident to try new things.	1	2	3	4	5

	NEVER	RARELY	OCC.	OFTEN	VERY FRE-QUENTLY

Interpersonal Relationships.

21. Is cooperative and shares things with other children.	1	2	3	4	5
22. Makes new friends.	1	2	3	4	5
23. Demonstrates acceptance of others different than himself (e.g. race, economic).	1	2	3	4	5
24. Resolves conflicts with peers easily.	1	2	3	4	5
25. Works well with the group.	1	2	3	4	5

Understanding Choices, Making Decisions, and Problem Solving Skills.

26. Weighs alternatives before making a choice.	1	2	3	4	5
27. Makes plans before going ahead with a task.	1	2	3	4	5
28. Shows confidence when making a decision.	1	2	3	4	5
29. Can work out solutions to her problems.	1	2	3	4	5
30. Works with the group to reach solutions to problems.	1	2	3	4	5

Adjustment Capacities: Coping Skills, Independence, Self Reliance.

31. Cooperates with other children in activities.	1	2	3	4	5
32. Follows directions and rules.	1	2	3	4	5
33. Helps other children.	1	2	3	4	5
34. Accepts leadership roles.	1	2	3	4	5
35. Deals appropriately with inner needs and external demands.	1	2	3	4	5

Appendix G

Parent Questionnaire
by D. Amato, J. Cox, C. Griffith, P. Harrison, D. B. Keat, F. Landy, P. Lynch, and M. Mezack.

It is our intention that this questionnaire will provide a broader background and clearer picture of the effectiveness of our communication with parents concerning the program in this school. We wish to tap the expertise which you can provide because of your experience in other schools, experience in this school, and your concern and expectations for your own children. In addition, the information which this questionnaire provides will form the basis for P.T.A. meetings designed to get closer to the specific information which you desire about our program.

We are doing our utmost to assure a high return of questionnaires; however, provision for assuring anonymity has had much careful attention, as you will note in the directions for returning your questionnaire.

Please check:

I have been a resident in the Park Forest School area:

a. 12 months or less _____ b. 1–3 years _____ c. more than 3 years _____

Person(s) answering this questionnaire:

a. Male _____ b. Female _____

Part One

Directions: Please answer each item by circling *one* of the given possibilities.

SA (strongly agree)	A (agree)	N (neutral)	D (disagree)	SD (strongly disagree)

1. My child is understood well by teachers in the Park Forest Elementary School   SA A N D SD

2. My child likes the Park Forest Elementary School   SA A N D SD

3. My child seems to be happy with the Park Forest Elementary School   SA A N D SD

4. I understand clearly how children are evaluated with regard to report card grades   SA A N D SD

5. Learning of facts is stressed sufficiently in this school   SA A N D SD

6. It is difficult for me to find out what

teachers expect children to learn in Park Forest Elementary School   SA A N D SD

7. I think it is better to have my child in one room all day rather than going from one teacher to another   SA A N D SD

8. A teacher should not expect children to study together, but should keep children busy by themselves   SA A N D SD

9. My child is too heavily involved in related projects, rather than in learning new materials   SA A N D SD

10. Student teachers are valuable members of the school's professional team   SA A N D SD

11. Sixth graders should be located in another elementary school rather than in Park Forest Junior High   SA A N D SD

12. I would like to discuss subject matter content at P.T.A. meetings   SA A N D SD

13. I would like to help evaluate the success of the school's organization and curriculum   SA A N D SD

14. Teachers should help to evaluate the success of the school's organization and curriculum   SA A N D SD

15. I understand clearly the reasons the Park Forest Elementary School is organized as it is   SA A N D SD

16. I feel that knowing what my child is learning is more important than knowing what grade he might be in   SA A N D SD

17. As far as the education of my child is concerned, grade levels (1st, 2nd, 3rd) are labels which are not really important   SA A N D SD

18. I feel that it is better to let my child learn at his own speed rather than to keep him necessarily in one grade all year long   SA A N D SD

19. In general, I feel that it is difficult for one teacher to be responsible for teaching everything to a group of children   SA A N D SD

20. My child has a better chance of being understood by a team of teachers than by just one teacher   SA A N D SD

21. Discipline in school is more important than what subjects are taught   SA   A   N   D   SD

22. If my child left this school, I feel that he would have an easy time fitting into another elementary school's classroom system   SA   A   N   D   SD

23. Students who go through this school adjust well to a junior high school   SA   A   N   D   SD

24. I feel that my child will be well prepared for junior high school work after graduating from Park Forest Elementary School   SA   A   N   D   SD

25. I feel that there are great advantages for my child to spend the school day with a group of teachers rather than with one teacher   SA   A   N   D   SD

26. My child seems to learn more in situations where several teachers work together than in situations where he works only with one teacher   SA   A   N   D   SD

27. This school is better for my child than most schools   SA   A   N   D   SD

28. Letting children work at their own speed in school provides a better learning situation for the bright child than setting an over all learning pace expected for all children   SA   A   N   D   SD

29. Grouping average children together promotes better learning for them than putting them with bright children   SA   A   N   D   SD

30. Letting children work at their own speed is better for the slow child than having the same expectations of all children   SA   A   N   D   SD

31. I understand how children are grouped in the Park Forest Elementary School   SA   A   N   D   SD

32. I feel Park Forest Elementary School is flexible in dealing with my child   SA   A   N   D   SD

33. My child does not feel anxious about competition from other youngsters   SA   A   N   D   SD

34. Teachers at this school work harder than teachers in most schools   SA   A   N   D   SD

Part Two

Directions: There are various ways in which you (as a parent) might become involved with your school. Please indicate your feelings, preferences, and observations for each item. (A) as they are today concerning the item, and (B) as you feel the items could be from a more ideal standpoint.
Please use the following key:

1. of no help
2. of little help
3. helpful
4. very helpful
5. extremely helpful

An example: Home visits   are $\underline{2}$

                              could be $\underline{4}$

a. Teacher conferences   are   _____
                                               could be _____
b. Principal contacts   are   _____
                                               could be _____
c. Elementary counselor conferences   are   _____
                                               could be _____
d. Special personnel (e.g., psychologist,   are   _____
    reading teacher)   could be _____
e. Home visits by school personnel   are   _____
                                               could be _____
f. Classroom visitation by parents   is   _____
                                               could be _____

II.   What are your reactions to the amount of information you are receiving in the following areas?

1. No help 2. Little help 3. Helpful 4. Very helpful
5. Extremely helpful

A. Language Arts _____   E. Art   _____
B. New Math   _____   F. Grouping and
C. Physical Edu-   leveling   _____
    cation   _____   G. Grade Report-
D. Music Program _____   ing   _____

III. The following are areas in which you might do volunteer work. Please indicate the amount you would like to work by circling the appropriate (for you) number.

	NEVER	RARELY	OCCA-SIONALLY	OFTEN	VERY FRE-QUENTLY
a. Lunchroom (cafeteria aide)	1	2	3	4	5
b. Library	1	2	3	4	5
c. Classroom aide	1	2	3	4	5
d. Committee work	1	2	3	4	5
e. Visitor tour guide	1	2	3	4	5

IV. In the area of your child's homework:

	NEVER	RARELY	OCCA-SIONALLY	OFTEN	VERY FRE-QUENTLY
a. You think that you should help	1	2	3	4	5
b. In reality, you help	1	2	3	4	5

V. Which of the following ways would you like to work in school? Please check a "yes," "perhaps," or "no" for each of the following.

	YES	PERHAPS	NO
a. P.T.A. Committee	___	___	___
b. Parent education programs	___	___	___
c. Parent advisory group	___	___	___
d. Study Committee (e.g., books, child development, etc.)	___	___	___
e. Orientation programs	___	___	___
f. Active participation in P.T.A. meetings (i.e. doing things there)	___	___	___
g. Passive participation in P.T.A. (i.e. sitting back and absorbing facts)	___	___	___

VI. In parent-teacher conferences, what kinds of things do you feel are important to discuss?

	YES	MAYBE	NO
a. Your child's good points	___	___	___
b. Academic problems	___	___	___
c. Social difficulties (children or adults)	___	___	___
d. Emotional problems	___	___	___
e. Physical troubles	___	___	___
f. Other _____	___	___	___

VII. With regard to *your child*, what would you like to know more about?

	EXTREMELY HELPFUL	HELPFUL	NO HELP
a. Play materials	___	___	___
b. Ways of relating to your child	___	___	___
c. Discipline procedures	___	___	___
d. Appropriate reading materials	___	___	___
e. Curriculum content	___	___	___
f. Child development	___	___	___
g. Sex education	___	___	___

VIII. Communication between you and the Park Forest Elementary School (a) check the three areas listed below which you *presently* feel are most important (b) also, check the three areas below which you *prefer* to use for better communication.

	PRESENT	PREFERRED
a. P.T.A.	___	___
b. Cluster Courier	___	___
c. Public newspaper	___	___
d. Information booklet	___	___
e. Radio	___	___
f. T.V.	___	___
g. Verbal reports by child	___	___
h. Written notices brought home by child	___	___
i. Conferences	___	___
j. Other _____	___	___

Part Three

Directions: The following paragraphs are descriptive statements of four "personal philosophies." As you read the four statements, attempt to determine how close *each* comes to *your* philosophy of education.

To the right of each philosophy paragraph there are the numbers 1, 2, 3, and 4. Circle only *one* number for *each* philosophy. Number 1 indicates the philosophy you feel fits *you* best, number 2 second best, 3 third best, and 4 the least. In other words, you are being asked to rank these four philosophies. An *example* might be that Philosophy 1 "fits" you best, thus you circle #1; Philosophy C "fits" you second best, thus you circle #2; Philosophy B "fits" you third best, thus you circle #3; and finally philosophy D "fits" you least, thus you circle #4.

Philosophy A: This philosophy emphasizes education as preparation   1
for a job. Social activities, school subjects, and extracurricular   2

activities are less important. *Persons holding this philosophy view* 3
education as the major way to prepare students to some day earn a 4
living.

Philosophy B: This philosophy emphasizes the study and under- 1
standing of school subjects. Social life and extracurricular activities 2
are relatively unimportant. *Thus, this philosophy attaches greatest* 3
importance to interest in ideas, knowledge, and improving the 4
mind.

Philosophy C: This philosophy emphasizes extracurricular activ- 1
ities, living-group functions, athletics, social life, and rewarding 2
friendships as being important to the well-rounded person. *Thus,* 3
while not forgetting school subjects, this philosophy emphasizes the 4
importance of the extracurriculum.

Philosophy D: This is a philosophy held by the parent who either 1
has values of his own or who has not really decided what is to be 2
valued and is searching for meaning in life. He believes there 3
should be deep interest in ideas and art forms both in the classroom 4
and in society. There is little interest in business or professional
careers. Many parts of the school extracurricular activities, athletics,
and school administration are ignored. *In short, this philosophy*
may emphasize individual interests and concern for personal
feelings.

   Please feel free to comment on the three sections of this questionnaire below.

Appendix H

Elementary Student Guidance Awareness Survey
by S. Baker, J. Johnston, K. Kissinger, F. Leu-
Buscher, and E. MacDonald
State College Area School District Counseling and
Guidance Department

Teacher's name _____   Full year or grade in school
                                                    _____ (01)
Counselor's name _____   (not including kindergarten)
School _____   Your Sex (check one)
                                          Female _____ (02)
How many years have you been at this   Male   _____ (03)
school? _____   Your Age _____

Place a check (√) in the blank which shows your answer to the
question.

a. Do you know who _____

     is? .... Yes ____ (04)

                                             No ____ (05)

b. Have you talked to _____

     about anything? .... Yes ____ (06)

                                             No ____ (07)

c. Has _____ ever helped

     you solve a problem? .... Yes ____ (08)

                                             No ____ (09)

d. Has _____ ever talked to

     your class? .... Yes ____ (10)

                                             No ____ (11)

e. Do you think _____ could

     help you better by talking to your entire class? . . Yes ____ (12)

                                             No ____ (13)

f. Have you ever been in a group with _____

     _____ and several other students? . . Yes ____ (14)

                                             No ____ (15)

       g. If you answered "Yes", did you like it? . . Yes ____ (16)

                                             No ____ (17)

       h. What did you like or dislike about the
          group?

          _____

          _____

          _____

i. Would you feel free to talk to _____

     _____ about something important to

     you? .... Yes ____ (18)

                                             No ____ (19)

       j. What might keep you from talking with
          the counselor?

          _____

          _____

          _____

k. Who has talked to you about jobs
     or careers you might want to do
     some day? (Check as many as you
     wish.)   a. Counselor ____ (20)

                                      b. Parent   ____ (21)

                                      c. Teacher   ____ (22)

                                      d. Friends   ____ (23)

                                      e. No one   ____ (24)

l. Who has talked to you about what
     you do best and what you like to
     do? (Check as many as you wish.) a. Counselor ____ (25)

                                      b. Parent   ____ (26)

                                      c. Teacher   ____ (27)

                         d. Friends   ____ (28)
                         e. No one   ____ (29)

m. In what areas would you like ____
_____ to be more
helpful to you ? (Check as many
as you wish.)

    a. Helping me to solve problems . . . . ____ (30)
    b. Helping me to get along with other students ____ (31)
    c. Helping me to get along with teachers . . . . ____ (32)
    d. Helping me to get along at home . . . . ____ (33)
    e. Helping me to know how to work better at
        school . . . . ____ (34)
    f. Others . . . . ____ (35)

n. If you checked "Others

_____

_____

_____

Subject Index

ABC theory, 75–77
"Achievement place," 260
Achievement tests, 40, 50, 294
Activity, physical, 193
Activity counseling, 87, 111–112, 126–127
Administration (administrator): defined, 266; in groups, 132, 146–156; of guidance programs, 266–286; and program coordination, 279
Adoption, 192, 240
Affective domain, 13, 174, 188–191, 199; curriculum materials, 192–195; procedures and process, 195–197
Agenda, building (in groups), 143
Ages of Man (Erikson), 163–165
Aggression, 80–81, 169–172
American Personnel and Guidance Association (APGA), 4
American School Counselor Association (ASCA), 4
Analytic (psychoanalytic) approach, 59–60, 163–164, 216
Anxiety treatment, 67–73
Appraisal, 19–52, 175–176; individual, 20, 28–48, 296–298; group, 48–52
Arts and crafts, 192–193
Assertive training, 70–71
Assessment, *see* Appraisal
Association for Counselor Education & Supervision (ACES), 4
Attainment record, pre-school (PAR), 48, 295
Attendance officers, 280
Audiovisual materials, 193
Autonomy vs. shame and doubt (Erikson), 163
Aversive conditioning, 83

Barclay Classroom Climate Inventory, 48, 295, 300
Baseline, 166, 169–170, 297–298, 301, 304
Bathroom technique, 82–83
Beatles, the, 79
Behavior: aggressive, 80–81, 169–172; assessment, 106–107, 140, 166–167; change, 168–169; –change target, 166, 169–170; consequences, changing, 167–168; contracting, 78–82, 107–108, 172; diagnosis format, 21–23;

disorders, 111, 172, 177–181; modification program, 169–172; objectives, 10, 12–15, 219, 288; observations, 304; and parental involvement, 88–89; rehearsal, 71–73, 115–118, 171–172; report card, 180–181
Behavioristic therapy, 60
Bender Motor Gestalt Test, 33–34, 282, 295
Benton Visual Retention Test, 34, 282, 295
Bibliocounseling, 78, 112–113
Blackboard drawing, 86–87
Brain dysfunction, *see* Minimal brain dysfunction
Breathing (in relaxation), 67
Bridges, test, 18–19
Broad spectrum approach, to counseling, 58–89
Buddy programs, 255–256
Budget, for guidance, 275–276

California: Achievement Test, 50, 294; Short Form of Mental Maturity, 50, 294; Test of Personality, 51
"Card carrying," and reward, 80
Career: 110, 206–233; development, 216–217; education models, 217–224; and elementary school counselor, 224–233; information, 231–232; theory, 209–216; and vocational perspectives, 244
Case(s): Charlie, 67, 70–73, 76–77; conference, 174–177; Harry, 69–70, 79–80; history, 20–21; individual case study, 296–298; Jane, 84–86; Nan, 86; staffing, 278–284
Center for Humanistic Education, 191
Chaining, 167
Character education, 9, 198, 247
Child: as consultant, 87–88; and consultation, 161–165; development, 6, 161–165; guidance groups, *see* Classroom, meetings; initial contact with, 25; interview, 26–27; mistaken goals, 63; observations, 23–24, 27–28; play, 25–26
Children's Apperception Text (CAT-H), 43–44, 295
Children's Personality Questionnaire, 51, 295

341

Role(s) of counselor, 4–6; reversal, 71–73, 116–118
Role playing, *see* Behavior rehearsal

Schedules, Counselor, 269–271
School board contacts, 275
School Counselor Attitude Inventory (SCAI), 6, Appendix B
School intervention, 241–251; disadvantaged child, 244–245; interpersonal relationships, 243–244; legal and ethical considerations, 245–247; organizational development approach (O.D.), 242–243; orientation programs, 248; paraprofessionals, 249–250; PTA/PTO, 248–249; referral, 250–251; school board contacts, 275; self-development, 251; vocational perspectives, 206–237, 244
School psychologist, *see* Psychologist, school
Scouts, 257, 259
Selection, of counselors, 7
Self-acceptance, 7; (-concept), 7, 47, 121; -control, 22, 78, 168, 181; -development (counselor's), 251; -development groups (teachers), 139–146; -esteem inventory (Coopersmith), 47, 295; -evaluation, 21; -knowledge, 206; -study, 301–303
Semi-structured group (parents). *See also* Parents categorizing responses, 136; didactic approach, 136–137; listing concerns, 134–135; problem situations, 135–136; ways of structuring, 133–134
Sentence completion tests, 44, 122–124
Sequential Tests of Educational Progress (STEP), 294
Sesame Street, 169, 253
Sex education, 78
Shaping, 167
Skill Training groups, 146
Sleeping problems, 89
Slosson Intelligence Test (SIT), 29, 294
Social development: measurement of, 47–48, 295; relationships, 22–23
Social interaction, 194
Social-problem-solving meetings, 9, 151
Social worker, 280
Sociodrama, 115
Sociometric tests, 48
Speech and hearing tests, 37–38, 295; therapist, 281
"Squiggle" drawings, 44–45
SRA achievement series, 50, 295
Staff case conferences, 174–177; meetings, 276–277; team approach, 278–284
Stages: of career orientation, 210–213;

of groups, 101–103; of treatment (existential), 61–62
Stanford Achievement Test, 50, 294
Stanford-Binet Intelligence Scale, 28, 29, 199, 294
Statistics, 291–292; chi-square, 305; correlation, 293; descriptive, 292–293; expectancy tables, 298; factor (cluster) analysis, 293; F-Test, 293, 300, 305–308; item analysis, 305; percentage, 300–301; t-Test, 300–302; Wilcoxon signed-ranks, 304
Stealing, 84–86, 86–87
Stick-man procedure, 45–46
Stimulus-oriented mode, 224–225
Story-book counseling, 112
Storytelling, mutual, 84–86
Students, description of, 298–299
Substitute homes, 260
Successive approximations, 167–168
Supper-time drawing, 36–37
Survey of former elementary students, Appendix I
Systematic desensitization, *see* Desensitization
Systems approach, to counselor functions, 268–269

Target-behavior change, 169–170
Teacher, 278–279, 282–283, observation system, 166–167; survey, Appendix K
Teacher groups: self-development, 139–146; skill training, 146–156; training, 195–196, 197–202
Team action for leadership and learning (club), 127
Technical eclecticism, 4, 66
Television, 74, 168–169, 252–253
Temper tantrums, 88
Templin-Darley Tests of Articulation, 37, 295
Test anxiety, 69
Test Anxiety Scale for Children (TASC), 293
Test development, 292–293
Tests: achievement, 40, 50; coordination, 30–37; development of, 292–293; group mental ability, 49–50; intelligence (individual), 28–30; interests and motivation, 50–51; learning disabilities, 41–43; perceptual motor, 31–33; 33–37; personality, 43–47, 51–52; program effects, 289; reading, 31, 38–40, 50; social development, 47–48; sociometric, 48; speech and hearing, 37–38; summary of, 294–295
Theory (ATOI): analytic, 59–60; behavioristic, 60–61; client-centered, 61; development, 61; existential, 61–62;

Author Index